AMERICA
BEHIND THE
COLOR LINE

Dialogues with African Americans

Henry Louis Gates, Jr.

WARNER BOOKS

New York   Boston

For Cornel West

If you purchase this book without a cover you should be aware that this book may have been stolen property and reported as "unsold and destroyed" to the publisher. In such case neither the author nor the publisher has received any payment for this "stripped book."

Warner Books

Time Warner Book Group
1271 Avenue of the Americas, New York, NY 10020
Visit our Web site at www.twbookmark.com.

Printed in the United States of America

Originally published in hardcover by Warner Books
First Trade Edition: January 2005
10 9 8 7 6 5 4 3 2 1

The Library of Congress has cataloged the hardcover edition as follows:

Gates, Henry Louis.
    America behind the color line : dialogues with African Americans /
Henry Louis Gates, Jr.
        p. cm.
    ISBN 0-446-53273-8
    1. African Americans—Social conditions—1975– 2. African Americans—
Interviews. 3. Social classes—United States. I. Title.
E185.86.G373   2004
305.896'073—dc22   2003020629

ISBN: 0-446-69390-1 (pbk.)

Acknowledgments

This book is the companion volume to the four-part BBC/PBS series *America Behind the Color Line*, which I wrote and narrated. It presents in essay form many of the interviews that I conducted for the television series, which is an attempt to examine the role of class distinctions within the African-American community at the birth of the twenty-first century. I decided upon this format because of the richness of the interviews, many of which transpired over an hour or two and which, of necessity, could not be included in their entirety within the time restrictions of documentary television. To accomplish this goal, I benefited from the advice and editorial skills of Hollis Robbins and Toni Rosenberg.

I want to thank Hollis Robbins for her generous assistance in thinking through and organizing the extraordinarily difficult work of transforming a four-part audiovisual work into a single, integrated, textual one.

My consulting editor, Toni Rosenberg, with a clarity and commitment truly rare, crafted essays from the interviews I conducted. Ms. Rosenberg brought a depth of vision to the work that equaled my own expectations for what the companion book to the documentary might convey. I owe my deepest thanks to her both for her tremendous skills as an editor and writer and for her unsurpassed dedication to the book.

I would like to thank my editors at Warner Books, Jamie Raab, Colin Fox, and Larry Kirshbaum, for their enthusiastic support of this project. My agents, Tina Bennett, Lynn Nesbit, and Bennett Ashley, offered sage advice at every stage in the development of the television series and this book. Henry Finder kindly read various versions of my manuscript and critiqued them, both closely and wisely, helping me to figure out what I was trying to say. Joanne Kendall, as always, cheerfully and expertly typed several drafts of the manuscript. William Julius Wilson, Pamela Joshi, and Edward Walker provided the demographic data that appears throughout the text.

I would like to thank Jane Root at BBC2; Sandy Heberer, John Wilson, and Mary Jane McKinven at PBS; and Alex Graham and Jonathan Hewes at Wall to Wall Television for supporting this film series from its conception. Our serious and superb crew consisted of the following extremely talented members: Simon Chinn (series producer), Mary Crisp and Daniel Percival (directors), Jonathan Hewes (executive producer), Helena Tait (production manager), Bridget Bakokodie and Stephen Barrett (assistant producers), Zoe Watkins (junior production manager), Annette Williams and Jason Savage (film editors), Bernard Mavunga (camera assistant), Anthony Meering and Adam Prescod (soundmen), Debbie Townsend (archive researcher), Tamsynne Westcott and Ida Ven Bruusgaard (production team), Quinton Smith (online editor), Lyle Harris and Paul Reaney (fixers), Scott Wilkinson (dubbing mixer), Murray Gold (music), and Ray King (colorist). Without their devotion to this project, the film series could not have been completed.

I want to especially thank my friend Graham Smith for his stunningly beautiful and poignant cinematography, as well as for the pleasure of his company during the shooting of these films and the analysis of the day's filming over dinner each evening of the shoot. Graham Smith is an artist.

Finally, I would like to thank all of the people who so graciously allowed the film crew and me to interrupt the rhythm of their lives to discuss, in some detail, the strange interplay of race and class within the African-American community.

Henry Louis Gates, Jr.
October 16, 2003

Contents

Introduction

I enrolled at Yale University in September of 1969, one of ninety-six black men and women to commence our matriculation at that time. We were the first large group of black people to be admitted to Yale as undergraduates in the same class. By contrast, the Class of 1966 had included only six black male graduates. We were the beginnings of what came to be called the affirmative action generation, though we did not use that phrase to describe ourselves. "Vanguard," a term being bandied about by the Black Panthers, seemingly omnipresent in those times in New Haven, where one of their leaders, Bobby Seale, was facing trial along with eight other Panthers, was the word that most frequently sneaked its way into our endless, late-night dorm room analyses of our "role," our "mission," our "responsibility" to members of "the community" whom we had left behind. Would they be locked forever outside all that those hallowed neo-Gothic ivy walls symbolized?

Like any fledgling elite, at once heady with possibility yet racked by the guilt of the survivor—that is, presuming we would survive Yale's academic rigors—we were desperate to succeed and desperate for role models who would guide us to that success. Because of a particularly fortuitous bit of good timing, Yale (and many other historically white elite universities) diversified its student body precisely when it introduced the new field of Afro-American studies into the curriculum. To be blunt, a cause and effect relation obtained between the coming of the black students and the creation of this new field. So role models, resplendent black intellectual role models, were in full demand if not in full abundance; there were still just a few on the Yale faculty then, but many more were becoming increasingly available in the curriculum of our black history courses. Like many of my classmates, I adopted the great W. E. B. Du Bois, activist and prolific author, as a hero, even if he was a Harvard man! But Frederick Douglass, Paul Robeson, Thurgood Marshall, and even Dr. King were favorites as well. The true "activists" among us favored Marcus Garvey, Frantz Fanon, even the slave insurrectionist Nat Turner. Harold Cruse's *The Crisis of the Negro Intellectual* was our textbook du jour:

in my sophomore year alone, I read it in three different classes. We were bound and determined to avoid the mistakes that our predecessors in our crossover roles had made; above all else, we wanted to be responsible "to the people," as we would put it, "representing" them somehow, determined to remain "accountable" to them, bringing them along with us as we scaled the historical barriers to racial progress, dragging them, if we had to, inside the cloistered walls of power and financial success that Yale represented. If we were not yet full-fledged intellectuals, we were in the midst of a crisis, a crisis of identity and representative responsibility, since it was we who had been chosen to leave the black community and integrate what C. Wright Mills had called "the power elite." And this power elite was determined, to modify the Children's Defense Fund motto, "to leave no black person behind."

While Douglass and Du Bois, Garvey and Robeson, Fanon and Marshall were our official role models, it is probably accurate to confess that we also drew an enormous amount of secret inspiration from the cult figure Putney Swope. Putney Swope? In 1969, the same year we went to Yale, the arts film *Putney Swope* was released, starring Arnold Johnson and Mel Brooks and directed by Robert Downey, Sr. We might think of it today as a prototype of the "blaxploitation" film genre, but it was in fact a utopia, one of the first fantasies, rendered on film, of how things would be different once we were to "take over."

The film opens at a meeting of the board of directors of a Madison Avenue advertising agency. One black man, Putney Swope, obviously a token, sits modestly among the eleven board members. When the agency's president dies from a heart attack during the meeting, Swope is accidentally elected chairman of the board, receiving nine of the eleven votes cast, because, as one executive puts it, "I thought no one else would vote for him." Swope, a nascent revolutionary cloaked in a bespoke suit, soon fires all but one of the company's white staff, hires black people from the ghetto to replace them, renames the agency Truth and Soul, Inc., and declares that he will boycott all advertising for tobacco, alcohol, and war toys. Soon, Truth and Soul becomes the dominant agency on Madison Avenue, amassing $156 million in profits by creating irreverent ads for products such as Ethereal Cereal, Victrola Cola, and Face-Off Pimple Cream.

Swope is "a brother who is going to make it right." And how will he achieve his revolution? There is "no sense rocking the boat," he declares. "Rocking the boat is a drag. What you do is *sink* the boat," but you sink the boat "with productive alternatives." "You can't change nuthin' with rhetoric and slogans," Swope argues. "The man's got the truth in his pocket. He doesn't talk about it. He hangs it on a shingle where people can see it."

We loved this hilarious movie, my new black friends at Yale and I, and we saw it again and again. For some of us consciously, and for many of us unconsciously, it was an allegory for the path that we should take in our new roles as the vanguard of our people, the black portion of a group that our president, Kingman Brewster, had described in his welcoming speech to freshmen a year before as America's "one thousand male leaders." (Our class included, for the first time, 250 women, so Brewster's speech adjusted for gender.) We would do our homework, integrate Yale's most exclusive and elite clubs, secret societies, and student organizations, and then we would take on Wall Street and every other venue of power and wealth, transforming them from the inside with truth and soul, leaving no sister or brother behind.

Putney Swope had laid out a path for our individual success within a context of "revolutionary transformation," "social responsibility," and "accountability to the people"—all key words in the heated oratory of radical black politics of the time. Above all else, we were determined not to allow our individual, or collective, success to be "used by the man" to justify the continued economic deprivation of all those black souls left behind in America's ghettos. No, we would not be tokens; we would not be sellouts; we would not be complicit in the use of the black people in the ghettos as scapegoats either for American prosperity or—more alarmingly—for our own individual success. Unlike Du Bois's group of leaders, the Talented Tenth of "college bred Negroes" at the turn of the twentieth century, we would be the catalyst for broad social change, saviors of our entire people. Du Bois's was the model to avoid. And Putney Swope inadvertently had shown us the way.

If the film gave us a rhetoric, a road map, for the mission on which we had embarked vis-à-vis the white establishment, it also gave us a language to use to defend ourselves against the sometimes deafening rhetoric of revolution that was swirling throughout the black community. As soon as Swope's agency appears to be succeeding, he is descended upon by four militants, each an archetype for a dominant political faction in the community, including the Black Panthers, the Black Muslims, Black Power advocates, and the National Urban League. ("There are brothers in the Black Room," Swope is warned ominously, so he quickly agrees to meet with them to hear their grievances.)

The first activist argues for "self-determination," "self-respect," and "self-defense," à la the Black Power advocates. The second declares that "violence is a cleansing force," while a third chimes in that "non-violence is non-functional," so "it's guns, baby," echoing the Ten Point Program of the Black Panther Party, which many of us had hung on the walls of our dorm rooms. "My organization is pro-integration," says a hapless, suited official ostensibly from the NAACP or the National Urban League; "a gun is not going to get you a job." "Yeah, but it will eliminate the competition," the Panther stand-in intones. When this mad round-robin finally ends, all agree on one thing and one thing alone: "Lay some bread on us!" they demand of Swope, who then dismisses them all as hustlers and shows them to the door.

The message was clear and simple, and we took it to heart: structural change would come only from the inside of the system *if*—and this was a huge "if"—we managed to keep our integrity as black people, as socially conscious members of a vanguard force penetrating the power structures of "the enemy" not for our own benefit, but for the benefit of the larger black community. Our job was to transform those historically white institutions like Yale by bringing more and more brothers and sisters inside when we could, and representing them from the inside when we could not. We would integrate America at its highest, deepest levels, and by doing so transform it forever, dragging "the community" along with us if we had to.

That was the plan.

I remember attending a political rally at Yale staged on behalf of Bobby Seale and his fellow imprisoned Black Panthers. One speaker—I think it was Jean Genet, the French playwright and radical—warned us that our newfound presence at institutions such as Yale was a ploy, representing a desperate act of window dressing for a power elite severely under pressure to diversify by race and by gender. We were tokens, he continued, admission to the Ivy League a clever ploy both to co-opt us with the trappings of privilege and to pacify the rumbling masses, the proverbial lumpenproletariat (whose true representatives were, of course, Bobby Seale and the Panthers), by serving up crumbs from the banquet table of international corporate capitalism in lieu of sharing the entire pie. Quoting Herbert Marcuse, whose *Reason and Revolution* was another text du jour in many of our courses that year, Genet spat directly into our shining black faces, claiming that the principal result of the Civil Rights Movement—which had led to our increased numbers in the student body at Yale—would be the creation of a new black middle class, rather than profound structural change. We were merely a mirage of such change, he scolded us, not the face of revolution that we thought we were, or hoped we would be. We were not a *part* of the problem; we *were* the problem, and our individual success was being fostered by the system as its safety valve to alleviate the pressure accumulating from genuine revolutionaries like Bobby Seale and, of course, "the people." Our presence at Yale wore a diabolical dual face: first, it allowed the system to placate, and therefore diffuse, attempts to reform it dramatically and radically; and second, the success that awaited each of us individually on the other end of our education, post-Yale, would render us useless as agents of meaningful—read "revolutionary"—social transformation. We were nouveau race-traitors: Ivy League Uncle Toms soon to have M.B.A.'s and J.D.'s, who would be far more invested in the proverbial bottom line and the American status quo than any generation of educated blacks before us, and certainly more so than the hapless sisters and brothers we had left behind in the ghettos, even if we were clad in colorful dashikis and coiffed with mile-high Afros.

How cynical Genet was, I found myself thinking. Genet was wrong, an aging misanthrope and French at that! What did he know? Our generation would be different. We would save our people.

I thought about Putney Swope and Jean Genet as I embarked on a journey to assess the state of Black America by talking to a wide range of African Americans.

Where are we as a people, at the dawn of the twenty-first century? I wanted to pursue answers in a documentary film series for PBS, by conducting interviews with famous African Americans and with not-so-famous African Americans. It has long struck me as curious that African Americans often speak differently—more colorfully and openly—when talking with each other behind closed doors, as it were, than they do in interracial settings; more spontaneously, say, in barbershops and beauty parlors, in church socials and their living rooms, than they do in the pages of sociological studies or in polling data. I wanted to capture that more spontaneous and less inhibited voice on film, and in transcriptions of my interviews, printed as the text of this book.

Du Bois wrote famously in 1903 that a racist experience when he was a schoolboy in Great Barrington, Massachusetts, had led him to the realization that African Americans conducted their lives in America behind a "veil":

> Then it dawned upon me with
> a certain suddenness that I was
> different from the others; or like,

mayhap, in heart and life and
longing, but shut out from
their world by a vast veil.
I had thereafter no desire to
tear down that veil, to creep
through; I held all beyond it
in common contempt, and lived
above it in a region of blue sky
and great wandering shadows.

In this series, I wanted, on a modest level, to provide a window, a peephole, through that veil, a veil that still, far too often, separates black America from white.

To do so, I traveled the country interviewing African Americans from Harvard to Harlem, from Wall Street to Watts, from the Lincoln Memorial to Memphis, from Fort Benning, Georgia, to Atlanta, the home of the black middle class. I walked the streets of Chicago's South Side and interviewed residents of Chicago's infamous housing project, the Robert Taylor Homes. I ended my journey in Los Angeles, where the fantasy world of Hollywood stands in stark contrast to the painful realities lived each day by the residents of Los Angeles's South Central neighborhood. In Los Angeles, the two black worlds of class and consciousness collide, sometimes bizarrely, but always in splendid living color.

As I talked to Black America all across America at the beginning of the twenty-first century, one thing became very clear. Everybody's a CEO. Everybody's talking about entrepreneurship, products, markets, and market share. It's all about getting the most out of people, empowering, creating wealth.

The critique of the Southern economy during slavery is that it focused entirely on growing staple crops and the suppression of what would otherwise be a market for food, clothing, housing, and other consumer goods. An ill-trained, ill-fed workforce had no incentive to produce a good product; neither was this workforce allowed to exercise consumer choices. What these interviews reveal is that apart from the moral case against slavery and the moral case against unequal civil rights, there is a damning business case against slavery, if the business case is defined as wealth creation and profitability. Economic historians may argue among themselves whether the slave system was economically efficient or inefficient, profitable or unprofitable in the long run, but the achievement and diverse economic accomplishment of blacks up and down the economic scale prove just how misguided those are who idealize the South as an economically cost-effective enterprise.

Colin Powell confirms that African Americans are becoming more and more economically successful. But Hollywood actress Nia Long states a more important truth: "Black people generate enormous amounts of money for the American economy." The success of black entrepreneurs and businesspeople around the country proves without a doubt that picking cotton was never the best way to generate that money. Young black kids have a new entrepreneurial spirit, Russell Simmons observes. "They're doing it. It's happening right now. That's all they're talking about. Getting money. Owning companies. They're not talking about how brilliant they rap; they're talking about how much money they're making and how they're making it. Legal money."

Willie W. Herenton, mayor of Memphis, Tennessee, for the past twelve years, speaks proudly of the economic successes of his city, the eighteenth largest in America, with $60 million in reserves, a double-A bond rating, a strong and vibrant financial center. "We have great purchasing power," he explains, but the next step is converting that purchasing power to wealth creation within the race. Tammie, a twenty-nine-year-old mother of six who used to live in the Robert Taylor Homes in Chicago, talks about the importance of targets and objectives and a diversity of options. If she were in charge, she says, she would find out what her fellow residents are aiming for, "what they do to set their goals, and see what they need to get to their goals."

Jesse Jackson states, "When one considers the economic origin of America, it was Africa and her people who subsidized America's development. After all, two hundred years without wages is an African subsidy to America, redefining what party is 'creditor,' and which is 'debtor,' in the African-American relationship." But while slavery "was woven into the fabric of the country," can we now critique it on other terms? What is the legacy of slavery—in purely economic terms, enforced servitude, labor without pay—for today's young people, poised to enter the workforce? The question has never merely been one of work and lost wages. The black work ethic is not the problem. As John Singleton puts it, whatever field you're in, success is a matter of being able to work in the field you choose and being able to back it up with blood, sweat, and tears. The problem, Franklin Raines explains, is that "having excluded such a big piece of the workforce, such a big piece of society, from being productive has hurt the country. We've taken all these kids who could be out creating something and we made them all dependent and put them in jail. Well, it's not just the cost of the jail, it's also the loss of what their productivity would have been in the economy. We've got to get that message through, but getting that message through the color divide is very hard." Ought we, as Jackson suggests, to wholly restructure a system that allows Russell Simmons to create the wealth he does? Yes, as Lenora Fulani explains, we need to educate black youth in how best to participate in this structure, but the goal of wealth creation and economic success is not in itself bad. Why shouldn't black America want to live in the Big House?

For every Vernon Jordan who says, "The one thing that we know is that white people like money, and that's why they sold us and bought us. It had to do with money. It had nothing to do with humanity; it was about money," there's a Chris Tucker: "What people gotta realize is—and I understand it, and it's fine—movie companies want to make a lot of money." Everybody's fighting for their job, he explains. The balance sheets have to look good. "I'd like to be in a position where somebody could bring me a script and if it's good and I can do it, I would get it done, or take it to the studios and get it done," said Chris. "We've gotta start opening doors; we gotta open them for ourselves. But to begin with, you gotta get through a narrow door."

This book is the result of these interviews, collected in the four parts that make up the film series. Above all else, I wanted these dialogues with African Americans to speak eloquently, as it were, for themselves, in an unmediated manner, providing a rare glimpse of black people reflecting to themselves on the challenges and ironies of their lives behind the veil, some thirty-five years following the death of the last great civil rights leader, Martin Luther King, Jr.

PART ONE

Ebony Towers

When I was growing up in the fifties, I could never have imagined that one of Harvard's most respected departments would be a Department of Afro-American Studies and that twenty professors would be teaching here at the turn of the century. Our experience at Harvard is just one instance of a much larger phenomenon. Since the death of Dr. Martin Luther King in 1968, individual African Americans have earned positions higher within white society than any person black or white could have dreamed possible in the segregated 1950s. And this is true in national and local government, in the military and in business, in medicine and education, on TV and in film. Virtually anywhere you look in America today, you'll find black people. Not enough black people, but who can deny that progress has been made? In fact, since 1968, the black middle class has tripled, as measured by the percentage of families earning $50,000 or more. At the same time—and this is the kicker—the percentage of black children who live at or below the poverty line is almost 35 percent, just about what it was on the day that Dr. King was killed.

Since 1968, then, two distinct classes have emerged within Black America: a black middle class with "white money," as my mother used to say, and what some would argue is a self-perpetuating, static black underclass. Is this what the Civil Rights Movement was all about? Can we ever bridge this black class divide?

What does the success of this expanding middle class—W. E. B. Du Bois's Talented Tenth, the college-educated black person, even now only 17 percent of all black Americans—mean for the progress of our people? Is this economic ascent the ultimate realization of Dr. King's "dream" of integration?

How do we continue to expand the size of the middle class? And most scary of all, is this class divide permanent, a way of life that will never be altered?

Writing in the *New York Times* on May 31, 2003, Jack Bass, author of *Unlikely Heroes: Southern Federal Judges and Civil Rights,* quoted from an interview with John Minor Wisdom, "the legendary jurist and scholar," which Bass had conducted just four months before the judge's death at the age of ninety-three in 1999: "He told me he was uncertain which was more important," Bass wrote: "how far blacks have come in overcoming discrimination, or 'how far they still have to go.'" This question arose in another form in an amusing, signifying interplay between the titles of William Julius Wilson's *The Declining Significance of Race* (1978) and Cornel West's best-selling *Race Matters* (1993). There can be no doubt that "race" is far less important as a factor affecting economic success for our generation than it was for any previous generation of African Americans in this country. Still, there can be little doubt that the fact of one's blackness remains the hallmark of our various identities in a country whose wealth, to a large extent, was constructed on race-based slavery, followed by a full century of de jure segregation and discrimination in every major aspect of a black citizen's social, economic, and political existence.

I decided to talk with some of the most remarkably successful African Americans of our generation who—because of opportunities created to one degree or another by affirmative action—have been enabled to excel in positions of authority that our antecedents could scarcely have dreamed of occupying, or even aspiring to hold. Had they become the Putney Swopes of our generation? I could think of no place more appropriate to begin than at the offices of the U.S. secretary of state, General Colin Powell.

Since 1963, we've had seventy-five black congressmen and congresswomen, two U.S. senators, a whole slew of mayors, and two Supreme Court justices, but only in the last few years have we penetrated the heart of executive political power in Washington. Just a generation ago, the idea of a black president was a joke we'd tell in barbershops. We figured that a black man could be king of England before he'd be elected president of the United States! Yet today one of the most important political figures in the world is a black man, a man fourth in line to the presidency. Many people think that he would have easily defeated Al Gore in the 2000 presidential election.

General Colin Powell grew up in the Bronx, the son of working-class Jamaican immigrants. He joined the army after college and saw combat in

Vietnam. Like many of us, his career benefited enormously from affirmative action. He rose rapidly through the ranks, becoming a five-star general and chairman of the Joint Chiefs of Staff. He commanded our troops in Desert Storm. As national security adviser to two presidents and now as secretary of state, General Powell is the most powerful black person in the history of the American government and is one of the most powerful people in the world.

I asked Powell if race had been a hindrance to his career path, or even to his aspirations. He replied, "I was raised in a family that never felt constrained by their poverty or by their race . . . And I was raised in a community that had blacks, whites, Puerto Ricans . . . a melting pot of the New York City environment. So I never really knew I was supposed to feel in some way constrained by being an inner-city, public school black kid, the son of immigrants. I just went into the army and I found an organization that said, no, no, no, we've changed, we're ahead of the rest of the society. We don't care if you're black or blue, we only care if you're a good green soldier. And if you do your best, you watch, you'll be recognized. If you don't do your best, you'll be punished. And I started out as a black lieutenant but I became a general who was black."

I asked him if his position as secretary of state had made his race a nonissue, had, in effect, allowed him to transcend his racial identity. "When you walk into a room," I wondered, "if you go to Asia or the Middle East, do the people you deal with still see a black man first, before they see you as the secretary of state?"

"Yeah, sure, but they also see the American secretary of state and they know that I'm not coming to them as a black man; I'm coming to them as a representative of the American people, as a representative of the president of the United States. I represent all the values of this country and the power of this country, its military power, its economic power and political power. Once they sit down and get past whatever color I am, they want to do business."

I asked Powell what he thought was the responsibility of those of us within the African-American community who have made it to those left behind, an issue that still plagues my friends and that especially worries me. "I want to continue to be a role model for the kids in the neighborhood I grew up in, and for other youngsters in America," he said. "Not just a black role model in that stereotypical sense, but an example of what you can achieve if you are willing to work for it. And second, those of us in the African-American community who have been successful financially ought to give some of it back to the community. You can do it through scholarships, through donations, through mentoring, through adopting or sponsoring a school. There are lots of ways to do it, and everything I've just mentioned I have done, or try to do. You don't have to scream and shout about it but just get it done, reach back and help these youngsters who are coming along."

But why do we have more of a responsibility, it seems sometimes, than our white counterparts? I asked.

"Our youngsters need us more perhaps, for one thing," he said. "And our youngsters are still living in a society that is really only one generation removed from racism, discrimination, segregation, and economic deprivation, and we're still suffering from that."

The tension between societal factors as the causes of our people's social and economic disadvantages, and those traceable to individual initiative or the lack thereof, would become a leitmotif within the interviews I conducted throughout the black community. I think it's fair to say that it is the largest single point of contention within the black community itself. Like General Powell, I, too, worry about the values of certain aspects of black urban street culture and the self-destructive behavior that reinforces the cycle of poverty—behavior that helps to keep the black poor impoverished. But the inner-city culture that General Powell says holds us back is also the source of the tremendous creativity found in hip-hop culture. If hip-hop is the culture of the black poor, it is simultaneously the face and voice of American popular culture. It is also rich with a few phenomenal success stories.

I traveled from Washington to New York to meet the king of hip-hop culture, Russell Simmons. Simmons has transformed black urban street culture into the lingua franca of American popular culture worldwide—and into a music and fashion empire that grosses more than $300 million per year.

"How old were you when you became an entrepreneur?" I asked him.

"When I was sixteen," Simmons said, "I wanted to be an entrepreneur, but selling weed was one of the few options open to me."

"Really? When did you become legitimate?"

"I used to give hip-hop parties when I was at City College. People would pay to get in—all the hip-hop artists, DJ Cheeba and all these guys. I had this music thing I loved, and I was lucky enough to get a job in the music industry."

Simmons's career took off in 1979 when he produced "Christmas Rappin'," by Kurtis Blow, on Mercury Records. It was phenomenally successful, and the rest, one might say, is the history of hip-hop.

Simmons's company, Def Jam, brilliantly punched hip-hop from the ghetto straight into the heart of middle-class, teenage white America, launching bands such as Run-D.M.C. and Grandmaster Flash. Simmons, a brilliant marketer, has branched out to fashion design. His Phat Farm label is the rage from Harlem to Harvard Square, from Watts to Westwood.

How did he create a business based on rebellious black culture and make it as American as apple pie? Simmons's genius was to take an underground movement and turn it into the common language of American popular culture. Where did his understanding of the entrepreneurial system come from?

"The entrepreneurial spirit came from within me," he said. "I was never offered a salary; they didn't like what we did. There was never an interest in giving me a job, or even making a record deal, so we started our own company . . . I wanted to be in the fashion business. Do you think anybody wanted to hire me or give me a job? I wanted to be in the advertising business. These things had to be forged with a little bit of resilience and vision . . .

"The independence that was forced on us by managing some part of our culture, or ideas, is the same independence that's creating a whole new lifestyle among young black people. All I had was drug dealers, some numbers runners, and an occasional pimp. They were the entrepreneurs. Now all these young people have images. It's true that a lot of them are hardheaded and kind of twisted and unsophisticated. That's why they did it in the first place. You think if they spoke the King's English, if they went to school and were told, do what you're supposed to do, that they'd be doing what they're doing? . . . They came from the street and they did what they had to do and they created what they've created."

Are these the new heroes in our community, people like Simmons, people like Richard Parsons and Ken Chenault, the CEOs of AOL Time Warner and American Express, respectively?

"Parsons and Ken Chenault and people like them are huge role models . . . But Puffy's a much greater hero, a much greater inspiration," said Simmons. "He's self-made. The same sophistication and education that guys like Parsons and Chenault have can come from some of our kids who will have enough experience to take on businesses that have smaller margins. We are spreading out. Do you know how many energy drinks are made by kids in the ghetto?

"I see the way young people are so excited about being entrepreneurs, and I believe that's the climate that will make a difference economically in our community. And the education part of it, they all recognize it's necessary."

For Simmons, the inner city is a font of entrepreneurial activity; the black entrepreneur is the true black revolutionary today, the inheritor of the legacy of Maroons and other renegades from slavery, the "bad nigger" characters in traditional black folklore and literature. These figures stole the white man's secrets, penetrated the logic of the system, and then used these acquisitions to attempt to liberate black people. Where once the means to our freedom was thought to be literacy, or reclaiming the principles of the Declaration of Independence, or utilizing the legal system—or taking up guns—for hip-hop entrepreneurs, the means, according to Simmons, is hardheaded capitalism, and the goal, massive profits. Is Simmons a visionary who has redefined the black entrepreneur as the new urban revolutionary? As he rightly argues, the black ghetto has always been full of entrepreneurs; moreover, success in that world doesn't even require a high school diploma or a college degree, opening up, as it does, economic opportunities otherwise closed to so many African Americans whose choices are limited because of their education.

We certainly need more entrepreneurs in the inner city, but not at the expense of education. In a highly technological world, formal education is the principal conduit out of poverty, just as it has been for our people since slavery and the days of Jim Crow. Our people's need to stay in school is even greater and more urgent today than it was back then, in harsher times under legal segregation.

Simmons is correct that success in this world doesn't require a high school diploma. But that also concerns me. Does the kind of success that Russell Simmons—and hip-hop—encourages also help our kids to get an education and expand their options?

From Simmons's office in Midtown Manhattan, I went to see another African-American icon, one who uses his particular genius to seduce inner-city children into the love of learning and the value of school.

Maurice Ashley is the world's first and only black Grand Master in chess—a title held by only seven hundred people in history. Ashley is the Tiger Woods of chess. As with golf, we think of chess as a pastime of the upper middle class. Ashley was born into poverty in Jamaica, then grew up in the inner city in Brooklyn. Perhaps more than anyone else, he has helped to make chess black.

I asked Ashley why chess, of all things, would be relevant to black people. "Chess transposes the imagination of inner-city black kids so they can see themselves in the back row where all the power pieces are . . . It's much harder for inner-city kids to understand why they should learn something that seems to have no meaning for their future life. But in chess, I'll show kids a move and five minutes later they can use it against their friend. In another five or ten minutes, they'll win the game and come back to me and say, show me something else, 'cause I just won that game and I wanna win again. It's self-reinforcing."

How did he get involved in chess? I asked.

"I learned to play many different games at an early age . . . By the time I was seven or eight, I could beat the other kids and I could compete with all the adults," Ashley said. In America, he told me, "in tenth grade, when I was fourteen, I had a friend who played chess a lot. I thought, I'm better at games than all the rest of the kids, so I'm going to play this guy and beat him. He crushed me. It was ugly. Then one day when I was at the library, I came across a book on chess . . . It was love at first sight . . . That's when I discovered that reading could open your mind to the wonders of everything you wanted to know. For the first time, I understood the power of books, because after I started reading them, I began crushing players I couldn't beat before."

In 1991, Ashley shook the chess world—and America—when his team from Harlem, the Raging Rooks, beat elite white private schools to become national champions. Stereotypically, black people weren't supposed to excel at intellectual activities, and these inner-city black kids had won a national chess tournament! This was news.

Ashley realized that chess could be the lure to hook schoolchildren into attending school regularly and focusing on their classwork. Chess could be a "black thing," its mental rigor and discipline transferred into new study habits in every other school subject. By kids learning chess, grades—and graduation rates—would go up. In 1991, at the Mott Hall School in Harlem, he and businessman-philanthropist Dan Rose helped establish an educational program in which chess was an integral part of the curriculum.

It amazes me in the generation of fast food and video games that kids would have the patience for chess, so I asked Ashley if this is a problem.

"I think fundamentally kids love to learn, as long as you make the learning engaging. . . . They sit and memorize and study so that when they get into actual competition they'll be ready . . . The great thing about chess is that it's practical."

I asked him if the kind of thing he's accomplishing with chess can be exported throughout the community.

"Chess is not the only solution, but I think of it as a direction. Chess insists that you use your mind. You can't play the game without it. But success does too; that's what success is all about, having a direction . . . I think we're approaching a time when kids' aspirations will be much, much higher than they were. We have a long way to go to put the structures in place that can finally bring about progress racewide, but we're closing in on the effort psychologically . . . We have people striving in all walks of life."

Ashley invited me to see another inner-city program, called HEAF, that is literally putting these ideas into practice. HEAF—the Harlem Educational Activities Fund—is dedicated to helping students who are being failed by their schools to get a solid education.

"HEAF takes kids in the community and makes them successful, that is, gets them through high school and beyond," Ashley explained. The program takes kids from junior high school and gets them all the way through college, teaching them that education is their ticket out. "These kids are hot," said Ashley.

And without HEAF?

"Without the tremendous support and direction that HEAF has been providing since 1992, thousands of inner-city kids who have gone on to college as a result of HEAF programs may have fallen through the cracks."

HEAF's after-school chess class helps draw these children into educational programs. Dan Rose is the founder of HEAF. He summarized his philosophy of education this way:

"The challenge of bringing inner-city disadvantaged children into the mainstream of American life is without question the most pressing, most important social challenge in American life. It is *the* challenge. Anyone who doesn't see it or who doesn't address it is not living in the real world . . .

"If a smart inner-city kid goes bad and goes to prison, it will cost the city, the public, $60,000 a year, and could cost him the rest of his life. Our goal is to turn these kids into professionals who make a couple of hundred thousand dollars a year and who pay $60,000 in taxes. I tell my archconservative friends that our goal is to take a $60,000-a-year tax eater and turn him into a $60,000-a-year taxpayer."

For Ashley and Rose, the long-term success of our people depends upon education, leading inevitably to a greater slice of the economic pie. And the economic pie is baked in the corporate world, symbolized by Wall Street—a world traditionally as "white" as chess.

Who would have believed just a few years ago that four of the world's largest corporations would be run by black men? For many of us, the corporate world was the last bastion of black exclusion. Quite visibly, that has begun to change.

One man I spoke to understood the importance of black representation at the top of the corporate world long before anyone else did. For him, economics, class, and wealth accumulation were the next fronts in the war for civil rights. He was a prophet of black class mobility. Vernon Jordan is the first person to retire from the Civil Rights Movement and take it to the next level—Wall Street. Among black Wall Street executives, Vernon Jordan is the proverbial chairman of the board. Jordan grew up in a black middle-class neighborhood in segregated Atlanta. His mother was a successful business-woman, his father a postal clerk. He was the only black student in his class in the 1950s at DePauw University, before earning a law degree at Howard University. Jordan recounts a bit of stark advice that his father gave him when he dropped him off at DePauw:

"I remember my father shaking my hand to tell me good-bye, but he didn't say good-bye; he said, you can't come home. I said, what do you mean? He said, the college counselor says your reading scores are far lower than those of your classmates . . . these white kids went to fine township high schools and private schools and you went to this old dilapidated, segregated, ill-equipped, double-sessioned, overcrowded school, he said, but you can't come home. And so I said, well, what am I supposed to do, Dad? And he said, read, boy, read, and he drove away." Jordan rose to prominence as a civil rights lawyer, then led several key black organizations, such as the National Urban League. In the early 1980s, however, he deliberately became an agent of another kind of social change, a pioneering force in the integration of the all-white boards of directors of corporate America. This led to the hiring of black corporate executives. Quietly, Jordan had taken the Civil Rights Movement from the segregated cities of the South straight to the heart of Wall Street.

As "First Friend" and confidant to President Bill Clinton, and as a member of some of the most influential corporate boards in the world, no one is better placed to explain what the presence of blacks on Wall Street means to our people than Vernon Jordan. New times, new duties: I asked Jordan if the integration of corporate America is the next phase of the Civil Rights Movement.

"The integration of corporate America has been going on a very long time. I went on my first corporate board in 1972 . . . but we've come a long way from the seventies if you think about Dick Parsons, CEO at AOL Time Warner, Ken

Chenault of AmEx, Stan O'Neal of Merrill Lynch, and Frank Raines of Fannie Mae. These four black men control in excess of $300 billion in market capitalization, and they employ some 300,000 people. That was inconceivable in my time, and now they are CEOs at companies that would not have hired their parents, except in menial jobs."

But how important to the progress of our people is it that individual black people are occupying these positions? I asked him.

"It's important in that it says to young people that they can do it too—that anything you want to achieve can in fact be achieved. But it says something else. It says that if you have the ability, the tenacity, the perseverance, the fortitude, and the smarts, they will put you in this job . . . when you think about Parsons, Raines, Chenault, and O'Neal, white people have put them in charge of their money, and my people did it. That's very serious! And the one thing that we know is that white people like money, and that's why they sold us and bought us. It had to do with money . . . But white people have entrusted their trust funds and the future of their children and their grandchildren to these brothers, because they are competent."

Jordan's dream of integration has affected every level of Wall Street, from the boardroom through upper middle management. Milton Irvin is one such executive, and he has excelled on Wall Street. Irvin grew up in a poor neighborhood in New Jersey. For the past thirty years, he has steadily ascended the corporate ladder on Wall Street. His lifestyle is on a par with that of his white upper-middle-class counterparts.

Irvin recently became the first black member of his country club. Fees are now $70,000 per year. Almost twenty years ago, he and his family moved to Summit, New Jersey, an affluent and still predominantly white suburb forty minutes from Manhattan.

"When I moved to Summit in 1985, there were not a lot of middle-class African Americans, and to a certain extent it was lonely being here . . . But something inside of me said, you know what, someone has to put a stake in the ground in a community like this, and show that we can be woven into this fabric."

I asked Irvin if he ever felt, as he integrated his golf club in Summit, for example, as if he had to ingratiate himself to the white people who were members there.

"When I've joined these clubs, I've never approached it with the attitude that I've got to make white people feel comfortable around a black person. It's more like I've felt they had to figure out, over time, that . . . you're really not different from them . . . I consciously try to be a full participant in the activities of these clubs. This done, it begins to give the others a sense and feeling of comfort . . . It's all a continuation of the Civil Rights Movement. Economic empowerment is a part of it. It's what we're building now."

Irvin and I visited the home of his friends Walt and Donna Pearson. Walt Pearson graduated from the Harvard Business School and was another Wall Street executive before recently assuming a new executive position in the Boston area. As with many affluent African-American families of our generation, their home is a splendid shrine to black history, art, and culture. I asked Pearson what he thought the constituent parts might be of our people being held back. "Nowadays there are programs to help bright and motivated African-American kids get out of the 'hood—whether it's ABC or Prep for Prep or private schools that offer some students full scholarships," he said. "However, if you come home to little or no family structure, you need something to keep you going, and that's the tough part. Beyond that, the playing field is far from level in terms of the ability to make connections in a white world."

Despite all of his success, did he and his wife, Donna, still experience racism?

"On Wall Street," he said, "what happens now is they let us in the door, but instead of blatant racism, you come across subtle things. For example, it seemed like they never wanted me to get too big an assignment, too big a client. When I went after those guys, I was always told I had enough clients, I had enough capacity, whereas my colleague could have even more clients than I did but yet he wasn't at capacity. It was things like that."

Donna Pearson agrees: "Racism still exists, but it's more quiet. It's kept behind closed doors. In Summit I saw instances, sometimes subtle, sometimes not, particularly at the school. Because I'm so fair-skinned, people sometimes think I'm white, and they'll say things and I'll say, excuse me, I'm African American too. And all of a sudden their face gets red."

I wondered how blatant this form of behavior could become. For example, did Donna ever hear these people say the "n" word?

"They don't say the 'n' word, but one time someone said to me, oh, that black person, they don't know what they're doing. And I said, excuse me? Or they'll think that the way I'm doing something is inferior to what they're doing and that I can't do a job like they do . . . you have to let them know right away that you can take the lead just as well as they can."

Did the Pearsons ever worry that their kids will be criticized by lower-class black kids?

"They will have to learn to handle being called white," said Walt. "I went to a private school, and I would come home to a housing project every day and was called 'schoolboy' a couple of times. I had to knock a few heads . . . But I tell my kids now, you're going to encounter a different kind of racism. You're going to confront the class system from your African-American peers, some of whom are going to call you 'whitey' or 'Oreo' . . . In addition, you will have racism from white people. It's going to be arduous. The kids . . . have to come home and be able to tell us everything. They have to realize they're blessed, but they must give back. It's nonstop."

As I conversed with these two families, it became clear that despite all of their personal success and wealth, the task of integrating the white power structure is far from over. Very few African Americans have penetrated the upper echelons of Wall Street. Just as painful, the success of those who have is viewed by some members of the black community somehow as a betrayal of the race.

I asked Melody Irvin, Milton's wife, how this bizarre attitude came to be, when social integration and economic success were cardinal virtues of the Civil Rights Revolution. How did it get to be that being successful is equated by some black people with being white?

"I think being successful has always been equated with being white," she said. "It's hard to change what's always been . . . Things are different for some of the young people that Milton has brought into the industry. But things are also still the same."

"Some of that perception," added Milton, "is driven by the fact that a lot of blacks who are successful, at least on a corporate level, have moved out of what have traditionally been their communities . . . [and] then that community feels a loss of one of its people . . . White people have done a pretty good job of creating wealth. We were looking for a community where we could begin to create wealth, and Summit was one of them."

Milton sensitively explained one of the most surprising dilemmas facing the continued success of our people: the growing gulf between the black middle class and those left behind in the inner cities. Wealth differentials *within* the race are becoming as large and potentially as unbridgeable as the traditional gaps between white and black were during the Civil Rights Era. And this is reflected in attitudes about education and values such as deferred gratification. It's a gulf that is often as much cultural and psychological as it is economic.

Traditionally in America, entry into the middle class and the accumulation of wealth are enabled by the ownership of a home. Blacks in many parts of America were barred from owning homes, whether they could afford to purchase them or not. No one in America has done more to facilitate black home ownership than the CEO of Fannie Mae, America's largest mortgage lender and our second largest corporation based on the size of its assets. Incredibly, it's run by a black man. I went to see him at his corporate headquarters in Washington.

Franklin Raines was the first African American to become the CEO of a Fortune 500 company, in 1999. Raines escaped working-class poverty through education. He was recruited by Harvard, became a Rhodes Scholar at Oxford, then graduated from Harvard Law School and Harvard Business School.

Raines has started a program at Fannie Mae designed to address the class gap among black Americans. By making it easier for African Americans to receive mortgages to purchase homes, Raines hopes to increase black home ownership by as many as 5 million people by the end of the decade. The ultimate effect of this on class distribution in American society would be profound.

His goal, Raines told me, is "to have the same class divide in the black community as . . . in the white community. I want the same percentage of middle class, the same percentage of rich, the same percentage of poor, in the white and black communities. Average is fine with me, because by all the measures, the black community is far behind average in income, in job status, and in education."

So how do we get more black people into the middle class?

"Step by step," said Raines. "There's no shortcut. To begin with, we've got to get folks the preparation that's needed. More people have got to finish high school . . . Then folks have got to get into these companies and persist."

I asked Raines how we can inspire those very people who are trapped in the inner city to aspire to be the next Franklin Raines.

"You've got to let them know it's possible," he said, "because most of them don't even know it's possible. When I was growing up in Seattle, I hadn't been to most of the city, let alone anywhere else. We'd go to day camp, and that was it. It was a big deal to go to another part of the city. My world was two or three square miles . . . Then I went to Harvard, across the country. After that I went to Oxford, and then it became the world. What I thought was possible just kept expanding. For many people it never expands; they never get off the block . . . We must make it clear that there are greater possibilities . . . We just have to make lots of kids aware of the opportunities and give them a chance, and if we give them a chance, we'll be surprised by how many will do well."

How do we drive that message home to black children themselves, whose attitudes are shaped in an environment of unemployment, teenage pregnancy, school dropouts, drugs, instant gratification, and the bizarre attitude that success in school or in the white mainstream is an act of racial betrayal, an act of selling out to the white man?

Lenora Fulani, a political activist and educator, has devoted the last decade to tackling these issues on the street. I met her at her project's offices in Manhattan. Her first observation echoed Raines's comment about parochialism:

"We have kids living in New York City communities like Queens and Brooklyn today, forget thirty-five years ago, who never saw the World Trade Center. They didn't know it existed until September 11. Almost none of the young men in these communities know the experience of putting on a suit and walking down a street in Midtown and finding a way of being related to that's so very different from the usual ways in which they're related to."

But what happens when they see Colin Powell on TV, or Condoleezza Rice? Doesn't this take them out of their environment? Don't the accomplishments of black people of our generation, people like us, inspire black youth? Isn't this the fundamental premise of integration, and the most important aspect of our individual accomplishments to our people?

"You want me to tell you what I really think?" she asked mysteriously. "Even on TV, the kids barely notice all the accomplishments of black people of our generation, the black role models of today, like Colin Powell and Maxine Waters. My experience is that when the kids recognize me on TV and say, oh I know Dr. Fulani, it's because they've seen me first in their communities. A lot of these kids don't know who Colin Powell is. It may seem impossible, but how could you have lived in New York and never seen the World Trade Center?"

For Fulani, successful black people at the top of the establishment can't possibly serve as role models if the children in the inner city don't know they exist. With Dr. Fred Newman, she founded the All Stars Talent Show Network and the Joseph A. Forgione Development School for Youth, designed to change dramatically the way that teenagers in the ghetto behave and think about themselves and their career possibilities. Fulani has designed a program that can be a class escalator, and she's campaigning for poor kids to step on board. Her theory of performance starts with a controversial premise:

"We don't have to negate the positive aspects of hip-hop culture, and I don't think that being black has to be equated with hip-hop. I think it's a cultural expression that's in our community . . . A lot of white kids who come from affluent backgrounds are influenced by hip-hop, and they have five earrings and the whole bit. It's a performance. We're trying to teach inner-city kids that it's a performance that they don't have to be trapped in. They, too, can wake up the next day, put on a suit, and go to work."

Fulani has "predominantly white, well-to-do businesspeople" who train the kids in her program to do corporate internships. "I tell them to teach the kids how to be white, and they almost fall off their chair. They have all the liberal reaction of oh my God, we're going to step on their cultural toes. I tell them, believe me, after the twelve weeks of training they'll still be black. But why don't you use this time as an opportunity to share with them some of the secrets of white success?"

Skeptical, I observed one of Fulani's programs. These teenagers, poor and from inner-city schools, were enrolled in her Development School for Youth. In just twelve weeks, the school promises to transform them from disaffected street kids to potential Wall Street employees. How can she possibly achieve this?

"What it means to use performance as a teaching method is that you put young people in situations that are way beyond anything they know how to do. This is totally new learning. You don't know anything about Wall Street; you barely know how to spell the word 'stock.' And then we have them perform as if they do know these things. And, in the process, they learn how to produce their own learning."

But what sorts of things does her program teach these kids?

"Oh, all kinds of wonderful things: basically, how to have conversations that are not in authoritarian situations. We teach them how to shake people's hands, how to look them directly in the eyes. 'Hi! My name is Shakimah Smith. It's great to meet you.'"

I have to confess that, initially, I worried that this program might be little more than a finishing school for poor kids. But I was wrong. As well as a grounding in finance, the students are taught practical skills—like how to comport themselves in the corporate world—that their schools don't teach them. They are taught, as Fulani humorously puts it, "to act white" to gain employment, without sacrificing the values of their home and neighborhood: in other words, how to be black and function successfully in a white world. Parents, schools, and churches did this when I was growing up but are failing at this acculturation process now. At the end of twelve weeks, Fulani's students are given paid internships on Wall Street.

These are ghetto street kids, and Fulani transforms them into potential Wall Street executives in twelve weeks? "I don't really care whether the kids in the Development School become Wall Street executives. I want them to know that Wall Street exists. I don't care what they do with that knowledge or that experience; I want them to have it," she said.

What Fulani is doing seems like a small miracle, but she would be the first to admit that it's just a beginning, a drop in an ocean of black economic misery. When I was growing up in the fifties, becoming a successful doctor, lawyer, or businessman was about the blackest thing you could be. For too many of our young people today, mainstream America will always be a closed shop for white boys, and we're better off on our own.

How we as people got here is, frankly, a dark and troubling mystery to me. Attitudes such as these are a perversion of Dr. King's dream, of all that he gave his life for. But perhaps it is not so very surprising, really. For as long as any of us can remember, the odds have been deeply stacked against our success in American society. But historically, our political leaders, our mentors in school and church, our parents and families, all insisted that we fight to succeed, despite the odds.

The great poet Audre Lorde once wrote that you cannot dismantle the master's house using the master's tools. But what other tools can we use, except those that built the house in the first place? Since Dr. King's death, as a result of the expanded opportunities of affirmative action and our own hard work, an unprecedented number of African Americans have succeeded in worlds once all-white, the doors to which were historically locked shut for more than a hundred years.

Despite the negative spin that Herbert Marcuse gave to it in the late fifties, the growth of the black middle class is one of the truly great victories of Dr. King's Civil Rights Movement. Each hire and every promotion of a black on Wall Street is a victory over racism for our people. The challenge facing the black middle class is to use their clout and wealth to fight structural and institutional racism, on the one hand, and to become more effective role models— living, breathing mentors of social mobility—for dispirited millions of black youth thus far left behind, to show them that you no longer have to be white to aspire to obtain our share of the American dream. The level of social consciousness among the new black middle and upper middle class is deeply moving; built as their newfound status is on political gains made only because of the Civil Rights Movement, perhaps this should come as no surprise. These people's lives and concerns, their political orientation and their social consciences, have refuted Marcuse's worry that they would be tokens, or raceless, soulless black men and women in whiteface who had left their people behind, as E. Franklin Frazier describes the old middle class in *The Black Bourgeoisie* (1957). But unless we do these things, the new class divide within the black community will be a permanent fixture in African-American life, with deep and profound economic and structural differences masked to some extent, as they are now, by a seemingly shared African-American culture. No one can believe that Martin Luther King, Jr., died for that.

COLIN POWELL

The Good Soldier

"The gulf between the two black communities—the middle class and those who have been left behind—need not be permanent, but it's going to take a lot of work to change it," U.S. Secretary of State Colin Powell told me. "It's going to take a lot of work on the part of both communities, the well-to-do and those who are striving. Those of us who have made it, white and black, need to give back with resources and mentoring. But there's something else we have to give back. We have got to get to our young people and tell them they can be successful."

When I go to the Middle East or China or wherever my job takes me and I walk into a room, people see a black man. But they also see the American secretary of state and they know that I'm not coming to them as a black man; I'm coming to them as a representative of the American people, as a representative of the president of the United States. I represent all the values of this country and the power of this country, its military power, its economic power and political power, and once we sit down and they get past whatever color I am, they want to do business with me.

Here at home in America, people sometimes ask what is the significance of my being the first African-American secretary of state. I hope it does have significance, particularly to African Americans, and I hope the significance is that it happened in America. It happened in a place where we were once slaves, nothing more than property. It happened in a place where at the time the Constitution was written, we were considered three-fifths of a white person for voting purposes. And it happened in a little over a couple of hundred years. Now that may be a long time by some standards, but by comparison with what's happened in other countries around the world, it's quite remarkable. When you also think that it happened to a guy whose parents just showed up in this country as immigrants off a banana boat back in the 1920s, it's remarkable.

I hope it gives inspiration to African-American youngsters, Peruvian youngsters, and white youngsters who might not have come from a black background but came from a poor background. Back when Desert Storm ended and there was all this celebration, parades everywhere, I went back to the Bronx, where I was raised, and I went to my high school, still in the inner city—and to this day it is bringing along other kids like me. I talked to the kids there, essentially Puerto Rican and black kids who were in the audience, and they were looking at me and they started to ask questions about me being a role model for them. And I said, well, I'm glad that I'm a role model for you, but I want General Schwarzkopf also to be a role model for you. Don't limit yourself by saying, if that black guy can do it, I can do it. If General Schwarzkopf can do it, you can do it, I tell them. Don't limit yourself any longer on the basis of your race, your color, your background, your creed. We've come too far to create our own limitations.

I tell young people a bit of a joke when they say, "Well, gosh, you're the black secretary of state." I say, "No, I'm not. There ain't a white secretary of state somewhere. I'm the secretary of state who is black, you know; there's a difference." I refuse to be limited by my race, and you shouldn't, I tell young people, allow yourself to be limited or stereotyped. Don't use your particular distinction as an excuse for you not to do your best. Take advantage of all the things that have been done for you over these 226 years. I wouldn't be secretary of state if I hadn't done that.

I was raised in a family that never felt constrained by their poverty or by their race. That had nothing to do with anything; we were as good as anyone. And I was raised in a community that had blacks, whites, Puerto Ricans, minority, you name it, we were it, a melting pot of the New York City environment. So I never really knew I was supposed to feel in some way constrained by being an inner-city, public school black kid, the son of immigrants. I just went into the army and I found an organization that said, no, no, no, we've changed, we're ahead of the rest of the society. We don't care if you're black or blue, we only care if you're a good green soldier. And if you do your best, you watch, you'll be recognized. If you don't do your best, you'll be punished. And I started out as a black lieutenant but I became a general who was black.

I want to continue to be a role model for the kids in the neighborhood I grew up in, and for other youngsters in America. Not just a black role model in that stereotypical sense, but an example of what you can achieve if you are willing to work for it. And second, those of us in the African-American community who have been successful financially ought to give some of it back to the community. You can do it through scholarships, through donations, through mentoring, through adopting or sponsoring a school. There are lots of ways to do it, and everything I've just mentioned I have done, or try to do. You don't have to scream and shout about it but just get it done, reach back and help these youngsters who are coming along. And to the extent we have benefited from this society, we can't just walk away from these youngsters.

In fact, so many African Americans have been successful, and have been able to improve their physical station in life—have a nicer neighborhood to live in, a bigger house to live in, fancier cars, nice clothes—that those who get left behind are left further behind than they might have been forty or fifty or sixty years ago. Before integration, the successful people in the community still didn't have anywhere to go, so that success stayed in the community and we had a thriving middle class. You couldn't break out too far. Then integration kind of changed all of that, and for those of us who became successful, it became easier to leave those behind who had not yet gained success, especially those children who needed examples to follow.

The examples were no longer there the way they used to be; the successful people had moved on to some other place. So the kids today, rather than seeing successful middle-class professionals in their neighborhood, are to some extent denied that kind of example. So, then, what example should they follow? They tend to follow people who may not provide them the right example, who may not exert the right kinds of influences. And we've lost something as a result. Those of us who have been successful and have escaped have got to go back.

There are reasons why those of us who are in the black community and who have made it have such a great responsibility. Our youngsters need us more perhaps, for one thing. And our youngsters are still living in a society that is really only one generation removed from racism, discrimination, segregation, and economic deprivation, and we're still suffering from that. It's different in that regard from the way our white counterparts may view their responsibility to youngsters in, say, a poor white community.

We're also living, to some extent, in a society that still sees people by color, much as we would like it to be otherwise. A few of us have been able to rise above that, to be frank. But there are a lot of youngsters walking down the street who get met with, watch out, there's a black kid. There's still that kind of discrimination in our society. Some people would call it racism. There is racism, but I don't call it a kind of discrimination racism; it's just there's a difference there that is part of our legacy, part of our history, that has not yet been overcome. And those of us who have been successful have an obligation to reach back to these youngsters and help them, more so than I think our white brothers. But I tell my white colleagues, you've got to reach down to the black community too. You've got to reach down to any community in need.

I also tell black youngsters, get a white mentor. If there isn't a brother, we'll get you connected up with a white mentor. I had lots of white mentors. Most of my mentors that made me successful in the army were white, and nothing wrong with it. We have to not limit ourselves because of our race or color, and we shouldn't limit ourselves with respect to where we go and get help from. More and more people in the white community are anxious to help those who are less fortunate, and especially those less fortunate in the black community.

I believe the most important thing that I can do, in relation to the black community and in relationship to myself, is to do the job. I have never been driven by ambition. I'm not unambitious—I wouldn't have gotten where I did if I was unambitious—but I'm not driven by that ambition. I'm driven by my desire to do the job. I've always tried to do a good job everywhere I've been. And it's been recognized and that's why I was successful. I try to do the best job I can for people I work for and for the American people, and I try to be a good family guy, as best I can. I try to keep a lot of friends on my side.

The gulf between the two black communities—the middle class and those who have been left behind—need not be permanent, but it's going to take a lot of work to change it. It's going to take a lot of work on the part of both communities, the well-to-do and those who are striving. Those of us who have made it, white and black, need to give back with resources and mentoring. But there's something else we have to give back. We have got to get to our young people and tell them they can be successful. We have to tell them, Rosa Parks did not ride in the back of a bus and Martin Luther King did not die so you could call young girls bad names, so that you could act like a fool, so that you could put stuff up your nose, or so that you could stick up somebody. Now, that is not acceptable. And these people did not die to create these opportunities for you that you refuse to seize. So let me not hear any excuses about why you don't want to go to school or how you go to a bad school. We all went to bad schools at one time or another, but guess what was in that bad school: some education. So don't allow these excuses to keep you from getting what is out there waiting for you if you will seize it.

We have got to teach our young people that as you come along and as you become parents, you have an enormous responsibility for the children you've brought into life. I'm sometimes disturbed by some of the television depictions you see on some of the channels and by some of the shows—and I don't want to get into any particular show—where we pander to this kind of deplorable behavior. If I had ever said these words, or if I had ever talked to an adult that way or ever said anything like this to peers or to anyone, it would not have been tolerated. I would have been told, we don't talk like that in this family. Or as Bill Cosby used to say, "I brought you into this world and I'll take you out!"

We've got to get back to those standards and stop making excuses, saying, I can't do this, I can't do that, this person's down on me, and things like that. Those are not reasons; they're all excuses. We have got to start weaning our youngsters away from this sort of thinking. Most of our youngsters are fine, they're in our universities, they're fine.

I was on the board of Howard University, I was on the board of the United Negro College Fund, another way of giving back, so I know what our youngsters are capable of doing. But there are too many of them who are adopting hedonistic lifestyles. That's simply deplorable and has to be stopped. Too many of our television stations are exploiting this kind of lifestyle and peddling it all over the airways, and other youngsters see it and hear this kind of language and see this kind of dress and this kind of behavior. Our humor has gone from Bill Cosby down to the worst kind, deep in the gutter.

I wear my blackness every day and I use it every day in one way or another, whether it's a check I write for something or a youngster I speak to or a kid I mentor via e-mail. When I was in private life, I was able to do a lot more, whether it was for the College Fund or Howard University or America's Promise, which is a youth campaign I ran. I never said we're going after black kids, but when I went after kids, most of the kids who were in the greatest need were black, and I knew that. With respect to people who may say it's no longer enough to do a good job, that we're not brothers anymore, that we have lost our blackness if we're not teaching in the ghetto at night, I can't spend a lot of time worrying about what people say about me or whether I'm doing enough. I do as much as I can. All of us should do as much as we can and just take whatever compliments or criticism comes with it.

VERNON JORDAN

Chairman of the Board

Vernon Jordan—lawyer, leader, adviser to presidents—sat on his first corporate board in 1972. "We've come a long way from the seventies if you
think about Dick Parsons, CEO at AOL Time Warner, Ken Chenault of
AmEx, Stan O'Neal of Merrill Lynch, and Frank Raines of Fannie Mae.
These four black men control in excess of $300 billion in market capital-
ization, and they employ some 300,000 people. That was inconceivable
in my time, and now they are CEOs at companies that would not have
hired their parents, except in menial jobs."

This is Martin Luther King, Jr., on the four girls who died in the 1963 Birmingham church bombing: "But I hope you can find a little consolation from
the universality of this experience. Death comes to every individual. There is
an amazing democracy about death. It is not aristocracy for some of the people, but a democracy for all of the people. Kings die and beggars die; rich men
die and poor men die; old people die and young people die. Death comes to
the innocent and it comes to the guilty. Death is the irreducible common de-
nominator of all men. I hope you can find some consolation from Christian-
ity's affirmation that death is not the end. Death is not a period that ends the
great sentence of life, but a comma that punctuates it to more lofty significance. Death is not a blind alley that leads the human race into a state of
nothingness, but an open door which leads man into life eternal. Let this dar-
ing faith, this great invincible surmise, be your sustaining power during these
trying days."

That is Martin's eulogy for the girls. One was eleven years old; three were
fourteen years old. Most people don't think about Martin's Memphis speech.
They think about "I may not get there with you." But the eulogy is unbelievable. They finally convicted Bobby Frank Cherry, who was a former Klansman, in May of 2002, thirty-nine years after the crime. Two other men had
been convicted in 1977 and in 2001.

On a trip to Tougaloo College in Mississippi, where I was giving the commencement in May of 2002, I landed at an airport north of Jackson. As we pulled out of the airport onto a highway, I looked up and the sign said MEDGAR EVERS BOULEVARD. Medgar was my friend. He was my colleague. I was the field director of the NAACP in Georgia; he was the field director in Mississippi. We did a lot of things together. Blacks have integrated institutions of learning at all levels in Mississippi in the years since Medgar was murdered, and from 1963, the year Medgar died, to the year 2000, the number of black registered voters in Mississippi rose from 28,000 to 450,000.

When we got to the Tougaloo campus that day, we went to the library and stood waiting for the commencement to begin. I saw a group of people moving toward the library, following a man who turned out to be the governor of the state of Mississippi, who had come to Tougaloo College—which was a hotbed of demonstrations in the sixties—to robe up, march, and address the graduates.

I remember when Paul Johnson, Jr., was governor of Mississippi, in the mid-sixties. I remember when I could not convince him to amend the articles of incorporation for Tougaloo College. When Johnson was lieutenant governor in 1962, he physically blocked federal marshals who were escorting James Meredith as he enrolled at Ole Miss. In those days at Tougaloo, what was considered a bastion of communists was bringing down the system of segregation. And here, four decades later, was the governor of Mississippi, who knew everybody and everybody knew him, and he was glad and honored to be there.

If you think about the March on Washington in 1963, you saw the best and the brightest of black leadership, and that march and what happened subsequently created four new leadership classes that had been virtually nonexistent. Black elected officials constitute one new class. The second class comprises blacks who pierced the corporate veil from the boardroom to management to CEO, blacks who manage, lead, run predominantly white institutions: Cliff Wharton becoming president of Michigan State, Frank Thomas going to the Ford Foundation, and now Colin Powell running the State Department.

Then there is a huge number of people who lead and run indigenous community organizations. This is a whole new class, because historically, all of the leaders were tied to a tent. The poverty program, the new urban program, brought in community people, and they told NAACP people and they told the tent brothers, move over! Make room. We have our own constituency. So there is a huge group of indigenous leaders at the community level that's a known leadership class.

The fourth leadership class is the new black entrepreneur. Historically, in our community, we buried our own, we had our own drugstore, we had our own little laundry, and they catered to the needs of that particular community. But now it is different. We not only have our street but Main Street.

There's a difference between black leaders and leading blacks. Leaders have to be certain who they are and what they stand for, and they have to be rooted and grounded in that process and stay with what they believe. I like to think that that's what dictated my decisions when I was a black leader. When I was head of the Urban League, and when I became head of the United Negro College Fund, I was a black leader, because I had a constituency. Today I am a leading black; I am not a black leader, although I get described that way. I don't have constituencies to which I am responsible and for which I have a responsibility for advocacy and programs, and I think that is the definition of a black leader. But a leading black is somebody who everybody knows. That means they have opinions but they don't have a constituency that they can take here, there, and yonder.

I had dinner recently with four young black businesspeople—two women and two men who decided to bid on me, won me in a raffle, for Project She, which disseminates information to young black women in this community about breast cancer. There was a fund-raiser and I was up for auction, and they put their pennies together and they won this auction. I never asked what the price was; I didn't want to know. So I had dinner with them. I loved it, because these kids, who are in their thirties, are all in the finance business and investment banking. One just left investment banking to go work for BET, where she's director of corporate development. They all have master's degrees, M.B.A.'s; they are all single, young, and ambitious; and they are very good friends and they came together in this project. I said to them, what you all are doing by supporting Project She is as important as your freedom rights. It's in a different context, but it is service, it is helping, it is making things right for black people. I think one of the frustrations is that people unfortunately think they have the same responsibility to do what was done in my time, but in the words of Shakespeare, "The occasion shall instruct you."

So there are not going to be any marches of freedom rights; we've moved beyond that. But these young people were taking their time out to support this project, to give their money to go to the fund-raiser, to make things better for black people. It is still the movement, but it's at another stage and another process that is equally important, and it was important for me to make them feel that this was their contribution. Now, it's not going to make the *New York Times* and it's not going to make the nightly news, but that does not make it unimportant. And I appreciate the frustration. I came out of law school in June of 1960. I finished law school on a Friday, and on Monday morning I'm with Don Hollowell, a black attorney, in the Atlanta Municipal Court getting kids out of jail. That's out of school, into that action. Well, it's not like that always, but the other thing is that those kids who won dinner with me at the fund-raiser had options after college and business school that were not available to me, not even well after I graduated.

It was just totally different for me. When I finished law school in 1960, there was not a job in Atlanta for a black lawyer—no matter what school you went to or what you were and regardless of any class standing—not in the city government, the county government, the state government, or the federal government, and certainly not in a private law firm. And so my only option was to choose between a black real estate lawyer, who was offering more money, and Don Hollowell, who was offering me thirty-five dollars a week to be his law clerk, and I chose it. I was as happy as I could be. I had a wife and child, and I was in the movement. I was a soldier, a foot soldier, and it was very exciting. Six months after law school, in 1961, I was escorting Charlayne Hunter through the mobs as she enrolled at the University of Georgia. And I understood why I was there and why I had gone to Howard University Law School, which was the only law school that had a course in civil rights, in 1957. At other law schools, they taught the Commerce Clause, but at Howard, we were taught the Commerce Clause and the Thirteenth and Fourteenth and Fifteenth Amendments, and it was a school with a great heritage. It was Durban Marshall's school and it was Spotswood Robinson's school and it was Robert Carter's school, and it was a forum where the dry runs for the Supreme Court arguments took place.

There was nothing better than going at night to the dry runs and sitting and watching Bob Maine, Bill Coleman, Frank Reeves, Jackie Owen, Don Hollowell, Jack Greenberg, and Constance Motley. You were seeing in action what you wanted to be. When they would take their breaks and stand around outside the courtroom, Doug Wilder and I—we were there at law school together—would just stand around and just listen and be in their presence.

The integration of corporate America has been going on a very long time.

I went on my first corporate board in 1972. Two years earlier, I first came to 30 Rockefeller Plaza, the building where I now work, with Dr. Fred Patterson, founder of the United Negro College Fund and third president of the Tuskegee Institute. Patterson was the son-in-law of Robert Moton, who was the second president of Tuskegee. Patterson married Moton's daughter, which is probably how he got to be president. I'd just moved to New York from Atlanta to become the new executive director of the College Fund. I believed with a passion in the mission of the fund. We had not gained a level playing field for blacks with respect to education, and still have not. I had always believed in the role of historically black colleges. The small number of openings each year for blacks in the country's white colleges cannot possibly serve the thousands of black students who seek an education and full participation in the civic, social, and economic life of this country.

So I was the new kid on the block, literally. The president of the College Fund, Dr. Stephen H. Wright, had recently left that post, and the fund had other troubles. The philanthropist John D. Rockefeller III had resigned from its board of trustees, as had advertising executive David Ogilvy and Andrew Heiskell, the chairman of Time Inc. Disputes about the management of the fund had led to an impasse.

Dr. Patterson thought it would be helpful to try to persuade Mr. Rockefeller to come back on the board of the fund. Mr. Rockefeller was not very nice to us; in fact, he bordered on being rude. And he said he was not going to come back on the board for the College Fund. Patterson introduced me as the new guy, as the young fella who was going to lead the College Fund. Mr. Rockefeller said, "I'm not gonna do it." White fellas are always stacked here at the Rockefeller Brothers Fund down on 54, 56. And I got back to my office and Datus Smith, an aide to Rockefeller, called me and said, "Young man, you made a mistake," and I said, "What was that?" and he said, "You shouldn't have come here with Dr. Patterson, he's mad with Dr. Patterson. I'm arranging for you to come back alone to see him."

I came back about ten days later to this same building to see Mr. Rockefeller. And I went in and he said, "Why are you back here? I told you I wasn't going back on that board." And I said, "Well, I came to make my case. I need your help. We need your help." And then he says, "I'm not gonna do it." And then I proffered to him the letter that his mother wrote to the five boys about social corporate responsibility. He said, "I know what my mother wrote and I'm still not gonna do it, and I don't know why you bothered to come back."

And I stood up and said, "Mr. Rockefeller, thank you for your time. I will do it without you." We shook hands and I walked out.

A year later, after Whitney Young had died, maybe a month or so after—Whitney died on March 11, 1971—Mr. Rockefeller invited me back. I come into the building and I go into his office and he's sitting there with Douglas Dillon, who was secretary of the treasury under Kennedy. "The last time you left here, young man, you were in a huff," he said. "But you said that you were going to do it without me and you did it. You've done a very good job," he added. We raised $10 million my first year for the College Fund. A lot of money. And Mr. Rockefeller said, "Now, I want to ask you to do something for me," and I said, "Yes, sir, what is it?" and he said, "I want you to become a Rockefeller Foundation trustee." And I said, "Mr. Rockefeller, I've got better judgment than you. The answer is yes."

And so, not every time that I come in this building, but many times when I come in and head up that elevator, I think about that moment, when Mr. Rockefeller told me again he wasn't coming back on the board of the College Fund. I felt okay, though; I didn't feel vulnerable. I'd asked him and he'd said no, that I was wasting his time and mine. It's very important to know when people are saying no and to get out of their way. I'd come back a second time thinking I had a chance, and I knew that he wasn't going to be better. The Rockefellers had been very involved with the founding of the College Fund, as they were with Spelman and with other important institutions, and I knew what I had to do at the time. Later, some good came out of it. Mr. Rockefeller eventually came back on the board of the College Fund, after my time there. In the Rockfeller Foundation context, we became friends. I became good friends with his son Jay and with his brothers Nelson and David, and I attended the funerals of Mr. Rockefeller and Nelson.

Now the integration of corporate America is in a different phase. A group of us, including Leon Sullivan, Frank Thomas, Jewell Lafontant, Patricia Harris, Bill Coleman, and others, were among the first blacks on corporate boards. But we've come a long way from the seventies if you think about Dick Parsons, CEO at AOL Time Warner, Ken Chenault of AmEx, Stan O'Neal of Merrill Lynch, and Frank Raines of Fannie Mae. These four black men control in excess of $300 billion in market capitalization, and they employ some 300,000 people. That was inconceivable in my time, and now they are CEOs at companies that would not have hired their parents, except in menial jobs.

Some people in the community say these guys and other successful blacks are not brothers anymore. But that's something you have to live with. People say things they don't even mean and certainly do not understand. When I was doing voter registration in the South, I was considered the militant. Then I'd go to work for the United Negro College Fund and find out I'd become a Tom. Same person, same beliefs.

It's important to the progress of our people that black people like Ken Chenault and Dick Parsons and Frank Raines and Stanley O'Neal are occupying these positions of power. It's important in that it says to young people that they can do it too—that anything you want to achieve can in fact be achieved. But it says something else. It says that if you have the ability, the tenacity, the perseverance, the fortitude, and the smarts, they will put you in this job. Ken Chenault is chairman of the board at American Express, and I'm the only other black member of the AmEx board, so we're a minority. But when you think about Parsons, Raines, Chenault, and O'Neal, white people have put them in charge of their money, and my people did it. That's very serious! And the one thing that we know is that white people like money, and that's why they sold us and bought us. It had to do with money. It had nothing to do with humanity; it was about money. But white people have entrusted their trust funds and the future of their children and their grandchildren to these brothers, because they are competent.

Bear Bryant didn't play those black football players to integrate the team; he played them to win. There are so many choices today that didn't exist when I was growing up, in sports as in education, business, community work, and politics. It's important to individuals that they have a place to pursue their happiness. And places are now available that were not available. I'm sort of a golfer. I love it and I do a lot of it, especially with my wife. It's being outdoors, the fresh air and the sunshine, green grass, a breeze from the lake or the ocean or wherever you're playing, and it's fun and it's competitive. It's a growing sport among black professionals, among this new leadership class of businesspeople. I played a lot of tennis for a time, after I moved to New York. I never put a tennis racket in my hand before I came to New York, and I don't play as much tennis now, but I love it. I have partners here who take clients golfing, but I've never made a deal on the golf course. I fundamentally don't take clients golfing, because golfing is my thing. And so I do it with my wife, Ann, and with my friends and my buddies.

When I grew up in Atlanta, the city golf courses were not open to blacks.

The only place you could play golf was at the Lincoln Country Club, and so most of the Talented Tenth, upper-class blacks played golf there, but the better golfers were the black kids who were caddying at the white country clubs, because every Monday they got to play there. I understand that sometimes I'd like to be Michael Jordan, especially when we play golf together, at the same golf course, and when I see him playing from the gold tees and shooting in the mid- to high seventies, I'd like to be Michael. I would like to have made that last shot when they beat the Utah Jazz.

I grew up in the first public housing project for black people in this country, University Homes, so called because it stood amid the web of Atlanta's black colleges: Morehouse, Spelman, Atlanta University, Morris Brown, and Clark. University Homes was not just for poor people; I had many adult role models there from varied social and economic levels, and my family would have been considered in the black middle class then. I can remember on a Saturday friends and I went to Ashby's Theater, and after your hot dog, your toasted-bun hot dog at Amer's drugstore at the corner of Ashby on Hunter Street, you walked home. I can remember walking home and seeing Dr. Benjamin Mays walking through the Morehouse campus. As a kid, I knew he was a giant, that he was important. He achieved an international reputation for Morehouse College, and he mentored Martin Luther King, Jr. He also persevered till he won a chapter of Phi Beta Kappa at Morehouse. Dr. Mays always walked erect, and so I'm walking twenty yards behind him, emulating Dr. Mays. Well, that's not all bad.

I loved going to the campus because I wanted to see Dr. Rufus Clement and Dr. James Rawley, President William A. Fountain, and I would see these professors. Rufus Clement always wore a vest, and I remember him in spats, and he always wore his frat Beta Kappa key on his vest. I have never forgotten those images, and when I would go through the campus, I would say, I want to be like that.

Black kids who grew up later, in the fifties, thought the blackest thing you could be, the greatest thing you could do for our people, was to become like Thurgood Marshall or Dr. King. Being an athlete was okay, and there was Hank Aaron and Willie Mays in the fifties. But when I was growing up, there was only one athlete—Joe Louis. When Joe Louis fought—he fought Billy Conn the first time in 1941—every radio in the court in our housing project was on. You could be out in the court and hear the fight, because every radio was on, and everybody cheered and he was big. We knew about Jesse Owens, but that happened in 1936. But we saw—heard, you couldn't see it—heard about Joe Louis on the radio. He was the man athletically.

I was in sixth grade, and during the annual Negro History Week celebration, my best friend, Frank Hill, who lives out in Kansas City now, was given the role of Joe Louis. This is the role that everybody wanted and it's the role I wanted, because you get to wear trunks and tennis shoes and boxing gloves to go on the stage. And you come out with these boxing gloves and you bow and then you get to the middle of the stage and you say, "I am Joe Louis," and you get cheered. So Frank got that role, and I was a little jealous. I was given the role of William Grant Still, which meant I had on paper tails and a baton in my hand, and I walked down and said, "I am William Grant Still and I conducted Tchaikovsky's symphony and New York's blah, blah . . . ," and no buzz, no cheers. But as I think about my life, that was a role I should have had, as opposed to Joe Louis, because it was more consistent. But it was not a happy moment. Everyone wanted to be Joe Louis because he was the man.

I always knew as a kid, growing up in the public housing project, that I was going to college. It was never a doubt in my mind, because the seed had been planted. And so it was not even a second thought. The role of economics, in terms of racial discrimination and the future of our people, takes a backseat to education. The problems affecting our people now have first to do with education. You can't get to the economic issues until you get the education. There was a time when you could work and not be educated because it was about brawn. Now it's about brains. Even if you have a job at McDonald's, you have to know how to work a computer. So you have to start with education, certainly in fundamental reading, writing, arithmetic, and computers. Then you are reasonably assured of some degree of economic security. Education is first. It begins there.

When I got ready to go to college, I had a falling-out with my best buddies, because we had talked since junior year about going to Howard—getting a house, having a car, being sharp every day, and dating the beautiful girls who we understood went to Howard. We didn't talk a whole lot about studying. But then this marvelous man came to my school from the National Scholarship Service Fund for Negro Students. He talked about the fund and he talked about going north to school, and I was absolutely intrigued by him, and I applied and got accepted. My buddies didn't like it, because it was going against the grain, and while they didn't accuse me of being white, they felt that I thought I was better, which is sort of the same thing, and that I was not a brother anymore.

One night I couldn't go out with my buddies because I had to work on my mother's business, but I went out the next night with a girlfriend who had been out with them the night before. We were sitting on this date and she says, I want to tell you something. I said, what's that? She said, your friends aren't your friends; you were the topic of conversation, and they said you are doing something different, so you are odd man out, and while I was bothered by it, I was not sufficiently bothered by it to change my mind.

But when I went home for Thanksgiving and Christmas, it bothered me, because a chasm had developed between us, and I raised it with the young woman who ran with me for vice president of the student body at DePauw University. I wrote her and I said, what have I done? What's wrong? It's not the same with me and my buddies anymore. She wrote me back and she said, you're walking with kings and you've lost the common touch, and I wrote her back a one-sentence letter. I said, "Dear Ethel, kiss my ass!" Because here I was the only black in my class, running twice as fast to stay even, and she's telling me I'm walking with kings, I've lost the common touch.

The answer to that, I believe, is that we have to work at giving our kids enough self-confidence and enough perseverance and fortitude to press on. You really cannot let other people create tensions for you in life; you have to create your own. Dr. Evans Crawford, at Rankin in 1958, preached that sermon, and I never forgot it, what he said about creating your own tension. I believe that we have to somehow ingrain that in the hearts and minds and souls of young black people, that they will create their own tensions and not be tempted by the tensions of others. Now, that's very difficult because the social pressure is difficult, but if in fact these individual kids are interested in achievement, then they have to create their own tensions, and that is true whether it's Michael Jordan or Vernon Jordan or whether it's Tiger Woods or Deval Patrick. They have to create their own tensions, and that transcends race.

You do not get to be a distinguished professor or public servant or successful entrepreneur letting other people create tensions for you. You have to create your own. When I gave the commencement at Tougaloo, I tried to make four points to these young people. First, you are what you are today because you stand on somebody's shoulders, and wherever you are going tomorrow, you cannot get there by yourself. That's point number one. Number two, if in fact you stand on other people's shoulders, you have a reciprocal responsibility to live your life in such a way that people can stand on your shoulders. Third, if in fact you have that responsibility to live your life in a way that others are going to stand on your shoulders, then you have to be prepared. You have to be committed to excellence and hard work and sacrifice. And fourth, if you do those three, then you have to have some moral and ethical boundaries and standards for your behavior. As Churchill said, you have to march in the ranks of honor. I believe that, and I think that those four principles have helped me in my own life.

I remember when my parents took me to college. They stayed that weekend, and I remember my father shaking my hand to tell me good-bye, but he didn't say good-bye; he said, you can't come home. I said, what do you mean? He said, the college counselor says your reading scores are far lower than those of your classmates, which means when they're in chapter six you'd be trying to get out of the preface. He said, these kids up here, these white kids went to fine township high schools and private schools and you went to this old dilapidated, segregated, ill-equipped, double-sessioned, overcrowded school, he said, but you can't come home. And so I said, well, what am I supposed to do, Dad? And he said, read, boy, read, and he drove away.

Well, I was stunned. Four years later at graduation, the graduation is over and you go to say hello to your parents. My father, with the same expression that he had four years before, walked to me and shook my hand. He didn't say, congratulations; he said, you can come home now. It's absolutely true. He said, you can come home now. And in a book of eulogies that contains the one I wrote for him, I tell the story about you can come home now. And then I say that there was another conversation between a father and son, a conversation between Dad and God, the father of us all. And Dad said to God, not long ago, I have fought a good fight, I have finished my course, I have kept the faith, and God said to Daddy, you can come home now. I like that.

But it was a mandate. My dad was telling me what I had to do, and he had accepted the fact that I was going to college and that it was a challenge. I remember at the end of my sophomore year writing home, I think I've had enough of this; maybe I'm going to transfer. My mother wrote me back and she said, there will be no transfer. It was like that passage that says, woe be unto him who puts his hand upon the plough and turns back. That would have been turning back; no way. And she was absolutely right. I'm going next Saturday to my forty-fifth college reunion. It seems like yesterday I was the only black in my class, only five in the student body. So I'm going back. I spoke at the twenty-fifth. You have to go to the forty-fifth just in case you don't make the fiftieth.

What was so clear to me in my early life was that there was a structure, there was a family unit, home, there was school. There was the Gate City Day Nursery, there was the Butler Street YMCA on Saturday, and there was St. Paul African Methodist Episcopal Church on Sunday, and every Monday and Friday at five o'clock I knew that we were going to choir rehearsal at St. Paul. I knew at five o'clock on Wednesday I was going to be at Boy Scouts, and I knew on Saturday that I was going to be at the Butler Street YMCA swimming. There was structure, and there was no doubt about it.

I think that my mother, as compared to my father, was a woman ahead of her time, and my father was a man of his time. So that if I had finished high school, got a job in the post office, married a nice girl, got a little white house with green shutters and a white picket fence, kept my car washed, my grass cut, my hair trimmed, my shoes shined, went to work every day, went to church every Sunday, listened to the news, read the news, and voted, my father would have said that was a good life, and he was not wrong about that. It is a good life.

On the other hand, my mother believed that was not enough, that there were other things beyond that I could do. And she pushed me. I had an extraordinary mother who was president of the PTA at every school I attended through high school. And when I was at one high school and my younger brother was at another elementary school, she was president of both PTAs. Unlearned and unlettered though she was, she understood, based on her own deprivation, the value of education. The value of going to the PTA meetings. The value of trying to make those segregated, dilapidated, ill-equipped schools that I attended as good for me as they possibly could be. Somehow she knew the importance of relationships with the teachers, relationships with the principals, relationships with the communities. How, why, I do not know. But intuitively she knew. So there was never any doubt in my mind.

I did not really get involved in the economic aspect of black people's lives until I came to the National Urban League, where I in effect took the baton from Whitney Young. He had the concept of a master plan for the inner cities, and I don't think he was wrong about that. It never happened, but he was the first to articulate it. I did not follow up on that; I talked about things in other ways. But I had come to understand some fundamental economics not from studying in college, but from my mother, who had a very successful catering business in Atlanta. My brother Windsor and I worked for her at the parties she catered and were paid as though we were her employees. Her business was also how I got my first exposure to lawyers. But when I went away to college, my mother wrote me every day for seven years. Every day. Some letters were short, some were long, some were sad, some were glad, some were angry, depending on what was going on, and they were always newsy about the church, about the neighborhood, about the family. However long or short, angry or happy the letters were, she always wrote two things, and the first was about economics. She would always write somewhere in the middle of that letter, "Son," comma, "if you make a dime, save two cents." That was her philosophy. And she'd never heard of Adam Smith.

The other thing my mother always wrote she put at the end of the letter. She would write, "Son," comma, "if you trust Him he will take care of you." That was her basic view of life. It was a simple faith that was a guide, a steering wheel for her life. It was so ingrained in my mind that it came to me at one of the times when I most needed it, though in the shock of the moment I wasn't sure I could believe it. I didn't pray, because the more you are in shock, the more you think you are gone. But obviously, a lot of other people prayed.

It was on May 29, 1980, Fort Wayne, Indiana. I had addressed the Fort Wayne Urban League's annual Equal Opportunity Dinner at the Marriott Hotel. Later that night, I had gone to the hotel bar with a group of Urban Leaguers. A member of the local board then invited me to her home for a snack and coffee, and drove me back to the hotel. As I got out of her car, I turned around to go and something hit and I went up in the air, then fell down on the ground. It was sort of an indescribable force that just has this impact on your back, knocks you off your feet and down on the ground. I was hit in the back with a bullet from a .30-06 hunting rifle that's used to shoot buffalo. People in the motel started making noise, and I lay there. I felt blood leaving my body and soaking my shirt, and I mean I thought day was done! That's why I love the sound of sirens. There's nothing like the siren, and if you're lying there thinking that this is all over and you hear the siren, the siren suggests hope and it suggests help. I was in Parkview Hospital for ten days. Then President Carter sent a plane for me to Fort Wayne, brought me to New York, and I was in New York Hospital for eighty-eight days.

What is interesting about being shot is that some good comes out of everything. Dr. Robert Stovall had attended the dinner that evening; he was a member of the board of the Fort Wayne Urban League. When he heard I had been shot, he rushed to the hospital. Why exactly he was there, I don't know, but he was there and he saw it was me and this white surgeon was on and it was his time to operate, on whoever was there in an emergency state and needed an operation. Dr. Stovall says to the white doctor, you cannot operate. He said, only Dr. Towles can operate, the black doctor. And he called Jeffrey Towles and said, you have to come here right now. Towles said, it's not my time; I'm not on call. And Dr. Stovall says, this is Vernon Jordan; you have to operate on him. Towles says, not my time to operate, goddammit!

Jeffrey Towles grew up in a small town in West Virginia. His mother was a single parent who worked as a cleaning lady, and one of the places she worked was a doctor's office at night, when she had nobody to take care of him. So this kid, Jeff Towles, would go with his mother, and as she cleaned the doctor's office, he just sort of went through the books, and he liked the diagrams. Then he went to school at West Virginia State, where Dr. John D. Davis was president, and left West Virginia State, went to medical school, and did his residency at Detroit General Hospital. The night before the trial, when I testified in South Bend, Indiana, on the shooting, he said, at Detroit General I saw all kind of injuries. He said, I never saw an injury like yours, and he said, based on what I saw when I saw you, I thought you would not live. But he saved my life. The same little kid who went with his mother to clean the doctor's office, this black kid saved my life. Because Stovall said to the white guy, you cannot operate. Now, it wasn't based on race; it was based on competence. He thought Towles was a better doctor.

The spirit of my mother, the commitment of my father—these are alive in our people. We have the determination to take on the poverty and ignorance that remain. The existence of the black underclass is the next fortress that has to be attacked, with the same kind of vigor we used to attack segregation in the 1960s but with different methods. I've never been into assessing blame. When the house is on fire, I think you call the fire department. I don't think you sit around and ask, who did it? You can do that at some other time, but I think you call the fire department. And I think that on the issues of poverty and ignorance, we need to call the fire department.

Poverty and ignorance in this country have to be attacked if we are to survive as a country. It is not in our own enlightened self-interest to have 37 or 40 percent of any group of kids, black or white, in America in this day and time who are uneducated, unemployed, and unaspiring. It's morally wrong, and it's a burden on the commonwealth. And so the commonwealth has a responsibility, as well as the citizenry, to do something about it. It is not just the obligation and responsibility of the Civil Rights Movement as it is now defined, but it is everybody's obligation. It's in everybody's enlightened self-interest to do something about it.

FRANKLIN D. RAINES

House of Dreams

Frank Raines, chairman and CEO of Fannie Mae, says that home ownership is vitally linked to employment and business productivity. "This
isn't a zero-sum game where because a black person gets a job, it means a
white person didn't get a job, and that's the whole story. That's not the
way capitalism works. When one person gets a job, he starts buying
things, and this creates the potential for more jobs."

I grew up in Seattle, in a working-class family. There were seven kids altogether. My folks were both janitors. One of them worked for the Seattle Park
Department; the other worked for Boeing. I went to public schools and was
active in everything kids are active in, from sports to student government.
And then I got a scholarship to Harvard, and that sort of set me off into the
world.

There were a lot of things we didn't have when I was growing up, but we
always were able to eat. There were some tough times. My dad was hospital-
ized for periods of time for very severe depression, and when he was gone, we
were on AFDC and didn't have a lot. I remember my mother used to give us
two dollars and send us off to the five-and-dime store to buy our Christmas
presents. And that was Christmas.

When my father would get out of the hospital, he didn't have a job, and so
he would go off to the bean fields south of Seattle and I'd go with him sometimes. There was a truck farming area that's now covered over with shopping
centers. To get to the farming area, you'd leave the house at three o'clock in
the morning, drive down to skid row, and catch the bus, and as soon as the
sun came up, you'd be out in the bean fields. You'd pick beans all day. You'd
do that for eleven or twelve hours, and a grown man could earn ten dollars in
a day and a kid could earn five, six dollars. You got two and a quarter cents
per pound. So we had a lot of beans sometimes because you could take home
all the beans you wanted. But through this my parents stayed together. They
owned their own home and they provided the basics, so I think of us as being

a working-class family, meaning that when bad things happen, you're on the edge, and when good things happen, you have a good Christmas.

I didn't ever imagine going to Harvard. Harvard sort of came to me. I didn't know anything about Harvard except that President Kennedy went there and that meant it must be a pretty special place. A Harvard recruiter came to my high school. Harvard was then trying to become more of a national university, to expand beyond being a New England university with all these prep school students, and so they started going out and actually recruiting. It's a little hard to imagine now when they have so many applicants, but Harvard was out recruiting. Jack Reardon, who's still at Harvard, came by my high school, and the counselors got a few of us together and he started talking about this place called Harvard. And then there were some young Harvard alumni in Seattle who also became involved. So for me, going to college was a big deal. I was the first in my family to go to college. The idea of going to Harvard was totally beyond anything I had even thought about.

I can't even imagine how my parents raised all these kids. At their peak my parents earned $15,000 a year each—at their peak—and it's just astounding to me. Their combined income wouldn't have paid for one year of college today. And so what my parents did was remarkable.

One of my earliest jobs was cleaning up. My father built our house. And when I say he built it, I mean he built the house. He dug the foundation with a shovel; he poured the concrete. He bought a house owned by the Highway Department. They were going to tear it down, and he dismantled it—took the nails out of the boards, brought the boards over, and built his house. And he built it as he could earn the money, because no one would give him a loan. He built the house by taking second and third jobs, and sometimes we would go with him and help on the second and third jobs, cleaning up offices and other things. As he got money, he bought more material and built more of the house. It took him five or six years to build this house. But he wanted it, and he decided to build it and did it step by step.

I'm still building houses with families. It's very inspirational being in a job like this where with our help, a guy like my dad now can get a loan because we would make that possible for him, whereas when he was coming up, there was nobody out there who was offering help to people like him.

Today there are black CEOs in four of the Fortune 500 companies, but this does not mean that the job of integrating the power establishment is over, by any stretch. What it means, I think, is that it takes thirty years to make a

CEO—thirty years of education and experience and trying, of being tried out at different jobs. Most blacks were not allowed into the major business schools and weren't allowed into major corporations until thirty years ago. So it's not surprising that once people are given a chance, thirty years later up will pop some CEOs.

What the emergence of blacks into the position of CEO at a few corporations really says, I think, is what a tremendous achievement it was to finally get on with the work of integrating former slaves into America after a 120-year hiatus. We went from the Civil War to the Civil Rights Revolution over a century later because the promise of the post–Civil War constitutional amendments was nullified. People just said after the Civil War, we're not going to do it, this equal opportunity thing. Forget about it; we're not doing that. And it was okay for them to do this, to abrogate these promises. Politically, they were allowed to do it, and so the aspirations of former slaves were totally eliminated. You had a few people who would pop up, but systematically, access to education, access to capital, access to property was just denied. We got to the 1960s and all that really happened was that the political system said, we're actually now going to enforce the promise that we made back in the 1860s.

And all of a sudden things started happening. Black folks started happening at Harvard and Yale, not because there are more who could do it now than in the prior hundred years; it's just that all those people back then had been stepped on and held down. My father might have been somebody if he'd had a chance to get a higher education, if he'd been allowed into the unions. He might have been somebody. The guy was hardworking, smart, but the system didn't make that possible for his generation. So it's making it possible now.

The financial firms on Wall Street are still predominantly white by a wide margin, but there are a few minorities there, more than there were. I was the first black partner on Wall Street, back in the 1980s, and I didn't make *Jet* or the other black magazines. Back in those days, African Americans didn't pay that much attention to Wall Street because it was so far out of the mainstream for most blacks. Wall Street still has a long way to go, but we're seeing a lot of progress.

You can see the progress if you look at a company like Fannie Mae, where we've tried to pride ourselves in our efforts to look like America. We don't mean look like America as adjusted by this and that factor; we just say look like America. This is a company where the majority of the employees are women, where 40 percent of our officers are women, where 25 percent of our officers are minorities—about 14 percent are African American. And we try to hire the best people we can. We have the luxury of having only 4,500 people, and so we look for the best people and we find them. If you look, you actually can find folks. And so we've got women and minorities running major operations in this company. This is not a situation where there's a black guy who's a CEO and that's it in the company. It's indicative of what we try to do. Not every company has been as successful, but I think they can be if they work hard at it.

There are no guarantees. You don't recover overnight from a hundred years of not having built up capital and educational experience. You can't just turn it on the next day. I've talked about this with people and I suggest that the miracle of compound interest—what we talk about in financial terms—doesn't just apply to money. A dollar back in the 1860s would be around ninety dollars today, at a very low rate of interest. But think about it in educational terms. If blacks had been educated three generations ago, what would the current generation look like? How many Nobel Prize winners would there be in the current generation if we'd started then? If the people had begun to have capital and could own property, how much property and capital would they have today, just simply from people adding a little bit day by day? So to me what's happened is that we're finally allowing the miracle of compound interest to start applying to black folks—the accumulation of wealth and the accumulation of social capital.

The accumulation of capital and the use of that capital is clearly the next phase of what I refer to as the integration of former slaves into the society. Civil rights to me is one aspect of that integration. Access to capital and the ability to accumulate wealth through that capital is another aspect of that integration. Political participation is another aspect. We're making some progress on all of these, but the longest haul is going to be on capital simply because we're starting so low. Our estimate is that if the average African American had the same wealth level as just the average white family, which is something like $40,000—so we're not talking about a lot—it would add $1 trillion to the wealth of African Americans.

For most people, what wealth means is that you've got the money to educate your kids, that if you get sick you don't lose everything, and you can retire with dignity. That's all wealth means. And for most people, wealth comes first in owning a home. Most of the wealth for the average family in the United States is not on Wall Street; it's in their house. So the fact that the African-American home ownership rate is below 50 percent and the white home ownership rate is over 70 percent is a huge part of that lack of wealth and capital. Wealth also means the ability to have financial growth through something besides simply the labor of your own hands; that is, growing your capital and wealth by investing in companies or, as many people do in this country, by investing in your own business. But if you don't have that little nest egg, you can't get going. And again the number one source of capital for new small businesses is borrowing against your home. African Americans are not used to talking about wealth in this country, but it is a fundamental differentiator today in the experience of black families and white families, this wealth gap. And the biggest piece of that wealth gap is the home ownership gap.

I was just down in Atlanta with President Bush looking at a project that we helped to finance, in which a bunch of severely run down public housing was torn down and replaced with wonderful, affordable apartments, senior housing, and home ownership townhouses for teachers and police officers. It totally transformed this community. We put probably $6 million to $9 million into that one. It's called a Hope VI project, and there are many of them in communities across the country. Some people who no longer live there look and say, I grew up there; I'm proud now. My neighborhood is now getting better. And they say that even though it's not their house. It's their neighborhood, and they feel a pride in that.

It's interesting for me that when I walk around in D.C. and in neighborhoods, sometimes people cry out, "Hey, Fannie Mae, hey, Fannie Mae man." Some of them actually know who I am. Yet if I could ask them anonymously how important is it that some black folks are running a few big corporations, people would say, these guys are in it just for themselves. This is what they believe if they don't see any of them around, don't see them contributing to the community.

I think the key thing, and one of the things we focus on, is you've got to have some tangibility to what you do. People have got to see it and touch it and feel it in their lives, and so even though they personally may not be benefiting, they know something good is going on.

We try at Fannie Mae to have tangibility so that people can see what it is that we do, but we find that it also inspires people—they say, I want to do something like that. So when people say it hasn't affected me, I want to be able to say, well, let me tell you some of the things we've done in this neighborhood; maybe you heard about them. They might not know we were involved, but then you go through it and they say, oh, you guys are in that, you're doing that, okay, I know about that one, yeah, that's kind of a nice thing. And if you can't bring that tangibility, then people ought to criticize you. They ought to say, well, where is it? If it's just numbers somewhere, I can understand their reaction. We're one of the largest companies in the world. I also have two- and three-person offices—we call them Partnership Offices—in fifty-four different places in the country, where all they do is work with people at the local level to see if we can make tangible differences. But as big a company as we are, we're always asking, what needs doing here that will start the ball rolling? So at the same time that we're buying a billion dollars in mortgages, we're also working on one twelve-unit project in Tucson that people have been trying to make work for the last ten years, and we go in and say, let's make it work for real.

The *Washington Post* conducted a poll a year or so ago in which they asked white Americans, do you think that equality has been reached now in terms of jobs, income, and education between whites and blacks? And the majority said yes. And so I did a measurement of what it would look like if it were equal. And that's where we came up with this number of a trillion dollars of wealth, millions of new homeowners, a couple of million additional college graduates, a million more jobs. If you just were working toward the average, not looking for anything special here, just wanting to be average Americans, it would be huge in terms of the change for the black community. If we'd spent the hundred years before the 1960s working on it, we'd be a lot closer. But we didn't; in fact, it was the other way around. Remember, this was a country in which home ownership was vital and property ownership was vital, and in many jurisdictions it was illegal to sell property to blacks.

So it's not so amazing that not much happened during that hundred years and that Du Bois had to talk about the Talented Tenth—blacks who are highly educated, who hold positions of leadership—because only a tenth had managed to emerge from this panoply of repression. The fact that a tenth did emerge is quite astonishing. Where did Du Bois himself come from? Where did that black man come from who had the temerity to get a doctorate from Harvard in the nineteenth century, in 1895? When you look back to these people who broke through back then, you go, now that's an achievement. For me to have had a chance to go to a public school, to go to Harvard, to go to Oxford, to go to law school, and people say, he ended up okay, well, it's in the range of things you expect. But for the prior generations to have done that, when they had none of that opportunity, none of that support, now that was an astounding achievement.

I think everybody in America who succeeds has a special responsibility for those who are left behind, who haven't had the opportunity to succeed. Those of us in the Talented Tenth have this responsibility, but we are not alone in it. I don't know that it was a voluntary thing for John D. Rockefeller to share his wealth. I think it was mandatory, morally mandatory, for him to share that wealth with society and to create the institutions he founded or sustained financially, whether it was the University of Chicago or Spelman College or the Rockefeller Foundation. I think it was mandatory in a moral sense. And I think it's the same thing for African Americans. Those who have benefited from the opportunities that the country provides have an obligation to give back.

It starts as a moral question. It is that we really do, I believe, have a moral compact with one another to look out for the well-being of others who have not had the same opportunities. Second, no one succeeds on his or her own; everybody benefits from this infrastructure that everybody supports. The soldiers who were in World War II preserving a democracy—folks who might've been a machinist from some small town in the South, or who came off the farm—they protected this system that has allowed other people to prosper. None of these megabillionaires would be able to have all that they have without the people who did participate in protecting this system. So no one gets there on their own. What's the old saying—if you're walking along and you see a turtle on a fence post, you know one thing for sure: it didn't get there by itself. I think that many of us are in that way turtles on the fence post and we have to acknowledge that as well. We have to acknowledge not just that there's a moral imperative, but also that we didn't do it on our own.

Third, I think we all share an obligation for this catch-up process of obliterating the impact of that hundred years of repression. I believe that we can't allow another and another and another generation to go by who haven't gotten into the system, haven't had the opportunity. So I think part of the obligation for those who have succeeded flows from that as well.

One of my goals as CEO of Fannie Mae is addressing directly this one hundred years of repression. It's fortunate that what we do in increasing home ownership is at the heart of the solution on the economic side. We finance one out of every four homes in America. But even with that, the home ownership rate among minorities is way too low—below 50 percent for African Americans, 47 percent for Hispanics, about 50 percent for Asians. And so what we do every day is gather capital around the world and bring it to the United States, and now we're trying to focus more and more of that capital on minority communities. We've signed on for President Bush's initiative to expand minority home ownership by 5.5 million families by the end of the decade, and we're going to provide $700 billion over this decade for this goal. The more homeowners there are, the better it is for Fannie Mae, and the idea that we should say, well, these folks don't qualify, would be like the soap company saying, well, we're just not selling you soap. This is a good business, one that has a profound impact on people, because of the multiplier effect that comes from home ownership.

It's not just the wealth issues, it's the social capital issues. Homeowners vote more. Homeowners stay in the same neighborhood longer. Homeowners' kids do better in school. Where you have more homeowners, there's less crime. Lots of good things come from expanding home ownership, and by our focusing on it as a business, we believe that we can do more of it than you can just by doing it out of the goodness of your heart. I want to have the same class divide in the black community as you have in the white community. I want the same percentage of middle class, the same percentage of rich, the same percentage of poor, in the white and black communities. Average is fine with me, because by all the measures, the black community is far behind average in income, in job status, and in education.

There's only one way to get more black people to the working class and from the working class to the middle class and into areas like Wall Street, and that's step by step. There's no shortcut. To begin with, we've got to get folks the preparation that's needed. More people have got to finish high school and finish it having picked up those basic tools, with regard to reading and writing and the ability to perform on a par in mathematics. Then we've got to get more people into college and taking courses that translate into the kinds of jobs they've prepared for. They don't have to major in economics, but they need to take economics, they need to understand economics, regardless of whether they major in literature or any other area.

Then folks have got to get into these companies and persist. It's hard and it's not always hospitable, but persistence, hanging in there, taking on the tough job, taking on the dirty job and giving yourself exposure, is the way you get ahead. For a lot of folks, there's an expectation where you get into a job that you just sort of automatically get what comes with the job. You move up in grade, for instance in the civil service. Well, that's not the way it works in business anymore. You've got to find ways to stand out. You've got to find ways that you can perform and show your stuff. A lot of times people say, that's risky. Yes it is, but you don't get a gain without risk. If you want to invest risk-less, people pay you very little interest. If you want to take a little risk, you get a little more interest, and the same thing is true in human development. You have to take a risk, a prudent risk, and you have to keep investing in yourself. Sometimes people say, I'm done; I've now gone to a school and I'm done. Well, that's not true. You've got to keep investing in yourself. You've got to keep learning and you've got to keep training, because your knowledge becomes obsolete much faster today than ever before. So you have to constantly invest.

Now, all of this can be helped by corporate America. A number of corporations have been tremendous supporters of education and improving education, particularly in our central cities, and insisting on quality education—not just having a good time, but having the kids learn. A number of corporations have been very helpful in supporting admissions to colleges. A number have training programs that can work, and more need to get involved. Expanding the pool of people is as important to the company as it is to the person, and investing in this human capital is important. As we become a country in which there is no majority, and where a significant percentage of new workers are going to be people of color, there's not going to be any choice but to dip into this pool and train and promote the best people. Otherwise, you're not going to have any people.

Companies are coming to realize this and are beginning to take the kinds of steps needed for success. Besides being a great moral principle, it's just fundamentally good business. If you limit yourself and the scope of who you are willing to look at for talent, you're going to limit the amount of talent you find. If you open it up to all the talent, you're going to find more and more people.

It's not that many years ago when the best job financially a woman could get was schoolteacher. And in fact, those of us who were in school then probably benefited from all these women who were teaching school but were also highly qualified in other areas. They were phenomenal and could have done a lot of things. Now as we've reached out to women, we've found all of this talent that's out there, and that's been terrific for our economy. I think the same thing is true as we look at different groups of minority Americans. As we look in there, we're going to find all this talent, and people are going to say, wow, I didn't know that was there. It is there, and it simply has to be found and developed. Not everybody's going to be great; on average, people are going to be average. But there are going to be a lot of great performers who are going to blossom, who no one had thought were capable of doing something, because they'd never gotten the chance. You've got to let them know it's possible, because most of them don't even know it's possible.

When I was growing up in Seattle, I hadn't been to most of the city, let alone anywhere else. We'd go to day camp, and that was it. It was a big deal to go to another part of the city. My world was two or three square miles. Then others helped me, and I got to most of the city. When I got into debating, we traveled around the state. Then I went to Harvard, across the country. After that I went to Oxford, and then it became the world. What I thought was possible just kept expanding. For many people, it never expands; they never get off the block. And when they look on the block and ask, what's possible here, there's not that much possible on that block.

We must make it clear that there are greater possibilities. Sometimes people shrink from talking with me about my being a black CEO and about wanting to be a CEO, but I don't shrink from that. The reason I don't is I've had too many kids come up to me and say, I saw an article about you where I heard you say this, and ever since then I've been doing this or I've been thinking about that. So I think it's important to be part of saying, look, I was a working-class kid from Seattle; my mother finished the sixth grade, and my father almost graduated from high school. If I can do it, this isn't rocket science. There are opportunities. We just have to make lots of kids aware of the opportunities and give them a chance, and if we give them a chance, we'll be surprised by how many will do well.

A couple of years ago, a *Washington Post* poll asked inner-city black kids to list things that were white, and they listed getting straight As in school, speaking standard English, visiting the Smithsonian, and so on. I think this shows two things. First, it's an observable fact that most people who achieve those things are white. So the kids were just reflecting a reality that they see. Second, though, is a protective mechanism that people use so they can tell themselves, if I'm not going to be allowed in the club, then I don't want it, that's not a good club. People start denigrating things that they really know are probably good things, but because they're not available to them, then they decide they're not important. And that's why it's so important that people see that the opportunity is available to them and that there are people like them in the club. Then they don't have to reject the opportunity for the sake of their own self-esteem—because if you're not allowed in, how do you deal with that? People don't deal with not being allowed in by saying, well I guess it's something about me. They deal with it by saying, it's them.

I saw this when I was growing up, and I went through it when I was in the ninth grade and decided I wanted to be with the brothers. There were only a few white kids in our school, and I didn't want to be in these classes anymore that were white and Asian and that had just a few blacks in a school that was 90 percent black. The so-called accelerated classes were these little segregated classes. I wanted to be with the people, and so I tried very hard not to get good grades. I understand that pressure to want to fit in, to think that my club is a good club and their club is not. A lot of teachers helped me out of this quagmire. They gave me a very hard time about my grades, and there were coaches who said, no, that's not going to work. We know what you can do and we expect you to do it. I had a lot of adult supervision beyond my parents, and lots of people who had very high expectations for me. At the time I was going, why have they all picked me? Why am I carrying all this weight? Well, it was a good thing for people to have high expectations of me, because I felt a need to respond to it, and the test of success for me was high. It wasn't a low hurdle that I could just get over. People were going, no, no, that's not you, your test is up here, Frank.

If what we classify as the club we don't want to be in is the club that creates success, we lose the opportunities to succeed. Far too many of our kids have lost these opportunities, or if they have them, it's episodic, and if they get in trouble, there's no one there to help them. We've got to change this dynamic. I benefited from people constantly showing me the power of example, saying, here's somebody who succeeded, here's what success looks like, here are things that you ought to think about. And they weren't crazy things; they were all things that were within reach. And then it was the possibility of going to college, going to a good college, and becoming a lawyer, that made a big difference.

How long it will take African Americans to catch up depends a lot on society. If the society makes a commitment and looks at things like affirmative action as part of that commitment of catching up, not giving an advantage to someone but just letting them catch up, I think we can make a lot of progress in another couple of generations. If not, it's going to take another hundred years, because as more and more make it, it gets harder for the ones who haven't made it.

We attitudinally have got to get the country back to understanding that the job is not done. People think it's done when they see a few black CEOs or a few other highly successful African Americans. It's not done. But the country will benefit when it is done, and everybody in the country will be better off. It's not just black people who will be better off. Everybody will be better off, because the more homeowners there are, the more entrepreneurs there are, the more workers there are, the better off everybody is. This isn't a zero-sum game where because a black person gets a job, it means a white person didn't get a job, and that's the whole story. That's not the way capitalism works. When one person gets a job, he starts buying things, and this creates the potential for more jobs. The miracle of compound interest is not just a personal thing; it also happens to a whole economy. Henry Ford understood this with his Model T. He was creating these cars and he said, I've got to pay these workers enough so they can afford to buy my car. If they can afford to buy my car, then I can afford to pay them, and the whole process went from there.

Having excluded such a big piece of the workforce, such a big piece of society, from being productive has hurt the country. We've taken all these kids who could be out creating something and we made them all dependent and put them in jail. Well, it's not just the cost of the jail, it's also the loss of what their productivity would have been in the economy. We've got to get that message through, but getting that message through the color divide is very hard. This us-versus-them—if they get something, I'm losing something—that thinking has hurt not just black folks; it's hurt the country. My message is, when those who have been left behind catch up, we'll all be better off, so let's get to it.

RUSSELL SIMMONS

Corporate Man

CEO, corporate executive, and producer Russell Simmons understands both individual and business success. It is a fact, he told me, "that you invest your money in corporations because they have longer lives than people. That's the reason you do it. That being the case, the karma and business responsibility of whatever it is that you did during your life lasts as long as the company is alive."

I got where I am through nothing but a lot of luck and blessings from God. I've been very, very lucky. I say blessings from God, but I don't know quite which God. The one inside me is the first one I try to aspire to, a relationship with God or with my higher self. Even if the relationship is not a great one, I'm always working at making it better. I think that's what has gotten me a fortunate kind of a circumstance in a worldly way. Then lately, I've been very happy, so I guess that's really the best fortune. I've been very lucky and very happy, and all of it comes, I think, from some of the sacrifice that turned into the greatest blessing.

I grew up in the drug capital, Queens. They call it lower middle class where I lived. I was very lucky. I was bused to school to a neighborhood where they had the same lower middle class living on the verge of poverty. But in my neighborhood, they had heroin openly sold on all the corners. Whenever you saw a white kid in my neighborhood, you might as well arrest him, 'cause he'd come to buy drugs. They had to come to my neighborhood to buy drugs. At that time, you had an unequal police protection program when it came to drugs. Drugs devastated our community. Until then no one gave a damn. Heroin destroyed the kids in that whole lower-middle-class black environment, and it didn't destroy the kids up by the school I was bused to.

The houses in my neighborhood and the houses where I was bused to school looked like Archie Bunker's. They looked the same. Drugs were the defining difference. Everyone in our neighborhood knows we had the Muslims and heroin addicts on our corner, period. You were selling drugs, you were taking drugs, or you were a Muslim selling bean pies or selling religion—you know, join the mosque and become a better person, which a lot of heroin addicts did.

When I was sixteen, I wanted to be an entrepreneur, but selling weed was one of the few options open to me. Today, however, young people are inspired to have higher aspirations because of hip-hop. Young people now have all these people visible who make the choice to be entrepreneurs and inspire them to do the same. It's now a cultural thing in our community. Being a teacher maybe, or a doctor, these used to be the hopes and aspirations of our community. But now hip-hop is all they talk about. Lower-middle-class blacks in New York City were the absolute dumbest young kids you could find anywhere, same as you would in the projects down the block. Well, it's the same dumb people who broke the mold, because they were so hip-hop and so angry and so fuck this, I'm going to make it on my own. It's like, own a company.

I used to give hip-hop parties when I was at City College. People would pay to get in—all the hip-hop artists, DJ Cheeba and all these guys. I had this music thing I loved, and I was lucky enough to get a job in the music industry. I made it big in 1979 when I produced "Christmas Rappin'," by Kurtis Blow, on Mercury. I got to go to Europe at that time. They met me at the airport in Amsterdam. It was unbelievable. I'm being treated like a king. I was twenty-one. "Christmas Rappin'" was the hot record. I'd never been on a plane before and never been anywhere outside New York. I got home to New York and I rented my own little apartment, big as a midsize car. I was in business. I had my own apartment and I had a hit record. I was a success. Rick Rubin and I started working on Def Jam together in 1983. We had the success of Run-D.M.C., really the first hip-hop crossover group, all set by then. Rick produced "I Need a Beat," which was our first record together. We put out the Beastie Boys and all those other records independently, and then we made a deal with Sony. That was the beginning of Def Jam Records. Def Jam was Rick Rubin's logo, his idea, his whole thing.

I'm doing something I love. That's about the most success you can have. That's a pretty big deal. When I started out, the most worldly belongings I had was a little job and a little apartment. Then I kept getting greater responsibility and greater worldly success. The number of talented people around me keeps growing. I'm blessed to have them. And I discovered how to let go so I can incentivize all these talented people properly and diversify and not be so hands-on. There's Kevin Liles, who runs Def Jam Records. I go in his office and sometimes he wants to know why I'm there. Lyor Cohen, the CEO, is the same way; it's like, what do you want? They're doing so well. One record after another is number one. Ashanti was number one last week. All the success they've had at Def Jam, I think, has come from having worked with them in the beginning and maybe giving them some idea of the vision. But their energy makes Def Jam what it is today.

The entrepreneurial spirit came from within me. I was never offered a salary; they didn't like what we did. There was never an interest in giving me a job, or even making a record deal, so we started our own company. There was never an interest in us doing any of the things that we were able to eventually do. I wanted to be in the fashion business. Do you think anybody wanted to hire me or give me a job? I wanted to be in the advertising business. These things had to be forged with a little bit of resilience and vision.

In other words, I had ideas. Everybody has great ideas, but I learned something. I learned not to quit. People always quit. Everybody quits. They go to work; they have this great idea. My brother, the Reverend Run, is a great motivational speaker. He tells a story about the 7-Up Company. It's not one of his great metaphors; it's like his joke, his funny thing. A guy went to work and made 1-Up. I'm not supposed to tell the punch line, but I already did. Then he made 2-Up and 3-Up and quit at 6-Up. The next guy goes to work one day and makes 7-Up. Stupidest thing you ever heard, but it's got to do with not quitting. A sage and a great spiritual teacher tells a story about digging a hole and running into a rock. He goes, oh, man, let me start over. No, you dig through the rock, 'cause there's another rock and another rock, and the rock teaches you what you really need to know to get where you want to go.

Quincy Jones is an entrepreneurial role model for me. He is a creative person that does his work from his heart and then just manages around it. The management of the work facilitates his ideas. He wasn't a business major; he was a creative person. That's what makes his work similar to what I try to do.

People say I'm smart because of Def Poetry Jam. They say, you are so creative, how did you think of that? Oh my God, it was hot in the ghetto for years. I had the access and I did something that was obvious. There was nothing creative or genius about putting poets on television. And it was perfect timing when Def Comedy began, which I've gotten a lot of credit for. There was already a Chris Tucker, there was already a Martin Lawrence, there was already Steve Harvey, there was already Jamie Foxx. It wasn't them that put it together, but they wasn't discovered. They were already there. I'm an expert on the tastes of people in the inner city compared to the people who think that I'm an expert.

It's been difficult for blacks to sell the American dream. Let me explain some of the roadblocks. Ralph Lifshitz had to change his name to Ralph Lauren to be the American dream. So a nigger being the American dream is not an easy thing either. But we somehow got past that roadblock. Even in the selling of my sneakers now, you've got a roadblock. People only want to wear Nike and Reebok and Adidas, so there was a roadblock that we're breaking through. I may be the American dream. I can maybe sell a pair of jeans and a pair of sneakers. To sell a $10,000-and-up watch is a bit of a stretch. But I just bought a piece of a watch company, and we're in discussion about me buying the company. The watches are already starting to explode. It's an Italian company. I haven't announced it officially, but I've purchased a piece, and I think my image buying into it is good.

Economically, some families in our community had more financial stability during segregation. We had the black dentist, the black lawyer, the black teacher. We had jobs. We had things we had to do for our community and services to provide. Integration tore that down. It damaged our economic stability in our little communities. But that went away for the better. No one really can see the full meaning of an event. All you can see are the temporary effects. It's a good idea, integration, it'll be great for us; we'll be able to move around. Boom! Bad idea. They took all of our business. Oh, good idea! Now we can take over our own business again and we can do anything we choose. Now we can emigrate into the mainstream business, so business is 85 percent bigger than it was. You have to hear God's sound track in the background of whatever happens to you and around you. If you do that, you will see the silver lining.

But as much as integration has hurt in the past, we now have to make it help. Relationships are critical, and part of our job is to take advantage of integration the way integration has taken advantage of us. That's an important one. You have to be able to take advantage now of a new climate, where racism is not so obvious. People don't recognize their own racism now, and they are willing to be partners and change the world if you give them the opportunity to participate.

I'm not saying that racism is completely gone and people should forget about it and not fight to make whatever civil rights issues that are still there go away. I'm saying that you have to recognize what opportunity you do have. In the clothing business, it was very difficult to convince some people of this opportunity. We're a multimillion-dollar company. Puffy's company and Jay-Z's company, a lot of companies, are doing a couple of billion dollars at least, I would say, in clothing. A couple of billion dollars is a big company. And there's no major distributor involved. There's no multibillion-dollar company breaking their neck to distribute urban clothes. They don't understand it. Just the way Time Warner didn't understand about the rap record business, and because of that, independent people flourished.

So our opportunity has to be to go independent, 'cause the major distributors have turned us down again. They turned us down in music, and they don't understand why my advertising agency is flourishing, or any of what we do. The thirst in young America is greater than the older guardians of culture understand. They don't believe that it's racism. When MTV was playing rap records, they used to feel afraid to put on a record because they didn't think their audience would get it. MTV was cool. They got it. But they thought the audience wouldn't get it. And when they put the record on, oh, man, the audience loves it. Surprise. So there is still rigid attitudes and backwards thinking by the gatekeepers of the culture, but you've got to get past it. You certainly can't be bitter, and you have to see where your opportunity is. You are making more money independently.

Look at it this way. If Irv Gotti was white and he was selling white music, we'd pay him a salary and talk to him later. But because he's doing something unique that's still not properly embraced by the industry, he gets a lot of money and he runs his company. He becomes independent. The independence that was forced on us by managing some part of our culture, or ideas, is the same independence that's creating a whole new lifestyle among young black people. All I had was drug dealers, some numbers runners, and an occasional pimp. They were the entrepreneurs. Now all these young people have images. It's true that a lot of them are hardheaded and kind of twisted and unsophisticated. That's why they did it in the first place. You think if they spoke the King's English, if they went to school and were told, do what you're supposed to do, that they'd be doing what they're doing? There would be no cash money collected if they was Harvard-educated. They came from the street and they did what they had to do and they created what they've created.

The record business was black music and still is to some degree. But the black music business meant low expectations, small budgets, and limited resources. We've gotten past that to the extent that rappers have proved they sell catalog. Certain rappers have been competitive—more than competitive—in the mainstream. In the clothing business, there was ethnic clothing distribution. I didn't know what that meant, but I knew about low expectations, limited resources, and small budgets. In the advertising business, you have a cake that's 100 percent. They give 20 percent to the black advertiser and they say that 80 percent of the budget goes to mainstream, because half of the blacks are covered by mainstream. So if you're in the black advertising business, you have limited resources and low budgets, and here we go again.

It's the same in the movie business. When they did the 1996 remake of *The Nutty Professor,* with Eddie Murphy, there was not one black film producer. I still think you can't name one. You cannot name one unless Chris Tucker or Eddie Murphy put their name on it and call themselves producers. But the guy riding around in the go-cart, doing nothing, that's reserved for white men. For me, though, there's been a change in America and I'm optimistic.

When I was living in Malibu, I lived close to Brian Grazer, David Geffen, John Davis, and Jerry Bruckheimer. There were many more. The whole beach was full of filmmakers. I was the only black person on the beach. No one knew any black film producers, and everybody wants to be my partner. Again, the integration thing that hurt us so badly has now given us inroads or possibilities, and you've got to take advantage of them. Puffy don't think he's black. Tell Puffy he can't do something. If he wants to make movies, he'll make movies. He'd be the only black film producer making a bunch of movies right now, but he's busy with records and clothing and things. My point is, part of it is being told you can't do something but believing you can do it still. And having that interest in doing it. It's your job to talk to people who are doing what you're doing. They're going to be interested in what you're interested in. They're going to learn a lot from you.

Our kids have a new entrepreneurial spirit. They're doing it. It's happening right now. That's all they're talking about. Getting money. Owning companies. They're not talking about how brilliant they rap; they're talking about how much money they're making and how they're making it. Legal money. You hear the Jay-Z song. He said, "Who would have thought I'd own a clothing company, who the fuck would have thought," he said. I'm doing my thing in every area. It's a business thing.

We're creating a culture that promotes entrepreneurship, and that's a very dramatic change that hip-hop has given America. Hip-hop culture is the driving force in mainstream American culture. Not only mainstream American culture, but in luxury brands. There was a Bentley that came out, a big silly

Bentley. I say silly, but really whatever you want is fine. My wife had it; Jay-Z had it; Puffy had it. I remember when the Franck Mueller diamond platinum watch came out, 'cause I ended up buying one for my wife, a very expensive new watch. The next thing I see, Puffy had one and Jay-Z had one. My brother the reverend, he's never outdone by nothing glamorous. Even though he's a reverend and God-fearing, God's given it all to him as well. The reverend says you can't help the poor if you're one of them. He had a watch. That's where I first saw the Franck Mueller diamond platinum watch. I first saw it on my brother, even though all my partners, from different facets of the Jewish community and lawyers who are in a group—the Syrian Jews, over on Ocean Parkway—are very in touch with what's hot with a watch. The company always advertises in *Lifestyles* magazine 'cause it's such a great group for choosing the next hot watch. My brother and I argue whether his wife or my wife had that watch first. My wife saw more white watches than his wife, that's for sure, and she had it first, and that's the argument and I've won and I'm right. Don't care what he says.

I recognize all of the very serious civil rights issues that still exist. And I work on them. But I get criticized all the time, for example for supporting Andy Cuomo in the New York governor's race. There's a whole chorus of civil rights leaders who are criticizing me. One friend told me I was a traitor to the race for not supporting Carl McCall. Carl is a very nice guy. He has a lot of integrity.

People are always beating up on me about the Minister Farrakhan business. I stood next to him 'cause the rest of the politicians won't go anywhere near him. But I watch his speeches and he sounds like a yogi to me. When he's talking about how he wants to be a great Jew and a great Christian, he reminds me of what I love hearing. I repeat it all the time. Muhammad wasn't a Muslim or a Christian. Christ wasn't a Christian. Abraham wasn't a Jew, and Buddha wasn't a Buddhist. For me, that stuff really resonates. I don't like organized religion so much. But I like Farrakhan. I like 99 percent of what he says. I don't agree with 99 percent of almost anything that anybody says, but most everything out of his mouth seems heartfelt to me. A lot of times it's true and people are uncomfortable with it.

But I'm trying not to deal with the anger. I read yoga scriptures every morning. I try to connect with my highest self, with the best I can be. But I still live at the same time. I still have this whole justice thing. On the Phat classic sneakers, the flag is upside down in the Phat Farm flag, the Phat Farmer image. The flag is not upside down because we don't love America. It's because we do love America. It's because we can make a greater America. For ten years, that flag has been that way.

I'm very active in the Foundation for Ethnic Understanding, with Rabbi Marc Schneier. It does outreach, but what it really does is fight anti-Semitism and antiblack racism and other forms of bigotry. So why are you on the board? people ask me. Why are you a senior member on the board, and why did you raise all that money to fund them this year? Because it's a great outreach and it's important for them to have that outreach and it's important for the black community and the Jewish community to be in sync.

Harlem was abandoned, and Jewish people invested in it. Why is anyone upset with that? Nobody else wanted it, obviously. People have to realize that when they talk about relationships with blacks and Jews. Don't be mad at them because they're there. They're there because other people aren't. They've been there for the Civil Rights Movement, and we've been there a lot for their causes and issues. Martin Luther King was certainly a big supporter of the Jewish initiative to protect themselves and to have a homeland. And Jews were big supporters of Martin Luther King. So we've been big supporters and they've been big supporters. We need that collaboration. We have a lot of the same issues today still.

So I'm not black when I'm flirting with Rabbi Schneier 'cause, you know, why are you doing it? 'Cause it's common sense. I love people. I try to live with a respect for what's in my heart as opposed to which way the climate blows. That's my answer as to whether I'm still black or just famous. I do what I think makes sense, and I do think I'm black. I know that the choices I make benefit my community when I talk about the poor people's revolution or ideals. I always talk about poor people and the reasons I make these choices. I believe the way our society is judged is based on how we treat those people in our community, and their suffering. So when I chose to support Andy Cuomo, which I've been badgered a lot about, I said, why are you telling me I shouldn't do it? No one can tell me. People who are much more sophisticated, I go to them first. I went to Hugh Price, president of the National Urban League. I went to some of the leaders who are not so political, and I went to Farrakhan even. I said, here's what I'm going to do, 'cause from what I can tell this makes sense. No one said a word. There are issues I take on and people don't understand, but I try to take on ones that suit my heart.

The reparations movement, which I'm so fond of and I'm pushing heavy on, no one knows the kind of effect we're going to have across this country on the level of dialogue about reparations. No one has any idea. I can see it very clearly. That whole rap, forty acres and a Bentley, that whole thing's going to happen. That whole rap is going to really resonate nicely. I don't know what I'm doing right; I don't know where it's going to go. The idea of reparations has been criticized as a way for black intellectuals to take advantage of white corporations. That's a stupid concept. Why are they white corporations? They're American and they're public. I'm assuming that blacks own some percentage of them. Reparations has also been criticized as a polarizing idea. Well, shit, man, Martin Luther King was a polarizing idea too, wasn't he?

The thing about reparations is they try to make it racial, but it's not a racial issue at all in my opinion; it's an American justice issue. There's not a soul alive in America who's responsible for reparations for the slave trade. There's not a soul alive who personally made any money off the slave trade. The fact remains that you invest your money in corporations because they have longer lives than people. That's the reason you do it. That being the case, the karma and business responsibility of whatever it is that you did during your life lasts as long as the company is alive. Let reparations come in the form of education or affirmative action, let them come in the form of health care, let them come in the form of leveling the playing field. We are going to start a campaign that's going to rattle America.

The type of remedy depends on whether a corporation or the government is involved. If a corporation says, we want to fund literacy programs all over the country and that endears them to the community and they somehow make more money because of it, then it was smart for them and for the community, and God bless us all. I'm hopeful that what I'm doing will inspire other people to do the same. I believe the more you give, the more you get. That's my spiritual thing. It works out that way in this case. It works out that way in almost every case. A lot of social and political causes that affect our community are the driving force behind my businesses.

I think keeping our community together is about communication. There are successful people who disappear from the community and people who are apathetic and separate from the community, and who don't realize that they have separation from the people, a separation from God. I think it's about spirit first, though I hate to say it, because people say, oh, man, you mean that? Spirit first. We are all connected. We breathe; we compromise someone's air space. And everything we do is political. Something was told to me and I never got it out of my head, 'cause it's very true: everything we do is political and has social implications. So long as we realize that, we'll start to support each other in our efforts to become better and happier.

People like Richard Parsons at AOL Time Warner are great. They show people we can make it and all that, and that's good. But there's an issue of language. How important is it that those people speak the language of the 'hood? They couldn't have forgotten their language. Or maybe they did. Maybe they're different. They do not speak their language. All these cultural levels we communicate naturally on, and we have to communicate more on those levels so that people can really feel connected to those who succeed. There's a disconnect between the successful, educated, and sophisticated, on the one hand, and the unsophisticated—in some ways unsophisticated, but in other ways much more sophisticated than others. There's a disconnect between the undereducated and the educated, and that disconnect has everything to do with how people aspire to success in America, with how they define success.

You learn a language when you're young and you learn language when you get older; but you don't forget the language you learned when you were young. It's a very cool language, very expressive. It's beautiful. But how the fuck we forget it when we get a nickel. Of course, when in Rome, you do the fuck what the Romans do. It's the marketplace. But you learn that when you go to school and they teach you the King's English. Then you go back to the 'hood, where you can be comfortable—where you can speak a dialect of this language too. You've got to communicate with people, encourage them, and be honest. I'm not knocking Richard Parsons, besides him being a Republican, which is none of my business and which is okay by me too. We need all kinds to reform this world. You need people on all sides. Parsons and Ken Chenault and people like them are huge role models. They work inside institutions; they haven't built institutions. They have jobs, and they're great. But Puffy's a much greater hero, a much greater inspiration. He's self-made. The same sophistication and education that guys like Parsons and Chenault have can come from some of our kids who will have enough experience to take on businesses that have smaller margins.

It's great to be able to speak the King's English, and it's good to be able to work in a corporate structure. Having relationships or having the ability to communicate in a certain way is important. You learn that when you go to school anyway, you hope. You speak a couple of languages. You speak street, but you also had to pass English tests. So you move around. You've got to be able to speak to who you're speaking to. But being an entrepreneur is outside the building in the beginning.

I don't think that young kids feel so much like they're selling out in learning to speak the King's English. I read something that Puffy said which I thought was brilliant. He said, what about his street credibility? He says street credibility is about hustling, not about being a gangsta rapper. He said he can't really live up to that image and he's not trying to. He's trying to get some money. He said it more simply and much smarter than that, about how they respect you if you're doing your thing and if you're building your life and you're building your career.

I believe that it depends on how you bring it back. A lot of people are so offended by you bettering yourself. I spoke at a seminar in front of three thousand people, with Irv Gotti and Kevin Liles, about entrepreneurship. I see the way young people are so excited about being entrepreneurs, and I believe that's the climate that will make a difference economically in our community. And the education part of it, they all recognize it's necessary. Some don't have an education and want economic success right now. But a lot of them will get an education, and the group that's coming along now will be more sophisticated.

At Harvard and Howard, rap is what black kids are talking about. They'll all come out of school and they can read and write. But if not for Cash Money Crew and Master P and the rest of those street kids setting an example, the cultural phenomenon of hip-hop wouldn't have been able to continue to evolve. All my Syrian partners, a lot of their kids don't go to college, because by the time you come out of school, you could've made millions. Look at so-and-so who made 30 or 40 million bucks and you're still in school, arsehole. That's the cultural space they live in, over on Ocean Parkway, the Syrian Jewish community, who are my partners in many businesses, who are my friends and my community in many ways. First of all, they own everything on every block in every ghetto in New York. Jimmy Jazz, S&D's, Ashley Stewart, the WIZ, Crazy Eddie, Dr. J's; I can go on. And they own most of the real estate and most of the retail businesses and all the electronic businesses. They all live at one little block at Ocean Parkway. They're there because the Wasps didn't want to be there. That's first. To all those who are going, well, they're exploiting us, they're there in space that you didn't buy, that the Wasps didn't want. It's not their fault, except that it's a cultural phenomenon. They are merchants. They rub off on us when we're their partners.

A great number of my partners are from the Syrian Jewish community, and they are very good partners. People used to say that a black dollar wasn't worth as much to white people as a white dollar. People still say a black dollar is worth ninety-four cents to a white person. But it's worth ninety-nine cents or a dollar to people in the Jewish community, who have suffered so much and who understand our plight. All my partners in the bags and belts and leather and shoes and underwear are all separate companies; they're all separate families. Some are Orthodox. Some are Hollywood Jews, not really the practicing sort. My partner Lyor Cohen is a CEO of Island/Def Jam. We've been partners for twenty years. We're going to be old together; we've been partners forever. Jimmy Jazz is a Syrian businessman. He did $100,000 of our sneakers last year, and he's already done $2 million this year. One set of stores. Jimmy Jazz in Brooklyn and Harlem. They have stores all over the city. They've done $2 million already, with just one sneaker. That line is just developing, and we donate the profits for reparations work. Certainly I've learned a lot from my Syrian business partners.

The street kids who developed hip-hop are inspiring other people, who have become more sophisticated and more educated. Our next generation of entrepreneurs will be a lot more sophisticated and will have a cultural base in being entrepreneurs. I had a number of runners and drug dealers, and now they will have legitimate businesses run by people they respect, that inspire them, that will make their lives different in terms of their possibilities, or make their belief in their possibilities different.

That's why I support people like Jesse Junior. One of the things that Jesse Junior talks about is equal high-quality education. A very important concept. That's the key. When I was campaigning for Mark Shriver, his dad, Sargent Shriver, said that the war on poverty and ignorance is the only war we can't win, because it's underfunded. When you come out of a really difficult environment and you walk into a beautiful school where you can eat and be treated a certain way, where you've got books and you've got computers and you can learn, it's exciting to go. You go to a school that looks like your house and you live in a 'hood, it's not good. It's obvious that we need to educate.

Do we think that blacks have found themselves where they are today because they're stupid? They're slave victims. They've had issues since slavery, but first they're slave victims and then they're other victims, and that's how they found themselves in their current situation, not because they're stupider than everyone else. This is a commonsense issue. If everybody in America had the same lack of opportunity, then everybody in America would be all mixed up. Under the circumstances, we've been very spiritual people. We have a lot of issues and there are a lot of problems, but they stem from a lack of opportunity and a lack of education and a lack of knowledge of our higher self, God, whatever you want to call it. Individual responsibility has everything to do with your heart and your leading, with having a connection to yourself and your truth. We are born love and born God and born good, and we get made something else.

Black kids ain't identifying success with being white so much as they used to. Their image of themselves is ten times better than it was, and it's getting better every day. I think that people even in our great institutions of learning have that rebel thing they learned from hip-hop and that is supporting their new energy, their new ideas of what they can be. Hip-hop is a new extension of poetry. Brand-new, and hitting the mainstream now. It has to keep evolving, like anything else. But rap is here to stay as long as it's got new energy and creative people to fuel it.

The thing about hip-hop culture that's so good is that it has a lot of honesty and integrity. It's not fabricated in any way. That honesty comes from the heart. It's a voice for people who have been voiceless. Its integrity allows them to transcend the environments and ideas they're accustomed to. These are big environments with big problems and big possibilities. But the poetry of hip-hop, and its description of the environment it comes from, is so honest that people who knew nothing about these kids are learning about them. They want to listen, because the articulation is true.

MAURICE ASHLEY

Chess Master

Before Maurice Ashley became the first—and still the only—African American to achieve the rank of International Grand Master of chess, he coached junior high school students in Harlem to the National Chess Championship in just two years. "We were a strong people coming out of Africa. We need to revisit what we had," he told me. "Chess is a mechanism for turning pawns into the power establishment. Chess transposes the imagination of inner-city black kids so they can see themselves in the back row where all the power pieces are."

Chess—the real thing—is what I'd call a reflection of life, because there are so many similarities between chess strategy and life strategy. The most important concept in chess is the center. Not just in terms of the physical space, the board itself, but in terms of you, because you have to be centered, same as the sun is the center of the solar system. You always want to control the center of the board: d4, e4, d5, and e5.

People point to these squares because geometrically they form the center of the board, but centrality is more a concept than a reality. It's about directing emotions this way as opposed to that way or out on the side. Sure, you know you'll make a move like e4, which occupies one of the four central squares and controls the squares f5 and d5. But it's not so much the move itself, although that's important. It's the idea that you're coming forward through your middle, through your center, and staying centered, and your pieces want to harmonize with that drift.

I said that chess is like life. To succeed in either one takes patience, planning, concentration, the willingness to set goals, and an inclination to see deeply into the nature of things. You can't just go for the first available option; you have to go for the thing beyond. The first option is generally not the best, and it's often terrible. Chess is about seeing the underlying reality. You have to get a feel for what's happening on the board.

Usually a strong player won't give you any holes. You start thinking about what's in front of you, slowly, rank by rank. You look at a rank and you see it's well protected because of all those pawns. Pawns are small, yet their importance is in inverse proportion to their size. They have tremendous influence. They're the peasants, the workhorses, the body. They go slow. But they're essential for making sure the structure stays together. A knight, a bishop, a rook, a queen—these are the flashy pieces, the fighting forces that do the big damage. But they follow in behind the pawns.

We're the workers, the peasants, the pawns, in relationship to the white community. Chess is a mechanism for turning pawns into the power establishment. Chess transposes the imagination of inner-city black kids so they can see themselves in the back row where all the power pieces are. The pawns are the people. And just because they have less power doesn't mean the others can take advantage. The others can't just go where they like. A bishop or a knight can't just decide to go right where that wimpy pawn is, 'cause that wimpy pawn is going to decide the game. Weak, so to speak, but deciding the whole future of the game. I can gauge a chess player from the way he plays his pawns. If players are carelessly sacrificing their pawns, they're not going to make it. They don't have a clue.

It's all about long-range thinking. The secret to success lies in the preparation. If you prepare for an eventuality, then your opponent is going to have to outprepare you, and if you keep working hard, they're going to have to work harder than you. To me, hard work is a challenge. Lots of us were told that in order to succeed we would have to work ten times harder than white people and be ten times smarter. But I've worked hard and I've prepared, and now they have to be smarter than me.

The forces on a chessboard are equal to start off with. Then you use your intellect to try to outwit the other guy. If you're prepared, and you bring on all the force of your intellect, you win. For me, chess has always been about achieving at the highest level. I remember hanging out in parks in Brooklyn, playing chess and watching other people play. For some guys, their whole world was playing in the park. It was the be-all and end-all. Then I had friends who were playing tournaments and who wouldn't try to bring their rating up because they might not win at the higher level. You might win some money staying where you were, but if you went higher in the rankings, you'd have to compete against elite players. But that's all I ever wanted to do. Some of the guys I knew wanted me to stay in the little pond so that I could be the big fish. I didn't understand that. I had learned as a child to strive to be the best. And chess can accommodate that because it's a fair game.

Where I come from in Kingston, Jamaica, to be working class was to be rich. There were few television sets. I learned to play many different games at an early age: card games, checkers, dominoes, all kinds. By the time I was seven or eight, I could beat the other kids and I could compete with all the adults. A friend introduced us to chess, and we all started playing. It was just one of the games we played. My brother is eight years older than I am, and I didn't know his friends that well. But I hung out with them and we played chess and I learned. I picked up little things from them. I remember even then catching on a little faster than they did. They were surprised that a little kid could play.

I think that being from Jamaica, we had a very strong sense of accomplishment, of trying to succeed despite the odds. There's a famous Jamaican saying: *Wi likkle but wi tallawah.* We may be small, but you can't break us down. We know we have our Bob Marleys and our Marcus Garveys. We've made it on the world stage. Even though we're from a very small island, we're all about excellence and success.

I was twelve years old when I moved in 1978 from Kingston to East New York, a tough section of Brooklyn close to the Brownsville area that formed good old Mike Tyson. My mother had done what West Indian parents often do. She had left her three children in the care of her mother and had come to America and worked as a nanny and done odd jobs and made some money. Ten years later, she brought us up to Brooklyn. So we were without a mother in Kingston for ten years. My grandmother had a very strong educational background. She was a teacher, and she made sure we were great students and we kept up with the intellectual side of things. When we came here, we were prepared to study hard and to consider our moving to America as an amazing opportunity to be successful.

When we arrived in America, we had nothing. I slept in a room with my older brother and sister. I remember wearing reject sneakers 'cause my mother said she wasn't spending money on the fancy $100 kind; she was just going to get us something we could wear to school. But the critical part of our experience was always that you'd strive and you'd strive to be the best you could be. You tried to be great.

My brother is a two-time world champion kick boxer, and my sister is currently a world champion boxer. I beat my brother in chess and then he beat me up. He beat me in the last game we ever played. He refuses to play me in any more games 'cause I got better.

The stereotype that chess is a white game didn't permeate our community because so few people knew how to play. The other stereotype about chess—that it's the epitome of intellectuality—didn't get applied either. I don't think the other students thought the kids in the chess room were geniuses. I think they thought we were just guys who loved to play the game.

In tenth grade, when I was fourteen, I had a friend who played chess a lot. I thought, I'm better at games than all the rest of the kids, so I'm going to play this guy and beat him. He crushed me. It was ugly. Then one day when I was at the library, I came across a book on chess. I was stunned. It was like, what? There's a book? There are strategies? It was love at first sight. I pored over the games and reveled in the majesty of the pieces. I remember my excitement one afternoon as I read about a famous game of Paul Morphy's, who was a top-grade American chess player in the nineteenth century. I was hooked.

It turns out, of course, that my friend was also reading books, and that's why he was crushing me. To beat him, you couldn't be just a chapter ahead of him; you had to be books ahead of him. That's when I discovered that reading could open your mind to the wonders of everything you wanted to know. For the first time I understood the power of books, because after I started reading them, I began crushing players I couldn't beat before.

When the American Chess Foundation, now the Chess-in-the-Schools program, asked me to coach kids in Harlem and the South Bronx, I was a student at City College and I was playing at the Senior Master level. The top 10 percent of all chess players are at the Expert level. Masters are the top 4 percent. Senior Masters are the top 2 percent, and International Masters are more like a fraction of 1 percent. International Grand Masters are pretty much off the scale. Back in the 1980s, to be a black chess player and an Expert, five levels down from the highest level, was considered fantastic. We were proud of that. If you were a Master, you were a freak of nature. There were one or two guys who were Senior Masters; we didn't even think of them as real people. But to me the only level that mattered was International Grand Master. When I broke that barrier in 1999, everybody and their grandmother started talking about being a Master and an International Master. You can't aspire to be just an Expert or Master anymore because now that's considered nothing. And that's what having aspirations is all about.

One group of kids I coached for a year in elementary school moved on in

1989 to the Adam Clayton Powell, Jr., Junior High School—also known as JHS 43—right in the heart of Harlem, on Amsterdam Avenue. Together these kids had a kind of synergy. There was Kasaun Henry, Charu Robinson, Brian Watson, Michael Johnson, Steven Yow, Jonathan Nock, and others. They may not all have been doing great at school, but they had a passion for chess, and I felt their passion.

I remember Kasaun clearly because he thought he was a chess superstar. When Kasaun arrived for lessons, he would march into the room and say, "World Champion Kasaun Henry." And the thing is, he backed it up. I can spot a kid with skills, and I said, this kid's got the attitude and he's got the mind to back it up. I used Kasaun as motivation for the other kids. They were furious that Kasaun was getting so much attention, and they wanted to beat him. Kasaun would be arrogant with them, the same way he'd been treated back in middle school. It's easy to motivate the kids to play against one another because they're so competitive; they all want to be superior and they all want to be the coach's favorite player. I remember Charu being furious and saying to Kasaun, come on, man, how can you beat us like this?

It was business when we went over games at the school. It was like, come on now, no messing around, no talking; why are you talking? Charu would say, if you start acting up, you gotta leave. We'd have a score sheet where we'd record everyone's games. If a kid didn't have all his moves written out properly so we could review his game, we tossed the game in the garbage. We didn't even want to talk about it. We'd say, what's the deal? This is your business. How can you conduct your business like that? The kids understood that, and they would get like, oh God, I can't believe I can't show this great game. We cultivated the attitude that we were about winning; we were about excellence. Mike used to say, gotta go to work, gotta go to work. This is a job. We've got to take care of business.

Some of the kids at first wanted to just grab the pieces, and I would say, uh-uh, you can't touch the board. There are eight of us; we can't do that. Articulate your ideas. Tell me your ideas first. Slowly, we learned how to talk chess together. We talked without having to move the pieces. They'd come up with an idea and I'd say, have you thought about this? Or this? Finally we'd move the pieces to check out our ideas, and the kids started learning to visualize the game. That gave them a bit of confidence and power. I coached the kids twice a week, but they played every day at lunchtime and they played at home. I guess my love for the game was infectious. I'd tell them about the competitions

I played in and how intense the battles were, and they'd start on me like, yeah, man, that sounds like fun, who can we go crush? I felt like the Pied Piper. They loved what they saw and what I was doing. And so we started a team. Someone came up with the name Raging Rooks, and we were like, yeah, we gotta call ourselves that.

We knew we wanted to compete in the 1990 National Junior High School Chess Championship in Salt Lake City. We wanted to participate against the best. So we traveled to tournaments on the weekends to practice competing. We'd go in totally confident, and we dominated the games. The other kids didn't want to see these kids coming. As a team the kids didn't do as well as they had hoped to at the 1990 Nationals, although Kasaun Henry won the top unrated title in the varsity section. After we lost, I walked to the park with the kids and said, you want to win the National next year? We're going to start working right now, and we're going to win next year. They jumped on my back; they were really into it. They said, come and teach us; we've got nothing to do in the summertime. I was on school break, so we hung out and I showed them ideas and they practiced and they read books. We spent the next year going to tournaments and playing and practicing. By the time we got to the National Championship in Dearborn, Michigan, in April of 1991, we were the most honed and practiced team there. We'd won a lot of tournaments in the city, and for us, the Nationals were just an extension of all we had prepared for. It was a tough fight, but in the end we tied for first. We weren't surprised.

On April 26, 1991, the Raging Rooks made the cover of the *New York Times*. The headline read "Harlem Teenagers Checkmate a Stereotype." It happens that on our team we had six African-American boys, one Latino, and one Asian boy. The mother of one of our boys put the *New York Times* photo in a store, and a black man walked in and looked at the photo. He saw Stephen, the Asian boy, and said, "So *this* is why they won. Now I *know* why they won." The mother who had put up the picture was mortified. What was curious was that Stephen wasn't on the first-string team; he was on our second-string team. It was the first-string team that won the championship. Stephen's team came in seventh, and did a very good job, because seventh in the nation was fantastic. But still, he was on our second-string team. So we could look at our own black faces, see black accomplishment, and still reinterpret it a different way, because we've been taught a horrible, horrible thing about ourselves: that we are not that bright, we are not that smart, we are not that capable.

I think it's a message we send to our kids. And it bothers me that we're still letting other people tell us what to think. We're long past that, in my opinion. One phenomenon I've noticed, and it's something that deeply disturbs me, is that my story is often first told by the white media and then told by the black media. I see that happen quite a bit, as if we need to be validated first by white people. When will we validate our own? We need to tell ourselves the truth. Lots of times people ask me, how did you get kids to believe they could be great at chess? I just told them they're going to be great. That's it. We didn't go to tournaments and think we were not going to win. We knew we were the best-prepared team there.

The ghetto of the mind is in some degree optional. The kids' attitude going into competition was, we're a group of finely tuned chess champions; deal with us. They knew my expectations for them were way up. Like, you're going to win the whole thing. We're not trying to come in second; we're trying to win. Letting kids know that all we're accepting are As is the message I'm talking about. We're not B and B minus. We're not accepting passing; we're not accepting Cs; we're looking at As. If you get a B, all right; you were striving for an A.

Kids can start learning chess at six years old. They can start at two. The older kids get, the more challenges they face. All kinds of influences start to seep in, particularly in high school. One person who struggled with these challenges was a brother named Kenny. As a teenager, he was an extremely talented chess player. At age sixteen or seventeen, he was considered the champion chess player of Harlem. He was also a drug dealer. Kenny was admired in the community both for his skill in chess and for his personal success in the game of drugs. He introduced Kasaun to chess in a park in Harlem. Kenny was a very important person in Kasaun's life.

After I began coaching the Raging Rooks, there was heavy tension between Kenny and me. Kenny was in his mid-twenties then, and he seemed to want control over the future of Kasaun's chess game. It was as if he felt that Kasaun was his protégé, and he was jealous or protective. But even if his motives were pure in trying to help Kasaun, he wasn't a good role model, because he was a dealer. I was on a serious chess path, and I was trying to show Kasaun the way to get to where I was.

Kenny was so furious that when he and I played chess he would fight me like a dog. It was almost like a fight for Kasaun's soul. He could have whacked me in a minute if he wanted to. But that's not what he was about. He was trying to prove on a chessboard who was better for Kasaun.

I would consistently win and make Kenny furious. Then one time Kenny saw me win at a chess tournament. After the game he came up to me and shook my hand and said, you know, you're a strong player. And all the tension lifted. He let me have Kasaun. Kenny was trying to turn himself around. Shortly afterward, unfortunately, his brother shot him in the back and killed him. They'd had an argument. The details aren't clear, but it seems the fight was over when Kenny was shot.

There are so many Kennys, so many guys who have the potential to be leaders of industry, to be doctors and lawyers. Kenny could have been anything he wanted to be. He could have been a businessman; he could have been a leader. He was a natural at so many things. It just happened that he was influenced to go down the path of drugs. There was no superstructure that fed into Kenny's potential as a human being. He found a structure in chess, and he found one in being a drug dealer.

Sometimes we look at our people and think they're not striving, or not excelling. They are striving, but sometimes in the wrong way—the way they think is possible for them because they don't see the alternatives or aren't able to access those alternatives in their community.

Many of our kids play basketball, for instance, as if their lives depended on it. Basketball is leading some people out of the ghetto, but very few. It's spawned some really classy players—like Dr. J and Magic Johnson, who are superlative human beings. In that way it's been beneficial for our community. But most of our kids are not going to be basketball players or football players. That should not be the dream. It's a wrong message to send. The dream should be that you're going to use your mind to become successful. We should be passing on the message that it's cool to be smart. Bill Gates will tell you that. He may be the biggest nerd on the planet, but he could buy out Harlem many times over.

Our people have been hypnotized by the hype of athletics. There's the lure of the glamour, of the great clothes and the big house. You lived in a small apartment. You were fine. But now you need a mansion with forty rooms and you need a swimming pool. I think about Mike Tyson, who came out of my neighborhood, and he needs seven cars, one for every day of the week. I mean, come on, what is that about? And then you get guys who have a $100,000 gold chain around their neck and you say, for what? What are we trying to prove? That we have money too? And is the money going to fill the hole inside that tells you you're not as good as they are? It's not. The point is to be as good as you can be, and not to judge yourself by other people's standards.

I can appreciate that deferring gratification is a problem for a large segment of our community. But I think the problem goes beyond feeling trapped and beyond reaching for the most obvious option. There are professional athletes who make millions of dollars and then five or ten years later are flat broke. Bankrupt. And no one can say these guys were without opportunity or hope. They were full of opportunity and hope. It's true that black America still faces grave economic inequities, but the fact is that even after we get certain opportunities—and this is what saddens me—we seem to defeat ourselves. We seem to go after the appearance of success instead of investing in our abilities for the future.

In life as in chess, you have to take care with everything you have, even if it's not much. A few wrong moves can end the game almost before it starts. It's not that all mistakes are irrevocable. It's not that you make one mistake and you're dead or you're in jail. But when you don't have much to start with and then you take yourself further back from the starting line, you're setting yourself up for some horrible obstacle that you will have to face later on. Maybe you're having fun or maybe you're frustrated, but you're setting yourself up. The obstacle you started out with was pretty big, but it wasn't the end of the game. You still had room to grow. But if you refuse to deal with it, the obstacle itself will grow until it's a wall in your face.

I travel all around the country talking chess. I'm always stunned when I go into a neighborhood and black adults are saying to their kids, look at Maurice Ashley. Look at how great he is. Look what he's done. And the kids have picked it up. They want my autograph and they want to talk to me and play with me. The point is that they, too, want role models and heroes. They want people to look up to. They want to be like people—like Mike, like Tiger, like Serena and Venus, and, God willing, like Maurice. That's why the black elite has to be visible. You have to see it to know it's possible. Look how many lawyers, how many cultured African Americans, came out for the Clarence Thomas hearings. I had never known that that many intelligent black people existed. They just kept rolling them out. That had an amazing effect on everybody, despite all the divisiveness caused by the hearings. Everyone was like, these cats and sisters in suits and so eloquent, where they come from?

People need to see an empowered community of African Americans. It's true that successful white people aren't expected to be a role model for every white person alive. And sure, African Americans who are successful should be able to do their thing and be respected for it. But I think African Americans have the additional burden of recognizing that their success rests in part on the sacrifices of those who fought for freedom and civil rights. In some way you have to try to give back.

My main obligation is to be a Grand Master. That is first and foremost. I can't be a role model unless I'm the man. That's a full-time job. People can't be expected to do everything. But they can also become complacent. They can believe it's enough just to do their job, without an eye to injustice or to those who don't have the same opportunities or talent.

Willie "Pop" Johnson was a huge influence on me when I was coming up as a chess player. Pop sustained me on many occasions both emotionally and financially. He helped me learn how to stay focused when I'd lose to guys who were better than me, and he made it financially possible for me to buy chess books and enter tournaments when I wouldn't have been able to do these things on my own. I also remember looking to Arthur Ashe and Jackie Robinson for inspiration. Althea Gibson and Zina Harrison and Debbie Thomas—women who led the charge in white-dominated fields—inspired me. I remember looking at a guy younger than me, Tiger Woods, who won at the Masters in April of 1997 and helped convince me to take my dream of becoming a Grand Master off hold and pursue it in earnest.

I can't assert that what's good for Maurice Ashley is good for Henry Louis Gates, Jr., or Ken Chenault or Tiger Woods or Venus Williams. All of us face challenges. But there are some who will say, it's downtime between tournaments. I can go check out some kids and see if there's any talent. For me, it's not a burden. It's selfish. I'm not helping kids because I ought to; I'm helping them because I want to. It cleans out my soul, keeps me fresh and young. I love seeing a new face, a black face that's going to be the next star, and deciding that this is a kid I could hang with. He gives me power. Hanging with him makes me feel stronger.

Kids survive in the schools. Survival is nothing. You lay low and try to duck the radar. You hope you're not one of the kids who gets beat up on. And you hold on to a set of strong values. People survive more horrific conditions than drugs and metal detectors and police officers. The question is, how do you thrive? How do you excel?

In *The Tipping Point*, Malcolm Gladwell writes about the small factors that lead to dramatic change. All you need is incremental advances; not everybody has to change all at once. At some point, things tip, and then suddenly there's an epidemic of change. I think we're approaching a time when kids' aspirations will be much, much higher than they were. We have a long way to go to put the structures in place that can finally bring about progress race-wide, but we're closing in on the effort psychologically. People can sit back now and say, we have Tiger Woods, we have Maurice Ashley, we have the Williams sisters, we have Ken Chenault and Vernon Jordan. We have people striving in all walks of life.

We were a strong people coming out of Africa. We need to revisit what we had. Egyptian kings and pharaohs played games like chess. The dark-skinned Moors brought chess to Spain in the early 700s A.D. and taught it to the Spaniards—along with mathematics, medicine, and architecture. This legacy was lost in their conquest and in our subsequent conquest. Much as we've become accustomed to thinking that we're less intelligent than other people, my dream is that we will shake off this delusion and recognize that we're as smart as anyone else.

Harlem is changing big-time. In 1991, the year the Raging Rooks won a National Championship, violence and divisiveness were at their height in Harlem, and David Dinkins was still mayor of New York. I was interviewed on *CBS News This Morning* after the team's victory. They asked me what I thought about Harlem, and I said, I think the success of these kids symbolizes a new Harlem Renaissance. Afterward I thought about what I said. I had asserted that the championship represented a fundamental change in the community. Well, the face of Harlem has changed in the eleven years since I made that remark. I could suggest that chess had a big part in it. But I think the deeper reality is that my success in working with the kids, along with my personal success, helped reveal to others the potential of the community. It helped make people start to think, what if these kids really did have a chance? What if they had a better school environment, a better teacher, a better education? What if we made enough change in the community that these kids could make a difference? If they didn't have to worry about violence on the streets, and if they didn't have to worry about drug dealers, what would happen? We showed that amazing things happen. Kids win national championships in chess after just two years of hard work.

I want the kids I teach to understand that no matter where you're from, you can succeed. I'm a living example. Many of us are living examples. We shouldn't have to deal with obstacles of poverty and inferior education, of violence and drugs in our communities. Sure we should work for parity. Your life can't go according to plan if you have no plan. Every star chess player knows it's the endgame where the competition is won. When somebody asks, how fast can you beat him, I say, it's not how fast, it's when. I know it's going to happen; it's just going to take time.

In 1999 I founded the Harlem Chess Center at HEAF, the Harlem Educational Activities Fund. "Where young minds come first" was my slogan. Without the tremendous support and direction that HEAF has been providing since 1992, thousands of inner-city kids who have gone on to college as a result of HEAF programs would have fallen through the cracks.

The kids come to the Harlem Chess Center every day after school, and on Saturdays they have tournaments. They sit and memorize and study so that when they get into actual competition they'll be ready. There's some explosive energy in that room. You can't mess with those guys. They're assassins.

The great thing about chess is that it's practical. It's not, I'm learning algebra and wondering what the heck I'm going to do with it. Not that algebra isn't meaningful, but we don't help our kids enough with translating what they learn in school to the real world. We try to convince kids that they should learn for the sake of learning. Now, that makes sense to adults, and maybe even to kids in affluent communities. It's much harder for inner-city kids to understand why they should learn something that seems to have no meaning for their future life. But in chess, I'll show kids a move and five minutes later they can use it against their friend. In another five or ten minutes, they'll win the game and come back to me and say, show me something else, 'cause I just won that game and I wanna win again. It's self-reinforcing.

Thankfully, the transformation that takes place in a kid's life through chess is not immediate. What happens is gradual. The kid who hasn't been doing that great in school, who doesn't have that focus and that concentration, suddenly sees a chessboard and is fascinated by the pieces, by the shapes, by the energy of it, and wants to learn. The board focuses the energy into sixty-four squares, and kids look at the board and start to think, because they can't help but think.

There's another very powerful aspect of chess, and that is that you learn when you lose. I don't love losing, but I love the lessons I get from losing. Losing hurts. Then I go home, sift through the feelings, and start to wonder, what is it that made me lose? I think about it very carefully, and then suddenly I see it. And I go, oh, I have to work on that. But I wouldn't have known what to work on to improve my game if I hadn't lost. I learn where my weaknesses are and I come back more powerful. I don't have to have a big ego. I just have to keep on learning.

Life is not about reality. It's about how other people perceive the world. When you can look at somebody and believe you intuit who they are because of their skin color or occupation, you're living in the land of perception. That world has meaning; it has impact. But it's not reality. By making chess as black, ideally, as basketball, I'm redefining the way other people perceive things.

Today you can be a member of the hip-hop culture and a member of the chess team and there's no contradiction. Smooth guys like Will Smith, Wynton Marsalis, Wu Tang Clan, Jamie Foxx, Jim Brown, all play chess. Black kids who play chess are no longer seen as wanting to be white. Their peers, both black and white, are more likely to think they're cool. Kids who play chess play basketball; they watch all the "in" TV shows; they participate in the popular culture. Chess has suffered from the same degree of stereotype in the broader culture that we as a people suffer from. And you have chess kids now who are much broader than the stereotype.

I hope that in another fifty years we will have arrived at a tipping point, or be fast approaching one. I have a funny dream that perhaps the NBA will be dominated by white players and the World Chess Federation will be dominated by black people. It could happen, with all the European players who are coming into the NBA and all the black people who are playing chess. How funny would that be?

DAN ROSE

Black and White Logic

Dan Rose insists: It's about teaching logic.

Chess is seen by the middle-class Caucasian world as something that requires excellence, something that takes brilliance. In the minority world, playing chess is not considered "acting white," because many uneducated people, many people in other worlds, whether it's in prison or on the streets, play it. It is considered a game—a competitive game. We think chess is an ideal vehicle for bringing inner-city children into the world of cerebration, of planning, of sequential reasoning.

When in interschool chess competitions our kids come in number one in New York City, number one in New York State, and then number one in the nation, they know they're good. Their family and friends know they're good. Their schoolmates and the people they beat know they're good. When we send our kids out to Ypsilanti, Michigan or Sarasota, Florida or wherever the national contests are, if our kids come in number one or three or whatever, the impact is great for everybody—black, white, middle-class, working-class. If someone who's racist, even without meaning to be or without knowing it—someone, for example, who wonders about how intelligent black people are—sees in the *New York Times* that the Mott Hall Dark Knights from Harlem have won a national championship, I love that.

The Harlem Educational Activities Fund—HEAF—helps kids succeed in school and in life, from junior high school through college. At the junior high level, where our kids learn chess, our goal is not to turn out good chess players; our goal is to turn out good people. We tell our kids, if you can be number one in chess, you can be number one in anything. We tell them that chess is a metaphor for life. In chess, if you don't get your pieces out on the board quickly, you're not in the game. In the real world, if you don't have a solid elementary and high school education, you're not in the game of life.

The midgame, in chess or in life, is where you set yourself up for the win.

In chess, you plan your attack strategy; the equivalent in the real world is your undergraduate and graduate college experience. You're setting up your life strategy. Finally, chess games are won or lost in what's called the endgame. We tell our kids the endgame in life is not a job; it's a career. It's not making a living; it's leading a life that is satisfying and productive and fulfilling.

So our theory, which we implement through HEAF, is a whole-life strategy. Our earliest consultant, twelve years ago, was Fred Hechinger, who died in 1995. Fred was really the country's leading voice in education journalism. The Hechinger Institute on Education and the Media was established in his memory. Fred's point—and it's one that we follow religiously—is that we're teaching and training the whole child. Don't fall into the trap, he said, of just teaching a kid to count. Don't just teach him to cram, to pass a test—you're teaching the whole child.

At seventy-three, I am getting on in years. I now understand what Archimedes meant when he said, "Give me somewhere to stand and I will move the earth." Speaking on BBC radio during World War II, in a 1941 broadcast aimed at President Roosevelt, Winston Churchill said, "Put your confidence in us . . . Give us the tools, and we will finish the job." You give me a place to stand and the tools to do the job—I'm mixing Archimedes and Churchill—and I'll move the world. We will bring the inner-city minority world into the mainstream of American life. It can be done.

I think that if the school boards were smart, they would open themselves to this idea. But we don't fight with anybody. We want only friends. We regard everybody else in the field as colleagues.

I've been involved in a great many endeavors and projects over the years. Yet in my mind, the challenge of bringing inner-city disadvantaged children into the mainstream of American life is without question the most pressing, most important social challenge in American life. It is *the* challenge. Anyone who doesn't see it or who doesn't address it is not living in the real world.

There are people who don't care, who cut back these social programs. At the same time, these programs have varying levels of efficacy. In some cases, it's like the fellow who refused to bail out of the leaky rowboat because the leak was not under his seat. We're bailing out of the rowboat. I tell our donors, if a smart inner-city kid goes bad and goes to prison, it will cost the city, the public, $60,000 a year, and could cost him the rest of his life. Our goal is to turn these kids into professionals who make a couple of hundred thousand dollars a year and who pay $60,000 in taxes. I tell my archconservative friends that our goal is to take a $60,000-a-year tax eater and turn him into a $60,000-a-year taxpayer. I think that's a good investment.

People are frustrated because they have lost confidence in the public system. They've lost confidence in the ability of the public school system to educate kids. They've lost confidence in the ability of the government to affect their lives positively. We've had a Great Society. We've had a War on Poverty. We've had endless governmental programs, and there's little to show for them. The service providers have become middle class, but the service recipients are exactly where they were thirty years ago.

The American public has not turned mean-spirited. It hasn't turned angry. The same public that voted for the War on Poverty, that voted for model cities, that voted for civil rights legislation, is still there, but it has lost confidence.

I believe it is important to shout from the rooftops that we can make progress! Environment is not destiny. All children can learn, and HEAF is demonstrating that. We can take any child in Harlem, regardless of the educational level of the parents and whether or not the parents can speak English, and we can help him or her succeed. You don't have to be a Nobel Prize winner to read at grade level in New York. If a child can read at the seventh-grade level, if the child is highly motivated and wants to come to the HEAF program afternoons and weekends, we can help that child. The child has to want to be helped, and if the parents are receptive, that's all to the good. Ideally, we want parents to be supportive, but at a minimum they cannot be hostile. Give us a kid who can read. Give us a kid who is highly motivated and who has parents who approve of what we're doing. And ten years later, we will give you a graduate of Columbia, Yale, Bryn Mawr, Cornell, Haverford, and Swarthmore, among others. This year, we got four students into Amherst alone.

The important thing is to convince the public that this is doable. And you do that by demonstrating what works. The history of social welfare has been to announce a new program with great fanfare and hoopla. You go back three years later and there's nothing to show for it. You go back five years later and it doesn't exist. That's what comes from looking for cheap, quick fixes. Nobody looks at what does work. Again, Fred Hechinger said it: Work with the whole child. Motivate him. Have him understand why he has to learn. Convince him that there are good role models. Convince him that you are there to help. Convince him that you are a loving, caring adult who is there to help him to move on.

And good things will follow!

(HEAF's Web site is www.heaf.org.)

THE IRVINS

Breaking Through

"There are times when I feel like I'm under a microscope at the golf club and organizations I belong to," Milton Irvin told me. "Is it taxing? Yes. That's why I came up with the term 'black tax' . . . If you believe in what our struggle has been, it's part of what you have to bring so that it becomes easier on the generations behind us. We really have to think very long-term." Melody Irvin works with "the low-income population in the non-profit world . . . In some of these communities, people have the Lexus and the Mercedes in the backyard, but they don't own a house . . . The changes have to take place both on Wall Street and on Main Street." Viola Irvin, soon to enter college, told me, "If you're a rich black person, it's just as bad because you've got the same racial profile. Our brother has been pulled over because he's a nice black kid driving a nice car. It's weird . . . I hope I never have to play the race card."

Milton Irvin

Summit is a town of about 21,000 people. Probably 5 percent of the population is African American, and 17 or 18 percent would be classified as minority. Of the total number of African Americans in town, probably only 10 to 15 percent are upper middle class.

I grew up in East Orange. When you think about it, Summit is only twenty minutes from East Orange, but the communities are so different. You go Route 78 to Garden State Parkway North and take exit 145, and it really begins to change. When I moved to Summit in 1985, there were not a lot of middle-class African Americans, and to a certain extent it was lonely being here. Before we purchased our home, we would drive around town, and every time we came through, we'd see African Americans walking around downtown and we said, yeah, this is it. Ultimately, we learned that 10 to 15 percent of the African Americans who live in Summit reside in two subsidized housing complexes, and that what we were looking for in terms of a peer group wasn't really here. Frequently, I'd meet somebody African American who was looking to purchase a home and I'd say, hey, why don't you move to Summit? South Orange and Montclair are traditionally more integrated communities; those were the towns that a lot of African Americans would gravitate to. But something inside of me said, you know what, someone has to put a stake in the ground in a community like this, and show that we can be woven into this fabric. We can become part of this community and act as citizens here. And my wife and I have done this. So that piece is gratifying.

It's part of what I call the black tax. I think that as African Americans who have caught some of the breaks, we naturally do more than what maybe our white peers would do in similar circumstances. It's important to let everyone know, when I'm a little different from them, that I'm really not that different. The color of my skin may be different, but in terms of what I want for myself, and what I want for my family, it's really no different than what you want. We have a similar class orientation. That was the whole notion behind my joining the Baltusrol Golf Club and the Beacon Hill Club. I did it because this is part of the American dream, and I wanted to experience everything that was out there. I'm just as qualified as the next person in that regard. I integrated both of those clubs.

Integrating the golf club, to me, was a step in our process as a people. Certainly, the risk I was taking was not the same type of risk that the Civil Rights Movement leaders took. It was the risk of alienating my African-American peers, who might say, who do you think you are? Some of them said, now you're trying to separate yourself from us even more. Or, why don't we get together and form an African-American golf club? Why do you have to join this high-society institution?

I responded by saying, well, there had to be the first African American who went to Harvard, and there had to be the first African American who went to Wharton. And quite frankly, there's going to have to be the first African American to join the Baltusrol Golf Club. And it might as well be me. And if and when we want to pool our resources and have the greatest African-American club in the country, I'm ready. Actually, I tried it a couple of times with a few of my colleagues. There was a golf course we were going to try to buy, and have it as not an African-American club, but certainly African-American ownership and something that we could be proud of. But I couldn't wait for all of that to develop. Nothing says you can only be a member of one club, so if and when it's feasible, I stand ready to move ahead with that plan.

When I've joined these clubs, I've never approached it with the attitude that I've got to make white people feel comfortable around a black person. It's more like I've felt they had to figure out, over time, that you're not scary and you're really not different from them. I always say, hello, how are you doing? I speak to everyone. I consciously try to be a full participant in the activities of these clubs. This done, it begins to give the others a sense and feeling of comfort. Golf is my passion. When I joined the Baltusrol Golf Club, all the staff treated me very well. The head pro went out of his way to make me feel at home. What was particularly gratifying was the caddies. There are a lot of black caddies at the club, and you wonder how they're going to react. They were just so proud; it was almost like they were joining the club themselves. They could have said, carry your own bag; I ain't going to carry it. But they took the exact opposite approach, and that was meaningful. I got letters from people saying, it's about time we did this and I'm glad you're a member of the club. I'm sure there was some negative reaction, but it never came to me.

To get in, you have to have a sponsor and someone who will second the sponsor's recommendation. You have to have six or eight people write letters on your behalf. Then you have to know about fifteen or twenty people from the club on a social basis. You get to know people in your community and you decide you want to go out and golf with them. The club doesn't do a financial profile. Your sponsor wouldn't sponsor you if he thought you didn't have the means, because it would reflect badly on him. You only sponsor people who you feel can afford to join. When I joined the club, the initiation fee was $25,000. The bond was $5,000 a year, which is like your equity stake in the club, and then dues were around $3,000 a year.

I think the initiation fee now is $50,000, the bond is about $12,000, and yearly dues are around $7,000 or $8,000. By club standards it's still not bad. There are a lot of clubs sprouting out on Long Island that could cost you between $100,000 and $200,000 just to join. So for what you get here, it's reasonable. It's a lot of money, but it's also a place you can feel proud about belonging to. And it's good for business. Clients like to come out here and play. It's a walking course, so you're out with somebody for four hours. You can learn a lot about a person in four hours. A golf course is a great place to establish relationships and lay the foundation for deals. By being excluded from networking mechanisms like these clubs, African Americans were excluded from deal making and deprived of access to capital. We were out of the flow and had no idea what goes on.

There are times when I feel like I'm under a microscope at the golf club and organizations I belong to. But that's also what I put in the black tax category. I just take it as a given. Is it taxing? Yes. That's why I came up with the term "black tax." You just do it. If you believe in what our struggle has been, it's part of what you have to bring so that it becomes easier on the generations behind us. We really have to think very long term.

My son's experience has been very different. Having grown up in Summit, he feels totally accepted by the white community. I have to constantly say, you've got to be careful. I tell him racism is alive and well. It's not that I want you to walk around with a chip on your shoulder, I say, but I clearly want you to be aware that some of the things that may happen to your African-American peers will happen to you. Have you ever noticed, when you're with a group of your white friends doing something, that you're always the one who seems to get caught or in trouble? It's not coincidental.

Initially, my son grew up blind to racism. But he experienced class isolation. Because of the neighborhood where we live, many of the African Americans here who are of different economic means felt prejudiced against him. They associated the middle class, or the upper middle class, with being white. They thought he was acting white. And that caused him a fair number of problems. So if you live in an upper-middle-class neighborhood, or if you talk differently, if you speak standard English, then you're not a member of the group. He never really talked about it much. He kept a lot of it in and masked it well. It's only recently that some of this has come out. But it was painful. And now he's beginning to come to grips with the right and proper balance.

I don't think there will ever come a time when either my generation or my children's generation will have more in common with the upper-middle-class white woman living next door than with the black people back in the inner city. In our soul, we'll always have more in common with our people. But I'd put the odds at fifty-fifty that one of my three children will marry outside our race. And if that happens, I won't look back and think that I did anything wrong. I may feel I did something right. In any case, how I feel about it will be a function of what that other person is about, rather than their race. It'll be about what's inside that person, what makes them tick. That's what I'm hoping my kids really get, the ability to choose a good person they can click with for a long time.

For my daughters in particular, I think the pool will be limited. We live in a society where you can be married two or three times. People marry for a couple of years and then divorce and marry someone else, which was pretty alien in my family. My grandparents and my parents took marriage as a very serious, life-long commitment. Now, people like returns on class and education, relative to what they have or grew up with. But I'll be happy if my daughter marries some-one she's happy with. If it's a black person of a different class, that's okay as long as she's happy. I would probably be upset if she married a white person from a lower class, so to speak. Perhaps I need to question myself here a little bit. Whatever would make her happy would be okay with me.

In terms of the behavior of black youth today, I'd say that when kids go wrong in the early years it's kind of our fault. You think about black kids who went to Harvard University as well as kids who grew up in black neighbor-hoods, went to all-black schools and an all-black college, and then became very successful. So somewhere it's our fault when kids get into trouble.

Now if you're talking about a kid who focused on his education and went all the way through college and then tries to get into corporate America and can't, even though he got his M.B.A. from Harvard, clearly that smacks of racism. I think it's our fault early on in the game. It gets less clear as kids start to approach their teenage years and then move out into the system. But whose fault is it that our schools are the way they are? Some of that could be the state. But who is responsible when kids in projects drop out of school and get into trouble? I grew up in a project for four or five years, and it wasn't all that bad. We lived right next to the Polo Grounds. Now that project is in horrible con-dition, and I do not understand why. It disturbs me not just that the project's in bad shape, but that I don't clearly understand all the things that went wrong.

My wife and I have talked about going back into our community in the in-ner city. Melody wanted to call up everyone and say, let's start buying up blocks in the inner city and let's live there. We send our kids to private school anyway, so what difference does it make? It could be a smart move economi-cally. If all the yuppies move back to the inner city, the values are going to go straight up. If we don't do it, in twenty years our people could be sitting around asking, why didn't we think of that?

I think that to most blacks, the notion of being successful means that you're becoming white. Some of that perception is driven by the fact that a lot of blacks who are successful, at least on a corporate level, have moved out of what have traditionally been their communities. You could say that if you're suc-cessful and you grew up in Newark or Paterson or Jersey City or Harlem or the West Side of Chicago and you haven't stayed there, then that community feels a loss of one of its people. And the only way they can describe that loss is by saying, well I guess they're becoming white.

The South Side of Chicago has done a pretty good job of embracing its leaders. There are many success stories on the South Side. I don't buy the perception that if you've made a determination you're going to live in Summit, New Jersey, or send your kids to a private school, that all of a sudden you've become white. I'm looking at Summit as real estate. Quite frankly, it's been one of the best investments we've made. So if you say you want to begin to think about creating wealth, is that being white? White people have done a pretty good job of creating wealth. We were looking for a community where we could begin to create wealth, and Summit was one of them.

One way to look at it is, my wife and I are creating wealth and we are in industries that create wealth for other people. The question then becomes, how do we increase the pipeline within the black community in terms of wealth creation, in terms of integrating Wall Street, in terms of integrating the financial world? First, it has to begin with education. I think you can make youngsters aware of the investment process in high school as well as in college. They can be taught in high school what it means to buy a stock or a bond, or perhaps more important at that age, the significance of owning a savings bond or a BMW. In our own community, I think, we sometimes lose sight of the importance of investing. The most successful kinds of investing start early on. I think that in other communities the notion of savings is huge in comparison to what it is in our community, yet as a community, we're still probably one of the greatest exporters of capital.

Even when we spend in the community, we don't save enough and we're not producing enough for our future. We need to begin to educate our young about capitalism and investment. Wall Street is trying. It's a big supporter of an organization called Sponsors for Educational Opportunity. The number of summer internships offered to undergraduate students of color through the SEO Career Program has reached nearly three hundred. I would estimate that between 60 and 70 percent of the professionals of color on Wall Street have come through SEO.

Education is the key, and there's an onus on those who have already made it to make sure they are helping to open up the pipeline. It's very important that we have Frank Raines, Dick Parsons, Stan O'Neal, and Ken Chenault because they show that it can be done. And there are other African Americans on Wall Street who may not be CEOs but who are working as managing directors, as chairmen, and as executive directors and are doing extremely well. The pipeline is slowly filling.

Some people distrust the notion that a handful of black CEOs could mean anything positive for the black community overall. They say these people are just a few tokens scattered around Wall Street. There is such a thing as people of color that come into your organization to fulfill a diversity count. We have to reject the mind-set that this is tokenism and ensure that the young people we bring into these businesses have the tools and support they need to ascend the ladder. But when you're talking about the Frank Raineses, the Ken Chenaults, and the Dick Parsons of the world, it's about money. They would not be in those seats if the board did not think they were going to get their return. Some of these exceptional men have been nurtured. Harvey Golub at AmEx took a liking to Ken Chenault and made it happen. All of us who are successful have been nurtured by somebody. What was traditionally missing in corporate America was the CEO who was going to be willing to nurture that African American to make him a CEO.

When you have Stanley O'Neal at Merrill Lynch, Dick Parsons at AOL Time Warner, Franklin Raines at Fannie Mae, and Ken Chenault at American Express all coming from various diversity initiatives, suddenly there's more than one agenda, and that's good. I think it allows young people to understand that they can make it. When everyone's in the same place, it's almost like, well, if I'm not Harvard caliber, I'll never be a scholar. People are reading about these guys who are black CEOs and seeing them dispersed across different kinds of companies, and I feel that you get a lot of mileage out of that.

The notion that you're somehow less black if you're upper middle class and comfortable with yourself and with your accomplishments makes no sense to me. I'm not less black. I have white friends, I have African-American friends, I have Hispanic friends, and I have Asian friends. I enjoy people, and I accept them for who they are and what they bring to the table. I don't know what the phrase "less black" means. I am who I am, and it took me a little while to come to grips with it. I've worked hard. My father worked two jobs, a sixteen-hour day, just to make sure that I could get a decent education and that I understood who I was as a person. He's a much smarter person intellectually than I am, and the way I followed in his footsteps was just by achieving those things he was unable to achieve.

I am of African-American descent. I've worked very hard for everything I've gotten. I am a product of the Civil Rights Movement, and I do believe in affirmative action. Anybody in our peer group that doesn't believe in affirmative action is not as good as they think they are, in my opinion. We needed some breaks. All people have to do is look back at their parents. Are you going to tell me your parents weren't smart and that's why they didn't get to X, Y, Z school? They were just excluded. It took some affirming action for us to get the opportunity to prove that we could do the same as our white peers.

At my firm, there's a handful of black people at my level. Not enough, let's put it that way. But there's a reasonable handful. I think the firm recognizes that it has to do more, and we've had David Thomas from the Harvard Business School meet with our board, a meeting I was able to put in place. So I think that the company understands it as an issue. But to David Thomas, it's a global workforce issue.

I don't say I feel vulnerable as a black man in my firm. I think that in the investment banking business, everybody is vulnerable. So while they make it hard to achieve in that business, if you can begin to achieve, they understand that more than anything. If you are really bringing some value added, that goes a long way. Your peers may be running the low hurdles and you're running the high hurdles and you're in the same race. But if you get to the finish line, you get rewarded. That's how I would put it. I think they make the hurdles high. They still question you about that. But if you go through that maze, once again it's the black tax. If you can't figure out the black tax, then you have a different dialogue. And I think that what we as a people have to get better at is just embracing that in its totality. Our kids don't have to pay the same black tax, but there's still that notion of "prove it to me." They still have to pay a tax.

In essence, what we have to do as a people is just continue to move forward. We have to put ourselves in a position where we're comfortable and we can make our kids comfortable, but to a certain extent we still have to be pioneers. Everything comes back to the black tax, at least for our generation. The Talented Tenth has not been able to carry us as a people. We're seeing a Talented Tenth, but most of the agenda is still dominated by 90 percent of the people, which is what you'd expect. It's all a continuation of the Civil Rights Movement. Economic empowerment is a part of it. It's what we're building now.

So you can look at it in a couple of ways. You can look at African Americans and major institutions moving forward in terms of the Talented Tenth, and you can look at the issue of economic empowerment for the remaining 90 percent of our people. Progress for both the top 10 percent and the rest of our people should be evolving in parallel directions. As a member of the community in which I live, as an African American working in a primarily white organization, and as an individual who has integrated two country clubs in the town of Summit, I do feel that I am part of the African-American movement for economic empowerment.

I'm optimistic about the long-term prospects. In the short term, I'm disappointed that members of my peer group are having so few kids. So many of my friends haven't had any kids, and many have had only one kid. And yet African Americans in urban centers, in places like the Robert Taylor Homes in Chicago, are having so many kids at such a young age, and then their kids are doing the same. I think it will take a generation before we fully understand the implications of that.

We may be unable to reach the current generation of urban blacks who are having so many children so young. Ultimately, we've got to get rid of the projects and build town homes. That's already starting to happen. If you can improve the housing situation and get more focused on the economic issues, and get people like Walt Pearson and other successful blacks to take an interest in a community, then I think there'd be reason to believe we could begin to see change. And I think when our children realize what an easy road they have, compared to us and our parents, they'll start thinking about giving back more. They still don't necessarily relate to what happened in the Civil Rights Movement. But it will dawn on them one day that they had an easy road, and all of a sudden they'll have this feeling that they have to give back.

I've had some success, but I'm not on the front cover of magazines and newspapers like Ken Chenault, Dick Parsons, Stanley O'Neal, or Franklin Raines. I consider myself an average individual who has done well with the tools I had to work with. And I hope that young people who are reading this book or watching the PBS series will understand that you can be a Ken Chenault but you can also be a Milton Irvin and have a good life and contribute to society.

Melody Irvin

When we first moved to Summit and our son was three or four, I thought it was absolutely great. Everybody was open. When the kids are young, they have a nice base of friends. Everybody plays. There's no big deal. All the parents get their kids together. You have huge birthday parties and

whatnot. But once you get to middle school, kids start to be a little more se-
lective. And in the teen years, they get to be more picky and cruel, and as
black students in a mostly white school, the kids get isolated a little bit more.
They lose some of the fun they had in primary school.

I think we imported most of our friends. We provided a base of support for
our children that was not dependent upon Summit, or at least we tried to.
The reality is that as middle-class or upper-middle-class blacks, we cross two
worlds, and I think we cross them very well.

I like Summit. I told my husband that my preference would be to renovate
a townhouse in Newark or a home in Newark. But if we were to move to
Newark, we'd have to buy a whole block with other African Americans. We've
talked about this with some of our friends, and we need to go out there and
just buy the block and be together and make it happen.

My kids are in private school already, so we don't have the benefit of going
through the public school system right now. We chose not to have our daughters attend public school. It's hard for me to explain why. There's a problem,
and it's hard to articulate. My children just didn't fit in. I think the economics piece is part of it, as far as relating to the black children in this environment is concerned. It's almost like our children were discriminated against by
black children who weren't from middle-class homes.

I grew up in a small town in Ohio. Very few of the blacks from that town
went on to college. I'm from a family where education was valued. My parents basically said, this is what you're going to do. Forty years ago, if you valued education and wanted to excel, people would consider that you wanted
to be white, or that you thought you were better than everybody else. Forty
years later, I think our children are experiencing the same thing. It's like we're
not going to get away from it.

It's almost as if we have two identities within the black world. Our son,
who is twenty, articulates it very well, the growing up here. He experienced
things differently from our daughters. We took them out of public school earlier. Brandon went through the public school system up through eleventh
grade, and then he finished in an independent school.

This sounds terrible, but even though the private school our children are
in is much smaller and the number of black children is smaller, they have
more in common with the children there than they did with the children in
the public school. It has to do with motivation. In the private school, you're
not teased because you want to do better. We're dealing with that in the

Summit public school system. I'm involved with an advocacy group that is trying to eliminate the gap between the performance of black children in the school system and the majority of children in the school system. So it's an issue that's recognized within the community, and that's why Summit is a good place to live. We are dealing with it. It just takes a long time to do the right thing.

I look at other communities, like South Orange and Maplewood and Montclair, that have larger populations of middle- and higher-income blacks, and I think there's a better networking opportunity. Even though a lot of the parents of means there might send their children to private schools, it's a better environment for the children than a community like Summit. There are more support networks for African Americans, and I think more commonality. Summit is not quite there yet.

A lot of our friends have seen their children bring home someone white that they're dating, and some of us have been talking about how we want to respond. If my daughter brings home a white boy and says, Mama, this is the one, I'm not going to refuse to support her. I value what's inside, and if that is the choice of my daughter, I know it will be the right choice for her, because it's what's inside, not outside, that matters. My preference would be that she marry someone of our own color. I think there's a comfort level in that; there's more support. We have a great history, and I want that to be built on and continued. Not that marrying white would change that. We have interracial marriages in my family and they're great. I think it just depends. I think if my daughter married someone of a different race, he would be very sensitive to being fair and equal and giving, and all those good qualities, because my daughter was well raised.

I think being successful has always been equated with being white. It's hard to change what's always been. It's important that we have more people working on Wall Street. Things are different for some of the young people that Milton has brought into the industry. But things are also still the same.

I work on the other end. I'm dealing with the low-income population in the nonprofit world. The community development corporations that I work with have fiduciary education courses. In some of these communities, people have the Lexus and the Mercedes in the backyard, but they don't own a house. This is where the education process comes in. We're encouraging home ownership, so people need to know how to qualify for a home and how to save for one. The changes have to take place both on Wall Street and on Main Street.

Viola Irvin

I'm sixteen years old, and I'm in the eleventh grade. I've been going to an all girls' school ever since sixth grade. I'm interested in applying to Morgan State, American University, and Sarah Lawrence. I love the Sarah Lawrence campus. I like the atmosphere. I think I read in *100 Best Colleges for African-American Students* that Alice Walker went to Sarah Lawrence. The only thing deterring me from Sarah Lawrence is its size. It's a small school. So I need to look at Morgan State, a Historically Black College, and American University to see which one I like better.

I'm considering Morgan State because I want to get that sense of black community again. I'm also interested in Howard, but I think I'm going to look at Morgan before Howard. I'm not going to Spelman or any all girls' school, because I don't like that all-girl classroom anymore. I need that male-in-the-classroom experience for college, I think, so I can get that male's point of view.

Summit is nice. I haven't felt cut off from black people living in a mostly white town, because I'm in a Black Achievers Program at the Summit YMCA. It's a good way to stay involved with my black community. It's for kids in sixth to twelfth grade from private and public schools. Kids in the same grade level meet once a week just to be together and focus on our schoolwork. We do lots of reading and writing. We get time to talk about racial issues and what it feels like to be discriminated against. Sometimes we watch a movie. We just kind of hang out as kids and friends. It's real fun, a nice group of people.

Some of the African-American kids in Summit make fun of me because I drive a Mercedes. It does make me feel bad, but I have a nice group of black friends too. It isn't my fault that my parents are successful. I'm proud of that. Do I have to go hiding the fact that I'm rich? No. It's not fair. Being black doesn't mean you have to be poor.

My best friend, Kim, is black. She lives in Maplewood and goes to Columbia High School. Her family is middle class and she hangs out with the white kids. The poor black kids don't like her because they think she's not black enough. I guess you just find that anywhere. Is it jealousy maybe? I don't understand why they would be jealous instead of proud of the fact that we are a well-to-do black community. Don't you want that for your community if you're black? Shouldn't you be happy for us because we are well-to-do and we're going somewhere?

The black kids who criticize the middle- and upper-middle-class blacks could make it somewhere. The kids at the Achievers Program are very smart people. The ones who aren't middle class have very strong opinions about blacks who are. They have the intelligence to succeed; it's just that they may not have the money to go to college. One of the things the Achievers Program does for us is provide a scholarship fund. They want us all to get into college so we have a future, and then other black kids will want to do the same. Someone will look at me and say, oh, why don't I follow in Viola Irvin's footsteps and become well-to-do? Not that I'm well-to-do on my own now, but someday I'll have a good career.

At my school I sit with the white kids more often, but I also like the black kids. I went to a prom yesterday and my table was black, because I hang out with most of them and I need to talk to them. I remember in seventh, eighth, and ninth grade, all the black kids sat together. I used to sit with them sometimes and then sit with my white friends sometimes. A couple of the black kids sat with the white kids. But now in sophomore and junior year, I'm finding that black and white sit at the same table more and more. There's a group of five white kids, and there were five black girls sitting at the same table. We need that. It's good, because we have to break that racial line. I'm not saying I'm going to marry a white boy. I mean, it might happen. I think it's okay, but I don't understand why there's all this racial tension.

Maybe I'm young and I'm growing up in a different time period. I'm growing up in the white suburbs. I guess I must be a very sheltered girl, compared to most black kids or at least black teenagers. I don't understand what they're saying sometimes, and then I use some words they don't understand. It makes me feel sheltered, but it doesn't make me feel bad. It doesn't make me feel not black. It doesn't make me feel white. Black is black. You have a history of slavery in your blood. You share in the history of Malcolm X and Martin Luther King.

It's not your money, and it's not your Ebonics, it's you that makes you black. It's the history, the blood that's in you from the past. If you're a rich black person, it's just as bad, because you've got the same racial profile. Our brother has been pulled over because he's a nice black kid driving a nice car. It's weird.

Sometimes you wonder, should I play the race card in school? Is it because I'm black, or is it because I'm me? I was getting a B minus in one of my classes and the teacher said I was doing fine, that there was nothing I could do to improve on my performance. But if I have a B minus, I can always do something to improve. Did he say that because I'm black? Or is it him? You never know. Is it a question of racism, or is it a question of me? Or him? Or her? Or is it being a woman as well, because sometimes women face discrimination in the classroom? It used to be that a woman's place was in the home.

You don't always want to play the race card, but sometimes you've got to. Personally, I don't think I find much racism, because lots of the kids are open about things. We have a very open atmosphere. Sure, there's those few people who are racist maybe, or maybe it's more the parents. I remember hearing girls say, oh yeah, I can't come to this place 'cause my parents said it's too horrible. Like the Newark area. I can't go to Newark 'cause it's bad. That is racism. There are white towns with problems too, but you don't stay out of the whole town.

One year there was a minor incident. A white girl I know was saying get out of the Black Achievers Group; you don't want to be part of that kind. But then a couple of years later something more serious happened. A certain black girl got a very specific note, and the bottom line was like, get back to Africa with the animals, where you belong. It was something along those lines. At that time we had a black headmistress at the school and we had an assembly to talk about racism. I'm not sure what else could be done, but maybe that's because I was in eighth grade at the time and it was a high school incident.

Then when I got into high school, we wanted a black teacher. As black students, we felt we needed a black teacher. We got a couple of notes saying we already had two incompetent black teachers at this school. If you don't want a black teacher, it's okay; we understand that. But you don't have to be mean about it. They called them incompetent people, so there is racism in there. So there have been direct incidents of racism, but never to me, and I hope I never have to play the race card.

THE PEARSONS

Living the Life

Investment manager Walt Pearson told me, "The two pillars of family and education must be in place if African Americans are to make further progress. If we can stabilize those two structures, then I think we can bring up most of our people. I'm optimistic. I see the glass half full." Donna Pearson expressed the concern that "we're losing a generation, because there's such a disparity between the black underclass and then people like our children in the black middle class. We have to do something to educate the children. Otherwise, I think there are going to be two classes of African Americans permanently."

Walt Pearson

We were comfortable in Summit, New Jersey. Our friend Milton Irvin was a big influence on us, because he was already living in Summit and he told us quite a bit about the area. My wife, Donna, is from Montclair, so she was also familiar with the area. Donna and I had a list of thirty indices for the community we wanted to reside in at the time. Ridgewood and Montclair were our second and third choices, but Summit was the only town that met all of our criteria. Summit has proximity to New York City, on the Midtown Direct, and it has good public schools and a diverse community. People are beginning to realize there's a significant African-American community there. There are four African-American churches in town. Baptist churches. A lot of people don't realize that, because when they hear the name Summit, they think of Wall Street affluence, white affluence. A long time ago, before they discovered the Jersey Shore, affluent whites from Wall Street used to have summer homes there.

I'm very happy with my new job in Boston, and with our home in a western suburb of the city. We've just begun to settle in, and someday we'll have a story to tell about our life here. But our thoughts are often with our friends in Summit, and our memories of our life there will always be vivid. I remember, for example, our introduction to our Summit neighborhood, which one could say was rather humorous. Our house had been built by a member of the Rockefeller family in 1972. They lived in it for a year and then sold it to the family we bought it from in 1999. On the second day we were there, I had the moving company come. But on the first day, a couple of buddies helped me out. Across the street were the Hubbards. I had a truck outside, and as I was moving some things into the house, Mr. Hubbard's housekeeper, who was Latino, came across the street and said to me, I'd like to meet the family that's moving into this house. I laughed and said, you've just met him. I was in dirty jeans and a beat-up T-shirt and my buddies and I were all looking terrible, and she didn't believe that I had bought this house. So that was the first day. After that, we were very welcomed by the neighbors here except for one next door, who chose to be unfriendly.

The person we bought our house from used to be chairman of the nominating committee at Canoe Brook Country Club, and he told us a great story. He said he was one of the first Irish members of Canoe Brook. He and his wife had been there for a few months, and he invited the president of Canoe Brook over to his house and said to him, well, how are things going at the club? I really enjoy it, but I'm new. And the president said, the club's going downhill because we are admitting a lot of big Irish families. Little did he know that his new club member was Irish, with six kids.

I don't think racism will ever disappear. The playing field still isn't level, and I don't think it will ever be, at least not in my generation or my kids' generation or my grandkids' generation. On Wall Street what happens now is they let us in the door, but instead of blatant racism, you come across subtle things. For example, it seemed like they never wanted me to get too big an assignment, too big a client. When I went after those guys, I was always told I had enough clients, I had enough capacity, whereas my colleague could have even more clients than I did but yet he wasn't at capacity. It was things like that.

In most of my jobs, I've been the only African American, or the highest-ranked African American, particularly on the Street. At Alliance Capital, I had to work hard to be as successful as possible, but I knew that my being successful was a way to help bring in other African Americans. As long as I'm successful in my work, and I keep bringing in more people and they're successful, that opens a door for more of us to get in there.

I do feel that by integrating the workplaces, the neighborhoods, and the country clubs, we are an extension of the Civil Rights Movement of the 1960s. Judge Ernest Booker, my brother-in-law, was the first black member of the Essex County Country Club, in West Orange, New Jersey, and Milton Irvin was the first African-American member of the Baltusrol Golf Club, which by the way will host its first PGA Championship in 2005. I felt comfortable at the Canoe Brook Country Club because I was out playing golf, but we didn't become members. I think the rest of my family would have been uncomfortable at Canoe Brook.

My kids are eight, six, and three years old. Two girls and a boy. When we chose to live in Summit, we weren't particularly worried about our kids' identity in a white environment. We knew there was another African-American family a few doors down, and Milton and his family were close by. We were active in Jack & Jill, an African-American social and cultural organization. We belonged to a black Baptist church in Montclair but visited Fountain Baptist in Summit, which we liked. And we had a network of like-minded friends, many of them my buddies from Harvard Business School, who live either in Summit or in South Orange and Montclair. I would have liked to see more of them move to Summit when we were living there, but it costs a nice piece of change to do that.

There's no question that my kids, as blessed as they are, will be criticized by economically disadvantaged African-American kids. They will have to learn to handle being called white. I went to a private school, and I would come home to a housing project every day and was called "schoolboy" a couple of times. I had to knock a few heads. Fortunately, I was a good athlete, which always helped me. A lot of people left me alone. But I tell my kids now, you're going to encounter a different kind of racism. You're going to confront the class system from your African-American peers, some of whom are going to call you "whitey" or "Oreo" because you talk a certain way, or because your daddy works in a firm that is identified mainly with middle- and upper-class white people. In addition, you will have racism from white people. It's going to be arduous. The kids need to have a strong foundation here at home. They have to come home and be able to tell us everything. They have to realize they're blessed, but they must give back. It's nonstop. You have to keep after them, keep warning them. It's not an easy thing.

We are trying to give our children a strong sense of identity as African Americans in a predominantly white environment. If my children decided to marry a white person, I would be a little disappointed. I'm open to it, and I would definitely support them. But I would prefer them to marry someone African American.

We thought about going back to the inner city and perhaps renovating a brownstone while living around more middle-class African Americans. But once we started having children, we wanted green grass and we wanted a sizable lot. I sit on the board of two nonprofit organizations because I'm very involved in the community, and that helps me a lot. The kids I work with are touched by the fact that I'm willing to keep up with them and keep track of them, that I come from the same situation they do, and I speak their language if I want to. Most of them don't have a father figure at home, so they're looking for a role model. As my own kids get older, I will get them more involved in community work.

In downtown Summit, there's a housing project that's pretty much all people of color. Every day when I got off the train, especially in the summertime, I used to see the brothers who live there hanging out, and I was reminded of where I come from. My kids saw the project all the time when we went downtown. They realize that there is a significant African-American community out there, some not as blessed as they are.

Nowadays there are programs to help bright and motivated African-American kids get out of the 'hood—whether it's ABC or Prep for Prep or private schools that offer some students full scholarships. However, if you come home to little or no family structure, you need something to keep you going, and that's the tough part. Beyond that, the playing field is far from level in terms of the ability to make connections in a white world. I've worked with young entrepreneurs of color in a program called the National Foundation for Teaching Entrepreneurship, and they complain all the time about insufficient access to circles of people who could help them get connected in business, or even get funding for their projects. They don't have the opportunity to be where those conversations happen.

Black-on-black crime is one of our biggest problems, and we can't simply blame white people for it. It comes back again to the family and the family structure. In my household, the last thing on my mind was joining a gang. I came home from school and my mom said, you're not going outside until you finish your homework. We had a structure. My father came home every night, and we had supper together and a routine. We went to church often. We had values put into us, strong, powerful values, so we never thought about gangs or sticking someone up. When we saw somebody's mother wheeling a shopping cart, we ran over to help her with the groceries. That's just the way we were brought up.

Savoy magazine recently published a disturbing article about a beautiful girl who was killed in Chicago. She was raised by her white grandparents, and her black grandmother always sent for her to come up to Milwaukee for the summer. She enjoyed spending the summer in Milwaukee seeing the black side of her family and learning about that part of her heritage. When her black grandmother died, her white family would not pay for her to go back to Milwaukee to see her other black relatives in the summer. So she started feeling she was missing something, and she ran away from Texas with a couple of friends and went to Chicago, where she hooked up with some friends on the South Side.

She was invited to a party on the West Side of Chicago. I lived in Chicago for four years, and I know it well. This beautiful mulatto child went to a party on the West Side, in one of the most treacherous neighborhoods. She went with two other girls, sat down at the bar, and was immediately approached by a bunch of cool, slick-on-a-curb brothers. The other two girls say, let's get out of here, and they leave. The mulatto girl gets in a car with three young black men, not knowing anything about these guys from the 'hood. It turns out that one of them has sex in the backseat of the car with the girl, later claiming it was consensual sex, and when she doesn't want to perform anal sex, he rapes her and then kills her.

If the girl had been able to see the black side of her family, she wouldn't have been so intrigued with being seen at the rough side of black life in Chicago. If her family had just kept letting her go to Milwaukee in the summer, the West Side of Chicago wouldn't have been something exotic for her, the forbidden fruit.

The two pillars of family and education must be in place if African Americans are to make further progress. If we can stabilize those two structures, then I think we can bring up most of our people. I'm optimistic. I see the glass half full. That's just my nature. When I see Ken Chenault, Stan O'Neal, Richard Parsons, and Franklin Raines, I see the barriers being broken down and the glass ceiling being cracked. I hope they bring along others with them. Realistically, you can't capture everybody. Even in the Jewish culture, which does a great job, there are some Jews that are lagging; there are white people that are lagging. I don't think we can get everybody. But those of us who are successful owe it to our community to go back and help as many people as we can. Furthermore, I encourage bright African Americans to seek out the investment management profession, because it is one of the few endeavors that has a scorecard on your performance every day. It's about as close to a meritocracy as one can get. Of course, it isn't perfect.

Lack of access to capital has deterred the movement and progress of all African Americans. But as a people, we are starting to gain that access. We had the late Reginald Lewis, the financier and entrepreneur who owned TLC Beatrice International. We have Bob Johnson, founder and CEO of BET. I just read in *Savoy* magazine about a brother I'd never heard of who's a billionaire out of Birmingham, Alabama, and I was like, wow! One of my classmates, Keith Clinkscales, founded Vanguarde Media, which owns *Savoy* and *Honey* and *Heart & Soul*. Catherine Hughes, a black woman, is doing great things in the radio/media world.

There was a group of brothers and sisters in my generation at Harvard Business School. A lot of them came through a program called ABC—A Better Chance—which helps young people from low-income households. Several, like me, come from modest means, but from a family that stressed education. We've all done well, and now we're pulling for each other, while helping each other out. We all try to support African-American dentists, doctors, and accountants. We try to patronize each other's businesses and keep it in the community. That's key. And the kids see that too. We live a bicultural life. We have a black base and a black nurturing environment; we live part of our lives in the white world; and then we come on home.

Donna Pearson

I'm very happy living in the Boston area now, and I also loved living in Summit. I like a family-oriented town. I'm always involved with the girls' schools. Before we moved to Summit, and then west of Boston, we lived in a similar kind of town in California.

I worry about our kids being in a mainly white upper-middle-class town. It was that way in Summit, and it's the same in the town we recently moved to. The girls go to school with a majority of white kids. So we try to keep a balance. We make sure our children are aware of being black. They're surrounded in our home with works of art by blacks, and they read a lot of books by and about African Americans. We're in Jack & Jill, and that's good. In Summit, there was an African-American teacher at the school and we asked, make sure our children get that teacher. And we kept our kids in touch with their friends in other communities, as we will do when they have had time to make new friends in the Boston area.

Racism still exists, but it's more quiet. It's kept behind closed doors. In Summit I saw instances, sometimes subtle, sometimes not, particularly at the school. Because I'm so fair-skinned, people sometimes think I'm white, and they'll say things and I'll say, excuse me, I'm African American too. And all of a sudden their face gets red.

They don't say the "n" word, but one time someone said to me, oh, that black person, they don't know what they're doing. And I said, excuse me? Or they'll think that the way I'm doing something is inferior to what they're doing and that I can't do a job like they do. I happened to be working as someone's partner in a club at one time, handling the organizing of something, and you have to let them know right away that you can take the lead just as well as they can.

We had a dinner club for residents of Hobart Avenue, and I was the only African American. They welcomed me very nicely, but it's questionable whether people realized at first that I'm black. In fact, shortly after moving to Summit, Walt and I heard someone say, well, there's an interracial couple on Hobart Avenue. And we said, really? Where? A taxi service that our friends the Irvins use told Milton about an interracial couple on Hobart Avenue, and he was scratching his head trying to figure out who it was. It's funny. A lot of them thought we're an interracial couple. I say, we come in all colors, shapes, and sizes.

When we first moved to Summit, all the neighbors were welcoming except for one. The property needed a lot of work. We had no grass in the backyard, so we cut down trees because we wanted to grow grass and make it friendly for the kids. I went over and said, hi, I'm your new neighbor; I want to introduce myself. And she said, you cut down trees, and you're going to destroy this property. Not long after, my husband, Walt, and I heard she'd said that some people moved in next door and the property value had gone down.

We renovated for close to four years in our home there. It was nonstop. I like interior decorating; it's my hobby. So we said the property value was going to go up, because we were doing things to make it nice. Every time we did something, we got the unfriendly neighbor standing there watching us. But every other neighbor, I must say, was very nice.

Our daughter Taylor, who is eight, had a difficult situation at school. A friend of hers told her she couldn't be in a club she was starting because it was just for white people. This was someone Taylor was having play dates with, so I was a little confused. I called the girl's mom and told her what happened, and her mom said, I think something's wrong, because Grace likes to play with Taylor. So I had a discussion with Taylor. I told her that sometimes kids say things and they're mean about African-American children. I told her how beautiful she is. Her skin color is so pretty.

In pre-K, I found out, they had all these clubs. The girl's mom called me back and said, Grace doesn't remember saying that, and she enjoys playing with Taylor. Then she invited Taylor over for a play date. Walt's response was to tell Taylor to start her own club.

I think we're losing a generation, because there's such a disparity between the black underclass and then people like our children in the black middle class. We have to do something to educate the children. Otherwise, I think there are going to be two classes of African Americans permanently. The problem has grown. It's more visible now than it has been in the past. I hear all the time about grandmothers in their early thirties, and it's scary. Walt's involved in an organization that's turning young kids into entrepreneurs. He works with really young kids, in the seventh, eighth, and ninth grades, who come from neighborhoods where they thought they were going to be dead at nineteen. It's just amazing the minds of these children nowadays.

Some people assume that black people aren't educated because of the hip-hop and their appearance. I think some of the kids are just learning that these are very educated people who come from good schools, like Princeton, Yale, and Harvard. They're showing their creativity through their hip-hop. They're educated people, and that's key. The kids need to understand that better. Everyone out there is not just singing these songs. They're not gangsters. You have to be smart also.

Some of the hip-hop is fine for my kids to listen to. Not the ones with all the curses in them, but some of it, yes. My older daughter loves music and wants to know all about the hip-hop artists. She said, one day I'm going to win an Oscar.

If my daughter brought home a white boyfriend, it wouldn't put me through major changes, but I would have a talk with her and see how serious this was. I would prefer she marry an African American, but I love my children, and whatever makes them happy is okay. And I have a saying: If you go back across the years, probably everybody has a little bit of a story to tell.

Taylor Pearson

When I was in pre-K, something happened with me and my friend. My friend was making a club and I wanted to be in it and she said no, it's only for white people, and that made me sad.

I cried. And I wanted to go home, and then I wanted to tell my mom and dad, and they said they were going to call her parents and discuss it with her parents. She didn't ask me to be in the club after that either.

And that's what I wanted to say.

LENORA FULANI

Résumé Stories

Political activist and educator Lenora Fulani teaches kids how to be successful in the business world. Her premise is that the workplace is a performance space, the world is a theater, and our kids have to learn how to perform. "A lot of performances black kids currently have, they think of as the essence of themselves as black people," she told me. "But they can learn a different way to perform, like they learn anything else. Because of the poverty they live in, what the kids know about the world is very narrow, and they know it from the street corner. Part of what it means to learn is that you have to be worldly in ways that a lot of our kids aren't. So our educational approach puts them in situations where they have to learn to be more sophisticated."

I grew up in Chester, Pennsylvania, a poor suburb of Philadelphia. It was very much a working-class town. Many people who live in Chester came up from down South and settled there because it had a lot of industry at one time. My father worked as a baggage carrier for the Pennsylvania Railroad. My grandfather used to work in the steel mill. My uncles worked for a linoleum company and for the Scott Paper Company. Chester was predominantly black and poor, and still is.

My father died when I was twelve, and my mother kept us going. She was my principal role model, which is interesting because she was working class and pretty much uneducated until she became a nurse. I think people don't see themselves as possible role models, but my mother was quite something. She's one of my heroes. Having worked as a domestic until she was around thirty-five years old, she decided to become a licensed practical nurse and did that until she retired. She had to drop out of school in the sixth grade, and she was always very ashamed of that because she couldn't spell. She would write me letters and apologize for her spelling in the midst of them. But she was a real go-getter.

I knew that my nephews and nieces were poor even when I was little. One of my sister's kids used to come to our house and eat nonstop. All the things that happen to people in poor families happened in mine. But I wasn't particularly self-conscious about our circumstances. I didn't walk around thinking, I am poor. Being the youngest in my family, I got everything they had to offer. My closest sister was eight years older than me. It was almost like being an only child.

I was aware that I had privileges my siblings didn't have, and I spent part of my childhood trying to be giving to people. That was always very important to me. I used to play the piano for youth choir in our church, from the time I was twelve until I left to attend undergraduate school. My mother had bought me a piano. She rented it for a year, and when she realized I was going to keep playing it, she began to pay for it. She used to do things that were pretty huge for us.

One of the reasons I feel so close to black communities and black kids is I think it was a miracle that I got out of Chester as a young woman not pregnant. I watched what happened to my sisters and cousins and I was scared to death. I was like, I don't want this to happen to me. But that wasn't because I was brilliant. Circumstances impacted me; I learned from things I saw. It was almost a miracle. People always say to me, there's something about you that made you different. I think a lot of what made me different was outside of my control, such as being the last kid of five. Many circumstances go into the choices people make.

By the time I left high school, I knew things were not going well for many of those around me. I made a list of all the people I was going to go back to Chester and save after I got my degree. When I really discovered that I too was poor, I was in therapy. I was in my late twenties and had separated from my husband. I was in graduate school, studying psychology. My husband and I broke up when my kids were five years old and two and a half. Because he tied his fatherhood to our marriage, I think he just disappeared when he recognized that I had really left the marriage.

I had my two kids. My mother used to always tell us that we should have a savings account. So every time I got paid, I would put money in the savings account. But by the end of the month, I would have to take it out to spend it, and I thought there was something wrong with me because I didn't have a savings account. I finally raised it as an issue in therapy, and my therapist said to me, do you know that you're poor? And I felt two things almost simultaneously: totally humiliated and extremely relieved. I felt like, I don't have enough money to have a savings account; this is not a character flaw. It was magnificent; it was liberating. I was working with a white Jewish therapist whom I'd also worked with politically. His name is Dr. Fred Newman. He's been a mentor, and we've worked together now in the All Stars Project for more than twenty years.

I was not raised to think I could become anything I wanted to be, or that I would end up with a Ph.D. My family was almost completely nonacademic. I'm the first person in my immediate family who went to college. I don't know if I ever saw my father read a book. I assume my mother read some, because she had to pass tests to become an LPN. My parents bought me *The World Book Encyclopedia,* with the red covers. I think that if I had just completed high school, it would have been fine with them. In some ways, what I've done with my life is incomprehensible to my family.

Two of my sisters work—one is a nurse, and another works for the post office. A third sister died when I was fifteen. My brother worked for the Ford Motor Company in Chester and followed the job when the company moved to Mahwah, New Jersey. He finished his career and retired, and lives in New Jersey now.

Kids in the inner city today are just as poor as those of us were who grew up poor in small towns in the 1950s. In some ways, they're poorer. Inner-city poverty has a particular look to it. It's become so chronic that the poor accept it as a way of life, as do people who aren't so poor. We grew up during the Civil Rights Movement. There was a sense of having someplace to go. Growth was possible. The *Brown* v. *Board of Education* ruling, in 1954, paved the way for increased opportunity for us. More funding became available to state colleges. Individuals were bringing cases against state schools saying they had to admit black students because the colleges were paid for by tax dollars. In the 1950s and 1960s, Historically Black Colleges and Universities were supporting black kids who got into college by offering them the secondary-level preparation they had missed because the schools they attended were so inadequate. All this had a huge impact on me and on many others who grew up at that time. And the HBCU became even more important in the 1970s and 1980s, with the tremendous increase in the number of blacks attending college in those years.

Unless they have huge fantasies about being the next P. Diddy or Michael Jordan, a lot of kids living in poverty today think their kids are going to be poor and their grandkids are going to be poor. Kids in the inner city lead blind and uneventful lives. They're filled with all the rage and anger and nondevelopmental displays that go on in poor communities. People fight and scream and turn to sex at thirteen or fourteen because that's what there is to do. One of the reasons I got out of Chester is I remember sitting on my porch and looking at the three cars that went down my street every other hour. Being bored is so overwhelming. To me, it was one of the worst experiences of my life.

The growing economic gap between the rich and the poor has real consequences in our community. Many of our people haven't gotten richer and more economically stable since the 1960s, even though we've produced a black middle class. I don't know if the class divide in the black community is permanent, but I would like for us to acknowledge it more. I have a strong reaction to affluent black people commenting on this country's current economic conditions as if they themselves are impacted in the same ways that the black poor are. When they say things like we're all a paycheck away from being poor, it's not true. It's a way of denying both the benefits of the Civil Rights Movement and the fact that there is a big grouping of black people who are dirt-poor. We're not all the same, and saying we're all just a paycheck away from poverty only masks the differences.

Legal freedom from racism has had a true impact. The Civil Rights Movement has raised new challenges and new responsibilities, choices like do I go to class, do I do my homework, do I not get pregnant, do I not do drugs? That sort of choice in some ways is a very personal decision, and in other ways it's not. The poverty in our communities today is chronic in part because young people do not have the sense of possibility we had in the 1960s. What's not working for the black community and poor blacks today is more subtle than it was then, when people were fighting to change the world for us and there was a sense that all of this poverty wasn't our fault. Today there is more of an effort to blame the victim. It's almost like kids who are poor and failing are told, you have all of this available; how can you not take advantage of it? But in many ways they don't have all of it available. They don't have access. I think the educational institutions in our cities are failing. They have failed the kids for a host of reasons, and the kids are bewildered.

Since the 1960s, too much emphasis has been placed on economic deprivation and not enough on recognizing that we live in a country where it's about superiority and inferiority. The white experience is seen as superior, the black experience as inferior, and most American institutions were developed for the superior people. Even things that have nothing to do with racial issues are seen in black and white. There is a sense in our communities that there is black behavior and there is white behavior. You can rant and rave about that and say down with the system, which I understand. But in a way that misses the point. That's how things are. The schools were not created for all the kids who go there. I think they were created for white kids in the 1890s, different sets of white kids who could function in particular ways. And one consequence of creating a pedagogy for white people, for the superior people, is that it doesn't work with the people who have been labeled inferior. White kids have a very different view of the world and a very different life experience than young black and Latino kids. White kids are insiders. They view themselves as insiders; they're connected to the American mainstream. The approach in poor communities is remedial. The statement and posture are that there's something wrong with you; you have to catch up. Our kids feel like outsiders because they are, and you have to deal with that.

When I think of who it is that has to take some responsibility for the failure in our community, I think of the black establishment, the people who have benefited from the Civil Rights Movement. Many activists in the movements of the 1960s and 1970s recognized this hierarchical arrangement in our society, in our schools, in our institutions. The problem is that they were nationalists; they used identity politics. I think they looked at black culture, poor black culture, and defended it on face value. They talked about it as being economically deprived but culturally rich, and I think that was a mistake. I understand what they tried to do. But I think we made a major mistake in saying that we were culturally different as opposed to culturally deprived, because being culturally different covered over the fact that we were culturally deprived.

In 1968 there was a fight in the Ocean Hill–Brownsville section of Brooklyn over local control of the schools. The mission of the coalition that led the fight was to educate our kids. But my God, at that point in 1968, the young people in the black community were two grades down in terms of reading scores, and they lived in mostly segregated communities. Nearly thirty-five years later, they're in segregated communities, almost overwhelmingly, and I think there was a test that showed black kids in eighth-grade English performing at 24 percent of their grade requirement compared to 57 percent for whites.

We have to deal with this, but we also have to take responsibility for it, because while the mission was to educate our kids, that movement failed. The failure has to do in part with an economic situation that hasn't changed dramatically. But some of it has to do with the fact that a lot of the activists and militants who participated in Ocean Hill–Brownsville got absorbed in the bureaucracies of the Democratic Party. They either lost a sense of the mission or they didn't have the political or conceptual tools to produce quality education. I think their efforts to solve the problem of undereducation in our communities, or miseducation, with nationalist identity politics devastated our community and miseducated us.

In the 1960s, our political movements were geared toward establishing equality in the sharing of power across all aspects of American life, and that made sense to me. But the shift in our communities toward black cultural nationalism did our community a disservice and does black people a disservice. As a people, we played a role in the shift toward that ideology. The idea that we are all the same is in part one of its aftereffects. It's probably also a result of our experiences in slavery and with the Jim Crow racism of the South. In some ways, you come together to survive. Even if you don't do so literally, you do conceptually, and I understand that.

I wasn't political as an eighteen-year-old. But I also didn't want to participate in documenting failure in black communities. In the mid-1960s I had read *Dark Ghetto: Dilemmas of Social Power.* Around the time of Ocean Hill–Brownsville, I had decided I wasn't interested in discovering any more crap about black people. Then as a graduate student in psychology, I reread *Dark Ghetto* and understood it better. One of the things Kenneth Clark talked about in that book was cultural deprivation. I think our communities were culturally deprived then and still are today. Lowering standards or artificially creating a sense of self-importance in black kids by throwing black identity at them or records of black achievement will not cover over that failure.

The black cultural nationalism of the 1960s affected a lot of people, and most definitely did so at the universities. We ended up saying you can talk about certain things in the black community but you can't talk about them outside of it. If you speak Ebonics, for instance, then you're more black than those who don't, even if that means you're failing out of the school system. So I think we participated in creating a situation where we've left poor black people behind. Glorifying the culture of poor people in our communities isn't helpful to them. They are over there, and we relate to them as hip or whatever, but they're failing in communities that aren't growing.

The academic literature suggests that if you're born in poverty, it's harder to move beyond poverty—that you can't get out. The way that poor people have been related to over the last twenty or thirty years suggests the same thing. I was a psychologist in training during the late 1960s and early 1970s, and I have a real passion for black people. I hated the cultural deprivation movement because of how it was being used academically. And because I was concerned about it, I wouldn't touch it. But at some point, you have to come to terms with the fact that we've been deprived, and that glorifying our culture is not going to change the failure our kids are experiencing in school. We need to come up with a methodology that accepts this failure and deprivation and moves us on to development.

So how do you do something about the hierarchy that's been built in to the educational system and that dominates what learning is for our kids? We have to create an environment where there's value to what kids produce. What we've looked to do at the All Stars Project is to build nonhierarchical models for learning.

The All Stars Project took shape as a nonpartisan, nonprofit organization after years of grassroots community organizing that began in the early 1970s. Dr. Newman and I founded the project in 1981. It comprises two youth programs—the All Stars Talent Show Network and the Joseph A. Forgione Development School for Youth—and the Castillo Theatre, an off-off-Broadway theater for people of all ages.

Castillo specializes in experimental, socially relevant work, a brand of theater it calls "developmental theater." Like the youth programs of the ASP, Castillo is concerned with human growth. It gives kids a connection to the world of theater and culture that they wouldn't otherwise have. Pam Lewis, who is codirector of the Development School and national producer of the All Stars Talent Show Network, is also an actress in the Castillo Theatre ensemble. It's not unusual for her to bring what she's learning in the performance ensemble into the work with young people in the talent shows and the Development School. Many members of the full-time staff of the All Stars Project are actors in the Castillo ensemble.

We raise about $4 million a year for our theater projects and the two youth programs. We wanted to establish the integrity of the educational program without all the bureaucracy of government funding. Our independent financial footing has made a huge difference. Without it, you have to dance to somebody else's tune, which means you don't get to develop kids. For years, many wonderful volunteers have sat around telemarketing tables raising money to fund our projects. I was on the phones raising money about three nights a week for ten years. We also go out and talk to people in the streets about the importance of investing in the growth and development of young people of color, and the people we describe the programs to often become part of our volunteer telemarketing operation.

All three ASP programs are based on the use of performance as an important technique in human development. What we mean by performance is a capacity for human beings to do things that take them beyond themselves, to try on different costumes or identities, different ways of being in the world. It's a technique that allows people to reinitiate growth, because you can step outside of who you are and who you think you are, outside of "identity," and become both more of who you are and other than who you are. We've developed a learning approach that speaks directly to the kids in the black and Latino community who have been underdeveloped by our society. That's why we want to grow this learning approach and why we want people to know about it.

What we're doing with the ASP is raising the idea with kids that they can have many performances, and that if you have only that one performance you grew up with, then when you go out into the work world, you're not prepared. You don't know what to do; you don't know how to participate. When people feel uncomfortable with them, the kids feel uncomfortable too. As an educator, I believe that part of what it means to learn—to be a real learner—is that you have to acquire a sophistication about the world. You have to be worldly in ways that a lot of our kids aren't. There are all these ordinary jobs and ordinary ways of being in the world that kids who come from very poor communities aren't exposed to and don't know about. We're teaching young people how to be more worldly and sophisticated, given that the dominant culture in our society is white, especially in the work world. We teach them how to perform onstage at a talent show or in corporate America on Wall Street. They're learning both how to be more of who they are, as young black and Latino people, and more of who they are not.

We work with about twenty thousand kids a year in the All Stars Talent Show Network—every kind of kid you could imagine, between the ages of five and twenty-one and beyond. We're saying to kids, if you've never been accepted for anything, if you've never filled out a form for anything, you should definitely try this. Young people who have already performed in shows go sign up kids on street corners in New York City, Newark, Philadelphia, Los Angeles, and Oakland. They ask, do you want to audition for a talent show? Some of them do the audition saying, yeah, yeah, yeah, and when we accept them, they're blown away. People bring friends and families to the auditions. Everyone who tries out gets in, though they don't know that before the try-out. For some kids, it's their first experience of success.

We have an audition, a workshop, and a show, and a parent meeting following each show. We put the kids onstage and they do hip-hop, and we don't censor them. They make their statement. But in the process they're creating a show, they're mentoring young people, and they're learning about performance, not just onstage but as producers of something that's successful. The shows are amazing. I'm not anti–hip-hop culture. I don't think we should crush CDs. I actually like hip-hop. It's been played a lot in my house, and I don't have any problem with that. What I'm saying to young people is that hip-hop is not all we are. Black people have led the way in other forms of cultural experience and entertainment. Hip-hop culture is youth culture, but it's not the beginning or the end. Everybody's not going to be P. Diddy. The kids come to think that everybody can make a million dollars if you make a few rhymes. On some level they know that millions of them are not going to be able to do that, given the other things you have to learn and do to get there. We don't have to negate the positive aspects of hip-hop culture, and I don't think that being black has to be equated with hip-hop. I think it's a cultural expression that's in our community. To the extent that people insist that's the only way we can be, we have to engage kids by giving them other opportunities and other experiences.

Most of the kids realize this is their one shot. So across the board they perform their butts off, to use their expression. They take it and run with it. I think there are millions of kids—African American and Caribbean American and African and Latino—who are waiting for somebody to come into their community and say, I'm going to give you this so that you can develop. The kids are eating it up. African Americans in our program are just as able to take advantage of the opportunity as black children of immigrants, such as West Indians, contrary to the stereotype that says African-American kids are less good at learning. I think that in general African Americans are more jaded, because they live so close to luxury and yet so far from it. They've been living with a different perspective for a long time.

One of the things that's different about us is we don't insist that parents participate. We go directly to the kids, both for the All Stars Talent Show Network and for the Development School. The parents then see what the kids are doing and they say, my goodness, they're getting up at six o'clock in the morning to be somewhere. They're getting dressed, they're rehearsing in the hallways, they're performing. All of a sudden they're doing things with their lives that are unusual. The parents then show up to see what the kids are doing, and their attendance has grown over the years. I think it's the way to go, because it's challenging the parents. It's also including the kids in their own development and not tying it necessarily to parental participation. In some ways, parents have to decide what they want to do with their own lives. These programs are built for the kids to make some decisions, and what the kids decide then impacts on what the parents do and say.

The parents are invited to come join a committee and be active builders of the All Stars Talent Show Network in their neighborhood. Many of our parents come out to get help on how to raise their young people, how to be more sophisticated and less narrow in what it is they're doing. The parents are isolated, and they don't often get a chance to ask questions of someone with a Ph.D., for better or for worse. There are things happening in the communities that parents are totally overwhelmed by. One of the dialogues I often have with parents whose kids are going to schools that are not supporting them is what it means to say to kids, you're in this school because we're poor. If I could do better, I would send you someplace else. I know that it's not working out, and I don't want to pretend about that, so let's figure out what we're going to do together, given that this is the best we have at this moment.

That's one of those conversations you're not allowed to have. But if you don't have it, you participate, I think, in both underdeveloping your child and creating a level of hostility between you and them, because you're sending them out into something that's not working and insisting that it work for them. Without this conversation, the failure at school reinforces the negative environment at home, and everybody hates everybody.

Our leadership training program, the Development School for Youth, was founded in 1997 as the result of ongoing conversations with some of our contributors who are businesspeople. They were looking for ways to become more directly involved with the kids' education. So we now have an after-school, supplementary education program for kids between the ages of sixteen and twenty-one that meets for three months, with three classes that meet once a week each in an after-school setting. After-school programs are where young people are learning a lot of things. I think white kids are better at what they do because they have exposure to after-school activities that make a huge difference.

The Development School enrolls 120 kids a year from more than thirty high schools in New York City and Newark. We go into the best high schools, the worst, and everything in between, and do outreach. We talk to the kids about coming on board and about what we stand for and about giving them a summer internship in Manhattan at the completion of the training, and I say to them that they can still grow. I'm looking for people who still want to grow. The kids come into the program, and when you ask, why is it you're here, one of the things they say is, because I thought I was finished, meaning they were stuck where they were in life—and they're fifteen and sixteen years old.

We mix kids who are doing great in school with kids who couldn't get an A or a B if their lives depended on it. That kind of diversity is very interesting because both groups of kids bring something different to the table. What I'm requiring them to do isn't particularly what any of them are so great at, and this creates an environment where all kinds of kids can grow. I'm not trying to get them to be like we were when we were kids, to re-create that environment that worked for us. I'm trying to give them an opportunity to be who they are and can be, based on what they bring to the table. That's a key aspect of the theoretical work we do.

After the kids go through our training at the Development School, we give them eight-week summer internships sponsored by Wall Street corporations like Blaylock & Partners and the CEO there, Ron Blaylock. We want the kids to be able to do what the affluent kids do. I tell them, we have a hip-hop show in the All Stars Talent Show Network. So wear those costumes to the show. But when you're going to Wall Street for your internship, I tell them, take the three earrings out of your ear, don't wear a nose ring, and put on a suit. I object to that being defined as "white behavior." That's ridiculous. The kids share experiences of putting on a suit for the first time and getting on a subway and having somebody move over and make space for them, for the first time. Or walking into a corporate building and having people respond to them as if they're people—not even people of importance, but ordinary people you don't have to defend yourself around. They like that experience, and then they start figuring out what else goes along with it. You can't blame them for not dressing like that without having someplace to go, or think they're going to just run around the streets of Bedford-Stuyvesant or East New York or Jamaica with suits on. That would be insane. In some ways, they are inspired to put on suits because they're participating in a new aspect of their lives. They're doing something different.

One young man in the Development School, a Puerto Rican student, said to me that somehow when he was in junior high school, he saw something about business and decided he wanted to be a businessman. But he didn't know how to get from his situation in the South Bronx to becoming a businessman. He was very frustrated and started not doing school and just hanging out. Then Pam Lewis showed up to do an outreach in his high school. Later this young man told me, Dr. Fulani, I felt like God had sent her. We hear stories like that over and over and over again.

One of our young men has an uncle who's a limousine driver somewhere in Florida. The young man had to put on a suit for a mock interview. Since the kids don't wear suits, for example, they don't know how to wear ties. So the young man called up his uncle and asked him how to put on a tie. He used the headboard of his bed to practice tying the tie. Then he came back and taught the other boys in the class how to do it.

Another young person was working with one of our adult corporate sponsors. The adult used to come in after the kid had already come to work. The kid came to work an hour early every day. Every time the adult came in, she would go in her office and close the door. The kid, because of her enthusiasm, would run to the door and throw it open to say hello without ever knocking. She did this for two weeks before the corporate sponsor said to her, you can't do that. In this setting, what you have to do is knock on doors.

I asked the sponsor why it took her two weeks to say this to the kid, and she said, well, because she didn't want to be racist. And I explained that it's more racist to assume you can't say it or that everybody knows this. Chances are the kid's family members don't do professional performances—they don't work in a corporate setting. It's also racist, in a more subtle way, to think there's going to be a problem in trying to teach the kid something new. People initially feel awkward at the start of the internships—both the kids and the sponsors. Everyone is learning a new performance.

We all learn through imitation in the better parts of our learning. When kids are learning how to speak, they creatively imitate people in their environment. We talk to young babies as if they know what we're talking about, and they don't. But we accept whatever they produce, even when they put words together in funny ways. We don't say, shut up until you know the grammar and the meaning of this word. We participate in the performance. The learning is much more interactive. And then they go to school and it stops. Imitation in school is considered close to cheating. In the Development School, we create an environment not too dissimilar from kids' early language environment, where young people together are able to perform. It's not a test performance. It's the use of performance and performed activity to promote growth and development for thousands of minority kids.

Many of us were told growing up that we had to learn to speak a certain way if we were going to get a job. We don't particularly try to change how kids in the Development School speak. We just put them in situations that are demanding of them, and they have to figure out that if they want to grow here, they're going to have to change a lot of things. I have predominantly white, well-to-do businesspeople who train the kids for me. I tell them to teach the kids how to be white, and they almost fall off their chair. They have all the liberal reaction of oh my God, we're going to step on their cultural toes. I tell them, believe me, after the twelve weeks of training they'll still be black. But why don't you use this time as an opportunity to share with them some of the secrets of white success and help them succeed in your world, given that your world is where we all end up having to work? "White" here is code for middle class, for upper middle class, but it's also code for moving beyond how many of us in these neighborhoods think of ourselves.

I'm meeting more and more black professionals whom I'm exposing to these very poor black kids. Black professionals want to immediately go and change the kids' language, like "aks" to "ask." White people do that also. This is remediation, and it conveys to kids that there's something wrong with what they're doing. This is very different from putting kids in an environment where they do new kinds of things. I teach white people that I want them to speak to the kids in the ways they themselves speak, because the kids can then grow off of what they're hearing. It's ridiculous if white people try talking hip to these kids. I'm trying to introduce these kids to a new world, not to hip white people. They learn the language that fits, and they start to speak it almost unconsciously. In a way they correct, if you will, themselves.

One of the things that white kids have that the black community doesn't have, going back to the notion of cultural deprivation, is a cosmopolitan worldview. White kids go through a broadening of life experiences that makes them more worldly and sophisticated. We have kids living in New York City communities like Queens and Brooklyn today, forget thirty-five years ago, who never saw the World Trade Center. They didn't know it existed until September 11. Almost none of the young men in these communities know the experience of putting on a suit and walking down a street in Midtown and finding a way of being related to that's so very different from the usual ways in which they're related to. That trip across the bridge is measured in obstacles much greater than miles.

I don't really care whether the kids in the Development School become Wall Street executives. I want them to know that Wall Street exists. I don't care what they do with that knowledge or that experience; I want them to have it. One of the reasons I'm concerned about the bottom 90 percent is that a lot of those kids don't ever leave our communities. Almost everybody focuses on the top 10 percent, the Talented Tenth, as W. E. B. Du Bois put it. Those kids are going to make it anyway, for the most part. I'm not saying that we shouldn't support the middle-class kids, but they're going to make it. They're going to be okay in the world. They're going to go out and do the things that black professionals do, and they're going to leave their communities. But there are millions of kids who don't leave their communities and who still deserve a better quality of life, who need to be related to and developed. I'm not so much interested in developing them to leave the community. Our All Stars shows focus on how we can grow people who are staying in the communities. A lot of people will decide to do that.

Dr. Du Bois is one of my heroes. But we were barely out of slavery when he spoke of the Talented Tenth. We were trying to do something very different then, which was to establish the fact that we were human beings. Today the concept is sometimes misconstrued to mean that only 10 percent of the black community can develop. That misconception could be a result in part of the poverty and failed education in our communities, and the sense of discouragement that's followed. I was saying to a white corporate manager that we were interested in developing young people who never get to see Wall Street, kids who are not among our top 10 percent. I said, never would the white community be told that only 10 percent of them can develop. And he said, that's a good thing, because he was in the bottom 90 percent and would never have made it if that philosophy had been applied to him.

I guess that in terms of a nationalist understanding, I'm trying to get the kids in our programs to de-racialize. It's not a black or white thing when young people say to other young people, where are you going all dressed up; you're being white. It's peer pressure; basically young people saying to other youth, this isn't for you. Dressing up isn't a "white thing." A lot of what we think of in terms of color, because of how the society is structured, is not an issue of color. It's a class thing too. And we often confuse class with race.

I don't quite know what "authentic black culture" or "black authenticity" is. I think that there is no such thing, and that we've gotten into a lot of trouble with those kinds of terms because they glorify narrow ghetto identities to the exclusion of other identities. It's fine that we know from where we've come and that we're knowledgeable about Africa. But I don't think that's the same thing as being able to perform in ways that are academically stable.

To me, blackness isn't monolithic. Most of the kids we work with are black by birth, but being black means many different things. I want them to have experiences of the larger world. They can figure out what the larger world is for them, and their experiences will then shape what it means for them to be black. The dominance of hip-hop images teaches poor kids this is how they have to behave to be authentic and successful. A lot of these images are crafted by middle-class black people who go to college and then come back with hip-hop and get cool. That's a choice, and they have the right to choose that. But then they put on their suits and go do their other things, and usually make a lot more money doing these other things. A lot of white kids who come from affluent backgrounds are influenced by hip-hop, and they have five earrings and the whole bit. It's a performance. We're trying to teach inner-city kids that it's a performance that they don't have to be trapped in. They too can wake up the next day, put on a suit, and go to work.

I tell the kids that we need more nerds in the black community. Who has benefited from all of our hipness? A lot of white record companies and clothing companies. These companies are able to make fortunes off of marketing hipness in a way that most black kids can't or don't. The kids have got the hip part down pat. We train them to go to Wall Street and to walk into huge buildings and be able to produce a performance that's in step with what's going on there, and these experiences help the young people to grow.

The kids in the All Stars Project typically find themselves challenged by their peers as being less hip, and those challenges are often framed in the language of being "less black." However, kids who are failing in the school system join our program, do a corporate internship, and then go back into their communities and engage in a dialogue with their peers. Their peers see their growth. And they then ask them, what are you doing? Where you going? How do I get to be a part of that? The kids in the community are then starting to experience their friends as role models, and to be influenced by young people just like them who are doing different kinds of things. They're told to hang in there, and it means something, because it's coming from people like them, and "like them" is not just a matter of skin color. All of a sudden the world beyond their community, be it black or white, is not so far afield that they can't connect to it, because for the first time they see young people they grew up with on a street doing something different with their lives, and that's an inspiration.

What we've produced is their education, or development. We're doing things with these kids that the schools can't produce. And once you demonstrate success among this population, you are in a position to figure out even more for them. I'm looking to those of us who are more well-to-do to participate in that fight. We have to be more than role models. I think that for us, being a role model to some degree ends up getting used for not doing more of what needs to be done. If I'm black and I'm doing well and people can see me as a role model, then that's all I have to be, and all the black middle-class and upper-middle-class people don't have to have a connection to black poor people. We can't afford simply to be role models. There are ways in which we have to fight for our communities. We have to be connected to our communities. We have to find programs that allow our communities to grow and develop, and not think that it's enough to be seen.

Even on TV, the kids barely notice all the accomplishments of black people of our generation, the black role models of today, like Colin Powell and Maxine Waters. My experience is that when the kids recognize me on TV and say, oh, I know Dr. Fulani, it's because they've seen me first in their communities. A lot of these kids don't know who Colin Powell is. It may seem impossible, but how could you have lived in New York and never seen the World Trade Center? Dick Parsons, Franklin Raines, and others are more recent role models than the ones held up as examples in the community control movements of the 1960s. But pictures hanging on the wall don't teach kids how to read.

I can't say I don't care whether successful black people give back. I do care. I have all kinds of opinions; I am opinionated. A black person doesn't have to give back, but then people can't claim that by virtue of their mere existence they are doing something to give back. You can't go around saying well, but if a kid has my picture in a tenement on a wall, that's enough to inspire them. I think the real deal is figuring out the challenge to successful black folks relative to what they need to do to give back. I think giving back has to be a commitment to developing not the top 10 percent, but the bottom 90 percent and all that entails.

People want more. They battle for survival, and we can't ignore it. The notion that you don't commit crimes if you're really poor but good, as opposed to the bad poor, I think is a highfalutin description that has very little to do with what goes on in the world. Kids in poor communities of color talk about the culture of poverty. I hear heart-wrenching stories from sixteen- and seventeen-year-old black boys who say, I go to school; I do everything I can do to stay close to home. I live in a project. I don't sit on the park bench because the cops come and they do roundups and everybody who's there gets picked up and you go spend one or two nights in jail. A lot of kids talk about being worried they're going to end up on the wrong path just by simply walking down the street.

There's a way in which we don't want to look at the realities of what our communities are, but we have to. We have to acknowledge the unhealthy and nondevelopmental things that are going on there that we want to end. We have to figure out what we need to do to grow the young people and the not-so-young people in those communities so they can have better lives.

What I'm saying to these kids and their parents in poor communities is, you can't wait any longer. I'm teaching young people that you have to work with what you have, and you have to create with poverty and crap if that's what's in our communities. You have to use that to go somewhere. I don't say to them, you have to do something first before I can participate in helping you develop. I take them with what they bring.

I think the black community in New York is reawakening to its political power. We have a long way to go, but one expression of our getting there occurred in November of 2001, when the black community did a magnificent thing. It broke with the Democratic Party and voted to the tune of 30 percent for Michael Bloomberg, our mayor, who was running both on the Republican ticket and with the Independence Party, which I helped to create. I went out on the streets and helped to build that party from the bottom up. This is something I'm very passionate about. One of the things I was teaching our community is that if for the first time we made a move to give someone other than a Democrat a significant portion of our vote, we would up our political clout overnight. It's taken thirty years and the right circumstances for people to learn that lesson, but it's had a tremendous impact on our community.

It's not about black people becoming the swing element and electing candidates when white people divide their votes. I think we should be the leadership in helping to create new political paradigms in our country. The Independent Movement is made up of people who are interested in independent politics and who care about political reform, about making the process work and having more participation from ordinary people. In the black community, there are some people who are of that sentiment and some people who are not. Introducing the Independent element into the voting process makes it possible for black people to give further consideration to who they are politically. A lot of blacks are not going to go back to the Republican Party. People who have both built and are committed to the Democratic Party project that party as the place you go when you're black. Putting a new party in the mix and raising the contradictions—the failures, in my opinion—of the Democratic Party relative to empowering our community help to make black people take themselves more seriously as voters.

We live in a capitalist society, and we sure could benefit more from it than we currently do. The system knows how to make us work for it, so we should figure out how to get something out of that. I think that's extremely important.

PART TWO

The Black Belt

If the new black middle class is far more socially conscious than skeptics like the philosopher Herbert Marcuse or sociologists like E. Franklin Frazier predicted they would be, perhaps one reason for this is a keen awareness that these dramatic economic gains were enabled by the Civil Rights Movement and its by-product, affirmative action. Few of the members of the middle class whom I interviewed have any doubts that without the hard-won gains of the movement, they would not have been privy to the educational and economic opportunities that enabled them to develop their talents and abilities and excel in the broader American society. Despite their individual achievements, and the great gains that these achievements reflect, however, most still worry about, and confront, racism, and most feel that their class positions remain somewhat perilous. Perhaps the two biggest surprises— certainly to me—about the collective behavior of members of the black middle class are, first, their deep and abiding embrace of black culture and of a black cultural–nationalist social identity and, second, the desire of many to live in their *own* neighborhoods with other black middle-class people, and to do so, in growing numbers, "back home," in the South. Reverse migration, from the North, Midwest, and the West to Southern cities such as Atlanta, is one of the most important cultural phenomena to have emerged within Black America since Dr. King's death in 1968.

In 1963, the largest civil rights march in history took place in Washington, D.C. Washington was located where it is because at the time that it was chosen to be the seat of government, it was geographically at the center of the United States. So it has always marked the gateway to the South. I was always afraid to go to the South, because the South for a black person was the home of racism, the Klan, segregation, a litter of crosses, and the corpses of black men. But it was also the home of the Civil Rights Movement and the greatest civil rights leader of all, the Reverend Dr. Martin Luther King, Jr. It was here that he gave the greatest speech of his life, in August of 1963, when he said, "I have a dream."

The Civil War may have freed the black population of the South from slavery, but life remained a nightmare of poverty and terror. Racial segregation was the law of the land. Right up to the 1960s, most blacks in the South couldn't vote, and they couldn't own land even if they could afford to. Black men could be lynched capriciously, arbitrarily. My father used to joke that all Southern cities had a sign hanging at their outskirts. The sign read NIGGER! READ AND RUN . . . AND IF YOU CAN'T READ, RUN ANYWAY! But if the South was the repository of our people's worst nightmares, it has always been our spiritual home, the cradle of the African-American culture.

As a result of racist terror, millions of African Americans fled to Northern cities in the first decades of the twentieth century, in search of a better life. Few of the migrants would ever have dreamed that, a century later, black people in the hundreds of thousands would be flocking back to the South. According to one study published recently in *Population Today*, 368,800 black people moved back to the South between 1990 and 1995; 233,000 left the Northeast. The South's black population increased by 3,575,211 in the 1990s, according to researcher William Frey. That is an astonishing phenomenon for those of us who remember the horrors of the Civil Rights Movement.

I met the actor Morgan Freeman at the site of Dr. King's famous speech to discuss this surprising development. Freeman was born in Memphis, Tennessee. As with many of his neighbors, his family migrated to Chicago when he was a boy. And yet despite his wealth and fame, he has chosen to return to the South and make his home in Mississippi.

"People asked me when I went home to live, after becoming a major persona in theater, in film, good Lord, what is wrong with you?" Freeman told me. "You can live anywhere in the world you want to. Why did you come here? And I said, because I can live anywhere in the world I want to, that's why. This is home. This is where my roots are. This is where my parents are buried. This is where I've always felt safest."

I wanted to know what it is about the South that's different for a black person than the North or the West.

"We built the South, and we know it," said Freeman. "What I own in the South isn't because I went and bought it. What I own is my place here, because my mother, my father, my grandmother, my grandfather . . . all the way back to my great-great-great-grandmother, who happened to be a Virginian—that's where they had the farms . . . Traveling around the country and living in different places, I could never see that any place was any better racially than Mississippi."

"You mean you never experienced racism as a kid in the South?" I asked him.

"Of course I experienced racism as a kid in the South. But that's not the point. Whether I experienced racism in the South is not it. It's where else I experienced it. I don't care anything about experiencing racism in the South; I don't and I won't experience it now."

When we were growing up, our image of the South was not that of a nurturing place. The image we were raised with of the South was as the home of the Klan, a place of racism. But "you weren't going to find any less racism in the North," Freeman said. "It was more painful than in the South because you were given to think in the North that oh, it's different here. You're free, boy."

So will he be buried there? I asked. Yes, he told me. "My mother and father are buried right here, in front of the house. I've come back to my home place."

Few of us, we agreed, can go back to our home place. "But those of us who can and do, I think will be very pleased in later years," said Freeman, "when they sit on the front porch in a rocking chair, eat watermelon, fan the flies, and say, why did we give this up in the first place?"

I have to confess that I was surprised by Freeman's deep affection for the South. It's not the South of my childhood memories. To find out for myself what this "New" South was like, I decided to start at Freeman's birthplace, Memphis, situated strategically on the banks of the Mississippi River. Memphis—home of the blues, B.B. King, even Elvis—was one of the front lines in the battle for civil rights. Dr. King staged his march here in 1968 to support the sanitation workers; it was here that he was assassinated. For many of us, the Lorraine Motel, where he was slain, is sacred ground.

Dr. King spent his last night at the Lorraine Motel. He roomed there with his friend Ralph Abernathy. I wanted to see the room, which has been left exactly as it was right after Dr. King was shot. The crushed cigarettes there are a real surprise, given our ethos today. Cups of coffee half full sit on the stand by Dr. King's bed. The bed is still turned down, exactly as he did it when he got out of bed that morning.

Dr. King was standing on the balcony with his friends. He was shot from a little window across the street. He fell backward, and the balcony, of course, was covered with blood. There's a famous photograph of all of his friends pointing to the window across the street as the place where the shot came from. It's astonishing and horrific that a whole political movement, a hundred-year-old movement, could be ended with one bullet shot from that window over there. Pow. Just like that.

Dr. King's life ended in Memphis, but did his dream of a fully integrated America die with him? I decided to ask a man who spent the last forty years fighting for racial equality in this city, Mayor Willie Herenton.

"I marched with Dr. King on behalf of the sanitation workers," the mayor told me. "We wore a sign saying I AM A MAN. I was twenty-eight years old and I had this sign on me. The reason we had to say we were men was because of the way we were treated. We were treated like less than men."

After a lifetime as an educator and a political activist, Dr. Herenton became the first black mayor of Memphis. Since 1991 he's served three terms in office, and now he's running for a fourth. Did he ever in his wildest dreams, I wondered, think that he would be the man at City Hall?

"Obviously, I never thought I'd be on the inside of this building as mayor when I was in the Civil Rights Movement. I was outside protesting against a mayor because Memphis was a mean-spirited city. Memphis was similar to many other Southern cities at the time. I remember one evening a white man got on a bus and forced my mother and me to get up. We were at the middle of the bus and he said, hey, girl, he said, you know you're not supposed to be sitting here. And my mother and I, we got up and we sat farther in the back of the bus. I remember the separate water fountains. I remember going in the back of restaurants. You couldn't go in the front. You had to go in the side doors of theaters. You had to go upstairs; you couldn't go in the front of theaters. If you wanted to try on garments for size, you could not do that if you were black."

I asked Mayor Herenton where he was when he heard the news that Dr. King had been assassinated. "I was in a leadership training program to become principal of a school," he said. "We were having in-service the night of April 4, 1968. And we got word that Dr. King had been shot. It was unbelievable. Couldn't believe it . . . I remember we terminated the meeting, out of shock; sent everybody home . . .

"I'd been at Mason Temple the night before when he gave his speech 'I've Been to the Mountaintop.' That church was so crowded. It rained that night. There was a storm. It was hot inside; I could see the sweat on Dr. King's face. The place was packed. I didn't know it would be the last time that I'd hear him speak.

"There was no other figure like Dr. Martin Luther King," the mayor went on. "He moved the conscience of America. And all of a sudden he's assassinated in our city, in Memphis. This is the city where I was born. This was an event that could have occurred in any American city, but it occurred in Memphis . . . So I've often said that if there's any city in America that should accentuate the values and the principles that Dr. King stood for, it's Memphis."

One of the most dramatic examples of how Memphis has embraced the ideals of Dr. King since 1968 is the transformation of its police force. During the Civil Rights Era, the police in the South were symbols of institutional racism, brutality, and state terror. They were the official face of white oppression. Even today I'm always frightened when I see a flashing police car speeding up behind me.

Like many black people growing up here, James Bolden was also terrified of the police. But in 1968, determined to change things, he joined the Memphis Police Department. He was one of only sixty-five black officers in a force of two thousand. Today he's the chief.

Chief Bolden was twenty years old when Dr. King was assassinated. I asked him what the police force was like at that time. "The force was male and white-dominated," he said. "When I came on the job, we didn't have many aspirations of ever achieving any type of rank, because black commanding officers were practically nonexistent. There were very few black role models holding positions of rank in the Memphis Police Department. Blacks had certain areas of the city we could patrol and others we couldn't, even as a police officer. The areas we were assigned to generally were occupied by the black community, and we didn't police outside that community."

In 1973, Bolden founded the Afro-American Police Association to make the police a force against racism, not an example of it. He petitioned the federal government to get more blacks hired and promoted to executive positions. "Leading an organization that was trying to bring about some change within the police department," he said, "I was not met with open arms. There were white officers who refused to ride in a squad car with me. There were black officers who would turn their backs on me, who wouldn't speak to me because they were afraid I would bring trouble to them."

Did he worry that maybe an "accident" might befall him from some of his white colleagues? The fear, he told me, was with him every day. "I would go to work and sometimes I couldn't imagine getting home at night, I was so terrified . . . Who wouldn't be when you had to face something like that and everyone working around you was wearing guns?" Because of the threats, Father James P. Lyke, a Catholic priest, stood by Bolden's side and rode in his squad car with him.

Finally, in 1978, the federal government agreed that there had been discrimination in the Memphis Police Department. A consent decree was entered by the city, five years after Bolden had begun his protest. Today the Memphis police force is highly diverse. "Two deputy chiefs who work under my command," said Bolden, "are African American. Precincts throughout the city are equally divided between black and white. When I came on the job, there were no women in police work. Now we have women in leadership positions in the police department. You cannot find an area within the Memphis Police Department where minorities or blacks are not represented.

"I've had the distinction of living through the times when we could not drink at a water fountain, when we could not go to the library on a certain day, when we could not go to a movie, and when we couldn't eat at a restaurant," Bolden told me. "So for anyone to say that the South has not changed, then they're fooling themselves."

In just thirty years, the police and the city government of Memphis have been able to make profound changes. But is that true of other institutions throughout the South?

To find out, I went to Fort Benning, Georgia, home to more than thirty thousand raw recruits. Twenty-six percent of the U.S. Army's active-duty soldiers are black. Historically, the army was just as segregated as the police and as the society it was charged to defend. Today the army recruitment campaign boasts that its troops are "an army of one." I asked Lieutenant Colonel Donald Sando if the army is as integrated as it claims.

"Within our battalion, I have six companies, and two of my company commanders are black. Of the six first sergeants, three of them are black. Of the five battalions here in the Infantry Training Brigade, one of the battalion commanders is black. Three of the command sergeant majors are black . . . What I can tell you from my experience, from twenty-one years of commissioned service, is that I truly believe the army is color-blind. I truly believe that I'm color-blind . . . We promote soldiers and officers based on merit and demonstrated potential."

How could the army achieve such spectacular results in terms of this color-blind society that he describes? Historically, the army was notoriously racist. My father was in the army during World War II; he told us horror stories when I was growing up, and now the army, of all things, is held up as a model of what a color-blind society could be. How did they do that? "I can't speak for the previous fifty years of racial integration," said Colonel Sando, "but the armed forces were the first institution in our country to be racially integrated. It works for no other reason than we have to make it work, and we're going to make it work."

To make this work, each barracks is assigned an Equal Opportunity officer to deal directly with any race complaints. The army as a whole may claim that it is color-blind, but what about the individuals who make it up? Can the army change the racial attitudes that recruits bring with them? And what about white recruits from the South?

"I grew up first through fifth grades with all white kids in the neighborhood and all white kids in my class," Colonel Sando told me. "Depending on where these kids come from today, they may have grown up in a similar situation. There's nothing but white kids out in the rural Midwest, and that's who they're going to go to school with. Maybe they haven't lived with people from different races or different socioeconomic backgrounds or religious affiliations . . . One thing we tell the parents during family days is that we get the soldiers, we give them a haircut, we give them a uniform and then put them in a room with sixty of their closest friends and ask them to get along . . . Are there some difficulties? Absolutely. It's hard enough to share a bathroom with a brother or two brothers. To share a bathroom with sixty kids, there's some growing up that has to go on. So that's part of it, and they realize that they will succeed as a group or they will not succeed as a group, and that they have to take care of each other."

Colonel Sando's right-hand man is Sergeant Major Kenneth Wilcox. I wanted to ask a black man if attitudes had really changed. As we walked through the parking lot, I spotted a Confederate flag on a license plate.

"But what about this, Sergeant Major?" I asked him.

"That's a Confederate flag," he responded. "I'm personally offended by that. It doesn't represent me as a black American."

Was this person a member of his infantry?

"This soldier is an officer. I've got to figure out who the truck belongs to," said Sergeant Major Wilcox. "The flag is flying high. So I will deal with him when I figure out whose car that is. It could be one of my cadets . . . So I'm gonna deal with him."

Sergeant Major Wilcox has been in the army for twenty-four years. I asked him if it was race-neutral.

"I come from South Georgia, from an environment where racism was an everyday way of life. The military has allowed me to grow a lot in comparison to my brothers who are down South. So I'm grateful for the military. It's a great place to grow, but you still have people in the military who display racist attitudes, who haven't made the mental change . . . The new form of racism is subversive, like the young man with a Confederate flag flying high on his car . . . It's underneath the surface; you can't see it, but you sense it. Our task is to root it out and expose how ugly it really is."

Colonel Sando recounted a tale: "I had a soldier when I was a company commander, fifteen years ago, a white soldier, and he had a black platoon sergeant. And the white guy was having trouble with that. He told me flat out. He says, 'My daddy told me I didn't have to listen to a black man.' He was told that. I'm not going to talk about his father to him, so I said, 'Well look, you know, that's not acceptable here, okay? He is your platoon sergeant. He is your superior, and you're obliged to obey him. We all share a common oath, to support and defend the Constitution and obey the orders of the officer who is appointed over us, and you have to do that, son. You're going to have to figure out how to deal with that, all right?'"

And what did the soldier say?

"He said, 'Yes, sir,' and went on. Now, did I change the way he felt about his father? Probably not. Did I give him another perspective on life and explain the fact that we were not going to accept that behavior? I can't change his attitude, what he's going to think, but I can certainly change how that attitude is manifested in his behavior."

Sergeant Major Wilcox explained the army's philosophy of social transformation as a kind of shock therapy. "We've been challenged not only to train these guys; we've been challenged to take all the abnormal behavior that society has taught them and turn them around. And psychologically, we do wonders in fourteen weeks.

"We talk about men who have died on the battlefield to give us our freedom and how all that blood is red. There are no colors, there are no boundaries; all men on the battlefield are brothers. That man, no matter where he came from, I tell the guys, is your brother."

So far, so good. But what happens if somebody's busting your buns and you're so pissed off that you want to call him a name, so under your breath, instead of saying "you MF," you say "nigger," and he hears that. What does the sergeant major do then?

"That soldier will be told to go to my office, and he is looked at very straightforwardly as being a racist. As a sergeant major I would probably deal with him personally, and he'll definitely get punished. He'll lose money in his paycheck at a minimum, and at a maximum he could be discharged just off that one statement."

And do about 10 million push-ups?

"No, well, the drill sergeant will probably do a little more than I do. But it's a serious allegation, and you can't not deal with it . . . Whether it be between two black soldiers using the 'n' word in their slang, it doesn't matter. It's wrong. No matter who uses that word, it's still degrading language, and I say to anybody, no matter who uses it or where, don't use it at all."

So even two black people can't use it? "Exactly."

In institutions like the army, the police, the mayor's office—where integration is enforced—there has been dramatic progress in race relations. But what about in the hearts of the people, their deepest attitudes about race? How far has Dr. King's dream been realized in the New South?

I headed to Birmingham, Alabama, to find out. Martin Luther King called Birmingham "the most thoroughly segregated city in America," and that was saying quite a lot, given the extent of segregation everywhere in the South at the time. It was here, in 1963, that white supremacists bombed the all-black Sixteenth Street Baptist Church, killing four girls. It was only in May of 2002 that a man responsible for the bombing was convicted.

I couldn't believe that I was standing so close to the Sixteenth Street Baptist Church. I was thirteen years old and I was sitting in the living room with my parents when we got the news on the television that it had been blown up and that children, my age, had been killed. I think the Civil Rights Movement came into my life, came into my living room, that day in a way that was scarcely imaginable otherwise. People like me, or people in school like me, were being killed as martyrs. Birmingham was a metaphor for all that was wrong within the South and with segregation. It was the symbol of the heart of darkness, the evil of white racism, of white supremacy. It was the front line for the movement itself. Dr. King knew that if he could win in Birmingham, then he could win throughout the South.

Understandably, Birmingham has worked hard to bury its past. Today it is a thriving service city of about a million people, a third of whom are black. It has a black mayor, an integrated workforce, and a growing black middle class. On the face of it, at least, Birmingham is a new city. And perhaps there are few examples of racial progress in Alabama more dramatic than interracial marriage. Chris and Lura both grew up in the South. They met two years ago in college, where they were music majors. What in the world is it like being an interracial couple in Birmingham, Alabama?

"We've never had a person come up to us while we were out together and make a racist comment," said Chris. "But you tend to feel the things that people aren't saying. You feel people checking you out. Once in a while if I'm by myself with our baby, I can see the look of concern on someone's face, either a black person or a white person. They'll look at Aria and look at me and notice enough resemblance to think she's my daughter, but I can see them wondering, is her mother white?"

Did anybody give them a hard time, either in the community or in their family?

Lura responded: "Chris's black girlfriends gave me a hard time in the beginning. They didn't say to me, how can you steal a good black man from us? But that was the feeling. They were mad at him for leaving behind all the great black women he grew up with, as if it was a slam against them."

"Black women friends of mine asked me, why would you date a white girl when there are so many perfectly good black girls to date?" added Chris. "I tried to explain to them that when I met Lura and developed feelings for her, I didn't have a grocery list of things I was looking for in a woman. We met; we became friends; we developed a relationship."

I wondered if he ever thought about the fact that he would have been lynched for sleeping with a white woman twenty years ago, thirty years ago?

"As much as I would like to think that no one would bury a cross in my yard and set it on fire in these times, every so often you hear of somebody getting dragged down the highway chained to the back of a car. Or some policeman is beating someone shitless for seemingly no reason. I'm not going to dwell on it. There are moments when I wonder, have I taken a step that my family could pay a price for? But the answer tends to be that Lura is worth the risk and my child is worth the risk."

"I usually shrink from confrontation," Lura interjected. "I walk away and figure, whatever you want to be mad about, you be mad about it in your corner and I'm going to be happy in my corner."

Would they raise their child in the South?

"We haven't decided whether we'll have our daughter attend school in the South," said Chris. "In most any school in the South, there's a predominance of black or white students, and that's still hurting race relations . . . So I would love to get Aria out of the South, to some area where there's a little bit more diversity."

Will the South ever be a place in their lifetime where race won't matter?

"In my lifetime?" Chris said, laughing.

"I'm sure Martin Luther King, Jr., hoped that day would come," said Lura. "Most people hope for world peace, but if people don't take steps to make it happen, it's not going to come any closer. Everyone can take small steps toward that goal."

The fact that Chris and Lura can build a family here is certainly a sign of change, even if some attitudes toward interracial marriage—among both blacks and whites—are still entrenched in the past. Astonishingly, interracial marriage only became legal in Alabama in the year 2000. But does this reluctance to accept mixed marriage extend to other areas of personal choice?

Dr. King once said that the most segregated time in America was at eleven o'clock on Sunday morning, which is why I was intrigued to hear about an interracial church in the heart of Birmingham: the Church of the Reconciler, founded by the Reverend Dr. R. Lawton Higgs, Sr. Higgs spent his adolescence in Huntsville, Alabama, and moved to Birmingham in the late 1960s.

"I was convinced in those days that I was a racist," Reverend Higgs confessed. "I was not a violent man, but I definitely concurred with the view that black people are less than human and that they needed to stay in their place. I had no relationships with any black people. None whatsoever."

What made him change? I asked.

"I read Martin King's 'Letter from the Birmingham Jail,' and it broke my heart. I cried for about three days. I discovered I was in opposition to God."

Higgs established the Church of the Reconciler ten years ago, after previous attempts to integrate his all-white church had been met with hostility by his parishioners. He won a special commendation from President Bill Clinton for his work with race relations. But outside of Birmingham's homeless and the poor, he has struggled to attract a large congregation. So far, the Church of the Reconciler remains one of Birmingham's few mixed-race churches.

I asked Reverend Higgs why it is important for a religious congregation to be mixed.

"If we don't integrate, we don't know one another. If we don't know one another, we're afraid of one another. If we're afraid of one another, we're gonna hate one another. And if we hate one another, James Baldwin's message in *The Fire Next Time* will cease to be prophecy; it will be realized."

I told him that many of my friends choose to live in predominantly black neighborhoods, with other well-educated black people. So what's wrong with that?

"Well, nothing is more wrong with that than white folks choosing to live in white neighborhoods with white folks. It's segregation!" he exclaimed, as if any fool should be able to see that.

Did Reverend Higgs believe that his fellow white Southerners were less racist today than they were fifty years ago?

"Yes, because they won't kill you. That's true. That's the major change that's taken place. The segregation is not enforced by active violence, and that active violence is no longer acceptable, and that is a glorious gift of God. Let's give God—and them—a big hand for coming this far!"

I had heard mostly optimistic things about race relations in Birmingham. It's held up as a city of great racial progress. To hear Reverend Higgs talk about it at the level of the spiritual, at the level of who goes to church together, where they go to church, where they live, how welcome people would feel, how slow the rate of progress has been, was quite a surprise. It would be marvelous if the larger transformations in race relations in the South are typified by what's happening in Birmingham, but judging from the commentary of Reverend Higgs, it doesn't sound as though the social transformation is complete.

My next stop in my quest to discover the New South was its spiritual capital, Atlanta, Georgia, the birthplace of Martin Luther King and now home to more than a million African Americans, including my daughter Liza, a student at the historically black Spelman College. In 1903, W. E. B. Du Bois wrote metaphorically about the Negro's place in the South:

And there in the King's Highway sits a figure veiled and bowed, by which the traveller's footsteps hasten as they go. On the tainted air broods fear. Three centuries' thought has been the raising and unveiling of that bowed human heart, and now behold a century new for the duty and the deed. The problem of the Twentieth Century is the problem of the color-line.

When Du Bois wrote those words a full century ago, he could scarcely have imagined that running straight through the center of Atlanta, the King's Highway would be named after a black man, Martin Luther King, Jr.—or that Atlanta would be the mecca of the black middle class.

During segregation, one of Atlanta's neighborhoods, known affectionately as Sweet Auburn, was home to a large black middle class that has been a source of a series of brilliant religious, political, and intellectual leaders for well over a century. Most notable among these was Dr. King himself. The house where he was born still stands here, as does the church where he began his ministry.

Today Atlanta's mayor is a black woman. Atlanta boasts one of the highest concentrations of black-owned companies in America. Atlanta is heralded as *the* place where middle-class black people can live together in their own neighborhoods, enjoy the same standards of living as their white peers, *and* retain their property values.

As a result, middle-class black families from all over the North are migrating here in the hundreds of thousands. Indeed, since 1980, the black population of Atlanta has increased by 648,000 people. And Atlanta leads the nation's metropolitan areas in total black population gains—459,000—in the last decade.

Mrs. Carmen Johnson is a real estate agent in Atlanta's wealthy suburbs. She helps Northern middle-class black migrants realize their dreams of returning to the New South. She took me to see the kinds of properties black people are buying.

"The culturally diverse upper-middle-class neighborhoods tend to cluster around DeKalb County, which is just east of Atlanta . . . When you hear of DeKalb County, people generally know that it is highly culturally diverse . . . The Sandstone Estates comprise one of the premier subdivisions of DeKalb County. There are write-ups on it all the time . . . A house that sold there several years ago for $465,000 would now go for about $700,000 plus. A single female doctor at Emory bought a house in the Sandstone Estates for $600,000. There's a new house going up, and I'm not sure how much it's going to run. The Sandstone homes go up to $2 million plus. Most of the owners are of color . . .

"An African-American CNN news anchor lives at Sandstone. We have the recording artists Kelly Price and Montell Jordan. I can't point to their houses because I do work with a lot of celebrities and their privacy is protected."

What Carmen Johnson is saying is that some of the most affluent of these "culturally diverse" neighborhoods are truly culturally diverse. What she *isn't* saying is that some of the wealthiest so-called culturally diverse neighborhoods are, in fact, predominantly black. Is it this that has made Atlanta the mecca of the black middle class?

Deirdre and Jerald Wolff are a professional couple from Detroit who moved to Atlanta with their two sons two years ago. Deirdre is an attorney, and Jerald is a manager for an Atlanta power company. What drew them here? Why leave the North and move to the South?

"I had heard tales about the South—stories that left me believing that black people were not treated fairly, had substandard living conditions, and feared for their safety," said Jerald. "Some of this was misinformation, but it spread within predominantly black neighborhoods and instilled in me a fear of living in the South . . . I had good friends in Atlanta who helped convince me to fully consider relocating there. Years later, when a job opportunity came up in Atlanta, I weighed my options in light of my largely unfounded trepidation. The real paradigm shift about living in the South," he added, "occurred when some friends I had met in graduate school relocated from Chicago to Atlanta and were extolling its virtues. I was ready to make a change . . . Atlanta seemed like a place where my family and I could progress and prosper."

"Most likely," said Deirdre, "had the job been in a city less desirable to us, we would not have relocated. But Atlanta made all the difference . . . There are many African-American professionals here, as in Detroit. The distinction I notice is that in Atlanta, African Americans hold a wider variety of professions. Not only do many successful African-American doctors, lawyers, and corporate executives live here, but African Americans in Atlanta also own golf courses, publish books, and own dirt businesses, meat companies, and a great variety of other enterprises . . .

"We did not live in predominantly white areas of other cities to escape our own people," Deirdre continued. "We sought the typical American dream: a nice house near nice grocery stores in a good school district . . . Atlanta is refreshingly unique in that it is not uncommon to find African-American communities with subdivisions of homes valued in the $300,000 to $500,000 range. Many of these subdivisions are large, consisting of more than two hundred homes, pleasantly spaced on rolling hills. Several are gated communities of affluent African-American families living in homes valued at half a million to a million dollars. So, why not?"

But this is the home of Martin Luther King, I countered, one of the birthplaces of the Civil Rights Movement. White people who were defending their right to live in all-white neighborhoods used to say, "We want to keep our neighborhood pure; we want to live with people who embrace the same values." How would they respond to that? What if somebody said to them, "You're all being racist. There is nothing but black people in this neighborhood"?

"Let me answer," said Jerald. "My neighborhood in Atlanta is virtually all black. I would not mind at all if whites moved in. I just want good neighbors. I honestly believe that if a white family chose to move into our neighborhood, they would be welcome. On the other hand, if whites do not wish to live around me, I have no complaint. Our neighborhood is open to anyone who has the income to purchase the homes that are for sale."

"I sometimes see white people looking at the model home in our subdivision," added Deirdre. "They come and they look, and then they drive around, and they keep on driving around and around. I imagine they probably peek at the pool and the tennis courts and then go on out. Why? Perhaps they see that the community is African American. It is their choice to stay or go. People have the freedom to choose among whom they will live."

The right of families like the Wolffs to choose where they live was a cornerstone of the Civil Rights Movement. But in the 1960s, this meant the right to integrate white neighborhoods, not the forming of all-black ones. In fact, integration was designed to end all-black and all-white neighborhoods. Nevertheless, the trend toward exactly these kinds of neighborhoods is strong and growing. Blacks are flocking to Atlanta. But is this really the kind of New South envisaged by the Civil Rights Movement?

Before I ended my journey, I went to talk with another Atlanta resident, someone who knew Martin Luther King personally and who marched in his movement: the legendary writer Maya Angelou.

"It was thanks to the Civil Rights Movement and the leveling of the playing field that we had the possibility of Maynard Jackson and Andrew Young as mayors of the great Southern city," said Angelou. "Then the congressmen and -women began coming from the South to Washington, D.C., to plan a better world. I believe that those events freed people from the painful memories of Southern treatment. They began to look south again and see it as they want it to be."

It's almost as if Angelou was saying that, ironically, our people had been in exile in the North for most of the past century.

"Yes, I am saying that," she responded. "Our people are coming home. The South is rich with memories of kindness and courage and cowardice and brutality. It is beautiful physically, and spiritually rich."

I have to admit that it astonishes me that black people are congregating in some of the most affluent neighborhoods in Atlanta: black people have chosen to live with other affluent black people. I asked Angelou if she found this troubling.

She replied: "Martin Luther King told a story that after the Montgomery bus boycott ended and the companies capitulated, a black woman got onto the bus and walked all the way back and sat in the backseat. A young man who had been so adamant about voter registration, so adamant, and about the boycotting, went back and he said, 'Ma'am, excuse me, we have walked eighteen miles so that you don't have to sit here.' And she said, 'Son, I walked with you, but now that I can sit anywhere, I'm sitting in the back. It's much more comfortable. I can relax, put my bags down, and stretch my legs out.' Then she smiled. With choices comes a different kind of criticism."

A hundred years ago black people begged, borrowed, and stole to get out of the South. They used any means necessary to escape the racism and economic oppression that were associated with the white racism in this area. And now, at the beginning of a new century, to the astonishment I think of just about everybody, black people are flocking *back* to the South. And they're doing it with alacrity; they're doing it with a sense of spirituality and passion and commitment to our history, to our people, and to their property values!

But something else is happening too. The black people coming back to the South—given the choice and opportunities for integration—are opting to live with people in their own class and ethnic identity, which is leading to a new kind of residential self-segregation.

I thought about how ironic that was, as I sat near the tomb of Martin Luther King. You think about what Dr. King lived for and what he died for, and in a word, that was integration. And I admit that part of me finds these neighborhoods attractive, warm, and comfortable—sort of like my childhood and adolescence back in Piedmont, except that all these people are rich. But I can't help but wonder what Dr. King would think of this whole thing. Is the right to associate freely and willingly part of the dream that he died for, even if it leads to a new form of segregation?

MORGAN FREEMAN

Home

Hollywood actor, producer, and director Morgan Freeman was born in Memphis, Tennessee, and intends to be buried there. "I believe the movement of blacks from the North back to the South is a way of getting back to who we are and what we built," he told me.

On August 28, 1963, as Martin Luther King spoke to hundreds of thousands of people at the March on Washington, I watched the speech on TV. I was working for the post office in San Francisco, delivering mail. I was also studying dance and doing some dancing. A few months earlier I had been knocking around with theater, making no money. Then I met a guy in San Francisco who was from Paris—the only black man I had ever met from another country. I'd been studying French since college days, so we conversed in French. He said to me, if you come to Europe, you and I will preside over jazz dance there. We'll open studios in Amsterdam, Copenhagen, Paris, and Stockholm. So I said, fine, that sounds like a working idea, and I decided, if I'm going to Paris, I'm going to have to build up a little kitty.

If you want to make some money, one way to do it is to get a job at the post office. I started delivering mail in March, so I had March, April, May, June, July, August, and September to get my stake together. On August 28, I was still working, but I was getting ready to fly to Paris.

Every time I hear Martin Luther King talk—I can name other speeches of his that had the same effect as "I Have a Dream," and that still do—I experience an upwelling of emotion that is hard to describe. I feel pride, and a sense of being present at a moment in history. On August 28, I was witness to what may have been the greatest speech of the twentieth century.

Dr. King's speech that day reminds me of a sermon by Adam Clayton Powell that brought tears to my eyes, called "What's in Your Hand?" You just weep when you hear it because it's the secret to life, the secret to success. He was saying, look at what's in your hand instead of complaining about what you don't have. Look around you. See what you have and work with it. Build on it. And that hope, that moving forward despite all odds, believing that in the end justice will prevail if we work for it, was Dr. King's message as well.

By April of 1968, I'd gone from a job at the post office to New York and a Broadway stage. I was appearing in *Hello, Dolly!* with Pearl Bailey and Cab Calloway. On the night of April 4, Pearl Bailey came onstage before the show was over, and she made the announcement. It was one of two announcements she would make that year. There was a hush in the theater. Sometimes you'll hear a sob in a situation like that, but we heard nothing. I don't think we finished the show that night. It's hard to remember exactly what you were thinking, because your mind was blurred. You walked home, or got home somehow, and you didn't know exactly what you were thinking about.

In Memphis Dr. King had said, I'm not afraid to die. That meant, I know you're going to get me. He had powerful enemies, like J. Edgar Hoover. You can't get much more powerful than that. It was foretold. He foretold it. And if anybody ever comes back and says Hoover had anything to do with it, I'm going to go, I knew it. Most black people think that. I'm not trying to solve the mystery. I accept that Dr. King was going to be martyred. He accepted that he was going to be not martyred, but murdered. But it is martyrdom. The Kennedys and King, they were like a single entity that had to be completely dealt with. Otherwise, from the perspective of their enemies, this nation was in serious trouble.

Pearl made the second announcement two months later, on June 5, the night Bobby Kennedy was shot. I think that caused more of a stir because now they'd gotten all of them. For some reason or other the black community had set a great store by the Kennedys. They seemed to speak to everyone rather than just to a select group of people. And they were inside the power structure, as inside as you could get.

We've realized quite a bit of Dr. King's dream of integration since 1963. I believe Dr. King could look upon today and see that he'd made a difference. One of the things that have helped bring about these changes is our media. What we see in our media is what represents us, as far as we know. And what we see now is just about everybody. There's an inclusiveness; everybody is represented. When you think of our print media and our visual media, you always think, what are the children seeing, because they're paying no attention to what you say. Children watch what you do. It's like people who say, I'm not prejudiced. Well then, how did your kid get to be prejudiced? He didn't pick it up through the blood.

I was walking down the street in Los Angeles one day and this cute little girl walked up, stood and looked at me walk past, and she said, mister, you're a nigger, did you know that? I didn't know what to say. I just stood there, having it wash over me that, gosh, this is a child. This was in 1959 or 1960. That's the only time I lived in Los Angeles. I'm from Mississippi. People tell me this was the sort of thing I was supposed to run into at home. But there I was in Los Angeles. And there it was, racism, on the street.

I was born in Memphis, Tennessee. My parents happened to be working at John Gaston Hospital, the colored hospital in Memphis. Everyone else in my family was born in Mississippi, quite a few of them in the little town I live in now, Charleston. I grew up in Greenwood, Mississippi, for the most part. I spent a few years in Charleston as a little boy with my paternal grandmother. She died when I was six. My biological father came and got my sister and me, took us up to Chicago, where my mother was. That was 1943. I got off the train in Chicago in December 1943. It was the first time I ever was slapped by cold. It was the kind of cold that makes your heart jump up and grab you. I don't think I ever got acclimated to Chicago's weather, and I was there, off and on, from age six and a half to eleven, back and forth.

It felt safe growing up in the South. I lived in a little village in a place called Baptist Town, part of the black communities of Greenwood. At that time we had two schools, an elementary school and a high school. But high school went from seventh grade up, so junior high and high school were connected. I had great teachers and received a wonderful education. I learned this subsequently, when I was out of school—out among other people who had graduated from high school or who had two years of college. I could quote Shakespeare when I got out of high school in Mississippi, and that's not the stereotype of Mississippi and black education.

In 1954, when I was a senior in high school, I spent some time in Nashville and attended the illustrious Pearl High School, which served only black students then and had a very high academic rating. They were giving PSAT tests to students in the area's black high schools. I could have gone to any university I wanted, places like Harvard, Yale, Princeton, because I qualified in the top seventh percentile of my senior class. So I was a bright young man.

My teachers were not only outstanding academically; they encouraged me. That's the thing; that's the key. You've got to have teachers—and there are many of them—who find the child and cup them in their hands and say you're special, and make you understand that all you have to do now is work.

People asked me when I went home to live, after becoming a major persona in theater, in film, good Lord, what is wrong with you? You can live anywhere in the world you want to. Why did you come here? And I said, because I can live anywhere in the world I want to, that's why. This is home. This is where my roots are. This is where my parents are buried. This is where I've always felt safest.

At the time I was growing up in Greenwood, most northerners were raised with the idea that the South was a place of the Klan, a place of racism—not warm and nurturing, but alienating. In reality, the idea that it was the best thing at the time for a black person to get out of the South had to do with the fact that there was no work. It had nothing to do with anything else. You weren't going to find any less racism in the North. Traveling around the country and living in different places, I could never see that any place was any better racially than Mississippi. The black people migrating north at the time lived in cities more than they had in the South, and they found themselves experiencing more racism. It was more painful than in the South because you were given to think in the North that oh, it's different here. You're free, boy.

What's different for a black person about the South, in contrast to the North or the West of the United States, is that we built the South, and we know it. What I own in the South isn't because I went and bought it. What I own is my place here, because my mother, my father, my grandmother, my grandfather, my great-grandmother, my great-grandfather, great-great-grandmother, great-great-grandfather, all the way back to my great-great-great-grandmother, who happened to be a Virginian—that's where they had the farms. They got my great-great-great-grandmother off a ship.

That was the image, though, that the South was a place black people had to flee from. Booker T. Washington gave a great speech in 1895 in Atlanta, at the Cotton States and International Exposition. He said to black people, don't go to the North—"Cast down your bucket where you are." And as soon as they could, black people got a railroad ticket and went to Detroit and went to Chicago. They got bottlenecked in the South Side of Chicago and lived a life that was horrendous. You can't raise a child in a situation like that. I was there and I know. Those were hoodlums. And they weren't hoodlums because they were living in Chicago; they were hoodlums because life—survival itself—was marginal. People were too crowded. There was too little hope. Too many people were trying to scrabble out these little piecemeal jobs they were giving them. People were going up there, and all they'd done was hoe cotton; what did they know? Gee whiz. No fresh air. None.

More than a hundred years after Booker T. Washington exhorted African Americans to stay where they were, many are migrating back to the South. I wouldn't say we lost something because so many of our people fled their Southern roots and went to the North. We didn't lose anything. We probably gained something, and it just took a long time to perceive that gain. For instance, having grown up in Mississippi, left, gone away, and learned something that I didn't know and probably wasn't going to learn there, I can now bring that back. The people who are going back are bringing their knowledge back.

Integrating in society only means that people receive equal opportunity; it doesn't necessarily lead to widespread miscegenation. The mistake was associating the South with a place from which to flee. What goes around comes around, that's all. The South is the new comfort zone for blacks. If Dr. King were back and he were told that, I think he'd believe it. Of course he would. That's what he meant to happen, that the South would be a place we don't have to run away from. As a matter of fact, we want to run home. We want to go back. So we're going.

Look at Atlanta. They're flooding into Atlanta. I said to my daughter, when she was going to college, where are you going to go to school, and she said, well, I don't know. I said, go to Atlanta; go to Spelman. And when you get out of Spelman, you'll have a network. Well, she liked Spelman, and she's still in Atlanta.

It would probably be arrogant to try to speak for anyone else, but in my case, I recognize the South as being that safe place, the womb of nativity. Whatever I am—and some people say that's a lot, and I'll accept that—whatever I am was nurtured there. I can't give that credit anywhere else; don't want to and won't. And I'm going to surmise that there are a lot of people who are beginning to feel the same way. A lot of people have been going back to visit, and they've seen a gradual shift in attitude among southerners.

What we have always been blessed with is a sense of hospitality. And we have that for the simple reason that we're not overcrowded. There's room. In Washington, New York, L.A., you'll drive down the highway and you'll give that finger to the guy coming toward you—Chicago, San Francisco, any metropolis, any place where people are stuffed so close together. You won't get that here in the South. As soon as you get here, you don't have that problem. It's not just the South; there are places in Montana and Iowa that have that hospitality, that sense of space. But what they have going against them is the horrendous weather, and in the South we have our temperate climate.

So I'll be buried here. My mother and father are buried right here, in front of the house. I've come back to my home place. Very few of us can go back to the home where we grew up. But those of us who can and do, I think will be very pleased in later years, when they sit on the front porch in a rocking chair, eat watermelon, fan the flies, and say, why did we give this up in the first place?

Of course I experienced racism as a kid in the South. But that's not the point. Whether I experienced racism in the South is not it. It's where else I experienced it. I don't care anything about experiencing racism in the South; I don't and I won't experience it now. It's back to that little girl in Los Angeles who said, mister, you're a nigger, did you know that? You're going to experience racism, and it had nothing to do with the South.

I never worried about going up to some hollow in Mississippi and having some Klansmen come jumping out from behind some tree to get me. Actually, I never saw the Klan when I was growing up; I only heard about them. And the whole idea of it pretty much doesn't exist anymore because the Mississippi legal system broke them. They've been tracking down every miscreant who was involved in those activities forty years ago.

On the one hand, the migration of blacks from North to South is bound to go a long way toward redressing all the social problems that our people still have—our people who are stuck in the ghettos, stuck in the North. On the other hand, one of the problems with dense poverty—with poverty that is both financial and mental—is that it's self-perpetuating. Poor people have babies; seems to be all they do. You're talking now about a self-perpetuating thing that's hard to stop. For a fifteen-year-old trying to raise a child and getting help from her mother, who is by now thirty-one, there's no hope. None. How do you stop that? We say, well, you've got to educate, give them sex education. No, it's not about sex education. You've got to teach them. You've got to say, you're fourteen; you keep your pants up, and you keep your dress down. No two ways about it. No liberalness here, because otherwise you're just going to continue to overcrowd.

I believe the movement of blacks from the North back to the South is a way of getting back to who we are and what we built. I don't think you can look at it differently; there is no other way to think of it. Why else go? We're still an agrarian society in the South. Of course, we've got cities like Atlanta sprouting up, New Orleans, Memphis, Nashville; they're coming along. But the cities aren't Mississippi and Alabama and Arkansas, the places where all the real comfort is. The place where you walk down the street and people say, "How are you?" and "How do you do?" and mean it. So I think the reason for the migration south would be to get back to that sort of humanness, the gentility that just imbues.

Many black people moving back to the South want to live with other black people, willingly. Strangely enough, people group themselves. It's like any other form of life. Oak trees need oak trees to cross-pollinate. Black people are always going to seek out black people because as long as we've been in this country, we've been the only comfort we have, the only surety. As time goes on, however, intermarriage becomes less of a bugaboo in the South. There are many interracial couples who move around the South just as freely as they do any place else, without any problems. People are going to group according to one criterion or another, be it race, class, income, what have you. That's always going to be.

It's a new day now for our people, and I think it's a great thing that people are moving back south. They're going to be happier. They're going to bring talent; they're going to bring something with them. And I'm for that. That was part of my reasoning in going home. I've received a lot. Now the question is, what am I going to do with it? If you've got all this money, where will you spend it? What will be your aim?

The answer, for me, begins with what I was most proud of growing up—my education. And I've learned the power of film to educate. With movies you can reach so many people. Without *Glory*, most Americans wouldn't have known about the first infantry of black soldiers that fought for the Union in the Civil War—the Fifty-fourth Regiment of the Massachusetts Volunteer Infantry. They wouldn't have known about the bravery of the Fifty-fourth in waging a hellish assault on Fort Wagner in South Carolina, when they were outnumbered and outgunned. I don't know and I can't tell you how many people have approached me and said, I'm so glad they made that movie; I had no idea.

Here's another piece of history that most people don't know about. In late 1944 in World War II, General Patton's spearhead in his Third Army was a tank outfit, the 761st Tank Battalion. It was all black, except for the commanding officer and maybe three other white officers. This all-black battalion spearheaded Patton's 1944 campaign across Europe. They battled the enemy for 183 consecutive days across six European countries, fought in four major Allied campaigns, and helped liberate prisoners from Nazi concentration camps.

Amid the segregation that still existed in the U.S. Army, Patton had asked for the best separate tank battalion still back at home. When the 761st arrived in Normandy on October 10, he said to them: "I would never have asked for you if you weren't good. I have nothing but the best in my army. I don't care what color you are so long as you go up there and kill the Kraut sonofabitches. Everyone has their eyes on you and is expecting great things from you. Most of all, your race is looking forward to you. Don't let them down and damn you, don't let me down." They kicked tall arse, and I'm going to make a film about them.

Very few people know about the 761st Tank Battalion or the two other black tank battalions of World War II, just as people had no concept of blacks fighting in the Civil War. The question arises, who do we blame for these omissions? One answer is, it was one of the most pernicious forms of racism, to deny black people their place in the textbooks. It's as if the message was, not only are you people not human beings, but you have no history and we're just going to wipe out all your contributions. Well, we are human beings. And we can talk and we can write. So another answer to the matter of omission is, why don't we talk and write and make films about our own history?

A country whose history is truncated—let's put it that way—is only half formed. You can't feel good about any group of people if you can isolate them by color, size, or some other characteristic—and in our case, it's color. You can't appreciate them if you have no idea of their contributions to your being, and to your well-being. Once we start redressing that, we change our entire national persona. That's what I'm trying to do, and what others are trying to do. What academicians do in the academy to inform, to motivate, we in the popular media have got to do in the popular media. Simply put, that's my aim in life.

MAYA ANGELOU

Choices

Poet, teacher, and civil rights activist Maya Angelou told me how pleased she is that African Americans are moving back to the South and reclaiming their home place. "Our people have been in exile in the North for three-quarters of a century. In exile, and in many cases, not realizing it but terribly uncomfortable . . . Wherever home is, the closer one gets to it, the more one relaxes. That's even if you're walking. If you've been on a trek, a few blocks or a few miles, you can almost spot your house. You start to breathe differently. I think this is true for all people."

With liberation comes choices. One of America's worst race riots occurred in Atlanta, in 1906, yet today it is home to many African Americans who choose to live there happily.

To understand the phenomenon, one could say if there is that much evil in the history, there is bound to be that much good.

The Civil War was fought all over the South, and alas it is still being fought in some people's hearts. But the fight for Atlanta was particularly fierce and particularly ongoing. I do not know the impact *Gone with the Wind* had on the resistance to change, but I suspect that many people whose ancestors were white sharecroppers fell in love with the romance in the novel and imagined that if we returned to slavery days, they could be served mint juleps by grinning butlers and hotcakes by loving nannies. The people, black and white, who fought to liberate Atlanta from her prison of ignorance were equal to the task. The organization the Southern Christian Leadership Conference, Martin Luther King, Maynard Jackson, Septima Clark, Andrew Young, Joe Lowery, C. T. Vivian, and others white and black won victory for Atlanta and for all people.

Martin Luther King told a story that after the Montgomery bus boycott ended and the companies capitulated, a black woman got onto the bus and walked all the way back and sat in the backseat. A young man who had been so adamant about voter registration, so adamant, and about the boycotting, went back and he said, "Ma'am, excuse me, we have walked eighteen miles so that you don't have to sit here." And she said, "Son, I walked with you, but now that I can sit anywhere, I'm sitting in the back. It's much more comfortable. I can relax, put my bags down, and stretch my legs out." Then she smiled.

With choices comes a different kind of criticism. There is surprise that in some affluent neighborhoods in Atlanta, black people have chosen to live with other affluent black people. But if your neighbor likes the same kind of music you like, and pretty much the same food and maybe goes to the same church, it's easier to go over and ask, excuse me, do you have some pinto beans, or have you got some Mahalia Jackson records, some Tabasco sauce? Most folks live in the same neighborhood with others like them and have very fine homes there where they choose to live. That should be unremarkable.

I can't imagine having a city place that wouldn't be Atlanta. After I moved from California, the first place I bought outside North Carolina was in Atlanta. I'm a country soul—not way rustic, but small town. I love my town, but 140,000 other people do so as well. But I need the city too; from time to time I need its vitality. There are city souls and country souls. I think a country soul could have been born in Times Square, but when he sees the country he says, this is where I'm supposed to live. And a city soul could have been born in the mountains of West Virginia, but when she sees the city she says, hm-mm, this is me. Wherever home is, the closer one gets to it, the more one relaxes. That's even if you're walking. If you've been on a trek, a few blocks or a few miles, you can almost spot your house. You start to breathe differently. I think this is true for all people.

The federal census for the year 2000 tells us that far more African Americans are now choosing to migrate south than the other way around. This reverse migration has its roots, I believe, in the first move north. Not the very first, because obviously slaves were escaping slavery going north. The move in the late nineteenth and twentieth centuries to the place Robert Hayden called the "mythic northern city" was caused by people who hoped they could find a better place. People thought if they could get away north, get away from the cotton, the worn-out South, get away from all the hatred, from the mean sharecropping days, they would find milk and honey in the streets of Chicago and New York and even St. Louis, and certainly Los Angeles. However, if the North did promise that, it never lived up to its promise, although many black people remained there.

So when the people sent their children back to the South, to the grand-mothers, to the grandfathers, to Sister and Bubba, they sent them to be looked after, I believe, because of the Northern disappointment. It was thanks to the Civil Rights Movement and the leveling of the playing field that we had the possibility of Maynard Jackson and Andrew Young as mayors of the great Southern city. Then the congressmen and -women began coming from the South to Washington, D.C., to plan a better world. I believe that those events freed people from the painful memories of Southern treatment. They began to look south again and see it as they want it to be.

Something basic and earth-shattering happened with the Civil Rights Movement. The fabric of old belief was shattered. The belief that in the South if you're black get back, if you're white you're all right. That was structurally shaken, so that black people in Detroit and Philadelphia and Tucson began to look back at the South. They began to remember not only the South's beauty, but that our people's bodies and sweat and tears and blood have enriched this soil, and thought, wait a minute, maybe I belong there too.

I am saying our people have been in exile in the North for three-quarters of a century. In exile, and in many cases, not realizing it but terribly un-comfortable. There's a wonderful cartoon by the great Ollie Harrington, who drew the character Bootsie for the *Chicago Defender*. In the 1950s, in a particularly relevant drawing, he showed Bootsie and his friend standing atop a mountain in Maine. They are outfitted in ski gear with the ski poles and this heavy, heavy, heavy clothing. Bootsie turns to his friend and asks, "Do you think Martin Luther King really wanted us to do this? Is this part of our liberation?"

Our people are coming home. The South is rich with memories of kindness and courage and cowardice and brutality. It is beautiful physically, and spiri-tually rich.

I live in the South because it's the best place to live. It's beautiful beyond the weight and even the ecstasy of my memories. If you come as far south as North Carolina, you see the lush, almost tropical growth and the fireflies and hear the birds in the morning and the cicadas in the evening.

Come south, walk along honeysuckled paths, and listen carefully to the sounds of good Southern music that will play so easily on your ears. You will be happy that you had the nerve and perspicacity to travel on a Southern train.

We can reclaim our home place.

We can stand for the good. That's why we risk our lives.

I see the work, the art and the music, and the lyrics of the poets, and the sculpture and the paintings, and I see that the culture is healthy. I do not believe that drugs and criminalities and venialities have total power over our youth. There is a core of health in our culture. Still we rise, out of the huts of history's shame, we rise. From a past rooted in pain, we rise. Bringing the gifts that our ancestors gave, we are the hope and the dream of the slave.

JAMES H. BOLDEN

Policing the South

Memphis Police Chief James Bolden likes to say that these days, instead of running away from the police, the community runs to them, and actually embraces law enforcement. "They take ownership. They say, these are our police officers. Hardly a crime occurs in the city of Memphis for which we don't get a call from a citizen wanting to help out."

I'm fifty-four years old. Now as most everyone in my generation knows, when I was growing up, black people did not look at the police force as a friendly presence in our neighborhoods. Friends have asked me what in the world possessed me to try to join the Memphis Police Department. Well, I was on my way home one night and I was a young man, maybe twelve, fourteen years old, and I had an encounter with two police officers from the Memphis Police Department, and it wasn't a very pleasant encounter. We had always been taught that if we were walking the streets and if we saw the police before they saw us, then we should run, because there was a basic distrust of police officers at that time. As I said, the encounter wasn't a real pleasant one. I was verbally abused by the officers. And instead of that driving me away from the police department, it made me want to become a part of it.

After talking with my parents concerning what had happened, they said a lot of times what you have to do to change things is to become a part of it and work from within. And from that day on I had decided that I wanted to be a police officer and wanted to join the Memphis Police Department. I knew some good police officers who patrolled my neighborhood; the police weren't all bad. But that encounter certainly affected the way I felt about police work.

Where I grew up, in Somerville, Tennessee, we did not have a lot of contact with white people. Some whites would come into our communities to sell products or insurance, but blacks lived from day to day in a self-contained world. We didn't go to school with whites. The integration of Memphis schools didn't begin until 1961, and it took years for the schools to really integrate.

The interaction that we did have with whites was fights. I never personally experienced any problems with fights in Memphis. But in Somerville, I did experience some problems. That was a place where you sometimes had to get off the sidewalk in order to allow a white person to pass. We were told we had to do that. Relationships with whites were based upon certain things we had been told. They were prohibited and forbidden.

Being a child, I did not understand the full ramifications of what was happening, but I knew there was something not right about the equation. We accepted it as a way of life; this was the way it was in the South, and so consequently we did it. But we knew that something wasn't right about it. We always wondered not only about getting off the sidewalk, but why there were certain places we couldn't go or why we could not drink out of a certain water fountain. We always realized there was a difference in the way whites and blacks were treated, and we felt bad about it. I think my parents even felt bad. One day I saw my daddy as he wept because of something that had happened in our community in Somerville. So I'm sure it bothered him.

I joined the Memphis Police Department as a patrol officer in September of 1968, six months after Dr. Martin Luther King was killed. I was twenty years old. At that time, there weren't many black people in the Memphis Police Department. I think the number was probably somewhere around fifty. The force was male and white-dominated. When I came on the job, we didn't have many aspirations of ever achieving any type of rank, because black commanding officers were practically nonexistent. There were very few black role models holding positions of rank in the Memphis Police Department. Blacks had certain areas of the city we could patrol and others we couldn't, even as a police officer. The areas we were assigned to generally were occupied by the black community, and we didn't police outside that community.

As a matter of fact, just prior to me joining the force, they had gotten away from having separate role calls. One role call was inside the building, and other officers who were black would assemble outside the building. That was something else. Even down to the kind of shirt we wore. It used to be that the white officers would wear white shirts and black officers would wear blue shirts. But that changed right around the mid-1960s here in Memphis.

If you look at the police force today, you see a lot more African Americans than when I joined. In the 1960s, the number of blacks in the force not only didn't represent the size of the black community in Memphis; it didn't represent the number of blacks or other minorities who might like to join the force. So to begin with, in 1973, we founded the Afro-American Police Association, which probably brought about some of the greatest changes that we've seen in the Memphis Police Department. Coupled with a federal consent decree that was handed down, it caused hiring practices within the Memphis Police Department to change dramatically. It simply stated that future hires had to represent that base of the population. Here in Memphis right now, we have a population of approximately 53 percent minority, and so, naturally, our hiring is commensurate with that.

As a result of the increase in the hiring of minorities, more opportunities began to open up. Never would I have dreamed in all my years that I could become chief of police in Memphis, after all we had gone through. But it tells you that there have been so many dramatic changes in the Southern region of the country. If you look at the South today, you see that things are quite different. We think that even though we had a lot of problems here in the South, we have made tremendous progress. We have mayors and we have police chiefs, we have county executives, we have chief administrative officers throughout government in Southern cities, and I think that's a tribute to the price we had to pay for voting rights and other changes in the South.

In 1968 such opportunities were simply nonexistent for blacks. We had only achieved our voting rights three years prior, with the Voting Rights Act of 1965. So to think that you could be a police chief or you could be the superintendent of the school system or mayor of this great city was virtually unheard-of. But here we are today.

When I was starting to make all these changes on the force, the white officers were openly defiant. Speaking for myself, I can say that leading an organization that was trying to bring about some change within the police department, I was not met with open arms. There were white officers who refused to ride in a squad car with me. There were black officers who would turn their backs on me, who wouldn't speak to me because they were afraid I would bring trouble to them. So it was a very, very lonely time for me, personally, in dealing with the situation within the Memphis Police Department. My family suffered as a result of it, and there were just some very unhappy times, very lonely times for me.

And extremely dangerous times. Numerous threats were made on my life, on the lives of my family, but it was almost as if I had taken that step and I couldn't retreat. There were times when I felt discouraged and wanted to go back. But Father James P. Lyke stood by my side. I have his picture on the bookshelf in my office. He was with me, and there were other white people who worked behind the scenes and were really sympathetic to the cause we were working for, and realized that it was a just cause. They were very helpful.

One time I had to meet with some top police officials. I got a call early one morning at home when I was in bed. It was the director of the police department saying he needed to speak with me. When I got to headquarters—and mind you, I was a patrol officer with five years on the job—I stepped in the room and they had fourteen commanding, high-ranking police officials lined up around a table, and then there was just me.

They said, well, we hear you say there's trouble in the police department and that there's discrimination. It was a bit intimidating for me, but I responded by saying, well, yes, sir, there is discrimination within the police department, and it's obvious when I look at you seated around a table here. I see no one that looks like me. And I said, I look at commanding positions around the police department and there is one black officer. They had him sitting there in a corner, and they looked to him and they said, now you tell them whether you've ever seen discrimination in the Memphis Police Department. And the officer, he said, well, no, sir, I haven't. But I realized that we had a problem; the officer was obviously intimidated by that, and I certainly understood. I could understand his position, but certainly I had to be true to my faith that discrimination did exist and that it had to change within the police department.

The priest, by now Archbishop Lyke, was always there with me. He would sit in a corner of the room while I would conduct an interview. When I would talk with police officials, he would be with me. He would pick me up in the morning, and he would ride with me during my daily chores or duties with the Police Association. We developed a friendship. At first the priest was a spiritual adviser to me, but then as we grew to know each other, he became a personal friend. He was my closest confidant. He never tried to change me. He was a source of strength for me. He gave me a great deal of encouragement. If I needed advice, he would advise me. I felt that having a priest at my side then somehow would make me a better person, because I'm not perfect by any means. I've had my transgressions; I've made mistakes. But I also feel that deep down inside I've always tried to do that which is just and that which is right.

I must have been the only policeman in America who had a priest traveling with him. As ironic as it was, the priest sought me out. I never knew him prior to entering this adviser-friend relationship, and come to find out that this very priest had been close to Dr. King. He had come into my life at that time. The fact that he was a veteran of the Civil Rights Movement only gave me more encouragement that this was somebody I certainly should pay attention to.

The fear that maybe an "accident" might befall me from some of my white colleagues was with me every day. I would go to work and sometimes I couldn't imagine getting home at night, I was so terrified. I was always aware of what it might mean when the phone rang or what could happen while I was driving down the street. And these fears were not unrealistic. I was working in an environment where I wasn't held in high esteem not only by the white officers but by black officers. My black officers were afraid to come near me. So I was like a man without a country. I was ostracized. I was told by officers who were around me that simply because of what I represented, I could not be trusted. I was one of the only officers in the city of Memphis who had to ride by himself, because no one would ride with me. Black or white. It was very disheartening. My response was often to be fearful, because who wouldn't be when you had to face something like that and everyone working around you was wearing guns?

My wife and my children, naturally, were always concerned about my safety. But we'd go about our daily living, and you have to stand up for something. Sometimes you can be so gripped with fear until all the fear is scared out of you. I've been that way. I've been down that trail, where I have been fearful of things, but I just figure you've got to try to do the right thing. You've got to try to see that justice prevails, and sometimes that means putting fear behind you. I think that most courageous acts really come about as a result of paralyzing fear.

It was probably the teachings of Dr. Martin Luther King that made me decide to fight back and change the system. I always admired Dr. King because he talked about what was just and right, and I felt so strongly about justice. I named my son Justice. Dr. King was always talking about doing the right thing and treating people in the way they should be treated, judging a person not by the color of their skin but by the content of their character. That really made an impression on me, and I've always said that if I ever had an opportunity to make an impact on this earth, then I would want to do something along the lines that Dr. King had done.

I had the distinction of participating in the last march that Dr. King led in Memphis. The city sanitation workers were striking for better working conditions. There were thousands of us marching on March 28, 1968. We were proceeding from the Clayborne Ball Temple to City Hall and had turned right at Main and Beale, where the Orpheum Theater is, when the violence broke out. And I think Dr. King, being an advocate of nonviolence, was disturbed about that.

One of Dr. King's staff members had tried to discourage him from returning to Memphis to plan another march, but Dr. King was determined. He wanted to have a peaceful march. On April 4, he was in his room at the Lorraine Motel discussing plans for another march with the Reverend Jesse Jackson and the Reverend Ralph Abernathy, and then he walked out onto the balcony of the motel.

At that time, I was a salesperson with a supply firm here in the city of Memphis. I left work that afternoon sometime around six o'clock. Dr. King was shot at one minute past six. I recall it was a cloudy day. It seems as though it's always raining when bad things happen. We got the word that Dr. King had been shot and that they had rushed him to St. Joseph's Hospital.

Everything just went up in flames throughout the downtown area. Shock gripped the community. Some whites in our community rejoiced over the fact that Dr. King had been assassinated and said that he deserved what happened, simply because he came into the community starting trouble. But the vast majority of the citizens of Memphis were appalled.

Dr. King's death hurt us and it hurt the nation. It hurt the world to lose someone like Dr. King. When we lost Dr. King, we lost a great leader. Our hearts go out to the King family. But I can surely say that Dr. King's death brought about many, many positive changes, not only in the city of Memphis but throughout the world. It created a sort of kinship among the people of Memphis that has improved race relations and brought people together. Much of the progress we have today came about as a direct result of the assassination of Dr. Martin Luther King here in Memphis.

The fact that Dr. King's life ended here makes Memphis—makes what happened to race relations in Memphis—even more important. I look at how Dr. King lost his life, and I guess it's only a bit of an irony that he died coming to fight for the rights of a garbageman, a garbage collector. But he did. And I think therein lies the significance of the struggle for justice and freedom. Certainly Memphians are mindful of that.

Cynics today would say, well, not much has changed in the South; you've got a few black people in positions of power, but things aren't fundamentally different. That is definitely a misconception. Things have changed dramatically in the South. I've had the distinction of living through the times when we could not drink at a water fountain, when we could not go to the library on a certain day, when we could not go to a movie, and when we couldn't eat at a restaurant. So for anyone to say that the South has not changed, then they're fooling themselves. If you go from Memphis to Birmingham to Montgomery to Atlanta, you see cities where minorities are on the move, where minorities are in leadership positions, and to say that things haven't changed, certainly you would have to be living with blinders on.

The Memphis police force today is highly diverse. We probably have about fifty-fifty whites and blacks. I'm the chief of police. Two deputy chiefs who work under my command are African American. Precincts throughout the city are equally divided between black and white. When I came on the job, there were no women in police work. Now we have women in leadership positions in the police department. You cannot find an area within the Memphis Police Department where minorities or blacks are not represented.

We've come a ways in recent history, because historically in the South, the law was used to enforce discrimination against blacks. The sheriffs and the police were the ones who enforced the Jim Crow laws. These laws were made unconstitutional under the Fourteenth Amendment way back in the 1860s, but they were still being enforced in the South past the middle of the twentieth century. The sheriff or the police could go in and they could arrest, they could take away rights, and it was sanctioned. This is just the way it was. It was the system's way of oppressing, and that's the reason why police officers were to be feared. You never knew what would happen if you encountered a police officer at night while you were driving down a lonely road. It always struck fear in you if you were pulled over, simply because the police were the arm of government but you couldn't trust them. They were the foot soldiers of racism.

I remember very well when we started the Afro-American Police Association in 1973. The first words that came out of the then director's mouth were that anyone who tries to start any type of association here is liable to be looking for another job. That was intimidation in itself. Everyone who had attempted to form something like an association of black officers prior to that time had always been fired or lost their job some way or other.

Around 1973, we filed an action with the courts concerning discrimination. Around 1978, finally the federal government agreed that there had been discrimination in the Memphis Police Department and a consent decree was entered by the city. It took them five years to admit what I could observe in five seconds. It was very frustrating because we knew that discrimination existed, but still there had to be an acknowledgment from the system saying, yes, this is happening. Once that happened, we felt that we were beginning to turn the corner.

Why we won, or what made us different—what made us succeed when so many others had failed—I would like to think had a lot to do with the ability to stay clean, to stay fair, and the help of prayers, the assistance of the priest. Somebody somewhere had to be watching over me. I know that, because there was no way that I could have done what I did without prayers, without help from something that's out of this world. Many who had traveled that road before didn't make it.

But it wasn't over with the consent decree. The government was watching and saying, you've got to do it this way, and still there was resistance. We were fighting. And the fight is not over. It's not over even now, and not even with me sitting where I am. You can't say the fight is ever over. But I've always felt that justice will prevail, whether I'm here or not. There will be someone else to pick up where we've left off and carry on.

Obviously, racism doesn't exist today in the same way that it did in 1968, but it does persist. If you look at, say, city government, it can take the form of discriminatory awarding of contracts or hiring for services. A lot of times it may be on an individual level, say in pockets within the police department. Certainly if I have an officer out on the streets now who does racist things, who may be guilty of profiling, it doesn't reflect my philosophy; it doesn't reflect the philosophy of the Memphis Police Department. We can't deny that racism exists in some of our members. But I think for the most part they do a pretty good job now of controlling themselves. We have to leave personal biases at home. You can't bring them to work. We go on record as saying that if we find we have people in our ranks who are abusing people simply because of the color of their skin or their religious beliefs or things like that, then certainly we're going to do something about it.

When school busing was introduced, the whites began to move out of the city schools and into the suburban areas. But our neighborhoods, for the most part, are integrated, and we have record numbers of whites moving back to the downtown area, which has been revitalized. Whites are beginning to move back to the inner city and downtown in many American urban regions, and Memphis is no different; in fact, downtown Memphis is predominantly white now. Some areas in the city as a whole are predominantly black or predominantly white, but I don't think you face what you encountered in the 1960s, when you could not move into certain areas regardless of your economic status. Now we have blacks and whites and Hispanics and others living together here.

Back in the 1960s, interracial dating was the last taboo of segregation. But if you come to Memphis now, you'll see interracial couples, not only dating but married. You'll see interracial families. An interracial couple walking down the street would not get the stares they would have gotten back in the 1960s. There's hardly a neighborhood in the city of Memphis right now where you won't see interracial couples.

I don't subscribe to the philosophy that the black community was better off when all the black people lived together, with their own doctors and lawyers and maids and janitors. I lived through that era and personally, I don't like to think there are places in my city or my country where I can't go simply because of the color of my skin. Thirty years ago, there were places in the city of Memphis where you could not go. Now we're free to move about. Some of the conditions that exist in the city right now leave a little bit to be desired, simply because there's a violent element in our society, a lot of blacks killing blacks. We didn't see as much of that thirty or thirty-five years ago as we see right now. But I certainly wouldn't want to turn back the hands of the clock and return to the days of Jim Crow.

The response to diversity in the police department has been very good. There was a time when the citizens of Memphis viewed the police as an occupying force. But now we have citizens who actually call in demanding, and I mean literally demanding, that they have police in their communities in the form of what we call our community action centers in the many precincts that are spread throughout the community. We can't keep up with the demand for police now. That is a big change. When I was growing up, the police were a nightmare. They were the enemy. They were people you were vulnerable around.

I like to say that now, instead of running away from the police, the community runs to them and actually embraces the police. They take ownership. They say, these are our police officers. Hardly a crime occurs in the city of Memphis for which we don't get a call from a citizen wanting to help out. We have precincts where citizens meet on a regular basis, hold community meetings. They come in and they actually prepare meals for our police officers. So it's quite different now.

The city of Memphis itself has a population of around 650,000. In the metropolitan area, the population is closer to a million. In the Memphis Police

Department, we have about two thousand commissioned police officers who actually carry the badge, and then we have another thousand civilians, for a total force of around three thousand. About half of them are minority people.

We have integrated the police force by neighborhood. We don't have all black officers in a black neighborhood, for instance. That practice changed some time ago. Police officers now are assigned to neighborhoods regardless of the color or makeup of the neighborhood. So black officers work in predominantly white neighborhoods and vice versa. Color has no effect on the assignment.

We do sensitivity training in the police force, not just for white officers but for all officers, because it's not just a white problem. There are many officers of color who need sensitivity training to a certain extent. It's a two-way street. Yes, you are asking whites to understand blacks. But blacks must learn to identify with different cultures within our society and to be sensitive to people who may differ from us as well.

Black officers also need to be sensitive to black people. In the wake of the many changes that have occurred in this city, a black officer may be a little harder on a black person than a white officer might be. So we don't miss an opportunity to expose all of our officers to sensitivity training.

Our downtown precinct covers the entire downtown entertainment district. It's really almost like a mini–police department because we've got a precinct commander and a number of commanding officers. It's a fully pledged place. Some of our officers downtown ride horses, some ride motorcycles, some do bike patrol, which lets them interact with the citizens or tourists. So we have a lot of community policing going on. It's like a community precinct.

Over the next five to ten years, I think, Memphis will become even more of a major player in the world. We've seen a proliferation of growth here. Businesses are relocating here; professional sports franchises are moving to town. Memphis is centrally located. This is Middle America. You can get to any point in America very quickly from Memphis and the mid-South area. So I think Memphis is poised for substantial growth. We have a good climate and great restaurants. You've got the Isaac Hayes and the B.B. King Blues Club and Rendezvous, Cozy Corner, and all kinds of clubs and restaurants featuring food from all over the world. And we have Beale Street.

Up till the 1960s, blacks were confined mainly to the Beale Street neighborhood. All the black businesses—the black lawyers, doctors, and other professionals—used to live and work and play on Beale Street. The blues and soul music America is famous for started here in Memphis, mainly on Beale Street.

In 1899, at a time when blacks in Memphis had no parks or cultural centers, Robert Reed Church, Sr., the South's first black millionaire, opened up a park with an auditorium for blacks on a six-acre site here. The auditorium was later torn down, but Robert Church Park is now part of the Beale Street Historic District. Booker T. Washington spoke there, and President Teddy Roosevelt, and the Fisk Jubilee Singers and W.C. Handy and others performed there.

Beale Street is now world-famous. But when it was predominantly black, Beale Street was to Memphis as Harlem is to New York. I think Rufus Thomas once said that if you were a white man and you came to Beale Street on a Saturday night, you would never want to be white again. I guess that was his way of saying that Beale Street was a mecca for blacks. Now it's an entertainment and music and cultural mecca for the world. The city of Memphis renamed a strip along Beale Street after Rufus Thomas, who was almost synonymous with Memphis culture and music.

I like to think that what we've done is capitalized on some of our more famous citizens. Rock and roll was born here in Memphis. This is the birthplace and home of Elvis Presley, who based his own style to a great extent on the black musicians he listened to as a young boy. We've got the new Rock 'n' Soul Museum opening up in the Beale Street entertainment district. Sam Phillips' Sun Studio, where Elvis cut his first records and Johnny Cash, Roy Orbison, and so many others recorded, is right here. The home of W.C. Handy, father of the blues, is on Beale Street. B.B. King was right here, and Stax Records.

We now have the National Civil Rights Museum in Memphis as well. In 1982, the Lorraine Motel was foreclosed. People didn't want to do business there in the years following the assassination of Dr. King. The Martin Luther King, Jr., Memorial Foundation wanted to preserve the motel and eventually bought the property. Now the museum sits on four acres of land, right where the Lorraine Motel once stood. The National Civil Rights Museum is probably one of the best contributions ever made to our community and the world. It not only keeps alive what it used to be like here in Memphis, but also what's being done here and all over the world for civil and human rights. Schoolchildren visit it regularly. It says to people who come here, the terrible treatment of blacks is something that happened in America, something we wouldn't want to see happen again. We don't want to go back there. And we are grateful that people are more sensitive now than they've been, probably, at any time during our history.

Memphis has lived through catastrophes and survived to be better. We've survived the worst scourge of racism and become a better people. In the nineteenth century, Memphis survived another kind of plague. In 1872 and 1878, when the yellow fever epidemic hit the city, more than 5,000 people died, and more than 25,000 ran from the city trying to save their lives. Lots more were in camps used as shelters. Most of the city leaders succumbed to the fever. For a while, blacks got hired as police officers simply because no one else was able to police the city. And I think we had blacks in City Hall. But as soon as the epidemic ended, they all lost their jobs. So the history of the black police officer actually began in the 1800s rather than in the middle of the twentieth century.

Memphis lost its charter as a result of the yellow fever epidemic. People were panicked; lots of people were ready to throw in the towel and let the city die. The city came back. But it came back with its racism fully alive, and it took another century to make real progress on that front. There's no doubt we have a long way to go in America and in Memphis, Tennessee, as far as race relations are concerned. But we've come a long way. I see great progress. I see tremendous growth among the citizens of this great city, and I'm proud to be a Memphian.

SERGEANT MAJOR KENNETH WILCOX

Training Days

"I try to teach people, don't let other folks characterize you," Sergeant Major Kenneth Wilcox told me at Fort Benning. "You have to characterize who you are as a person. Remember, we've been challenged not only to train these guys; we've been challenged to take all the abnormal behavior that society has taught them and turn them around. And psychologically, we do wonders in fourteen weeks."

My men call me Sergeant Major. I've been in the army for twenty-four years. You hear that there's no more racism in the army, that it's a model for society. Racism itself is not visibly seen, but when you look at who has the opportunity to get to the highest level of command, it seems as if we've missed the boat on that one. General Powell and other black generals have served as examples of how far we can go, but his kind are few in number.

I come from South Georgia, from an environment where racism was an everyday way of life. The military has allowed me to grow a lot in comparison to my brothers who are down South. So I'm grateful for the military. It's a great place to grow, but you still have people in the military who display racist attitudes, who haven't made the mental change. They can't display their racism openly, but the attitude is still present. The new form of racism is subversive, like the young man with a Confederate flag flying high on his car. He has no idea how offensive that is to me, or maybe he does and really does not care how it makes me feel. This is the subversive behavior I am talking about. It's underneath the surface; you can't see it, but you sense it. Our task is to root it out and expose how ugly it really is.

I can tell a racist soldier when I meet him. His attitude and demeanor give him away. He can't openly state his racist attitudes, but you can tell. What I try to do is make sure he hears my perspective. You never know what's going to change a person's attitude, so what I try to do is interject myself into his life.

Whether he wants me to or not doesn't matter. I must seize every opportunity to turn a negative behavior into something positive. As a sergeant major, I have the authority and right to do that. We're talking about an attitude that has been part of someone's life for a long time. Sometimes these men have grown up from kids believing in this attitude about different races, so you can't change that in one day. I look at this job as a blessing because it allows me to reach out to the world and interject something positive. I tell the soldiers, I care about you as a person, regardless of your attitude toward me; I'm a professional and I care about you. I tell that to every soldier.

If I see a Confederate flag on a cadet's car, I'm personally offended by that. It doesn't represent me as a black American. Many would say that it symbolizes a love for the South, but it represents oppression for me. So I'll say to this guy, you've got a right to display that Confederate flag on your car, but I find it very offensive. It's your right to display it on your car, but if you need a favor from me, you understand I'm offended and therefore I have the right to not give a favor to a person that offends me. I'll do what I can do for you professionally, but once in a while people need a favor, and I won't give you one.

I will just talk to him personally and give him my perspective on things. And whether he changes or not is basically irrelevant. My responsibility as the offended black American is to tell people when I'm offended. It then becomes that person's responsibility to either change or continue the same way. The choice is theirs. I've given them a choice to change or not. Then I leave the situation as is. I can't make someone take a flag off his car. I can't twist his arm. But if he respects me and I respect him, he should be willing to remove the flag.

If a soldier makes it known that he just can't stand black people, and that his dislike or hatred of blacks is a hindrance to his becoming a soldier, we won't kick him out for that. We will counsel him and we'll try to help him change his attitudes. We have guys come in here with different tattoos that show they came from a gang environment or from an extremist group. Or you get a black guy and a white guy who are always fighting, and you interview the white guy one-on-one, and the bottom line is there's a hatred towards the person's color; it's not because of anything in particular the black guy has done. Or a white guy might say something to the black soldier like, you're just lazy, and the black soldier will get irritated by that.

It's a stereotypical thing that white guys look at black Americans as being lazy, as not wanting to work. And so I bring those guys to my office and I'll spend sometimes an hour with each of them. Often my drill sergeant becomes upset because of me spending so much time with each soldier. But I use that time to break through the hardened outer shell of the person. When I break through to the core and that person breaks down in tears, he knows and I know that I've gotten to him. I feel like I have been successful. Whether he goes back and builds his character up is irrelevant to me. I've done what I've been chosen to do, whether by the army or by society as an American, and also as a person who has the opportunity to change some of these abnormal behaviors and attitudes in the army.

Some of the soldiers leave here with what we call an EPTS—Existed Prior to Service—meaning they had a medical problem prior to enlisting in the army and this problem will not allow them to adapt to a military lifestyle. That's the easy way to get them out of here. A guy can go out and he can come back in six months later. When we attempt to discharge a soldier for being a racist, it can take a long time. But when that person does not want to continue his service and wants to go home, we just get them out of the way with an EPTS, and those guys usually don't come back. Occasionally we have one or two guys who come back, but hardly ever do you see those guys back in the service again.

A person who belongs to an extremist group, or wants to join one, comes into the military for one purpose only: to get the training. When they're face-to-face with the training, and discover that it's more difficult than they expected it to be, they soon start seeking ways to get out. But they come here to get the training. We've been told—I haven't had any firsthand experience of this—that they go out and utilize the military tactics they learned here.

Knowing that the training I've given might be used to fight against me just because I am black, how do I detach myself from resenting those I have been chosen to train? I tell myself, your job is to train all who come to you, and in terms of political extremists, we are talking about a very small number. And second, your job is to be a citizen of the United States and carry out your obligations as a citizen. This means rooting out that person from the military before he can achieve his goal. But my first job is doing my mission, which is to train those guys whether I like them or not. It is basically irrelevant whether I like them. My job is to train them.

I don't encourage my trainer to treat the extremists any differently from any other soldier. We do not make them do more push-ups or run more laps. As a matter of fact, these are the guys we don't focus our attention on. Knowing that they are looking for any excuse to hate and blame others for their own attitudes, we do just the opposite. We treat everybody the same way. At least I try to teach my drill sergeants to exhibit this attitude. And I learned as a drill sergeant that this method works.

When I was a drill sergeant, I had some guys come in who were either Muslims or white extremists. They put them in my platoon, and those guys learned to perform to the same standard. I didn't change my way of dealing with them. Whether it be a white guy like them or a black guy, they got dealt with the same way. You can't deal differently with them or you become just as bad as they are.

We call Eagle Tower our confidence builder. The first week of training, we bring the young men to the tower and we make them display their skills at handling themselves at a great height. By requiring them to rappel and negotiate the apparatus on the tower, we help them to overcome their fears and mistrust. They are going to climb up and rappel down. And then they've got to go climb up on the back side of the tower and walk across a rope bridge, swing across an open hole in the tower, and then climb down the cargo net on the other side. This will help them overcome their fears of height and fears of where they are falling. Then they come back and they climb up an apparatus and slide down the harness to the other side. You have soldiers who will get stuck on part or all of the apparatus. The first time they get up there, you have soldiers who will shake in their boots, crying and doing all kind of things. So you've got to do some discipline stuff with them, like making them do some push-ups to get their mind off their fears. You don't have to look pretty as you negotiate the apparatus, but you must negotiate it. The bottom line is that everybody will come off the tower whether they want to or not.

You'll see some guys, you think they may be having a heart attack. They cry, they slobber, they kick. You'd be surprised at the kinds of facial expressions you get up on top of that tower. Up there these soldiers are not concerned what color the sergeants are. They focus on how the sergeants can help them not to die. There is no color; there is only "please help me." The hardest thing to do is to get a person to trust in you and your ability. Everybody learns to trust their drill sergeant eventually, and the soldiers learn to trust one another. The idea is, hey, guy, you're here to train. We know that at times you're going to face some things you're probably not confident in doing, but trust me, I'll get you through it. That's why we do the confidence builder in the first week of the cycle, and then they come back to do it about two other times. By that time, a soldier has been through a lot of training. He's learned how to trust the drill sergeant and it's not a big issue anymore. Same thing about jumping out of an airplane. You've got that fear and the sergeant says, trust me, go out there, the chute's going to open up. You don't trust anybody till that chute actually opens up, but now I trust you. I had no faith in you at all till the chute opened up.

I've never experienced racism in the army face-to-face. I've suspected it and I've confronted it. And when I confronted it, the person did the right thing. I can't say I've been treated unfairly as a soldier at any time in the military. It's one thing to say that a person's racist, but it's another thing to prove it. All I say is that when a racist is revealed, at any level of the military, he or she must do the professional thing, and each time, that person has. I've never been held back; I've always been able to make my rank. People have always treated me favorably because of my self-discipline.

The military is the place where I feel most secure and where, as a black American, I can achieve the goals I want to achieve based on my character and my ability. I've got a bachelor's degree and I'm going for my master's degree now. I would not have had either of these aside from being in this uniform, so I am grateful, and it's an honor to serve.

Take Fort Benning, for instance. When I go to staff meetings at post level, I don't see a whole load of my folks sitting at the tables as heads of departments. This was first brought to my attention by a civilian. He spoke of other black soldiers who had retired and applied for civilian jobs to no avail. This particular civilian had obtained degrees and came highly qualified for the position he applied for, but didn't get it. The person who was hired was not highly qualified, nor did he have a degree. But he was white. So the norm in the army has changed, but in the civilian sector, at least at Fort Benning, there's still work to do.

The army has made it difficult for a person not to treat you equal, because I've got the ability, and I've got the authority, to challenge you or your decision on me based on the regulations. And you must adhere to the regulations whether you want to or not, or else you get egg on your face. Let's say somebody is very irritated and wants to call the guy who's irritating him a name, under his breath even. He goes "you nigger," and I hear it. That soldier will be told to go to my office, and he is looked at very straightforwardly as being a racist. I would probably deal with him personally as a sergeant major, and he'll definitely get punished. He'll lose money in his paycheck at a minimum, and at a maximum he could be discharged just off that one statement. The drill sergeant will probably do a little more than I do. But it's a serious allegation, and you can't not deal with it. If you don't deal with it, it becomes okay to do. Whether it be between two black soldiers using the "n" word in their slang, it doesn't matter. It's wrong. No matter who uses that word, it's still degrading language, and I say to anybody, no matter who uses it or where, don't use it at all.

Today you frequently hear people referring to each other with the derogatory slang "my dog." I don't let people call me their dog. I'm not your dog. I tell people, you don't determine my character; I tell you what my character is. You don't put me on a piece of paper and say this is your character, Wilcox. No. I will tell you. As a matter of fact, anytime I find you're mischaracterizing me, I will correct you, because that's not who I am. I've been in front of senior officers and said, I am not a liar; you're saying that I'm a liar. Now you do what you want to do with it, but I'm not a liar. I must make that statement before you now, because if I let you continue that way, you are characterizing me as a liar and everybody will see me as a liar. I don't want you to do that. So I try to teach people, don't let other folks characterize you. You have to characterize who you are as a person. Remember, we've been challenged not only to train these guys; we've been challenged to take all the abnormal behavior that society has taught them and turn them around. And psychologically, we do wonders in fourteen weeks.

We talk about men who have died on the battlefield to give us our freedom and how all that blood is red. There are no colors, there are no boundaries; all men on the battlefield are brothers. That man, no matter where he came from, I tell the guys, is your brother.

And if any of these guys think I'm a racist, if they think I'm a black man who hates white people—since most of these guys are white—there is a procedure they can call me on. All they've got to do is make a complaint. That complaint goes straight to EO, the Equal Opportunity officer, at the post, and somebody must act upon it. That person will come down and conduct interviews. He'll do a racial profile of the battalion. And then he'll let the commander know whether or not there's validity to the allegations. Whenever a complaint goes up, everybody's ears come up; everybody's antennae go up. It's not something that's taken lightly.

I was up to get another higher position, a brigade position. Lately, the brigade position has been given to other higher, enlisted soldiers, and all of them have been white except for one. And my subconscious says it's a racial issue. But on a professional level, I'm saying it can't be, because we live in a society in the army where you can't do that. There have got to be other issues involved, and I wouldn't allow myself to think that it was a racial thing. I still believe that to be the case.

Every soldier has the ability to get the attention if they want. Every person in a leadership position in the army, every person in a junior leadership position and a senior leadership position, knows that when somebody makes a racial complaint, everybody has to act. If you don't respond to the allegation, you find out later on that you should have acted. Sometimes a guy says it's a race issue when it's not. And when a complaint is made that shouldn't have been, everybody gets in an uproar. But every one of those guys can make a statement and say, hey, this guy is racist and getting on me and I can prove it and everybody heard him say racial swear words at me. Everybody's going to start acting on the allegation, and that guy who was accused is probably going to get moved. We have several senior guys on this post alone that have been moved because of racial issues. They don't stay long. There'll be some repercussions if you're found to be the one that perpetrated that kind of stuff.

Take the issue of homosexuality. It's not an issue until it is brought to you face-to-face. I cannot act prejudiced toward a person just because I think he's homosexual or I think he's this or that. Everything's got to be factual, and that forces you to act professionally toward that person regardless. The army as a whole has made that transition over the years.

The army has come a long way from the days when it was a racist organization. Education has a lot to do with it. I came in right at the end of the Vietnam era. You had no reason for not being educated. Today the black person, the white person, or the Hispanic person in the army has no excuse for not being educated, because the army has laid out the carpet. When I went to school, they paid 75 percent of my tuition and I paid 25 percent. But now they're paying 100 percent. Education has given people the ability and skills to move to a higher position in the army. In an infantry battalion, for instance, we may get three or four blacks out of about sixty people in the platoon. But when I came in, it was just the opposite: the majority of them were black. Maybe I'm wrong, but I think most of the black people are going to technical schools. They want technical skills, and they want to go where the money is and where people move up. So they're getting away from the infantry, and I predict that in about twenty years, the infantry is going to be mostly white at the high echelons. Artillery is probably heading the same way. Artillery has a lot of whites and maybe some Hispanics but not many blacks, because all your blacks are gravitating toward learning computer skills. Remember, the stigma is that a black man can't learn; a black man is not intelligent.

The youth coming into the military today like discipline. Most of the black kids, especially male, don't have a father in the house. They don't have the strict discipline of someone saying, you've got to do it because this is what you've been chosen to do and it's what I told you to do. And this is where they can get it. They can get a good fit on society and life right here. They're going to learn what it means to be part of a team; they're going to learn what it means to accomplish something that's more difficult than you can ever imagine you could accomplish. They will get to understand that the world is bigger than all the neighborhoods or towns they came out of. And they're going to feel like I feel, the sense of, hey, I can do whatever I want to do in the world. I came from tobacco fields and cotton fields. I used to look up in the air and see the airplanes go by and say to myself, you're going nowhere.

I know racism when I see it, and I feel racism when I go home now to South Georgia. When I go home, people can't comprehend that I'm a command sergeant major and I've got fourteen hundred men at my beck and command who do what I tell them to do. They still want to treat me like I'm from South Georgia. And I want to say, guy, you're not a sergeant major, and right now I've got more people in my control than you ever thought of. But I don't go there because that becomes boastful, and that's not me. The environment down there is still the same, and they see me the same way they saw me when I left there.

Race relations back in South Georgia need help. I can tell you, they are backwards. Everybody still lives in a box. I try to tell my siblings, you've got to get out of this box. You've got to experience the world, because the world is a bigger place than where you're at now. And you don't have to settle for minimum wage; you don't have to settle for bad compensation on your job. There are other places you can go. Don't think you've got to stay here. The army is a good place to be. Come and see me, and I'll take care of you.

WILLIE W. HERENTON

Keys to the City

Dr. Willie Herenton was elected mayor of Memphis in 1991. What he's most proud of, he told me, "is that this city, which is led by African Americans, is financially sound. The state of Tennessee is having tough economic difficulties, Shelby County is having tough economic difficulties, but this great American Southern city, we're strong financially. And the paradox of this is, in the old days there was this thought that blacks could never manage a multimillion-dollar governmental institution."

I was born in Memphis in 1940. I'm sixty-two years old, and I've been mayor of Memphis for twelve years. Obviously, in the 1940s and the 1950s, racial segregation was flourishing, especially in the South. We had jury segregation by law. In the North, there was the fact of segregation, but it was black and white. Where you lived was determined by race. In the South, we were forced to ride at the back of the bus. People drank from separate water fountains marked COLORED and WHITE. We were relegated to menial jobs and low pay. Police brutality was rampant. It was open season on blacks for no justifiable reason.

This was the order of the day. I well remember in the old days black people got life insurance policies—they called them burial policies. So the insurance guy would come to collect from my grandmother. My grandmother was old enough to be this guy's mother, and my grandmother would say, yes, sir. And I said, Grandma, why you call him "sir"? You're old enough to be his mother. That was the order of the day. Growing up in a segregated society, it was a way of life. You just accepted it.

Of course, I experienced racism myself growing up here in Memphis. I remember vividly being forced to ride at the back of the bus. I remember one evening a white man got on a bus and forced my mother and me to get up. We were at the middle of the bus and he said, hey girl, he said, you know you're not supposed to be sitting here. And my mother and I, we got up and we sat farther in the back of the bus. I remember the separate water fountains. I remember going in the back of restaurants. You couldn't go in the front. You had to go in the side doors of theaters. You had to go upstairs; you couldn't go in the front of theaters. If you wanted to try on garments for size, you could not do that if you were black. Well, then we weren't "black," we were "colored."

There were certain jobs that were menial, that were allocated to people of color. Schools were segregated. I remember getting the hand-me-down textbooks from the white high schools. Three years out of date, four years out of date. Or longer. This was a whole way of life. And if you saw an attractive white female, you were afraid to look at her. In those days, they were lynching people. If you saw an attractive white woman, you wouldn't want to be caught taking a glimpse, even accidentally, during those days. It was just crazy. It was hard.

Dr. King came to Memphis for two marches during the Civil Rights Movement. I marched with Dr. King on behalf of the sanitation workers. I was out in front of City Hall protesting against the mayor, who was then Henry Loeb. We wore a sign saying I AM A MAN. I was twenty-eight years old and I had this sign on me. The reason we had to say we were men was because of the way we were treated. We were treated like less than men. So I AM A MAN was a sign that you wore to demonstrate to America that we were not subhuman, but we were men. Obviously, I never thought I'd be on the inside of this building as mayor when I was in the Civil Rights Movement. I was outside protesting against a mayor because Memphis was a mean-spirited city.

Memphis was similar to many other Southern cities at the time. The sanitation workers were not afforded decent wages or working conditions. They were treated like subhumans, and I felt the need to protest against those kinds of injustices. So I marched. I couldn't imagine then a day when any black person would be mayor of Memphis. I didn't think in my wildest dreams when I was growing up that I would be the man at City Hall.

I will always remember where I was when the tragic murders of Dr. King and President John F. Kennedy occurred. The night that Dr. King was killed I was in a leadership training program to become principal of a school. We were having in-service the night of April 4, 1968. And we got word that Dr. King had been shot. It was unbelievable. Couldn't believe it. A silence went over the room, over an audience of about fifty whites and maybe two blacks. I remember we terminated the meeting, out of shock; sent everybody home.

I was driving back to the inner city of Memphis. I had my radio tuned to a black radio station, and then it came on. They said, we have bad news: Dr. King was not only shot but he has died. And I was just overwhelmed with emotion. I couldn't believe it. I'd been at Mason Temple the night before when he gave his speech "I've Been to the Mountaintop." That church was so crowded. It rained that night. There was a storm. It was hot inside; I could see the sweat on Dr. King's face. The place was packed. I didn't know it would be the last time that I'd hear him speak.

There is something else I will never forget besides Dr. King's words that night. I watched his face when he spoke. It's hard to describe, but there was something about this man. He glowed when he gave that speech. There was something about him that looked totally different. In the Bible, it's called transfiguration.

The death of Dr. King was a tragedy of enormous proportions to the Civil Rights Movement, to justice and equality. He was a man who probably did more for world peace, and certainly did more to ensure equality of opportunities and to deal with inhuman treatment in America, than anyone else in the country. There was no other figure like Dr. Martin Luther King. He moved the conscience of America. And all of a sudden he's assassinated in our city, in Memphis. This is the city where I was born. This was an event that could have occurred in any American city, but it occurred in Memphis. So I felt a great loss in the death of Dr. King, but also a tremendous embarrassment and a blemish on my city, on Memphis. One that we could never live down.

So I've often said that if there's any city in America that should accentuate the values and the principles that Dr. King stood for, it's Memphis. Memphis ought to be that example of a city where you have a mosaic of God's people who are treated with equality, with justice, and in accordance with just, noble principles of how people ought to live and work and be together.

Dr. King's death sent a shock wave across America, really the world. All kinds of emotions were rampant throughout Memphis, in the white psyche, the black psyche. I think black people immediately commenced to have a deep hatred for whites. I think this was true all over the world. And I think the whites of goodwill were profoundly saddened and hurt. Those who were racists probably were happy. That's sad to say. The racists were not remorseful. But people of goodwill, I think, were remorseful and felt a deep loss and embarrassment for our country and for Memphis.

If Dr. King were here today in Memphis, he would see a different city. He would see a city in which blacks are empowered politically. The per capita income for blacks in this city is equal to the per capita income of whites and blacks across America. He would see a school system that is no longer segregated by racists. He would see a city where the sanitation workers are treated with dignity and respect, where their wages have increased greatly, where working conditions have improved. He would see a city where blacks and whites have a greater mutual respect. Institutions are more accessible to blacks, whether it's in the private sector, government, or nonprofits. So we are faring much better than we fared in the early days of segregation.

Everything has opened up to blacks. The president and CEO of Memphis Light, Gas and Water—MLGW—is African American. MLGW is one of the largest three-service municipal utilities in the country. The director of our Housing and Community Development and the president of the Memphis Area Transit Authority are both African American. Will Hudson began in MATA as a bus operator in the mid-1960s and advanced through the ranks to become president and manager. We have African Americans on the airport authority, on the boards of all major governmental institutions.

Memphis is a place that black people are coming back to. They're coming back home. We had the Great Migration from the South to the North in the 1920s and 1930s. At that time blacks considered the North to be earthly heaven. They thought, you leave the South, you go to the North, there's no discrimination. Now they're coming back in large numbers. Why? We have big corporations here. Our tourism, health care and biomedical research, high tech, are all major industries. We're known as America's distribution center. The national headquarters for Federal Express are here. We have America's third largest UPS facility. We're the largest air cargo destination center in the world.

We have blacks who are in positions of great political power. We have blacks who are entrepreneurs, who are doing well with their own businesses. Memphis is destined to be the next Atlanta for African-American colleges. We have a great location, right in the middle of the United States. That's our major strength. We're a hub between the North and South. We have one of America's largest inland ports, on the great, mighty Mississippi River.

When you look demographically, we're about 55 percent African American. In a matter of five years, Shelby County will be majority African American. Today in Memphis you could come here as an interracial couple and some people might glance at you but they wouldn't stare. The South represented the battleground for the Civil Rights Movement, and look where we are today. The first time I ran for mayor, the campaign was divided on the issue of race. I'm the first black mayor of Memphis, and I've been reelected twice and we plan to run a fourth time, God's will. In the last race, we had a plurality of votes. I think we've proven to all of Memphis that excellence in leadership is not based on the race of the individual who holds the leadership role, but that it's about the quality of a person's leadership and work.

Now, I would be less than honest if I were to say that every vestige of racism in Memphis has been removed. Racism manifests differently now. I think the battleground in this new century will be set along economic lines. Black people are no longer impoverished politically and economically, but we are still disenfranchised economically. We represent labor but very little wealth. There is very little wealth creation in the African-American community. We have great purchasing power, but we have not converted our purchasing power to creating wealth within our race. So the economic gap is where I think we have a great challenge. It's about economics and where people choose to live and the choices they have available.

There are also huge educational disparities in terms of achievement, despite integration of the schools. Black kids have got to do better in school. Somehow or other, a lot of our kids today are forgetting the power of education. We knew it years ago. My grandmother and mama would always say to me, Willy, get a good education; that is something no one can take away from you. I didn't understand it then, but what they were really saying to me was, the segregated society and the white man will have his foot on you, boy, but if you get an education, you can make it. The power of education. Your folks told you, boy, you're going to school. And you've got to be better than the white boy. You've got to be better.

In the flat where I grew up in Memphis, we did not have indoor bathroom facilities. I could not go to the parks to learn to play ball; we played ball in a little alley. When I became superintendent of the Memphis City Schools, they wanted to go out to my home to interview me in suburbia. I said, no, I want you to go where I was born. I keep a picture in my office of where I was born to remind me of where I came from, because if you don't remember where you came from, you can come in here and with all of this power and responsibility and prestige, you could get disconnected from who you really are.

I worry that our people are disconnected. We've lost a resilient faith and the belief in God that helped us endure the harsher treatments we received. We've lost the work ethic we once had. We provided this country with labor; that's what we did. Now there are a lot of other groups coming to America that are outworking black people. And young people today don't want to work for six and seven dollars an hour. I grew up chopping cotton, picking cotton, working for three dollars a day. But there was a work ethic, and our people believed that despite harsh conditions, if we got a good education and we worked, we were going to achieve. I chopped cotton for three dollars for twelve hours, in a hot sun. Today everybody wants it instantly. They don't know that you've got to burn the midnight oil. We struggled. Every achievement we made in America didn't come easy. We struggled to achieve and they want it easy, and they don't give it to you that way.

I get guys now, they're crying, and I say, look, man, I don't cry, I don't expect people to be fair to me. I don't care how they bring it to me, I'm going to handle this. I don't care how hard it gets, how tough it is, I'm going to handle it. But these guys go, man, they're not fair to me, not treating me right. What's new about that? You succeed anyway. But they don't have that perspective, and this deeply troubles me. It's tough out there, and it's more competitive today, because blacks have access to the opportunities that were denied us for so many decades. But we're not taking advantage of those opportunities.

So in terms of the quality of life and how people relate to each other, as blacks and whites, the difference between the 1960s and now is as vast as between day and night. But we've lost a lot in terms of core values. We lost a lot of resiliency when we were oppressed by segregation. Far too many of our children have been removed from those values that sustained us while we were being beaten up by dogs and water hoses and we were being relegated to the back of the bus. We're not the same people, so that's good and bad. It's both good and bad.

In retrospect, it seems almost peculiar that we believed the system could work for us if we worked really hard, much as white people believed. We believed in the system despite the enormous odds of racism. And now the kids have more opportunity and they're taking less advantage of it. This disturbs me. In America today, you can make it. You can literally make it. Doesn't mean it's going to be easy, but you can make it. You've got to work hard, and you can't expect everything to be fair, but you've got to achieve. I always say to these kids, look, in America you've got opportunity. Doesn't mean everybody's going to treat you equal even today, but you can make it in this country. You can make it.

What I'm proud of is that this city, which is led by African Americans, is financially sound. The state of Tennessee is having tough economic difficulties, Shelby County is having tough economic difficulties, but this great American Southern city, we're strong financially. And the paradox of this is, in the old days there was this thought that blacks could never manage a multimillion-dollar governmental institution. Today this institution that I lead, the eighteenth largest city in America, has about $60 million in reserves and a double-A bond rating. We are a strong financial center, stronger than many cities that are headed by white municipal executives. And we're proud of that.

I've always loved cities, the great cities of the world. Cities in America went through a decline, and now there's a rebirth. For whatever reason, you were considered a success if you lived in suburban American. You had made it when you could move outside the city limits. That was milk and honey for white affluents. Then as blacks' economic conditions improved, blacks fled the cities as well. Now we're seeing people come back to the city. Memphis is among the top five cities whose majority white population lives downtown. That has occurred here within the last decade. Ironically, there are now more white citizens who live and work in downtown Memphis than blacks.

Some folks may question whether that's good for black people or bad. I think it's healthy. My perspective is that it's healthy for cities to have a diverse population. It's healthy for the economy of the cities; it's healthy for the quality of life; it's healthy for diversity. I don't think that cities ought to be the exclusive domains of poor minorities. You lose your tax base. We're building affordable housing here. The real challenge is to make cities a haven for all people—affluent, middle income, and those who are poor. We are revitalizing public housing in Memphis. In about another five years, all dilapidated public housing in the city will become mixed-use housing. You won't even be able to identify the lower-income housing. We want to blend in low- to moderate-income people with middle- and higher-income people. We want people from all economic strata to live within proximate vicinities of one another. That's what America ought to be about.

I'm not concerned about losing either black or white voters as a result of this approach to housing, and I'm not naïve about it. Memphis has grown to a level of maturity where people respect capable leadership irrespective of the race of the leader. Now, I'm not on an ego trip, but we have earned the respect of white Memphians. They didn't give this to us. They fought me in the first election. But I've been in this job for twelve years, and we're financially solvent, we've raised per capita income, and we've brought more jobs here than any other previous mayoral administration. So we have performed. The mark of excellence is not defined by the race of the officeholder. It's about the quality of your work.

We have brought the white people along with us. We've earned that. They didn't give it to us. I was on trial. The difference between then, when Dr. King was alive, and now is that they would have never let me even be on trial. They never gave me a chance then. You couldn't get on the stage. So we're onstage, we're front and center. We win an Oscar, Grammys, for performance.

In a profound sense, though, in terms of our essence and ethos, we've lost a lot. In modern-day society, we're much better off, by American standards. But in terms of who we are as a people, how we got here in our struggles, I think we've lost a sense of that. I think of Dr. King at Mason Hall on April 3, 1968. He said, "I've seen the Promised Land. I may not get there with you. But I want you to know, tonight, that we, as a people, will get to the Promised Land." Dr. King recognized that the spirit of African Americans has been deepened through all our troubles, and that it needs to be preserved—that the Promised Land is of the spiritual as well as the secular. I think the challenge today for our people is to build a future while preserving a sense of who we are.

THE REVEREND
DR. R. LAWTON HIGGS, SR.

Word of God

For Reverend Lawton Higgs, Sr., the word of God is clear: "Jesus said, 'You shall love your neighbor as yourself.' That's why it's important for the congregations to be mixed. Because until you're together in worship and in community, you don't know how to love. Until you can love somebody who's different than you are, you don't know how to love. Racial integration is a schoolhouse of love."

> *It's me, it's me, it's me, O Lord,*
> *Standing in the need of prayer.*
> *Not my brother, not my sister, it's me, O Lord,*
> *Standing in the need of prayer.*

—AFRICAN-AMERICAN SPIRITUAL

Birmingham is in need of prayer. A lot of prayer, for sure. We have too much poverty, and still too much hate hanging around. We're still too segregated in too many ways. We're segregated in public education. Birmingham city schools are now around 98 or 99 percent black. Many of the suburban school systems are 98 or 99 percent white. Some Jefferson County schools are integrated. But it's not about the growing, energetic engagement of an inclusive, multicultural society looking forward to building those bridges. It's more about how blacks and whites can be kept separate.

It's a matter of both class and race. The notion of contamination is still current. Recently, my wife was talking to a lady out in the northeast section of Birmingham known as Centerpoint. She said, if they just wouldn't stand in their yard, it would be all right. She meant it's all right if blacks move in, if they just wouldn't stand out in their yard. *Their own yard.* They just don't understand they're destroying our neighborhood by standing in their yard.

It's better than it was in the days of Dr. King, because they won't kill you.

That's true. That's the major change that's taken place. The segregation is not enforced by active violence, and that active violence is no longer acceptable, and that is a glorious gift of God. Probably one of the greatest accomplishments in human history is that Birmingham is not Jerusalem. And the reason it's not is the work of the Reverend Fred Shuttlesworth and Dr. Martin Luther King. I love those men. They have a lot to teach the world.

I entered ordained ministry from the West End United Methodist Church in Birmingham in 1974, six years after Dr. King was killed. That congregation was heavily racist and was all white, and people were leaving the community. I was convinced in those days that I was a racist. I was not a violent man, but I definitely concurred with the view that black people are less than human and that they needed to stay in their place. I had no relationships with any black people. None whatsoever.

I would not have wanted members of my family to have friendships with black people. I would not have even wanted to have a black person as a member of the church I was a member of. We did not have any black members. Let's say a black Methodist family had shown up at our church on a Sunday to take communion. That would not have been good. Oh, no. They would have probably been served reluctantly, but the preacher would not have made an invitation to church membership the day they were there.

Well, I read Martin King's "Letter from the Birmingham Jail," and it broke my heart. I cried for about three days. I discovered I was in opposition to God, and began to read a lot more of Martin King's work. I found out he preached the same thing that John Wesley preached, exactly the same thing. I was caught in a real bind, a spiritual bind. So I decided I would stand against racism.

It was a slow decision. I didn't become an overactivist. I didn't join the NAACP the next day or the Southern Christian Leadership Conference or any of the others. And I had no idea how deep all this was. The first thing I lost when I began to change was my dad. He threw me and my wife and our children out of his house because I said that black children can learn as well as white children. My own father. In a very violent rage. I mean I thought he was gonna physically attack me.

It was very painful, very difficult. Across the years, my dad and I developed a good relationship. He had grown a lot, as I had grown. My dad died two years ago, when he was ninety-three years old. He had changed a lot, but he still held a lot of his beliefs. He was a lot more reserved in his expression, at least while I was around. But I don't know that he ever fundamentally changed his view.

Racism is a deep, sick thing. I guess the real turning point in my life came when I was appointed to the McCoy Church here in Birmingham in 1983, nineteen years ago. McCoy United Methodist Church was one of the larger historically white dominant churches in Birmingham. I was appointed pastor after it had lost its dominance because of racism. The day I moved into the parsonage, I had an amazing encounter with God. I was walking across the street, thinking about McCoy Church and the church growth business—the whole philosophy of building church membership, connecting with people in ways that make the church grow. And one of the axioms of the Church Growth Movement is if you see a moving van, invite the people to church, because they're in transition. They're moving into the community; they're looking for a home. So you invite them to church.

I was in the middle of Eighth Avenue, north of Birmingham-Southern College, and I saw this moving van and God said, Lawton, invite those folks to church. They were black. I knew they were black. And I could not invite them to church. I thought I had grown a lot about this business, but I was paralyzed and could not invite that family to the church that I had just moved to. I knew the history of rejection in the Methodist Church, the history of the white church in Birmingham, and it just seemed more than I could do.

So I stood there in that turn lane on Eighth Avenue for what seemed like an eternity. I don't know how long it was. Then finally God said as clear as me talking to someone next to me, he said, Lawton, you've got to go over there and invite those folks to church, or you go back across the street and pack your bags and leave, 'cause I can't use you in this city.

Well, I was too ashamed to go pack my bags and leave, and God was not in a negotiating mood. So I reluctantly went across the street and invited those folks to church. They didn't come, because they knew my reluctance, and they also knew the history of the church, I'm sure. What this did to me was, one, I discovered how sick I was. As a white male preacher, I'd invited thousands of people to church. Everybody—people who had stolen, killed—all whites. And I could not invite a black person to church. And two, I essentially became a recovering racist at that point.

This was a euphoric event for my ministry, a great victory for me personally. It was as though I had broken some of my chains. The next day, I went in to a meeting some folks were holding in the basement of the McCoy Church. The Greater Birmingham Ministries—Scott Douglas was there, a great man; now he's their executive director—had been working with a group of folks who had been in a labor struggle with some of the food distribution people and were on strike. They had started the Greater Birmingham Unemployed Committee, and I went in and I invited them to come to church.

I was on a roll. And it scared them absolutely to death. Matter of fact, it terrified the black folks who were a part of the Greater Birmingham Unemployed Committee. They had just had to leave a Presbyterian church in town because the church was afraid they were going to start coming to worship. They thought this new white preacher coming into town was setting them up to get them out of the McCoy Church basement by inviting them to church to get them to show up so they'd get run off. They were terrified. But then we had a wonderful time together, and of course this turning point is really what saved my life. It was the beginning of the journey that changed my life.

Dr. Louise Branscomb, one of the great white leaders in civil rights and human rights, was a member of the McCoy Church. The Greater Birmingham Unemployment Committee went to her because she was on the board of the Greater Birmingham Ministries, and they said, what's this crazy creature doing trying to get rid of us? She worked it out with them, and they came to church later on but never did have to leave. All this reveals the other side of the story: the black folks were afraid to come in. So I decided I would work on my racial attitude, and I began doing all I could with them.

For nine years, I worked on a doctor of ministry degree on urban congregational development at Drew Theological Seminary. The faculty there and my advisory committee would not let me go by without really dealing with the issue of racism. So I had to work on that in lots of ways. They worked me over pretty hard. Among the many texts I had to grapple with was George Kelsey's *Racism and the Christian Understanding of Man*. Kelsey describes racism as "idolatrous faith," because a racist is really saying that someone's skin color is more important than divine creation in settling the worth of human beings. I had to come to grips with this misplaced faith in my own experience as a young person and as a man.

We did everything we could possibly do to build an interracial, missional congregation in the McCoy Church. But it kept declining. After nine years, we admitted failure, and the church died. The church I had first entered as an ordained minister died the same year. I had worked in our United Methodist structures here in Birmingham and in Anniston, trying to make some headway with racial inclusiveness. I was not successful. Churches die because of racism.

Eight churches closed in Birmingham the same year the McCoy Church closed, all over the issue of race. I have tried to work with the Alban Institute, which helps congregations across the country deal with human relations in their congregations and with all the things that affect the well-being of congregations. I've worked with the general board of the United Methodist Church and with an urban center that helps congregations grow in their capacity to relate to their neighborhoods. All of that was pulled out from under me. There wasn't any interest in it in the white church. Only tokenism.

When we tried to lease the storefronts for the church, the people we were leasing them from told us—it was in the lease, and I've got a copy of it—that all you can do is have the church. You cannot feed anybody, you cannot distribute any clothing, you cannot house anybody. All you can do is have the church.

I have since read *But for Birmingham*, by Glenn Eskew. An area of Birmingham now called Smithfield used to be called Dynamite Hill, because segregationists blew up several explosives there. From the late 1940s to 1965, between forty and fifty bomb attacks in Birmingham targeted blacks to try to prevent their exodus from all-black areas into white areas of the city. Twenty or more of the bombings targeted ministers and churches. Eskew said that some of the meetings to plan the bombings on Dynamite Hill were carried out in the basement of the McCoy Church. That was before I got there, but the neighborhood knew that about that church. That was corrupt, evil, carried out right in the heart of God. For a church, which carries the revelation of a gospel, the highest standards of human history and experience, to be so corrupt at its core is the most powerful expression of evil that can be present in the world.

Since I've been in Birmingham, we've had the battle with the FBI, which assaulted Dr. Richard Arrington here. We had a march in the streets about that. They pursued him to try to destroy his political career here and essentially broke his spirit as a human being. He was the first black mayor of Birmingham and served for twenty years, till 1999. I'm on the board of the Southern Christian Leadership Conference in Birmingham. The Reverend Abraham Woods is president of SCLC here and was instrumental in getting the FBI to reopen the case of the 1963 Birmingham church bombing that killed the four young girls and injured twenty-two others. Reverend Woods and I and many others, we had to organize and protest 'cause they were gonna reverse the name Richard Arrington Jr. Boulevard; they were gonna put it back to 21st Street. They wanted to put it back to 21st Street 'cause they said it was too long a name to put on the envelope. Franklin Delano Roosevelt Boulevard would have been all right.

What I'm doing today in integrating the Church of the Reconciler is not typical in Birmingham. We are a multicultural, multiracial United Methodist congregation. It's radical. There's nobody else doing this in Birmingham. Despite all the press about the New South, nobody else is doing it. Come let us make money together, and let's don't go to church together. Let's don't go to school together. You might live near me if you're as rich as I am, but don't stand in your front yard, please.

There's one black minister in a white church here, and there are a few black members, but not many. They have additionally been serving another church that was totally white, so everything is on the back of that black minister. He has to be white; he has to carry all that burden as the pastor. There's not any power sharing with the community or interest in sharing the power of building an inclusive experiment. I have two sons who are Methodist preachers, and they're both with churches here in Birmingham that are completely white. My older son is married to a Methodist preacher who is one of the pastors of First Methodist, a predominantly white church. I think they may have some African-American members, but it's not an interracial congregation. So as Dr. King said, eleven o'clock on Sunday remains the most segregated hour in America. And that's still pretty much the case in Birmingham.

Yet integration has to come to Birmingham, because if we don't integrate, we don't know one another. If we don't know one another, we're afraid of one another. If we're afraid of one another, we're gonna hate one another. And if we hate one another, James Baldwin's message in *The Fire Next Time* will cease to be prophecy; it will be realized. Integration is necessary for life, not just for Birmingham but for the world. If we can't integrate in Birmingham, they're not going to be able to integrate in Jerusalem, and we've got to learn how to love enough to do that. Not to change you or change me, but for me to be able to love you and you love me even though we're different, and for us to have the strength that comes from that, so we can address the problems of the world.

This is going to happen only through work. Hard work. Time will not solve it. Building churches that go through the healing process, that work through the separation of black and white, will help solve it. Suffering. Suffering. If Dr. King came back from the grave right now and took a tour of Birmingham, he'd be sad. I haven't done the statistics, but I bet when he preached the sermon on the American dream, he was talking about the number of black children who were in integrated schools and the number of black children who were in poor, low-quality schools. The quality of a school in America is still determined by whether it's white or black, and he would be very sad about that. He would also be brokenhearted that the black leadership in America is not continuing his struggle for justice and inclusiveness, but has gone after the greed thing as the form of integration. Bad. Bad. Learning to be as greedy as us white males.

Dr. King would also be devastated by the poverty in America today. Poverty in America is atrocious, and it's being hidden. He would be deeply devastated by the prison system and by what's going on in the prisons, and by the number of black men and women that are in prison and the unbelievable abuse they're receiving. He would be terribly devastated, without question. The percentage of women in prison in America who are black has gone up about 800 percent since the federal drug laws brought on mandatory sentencing in 1986. That's compared to a 400 percent increase in the number of all women in American prisons since 1986. The number of black women in jail rose twice as fast as the number of women prisoners from the population as a whole. A third of black men in America are in prison, on parole, or on probation. The percentage of black men in jail in America is eight times what it was at the height of apartheid in South Africa. And it's still legal in America to have slavery. The Thirteenth Amendment is still legal. Slavery has been eliminated except in the punishment of a crime. All those work gangs in the prison constitute slavery. They make you a criminal, then they make you a slave.

My daddy was a manager of the Norton plant in Huntsville. The way they dealt with the labor issue in Huntsville was to make sure the guy that was stirring up the labor trouble got hired at the Redstone Arsenal, got a big job that pulled him out of the way. All the black leadership was getting the big jobs; they're moving into the white system. So the American dream becomes the equivalent of being white American, of having what white America has, not the vision of justice and human dignity for all people. Come, let us make money together. And you use the criminal justice system to keep the poor and the blacks down.

We have a black mayor, we've got a black city council, we have black people everywhere in Birmingham. But that's not progress. Power is not in the elected officials anymore. It's in the same place it's always been. One of the real pains of my journey in Birmingham has been seeing our elected officials made out to look like fools all the time, 'cause they're elected by the populace but the populace has no power. The black elected officials have no power to do anything, so they become the pawns of the same power structure. They're just a different color; the same kinds of things get done.

That's how it was with the Metropolitan Gardens. It's the best public housing community in Birmingham, probably the best in the southeastern United States. It was torn down, and the people who lived there dispersed. It's the same thing that took place in South Africa, same thing that's taking place in Israel. They didn't sell the property to yuppies; they gave it to yuppies. They gave it to contractors to build a new public housing community that is inclusive and mixed income. But they used the Greater Birmingham area as the basis for determining the city's median income. They came up with $35,000, $40,000, when the real mean income of the city is much lower. The average income of the population that had been there was six thousand. So everybody who lived there is excluded from moving back there.

This may appear very clever politically, but you can't keep doing that without someday incurring massive violence. You cannot do it. You cannot continue to relocate poor people who live in areas with the greatest concentration of poverty and crime—shove them out, use the police to keep them out, and criminalize them if they come in. The legal aspects of things are very different from the real power. Public accommodations are pretty well integrated. You can go just about anywhere you want to. But you're not gonna have any power sharing.

Jesus said, "You shall love your neighbor as yourself." That's why it's important for the congregations to be mixed. Because until you're together in worship and in community, you don't know how to love. Until you can love somebody who's different than you are, you don't know how to love. Racial integration is a schoolhouse of love. If all you do is be with people like yourself, you don't even know what Jesus was talking about. You don't know what love can be or what it is being until you're placed in the situation where you can't ever do anything right, where you're at cultural odds, caught between the culture and the counterculture, and you discover you can still love across those gaps.

Many well-educated black people choose to live in predominantly black neighborhoods, with other well-educated black people. Well, nothing is more wrong with that than white folks choosing to live in white neighborhoods with white folks. It's segregation, and it will breed supremacy and inferiority. It cannot but do that.

Segregation is still a sin. Human beings ought to be able to interact together equally and freely. We can be as black as we can be and as white as we can be and we can love one another and we can care. You can care for my children and I can care for yours with all the passion of our heart. And until we can do that, then we're headed down the road to hell.

We hear so much about the New South, so much about the new Birmingham. We hear that Birmingham has shed its skin, has turned the corner. There's a new horizon. Well, all right. It is new. It is very new, very good. We have started an interracial church in Birmingham. That's it; that is the new. Of course, we're not primarily considered interracial anymore. We're a church for the homeless, and so we've been categorized as the church for the poor.

Finally, thank God, on May 22, 2002, a jury convicted Bobby Frank Cherry of first-degree murder in the killing of the four girls in Birmingham in 1963. Thomas Blanton, Jr., was convicted in 2001. And so it is a new Birmingham. Richard Arrington Jr. Boulevard runs all the way from the crest of Red Mountain to the Birmingham Jefferson Convention Complex, and it encompasses about twenty-five city blocks in the heart of downtown Birmingham. It's been a battle, a horrendous battle. And Birmingham knows that Birmingham cannot exist if we don't first deal with the racial issue and then put forth that better image. We work hard at an image. We spend a lot of money on image and sharing that image and sharing that history. King said the thing he feared the most was going from a small ghetto to a bigger one. In Birmingham, there's a big black ghetto, except for the city center.

We want to let people know that people who are different can love one another and worship together and be in church together. You can write all the books you want to about this, you can do anything else you want to, but if you haven't got money, it doesn't mean a thing. We have a black and white church; rich and poor church. We have to work on both race and class issues. Racist attitudes have never been addressed theologically in Birmingham. The Southern Methodist and Southern Baptist Churches still hold the theology of America, not just in the South but throughout America.

Over the years, I've turned to four spiritual friends who help sustain me. I read and listen to Martin King's sermons, and they never dry up. A second friend is John Wesley, the founder of Methodism. A third is the great African-American theologian Howard Thurman, whose book *The Strange Freedom* has nurtured me. And then William Stringfellow, a lawyer, a layperson who worked in Harlem in a ministry similar to mine and who was a great theologian even though he was not trained as a theologian. I spend a great deal of time with these guys. I live with them. I interact with them. And I ask them a lot of questions.

I got a call from the Promised Land at midnight one night. I answered the phone and it was a couple and they said, Preacher, we've got an apartment with carpet on the floor. Our kid is in day care. I'm enrolled in the community college, and there's public transportation here; we don't even need a car, Preacher. And they called from the Promised Land. It was a dream. There's still no landlord-tenant bill in Alabama. Our constitution is still the same old constitution. Change is slow, but it's happening. Scott Douglas went to Huntsville to a meeting on constitutional reform, and that's wonderful. It's a beautiful thing. In twenty or thirty years from now, race relations in the South will be better. A lot better. It's different now; it's better. They haven't killed me; they don't kill people who stay with it. Right, now. All right. That's a big thing. I honor that big thing. It is a huge thing. The laws are better. If a black couple goes out together in Birmingham, nobody's gonna lynch them anymore out in these hollows. But they better be careful. It's sad, but it's for real.

I did a wedding for a mixed couple—black man, white woman, married right here in the church—and they suffered massively. It was probably three years ago. The woman had a baby boy from a previous relationship with a black man. They were living in an apartment and the landlord would not fix the gas leak and the kid got CO_2 poisoning. They called me, and I had to carry the child to the hospital 'cause their car was broken and the guy where they'd had it in the shop wouldn't fix the car because they were an interracial couple. Now, that was a black mechanic, and he wouldn't fix the car because the black man was married to a white woman. The man's rage was unbelievable because of the experience that he had, suffering like that. They finally bought a ticket to California and left Birmingham.

Racism is an addiction. It's an addiction to power. An addiction to privilege and supremacy, and that's very addictive stuff. And to lay that down, to acknowledge that you're powerless over those things, is to begin to relate to people and identify the humanity and value of every human being, and to give up what the white male God provides for you. But doing that is a lifetime journey. Recovery from racism is recovery for life. It's a healing, a wholeness that you have to work through in order to get reconnected with human life. Crack cocaine is the flip side of racism. That's why we have such a huge hunger for crack cocaine. People have internalized the racism, so they stone themselves, they get stoned. We even use that language. And so the racists stone people, dehumanize people, classify, categorize, and discriminate against people. Recovering from a crack cocaine addiction is the flip side of recovering from the racism addiction—from addiction to the power and privilege and domination.

Birmingham was the center of so much hatred and so much evil. It's a symbol for racism. So many terrible things happened here that it would be marvelous if Birmingham could symbolize the transformation in American race relations. But Birmingham as a city is not yet a recovering racist. We want to deal with the image, not the reality. We want to do the things that look good, that make us feel good. But when it comes down to walking down the street and dealing with all of these issues, we don't want to do that. We're a whole lot more comfortable, black and white, in our respective segregated contexts.

CARMEN JOHNSON

The Big House

"What we're finding is that when we sell to someone coming down from the North," Atlanta real estate agent Carmen Johnson told me, "within a month or two we have their sister looking down here, their mother, and their best friend . . . Georgia now is a melting pot, and a black mecca . . . The white businesspeople here have opened the market to us. I think they have realized the power of the black dollar."

When I first moved to the East Coast from California, I lived for five years in Atlanta and then moved to Snellville, where I've been for the past seven years. Snellville is about twenty miles northeast of central Atlanta, in Gwinnett County, which is known for its school district. I'm a Realtor.

My mother was in computers before they were widely used; she worked as a data processor at Hughes Aircraft. My father was a car salesman in Los Angeles. He was born in Macon, Georgia, in 1913. But once he moved away, he never wanted to come back because of the prejudice that existed here in Georgia.

My father has been dead thirty years now, and he would never have dreamed in a million years that his daughters would want to move back to Georgia. But Georgia now is a melting pot, and a black mecca. It is culturally diverse. Entrepreneurs are drawn here. My sister and I own a Coldwell Banker franchise in Snellville. I don't think I would have ever been able to own a Coldwell Banker in California. Several other black franchises have opened here in Atlanta this past year. The white businesspeople here have opened the market to us. I think they have realized the power of the black dollar. In the past year, Coldwell Banker has actively recruited minorities to come into the franchise. So with all the big corporations that have relocated here in the last twelve years, along with the highest percentage of black entrepreneurship and black-owned companies in the Fortune 500, Atlanta has drawn blacks from the North.

The first black woman mayor in the United States was elected here in Atlanta. Shirley Franklin won the election of November 2001 and was inaugurated on January 7, 2002. We're very proud of that. It has helped African Americans to feel very comfortable about relocating in this area and starting their businesses here. Of course, when Maynard Jackson was elected mayor of Atlanta in 1973, he was the first African American to serve as mayor of any major Southern city in the nation. And then we had Andrew Young and William C. Campbell as mayors. So since 1973, every mayor of Atlanta has been African American.

I think Atlanta is the only place in the world with such a high incidence of black entrepreneurship. The government is predominantly minority. Therefore, it's very easy to come in with a company and get a network among your peers here in Atlanta. The ethnic makeup is so diverse in Atlanta that it is easy for someone to come here and go into business and be successful.

People of African-American descent from the North are coming back to the South. They're coming back for all the economic advantages we have here, like employment opportunities and the affordable cost of living, and they want to live here with other black people. I think it's no different than in other cultures. People tend to want to be around their own for social reasons. They want their children to be exposed to their own culture. Those are the types of reasons I've heard from people moving down here. They want to live near family and friends from their own communities.

And then there's the property tax. You can get so much house down here at such a low property-tax rate that it's a win-win for people retiring out of the North with big homes they can sell. They come down here and pay cash and live regally. Our property tax, on average, is 1.25 percent of the sales price of the house, whereas up in New York it's 3 to 4 percent. So you could come here and have a beautiful home for half a million dollars while up in New York, for the same amount, you'd have a relatively small home on a very small lot.

People from the North come down and ask, how much is that house again? How much land is that house on? They are so pleasantly surprised. What we're finding is that when we sell to someone coming down from the North, within a month or two we have their sister looking down here, their mother, and their best friend. The referrals just keep coming, because once they get down here and get situated, they scope out everything for the family. Then the family starts coming down here piece by piece as they put their affairs in order up in the North. Whole families are moving down here together, and friends are too.

I moved from California to Atlanta because of my children's education. In California, a lot of the children don't go on to college, and I knew that in

Georgia, a higher percentage of the children do attend college. I'm very glad I made the move. Both of my children turned out to be college graduates and have a great career ahead of them. My older daughter is a computer database manager. My younger daughter did her undergraduate work at Clark, and now she's at Meharry Medical College.

Two weeks ago, I moved into a house I built for myself, and I'm already thinking about selling it. It's too big for me—8,100 square feet. It's got five bedrooms, five baths, two half-baths, and five fireplaces. If I decide to sell the house, I'll put it on the market for $850,000—a steal for 8,100 square feet of new construction in Atlanta. For this neighborhood, $850,000 is at the high end, but it's an incredible value for the money. Because I built it myself, I was able to save a lot of money and pass on those savings to the new purchaser. The standard building in this area runs about $150 a square foot, and a buyer would be getting this house for about $110 a square foot.

I designed my house, and it took me two years to build it. But I can give it up because I can go and do it again. I'm in the business. If I were to buy a new house, it would be somewhere around 6,000 square feet with a finished base-ment. I'd be saving 2,100 square feet compared to the house I'm in now.

We're still doing some of the punch-out. It's a nice house. We did a lot of millwork, which you don't find in many large homes here in Atlanta. There's lots of detail—dentil and pilaster moldings on the sides of the doors, and lots of arching. The house has a limestone foyer with granite squares and a dome ceiling, and crystal chandeliers almost twenty-five feet high. You change the lightbulbs with a very tall ladder. There are crystal chandeliers and sconces throughout the house, and it has an overlook where you can stand and see your party arriving and greet them as they come in.

The breakfast room overlooks the water. Near the kitchen there's what we call the keeping room—an informal family room—where the family can relax while dinner is being prepared. Above the fireplace in the keeping room is an outlet for a large-screen cable-ready television. The fireplace vents out and not up, so the TV is completely safe. The grand room serves as both a formal din-ing room and a living room, like the Schultz plans designed for South Florida. The dining room goes where the chandelier is, and then the living room is sep-arated off. But the two rooms are combined, which makes the area a lot more functional.

The master wing is on its own level and has its own foyer, with a dome ceil-ing and crystal chandelier. The bathroom in the master wing has mosaic limestone tile and a steam shower, with full walk-in double heads. There are three guest suites on the second floor, all with huge walk-in closets and private balconies overlooking the lake. One of the suites is for my granddaughter, who is ten years old. She has the witch's hat ceiling in her bathroom, the kind of ceiling that comes to a peak. And I built a princess tower for her.

The basement is finished and is waiting only for the floors to be done and the carpet to be selected. The bar itself is being custom-made and will be here in about six weeks. There's room for a billiard table next to the wet bar. The basement is the biggest recreation center in the house.

Then there's the home theater. Depending on how it is outfitted, it would have three platforms with three rows of captain's chairs. There's a place to store all the equipment for watching movies, like a projector and a screen. And over in the corner will be the bar with the popcorn and such.

The deck is almost eighty feet long, and down below you can enclose the patio to create an outdoor kitchen. The plumbing is already there, and the patio can be fully insulated. We have full sun at the back of the house at all times, which is great for a pool lot.

The subdivision has three lakes, and about eight residents in my neighborhood have houses on the first lake. My house has the best view of the water—high and unobstructed. Boats that use the lakes cannot be gasoline-powered, only electric-powered. The lake is thirty feet deep in some places and stays clear all the time. It's fully stocked. My granddaughter pulled out thirteen fish in one hour.

I don't have a dock yet for the house. That was going to be the next project, after I got all the landscaping in. We've been having a lot of problems with the beavers this year. My lot was full of trees, and even with metal wrapped around the base of the tree, the beavers crawl up the metal and cut the tree off. Bucky Beaver took a thousand dollars' worth of trees so far this year, just in the last three weeks. We went out and sprayed the remaining trees with a repellent to keep the beavers from gnawing. It gets rid of the beavers without harming them. The last couple of weeks, it's been so hot that with the beavers taking the trees it's been hard to get down there and do any landscaping. When it gets a little cooler, we'll start with the landscaping again, once the beavers go into hibernation.

I love houses. I do. I build them, and then when I've finished them, it's like, oh, well, I go on to my next project. When I travel, all I do is look at houses. I have the cabdrivers take me to the affluent neighborhoods so I can look at the houses. Everybody asks me, aren't you tired of real estate when you go on vacation? It's like, no; houses are my life.

People looking at houses here sometimes ask me how many black people live in a particular neighborhood. Well, I am not allowed to answer that. Realtors are governed by the Sherman Antitrust Act, and we're not permitted to give information based on sex, race, or creed. I can't go in and say that this is a black neighborhood. I can say it's culturally diverse, but I can't tell someone that it's black. If someone comes down from the North and says, I want to live with other black people who were successful, I take them to those neighborhoods. But if they ask me how many black people live there, I cannot tell them. I can tell them to come back on Saturday and watch people washing their cars and mowing their lawns, and see the kids playing out in the yards. See for themselves. I can take people to the neighborhoods that I know to be culturally diverse, but I cannot tell them or name the people that are there. Nor could I say whether I know any white people who live there. I would simply suggest that someone look at who's driving down the street.

As Realtors, we can be fined a stiff penalty and sent to prison if we answer any questions related to race, religion, or ethnic background. Women are protected; gays are protected; people with AIDS are protected. If someone asked me, I couldn't say whether a person living in a particular house had AIDS even if I knew. If I don't want to sell real estate—if I want to trade in my suits for a striped jumper—I would answer those questions.

I think the law was designed to keep everything integrated so that white people couldn't come down and request to be in a white neighborhood and say, if there are any blacks that live in here, I don't want to live here. So when a white person asks a Realtor, do any blacks live in here, she cannot answer that question. And if a rich white person says, I want an exclusive neighborhood, I tell them there are no exclusive neighborhoods. All neighborhoods here in Atlanta are integrated; by law, people can live wherever they choose to.

In many urban areas, the black people were left in the inner city when white people moved out to the suburbs years ago. Now it's the white people who are reclaiming the cities, and black people are moving out to the suburbs. That's how it is in Atlanta. A lot of the houses in Atlanta are being given away, pretty much. The African Americans who owned them are getting good dollar for them, but they're coming out to the suburbs and getting a brand-new house. They're thinking that they've made out, when actually the people who are buying those beautiful old homes in town are the ones that are making out. So we're losing out once again. And the African Americans who are selling those old homes don't understand it, because all they can see is that they're going to have a bright new house out in the suburbs. Whereas if they just held on a couple of years more, they could almost make another 100 percent equity on top of the properties.

At this point, as far as choices are concerned, we all have a choice. We can live anywhere we want to live. And we choose to be with our own. So all that segregation, what was that all about? Because when it comes down to it, most of us choose to be among ourselves anyway. The difference now is that we do it willingly. It's a willing decision to associate, not mandated by the law.

I believe Dr. Martin Luther King would be happy to know that we have the choice to live in all-black neighborhoods. That's the difference: we have the choice. Dr. King's wife still lives in the same house she and Dr. King were living in when he died. She has chosen to remain in their home and in that area. I don't think Dr. King needed to prove himself by moving to an affluent neighborhood.

Yes, the Civil Rights Movement was about giving us a choice to live in white neighborhoods, but people can live where they want now. Blacks are no longer legally required to live in all-black neighborhoods, the way they once were. Many African Americans choose to live in the same neighborhood, and white home buyers often choose not to move into those neighborhoods. But they are welcome to move there if they want to. No one is keeping them out. Those who choose to are living in Buckhead, the prime neighborhood of Atlanta, which is less diverse. They don't wish to live in a black neighborhood because there are fewer amenities, like malls and fine restaurants, though that is changing too.

The culturally diverse upper-middle-class neighborhoods tend to cluster around DeKalb County, which is just east of Atlanta. We have the city of Lithonia in South DeKalb and Stone Mountain in North DeKalb. When you hear of DeKalb County, people generally know that it is highly culturally diverse.

Lithonia has the two Sandstone Estates and the Belair Estates. The Sandstone Estates comprise one of the premier subdivisions of DeKalb County. There are write-ups on it all the time. I sold out the subdivision. A house that sold there several years ago for $465,000 would now go for about $700,000 plus. A single female doctor at Emory bought a house in the Sandstone Estates for $600,000. There's a new house going up, and I'm not sure how much it's going to run. The Sandstone homes go up to $2 million plus. Most of the owners are of color.

About two-thirds of the residents in the Sandstone Estates are entrepreneurs, or they work from a computer base in their home. The other third commute to jobs in town. It's a thirty-five- or forty-minute drive, which is not bad considering other areas in the world where it takes two or three hours to go thirty miles.

An African-American CNN news anchor lives at Sandstone. We have the recording artists Kelly Price and Montell Jordan. I can't point to their houses because I do work with a lot of celebrities and their privacy is protected. Their houses are well secured, so people think, okay, they must be someone famous.

A guy who's a black golfer owns a very contemporary house in the Sandstone Estates. He even has a putting green down in the basement, with a simulator and a golf screen. He's a pro golfer and his wife is a computer consultant. They're a young couple. They probably bought the house for about $800,000, and in the three or four years they've been building it, the value has risen to about $2 million. A single black doctor is building a house in a cul-de-sac in Sandstone Estates. Her house is worth about $1.7 million, and it's a very safe area.

The only problem they have in the Sandstone Estates is that so many people know which celebrities own all the beautiful million-dollar houses. When friends and family come to town, you want to show off your neighborhood. So during the weekend, it is nothing but constant cars up and down. They're trying to vote to gate the community to keep people out, because there is no privacy.

Ten or twelve years ago, we had an all-black neighborhood called Sandstone Shores. It was completely built up with nothing but doctors, builders, and professionals. Then five of those owners, including a CNN executive, bought some land on the back side of Sandstone Shores and developed it into Sandstone Estates. So we had a successful minority neighborhood twelve years ago with all million-dollar homes in it. That was the original Sandstone Shores.

We can all speculate on whether homes in DeKalb County would sell for more if white people owned them. I think yes, they could command a higher price. But many of the builders are of culturally diverse backgrounds as well. There are forty-eight homes in the Sandstone subdivision. So we have black builders, black real estate agents, and then black people buying the homes. It's unique, and it works.

Belair Estates, five miles from Sandstone, is another subdivision with million-dollar homes. Physicians, attorneys, CEOs, bankers, entrepreneurs, all types of people who own their own businesses and live in the Belair Estates are just like people who live in Buckhead, but they happen to have a different skin color. The average price of a Belair home is about $900,000. The homes are sold out even though all the lots are not built on. I just sold a house there for $1 million to a couple that are both dentists.

There's a contemporary house in Belair that everybody calls the library, because here in Georgia they're not used to that type of architecture, and so they don't understand it. The house is about 6,000 square feet and is on the market for $750,000, again a great value compared to places up North. There's another house for sale in Belair for $1.5 million that's about 12,000 square feet. And there's new construction that's going to be about 10,000 square feet, and that will sell for $1.4 or $1.6 million.

Stonecrest Mall is two and a half miles from the Belair Estates. It's one of the new amenities, because there are so many people moving out to the area and building homes for between $500,000 and $1 million there. They had the mall on the books for ten years, and finally, when all the subdivisions started coming up, they decided it was time to go ahead and put it in because we were demanding it. We had to drive in to Buckhead and other areas and we had nothing to serve our subdivisions. So they considered it and here we are. The mall is less than six months old, and the outparcels across the street from the mall are still being built with freestanding stores like Sam's Club, Best Buy, Toys "R" Us, and McDonald's.

Buckhead is situated in the center of Fulton County. The county is on a strip of land that runs from the southwest to the northeast of the Greater Atlanta area. Buckhead is where the most affluent businesspeople and millionaires live. It's culturally diverse, though less so than DeKalb County. Most subdivisions in Buckhead start at $1 million and go up to the $12-million-plus price range. The cost of living is much better in Stone Mountain. You don't have the same amenities there that folks have in Buckhead; you miss out on the fine restaurants and things like that. But you do have shopping and movie theaters. And if you want to go to fine restaurants, they're only seventeen miles away.

In the Stone Mountain area, in North DeKalb, houses start at around $150,000, so DeKalb County has something for everybody. In the neighborhood of Stone Mountain that I specialize in, called Smoke Rise, there are a lot of culturally diverse, affluent owners and lots of million-dollar homes. In one part of Smoke Rise there's an area where diverse buyers are purchasing homes from $500,000 to $1 million plus.

A house that would go for $3 million in Buckhead would sell in Stone Mountain for between $700,000 and $1 million. It's approximately seventeen miles from Stone Mountain to downtown Atlanta—about a twenty-minute ride. People want to move out there because of the space and the beauty—even if it means they can't walk to work or walk around in downtown Atlanta whenever they like.

There are country clubs and organizations in Greater Atlanta that are not considered to be black courses, but they are majority black. For example, in Stone Mountain, there are many golf courses close by, and when you go on the courses, you see African Americans. That's where everybody seems to migrate to.

Stone Mountain was incorporated in 1839. The Confederate generals are carved on the mountainside in Stone Mountain Park, which covers close to six hundred acres. The park used to be Ku Klux Klan headquarters. A new Ku Klux Klan was started in Stone Mountain in 1915. In 1963 Dr. King said, "Let freedom ring from Stone Mountain of Georgia!" He spoke those words to more than 200,000 people at the Lincoln Memorial in his "I Have a Dream" speech. And the irony is that we have come full circle and we now monopolize Stone Mountain. It's rumored that Stone Mountain's first African-American mayor, Chuck Burris, lives in the home that was built by the former Grand Dragon of the Georgia Ku Klux Klan. The Klansmen are turning over in their graves. We bought up all the property and built big houses. Who would have known? Isn't it ironic how things turned completely around, and now we occupy their area. We ended up winning anyway. It's amazing.

DEIRDRE AND
JERALD WOLFF

"Why Not?"

Three years ago, attorney Deirdre Wolff and her husband, Jerald, bought a house in one of the growing number of affluent, predominantly African-American communities in Atlanta. "It means our children have playmates who look like them," Deirdre told me. "They have role models who look like them. They are surrounded by traditional families who look like them. In other places, lifestyles are often color-coded. But in Atlanta, African Americans are able to choose the lifestyle they want to live and the color in which they wish to live it."

Deirdre Wolff

Jerald and I lived in West Bloomfield, Michigan, a suburb of Detroit, for ten years before we moved to our new Atlanta home in September 2000. When we first saw our home, it was in the framing process. We were blessed that our property value had escalated in West Bloomfield, so we were able to sell our old house for more than the cost of our new home in Atlanta. We were also pleased to find that the price of new construction included features that hadn't been part of our home purchase in Detroit, such as kitchen and bath wallpaper, a finished garage, and basic landscaping, with a sprinkler system. Property taxes were much higher in West Bloomfield, and property values continue to rise here in Atlanta. All these economic advantages allowed us to finish the basement of our new home, something we had not done in Michigan.

Michigan is much colder than Atlanta, and although I don't miss the snow, my fourteen-year-old son, Jerald, missed playing ice hockey during our first winter in the South. Ice hockey rinks are a lot harder to find here. Many schools in the Detroit area have hockey teams. However, football is an adequate substitute, and Jerald has enjoyed playing for his school team in Atlanta. Our younger son, Quincy, who is seven, continued playing baseball and basketball for the community without even pausing to get used to living in Atlanta. Both the community we left and the one we found seem to share equally in the excitement of youth sports programs.

My husband and I joke that we had more visitors in the first ten months we lived in Atlanta than we did in the ten years we lived in Detroit. Atlanta is so dominated by people who have moved here from other areas that everyone seems to know someone who lives here. It's a popular venue for conventions and cultural events, including art festivals. For the most part, our friends who visited did not come to Atlanta to visit the Wolffs; they visited the Wolffs because they were coming to Atlanta. For instance, my dear TLC Book Club sisters from Detroit came here during the National Black Arts Festival last year. TLC Atlanta hosted their visit, and all fifty of us thoroughly enjoyed the fellowship and events we shared, including the twenty-fifth anniversary production of *Dreamgirls,* starring Jennifer Holliday.

Like my husband, I am a middle child. My sister is six years older and my brother is two years younger. I suppose that the memory of our middle-child experiences contributed to our decision to have an even number of children.

I was born and raised in St. Louis, Missouri. My father is a Baptist minister and has been since before I was born. In fact, he is still pastoring his first and only church, Antioch Baptist Church, where he has been for over forty years. My precollege days were spent at Waring School, which was predominantly black, and Southwest High School, which was predominantly white.

The process of desegregating the St. Louis public schools began in 1980, and my family and Jerald's family were there, in the midst of the transformation. In 1981, a federal district court asked the public school system to submit plans for a voluntary desegregation, and the schools began redistricting students to achieve racial objectives. It was the first time that a federal district court had rendered a decision with regard to the St. Louis public schools. John Ashcroft was attorney general of the state of Missouri at the time, before he became governor. The 1981 decision was the prelude for the mandated desegregation, which occurred in 1983. At that time there was a lawsuit involving the city of St. Louis and twenty-three suburban school districts, the state of Missouri, the NAACP, the U.S. Department of Justice, St. Louis residents, and a plaintiff named Minnie Liddell. That was the beginning of the real fight to integrate the schools.

Jerald and I met when we were fourteen, but of course I never imagined that he would one day be my husband. We met in the Inroads Pre-collegiate Engineering and Applied Science Program. Through Inroads, talented minority students selected from the metro area took math, science, and standardized test preparation classes at Washington University on Saturdays during the school year and throughout the summer. The program was designed to better prepare us for college success. Jerald and I became friends, and eventually, in our junior year of high school, he invited me to his prom. We continued to date and eventually got married. But during our teen years, we were far too busy with our books, sports, friends, and extracurricular activities to monopolize our time with each other. After high school we both left St. Louis. Jerald headed to Northwestern University just outside of Chicago, and I went to Washington, D.C., to attend Georgetown University.

With graduate school behind me—I had earned an M.B.A. from Washington University—I received a job offer that took us from St. Louis to Detroit. At that time, some ten years ago, Atlanta was one of the cities where I thought I might like to live, but nothing had come through for me in terms of work. Jerald was not interested in moving anywhere south in those days. Years later, however, his anti-South attitude softened when he was offered a good job in Atlanta. By then, we were well settled in West Bloomfield. The kids were involved in their activities, we loved our church, and we were happy in our community. So when Jerald was presented with the job offer in Atlanta, I needed time to consider it.

Most likely, had the job been in a city less desirable to us, we would not have relocated. But Atlanta made all the difference. Like many people, we already had friends who had relocated there. Atlanta still enjoys a reputation for being a place where African Americans love to live. It's something of a mecca.

Currently, I work as an associate general counsel for a major hospital in Atlanta. There are many African-American professionals here, as in Detroit. The distinction I notice is that in Atlanta, African Americans hold a wider variety of professions. Not only do many successful African-American doctors, lawyers, and corporate executives live here, but African Americans in Atlanta also own golf courses, publish books, and own dirt businesses, meat companies, and a great variety of other enterprises. We have neighbors who are state-elected politicians, news anchors, inventors, and builders of subdivisions and schools. Such professional diversity generates networking opportunities among ourselves, and offers our children exposure to varied career options within the African-American community.

Before we moved to Atlanta, we lived in predominantly white neighborhoods where people did not openly object to living near successful African Americans. Now we enjoy living in a neighborhood filled with successful African Americans. Though most of us lead busy lifestyles, we find time to socialize and develop friendships. The swim, tennis, playground, and basketball facilities within the subdivision draw neighbors together all the time. Parties and events for youth and families are planned each year for residents and are held at the subdivision's clubhouse.

We did not live in predominantly white areas of other cities to escape our own people. We sought the typical American dream: a nice house near nice grocery stores in a good school district. We wanted neighbors who shared similar religious and family values and whose children would likely make fitting playmates for ours. We like Starbucks coffee, Einstein bagels, and Barnes & Noble. We wanted the amenities and nice restaurants that, unfortunately, are typically exclusive to white communities. We also wanted to feel safe; thus, we were not attracted to areas with higher crime statistics. And so, like many thriving African Americans, we were led to live in white neighborhoods. Atlanta is refreshingly unique in that it is not uncommon to find African-American communities with subdivisions of homes valued in the $300,000 to $500,000 range. Many of these subdivisions are large, consisting of more than two hundred homes, pleasantly spaced on rolling hills. Several are gated communities of affluent African-American families living in homes valued at half a million to a million dollars. So, why not? It means our children have playmates who look like them. They have role models who look like them. They are surrounded by traditional families who look like them. In other places, lifestyles are often color-coded. But in Atlanta, African Americans are able to choose the lifestyle they want to live and the color in which they wish to live it. Why should African Americans who want the big house, kitchen fireplace, extended deck, and gazebo be compelled to live in a white community? African Americans should have access to the same variety of lifestyles enjoyed by other Americans.

I sometimes see white people looking at the model home in our subdivision. They come and they look, and then they drive around, and they keep on driving around and around. I imagine they probably peek at the pool and the tennis courts and then go on out. Why? Perhaps they see that the community is African American. It is their choice to stay or go. People have the freedom to choose among whom they will live.

For fourteen years before moving to Atlanta, our family lived in barely integrated communities. Each year, our son was the only African-American child in his classroom until the fifth grade, when there was one other. Now our children see something different. They know many other intelligent African-American children. They see them as the rule, not the exception. I imagine that Dr. King would have been delighted to see what is happening today in Atlanta. Our people are fully exercising the freedom to make a choice. We are not forced into segregated areas. At the same time, we can choose to live in predominantly African-American areas without sacrificing lifestyle, education, or traditional values. With no sisters or even girl cousins living nearby, my sons might have embraced the BET image of young femininity, with the possible complications that might have attended, had they never had real opportunities to interact regularly and develop close friendships with female African-American playmates.

In some places, credentials carry clout. However, many of Atlanta's African-American professionals have graduated from prestigious Ivy League schools. Having a degree, or two or three degrees, is common among African Americans in Atlanta. Therefore, networking becomes very important to professional success. Entrepreneurs often need to make the right connections in order to gain potential business. Opportunities for making networking and social connections are abundant here. Just about every African-American fraternal, professional, or social organization is sure to have a local Atlanta chapter. More than that, you can count on the Atlanta chapter to be one of the most progressive and dynamic in the national organization.

I have found much more race consciousness in the South. At times, I have seen both blacks and whites attempting to even out the number of blacks and whites within their departments, or at least ensure that they have the representative token. Even at my son's school, the principal assured me that they would carefully group the African-American children so that none were left alone in any class. While I doubt these situations were nonexistent in the North, they would be far less likely to be up for discussion. Behind closed doors, educators may have decided how they would divvy up the black children, but they would probably feel less comfortable speaking openly about it to a parent. I suppose that in the South, the issue of race is so deeply rooted that white educators want black parents to know they are addressing it.

I have personally encountered racism in Atlanta, sometimes in the ignorant embracing of stereotypes. For instance, I was walking with four young African-American male scholars coming from a science enrichment camp at Emory University's School of Medicine. When we arrived at my office, a white co-worker took one glance and commented that I must have found a basketball team. All of these young gentlemen were less than six feet tall. Much has changed in the South, but some people are clearly holding fast to old racist attitudes.

Jerald Wolff

My wife, Deirdre, and I moved to Atlanta a couple of years ago. We are enjoying our life here and have no immediate plans to relocate. We are pleased with the school where our sons are enrolled. We like our neighborhood and hope that the property values continue to rise.

Deirdre and I met as we began our sophomore year in high school. We both participated in Inroads, a corporate-sponsored program designed for minority students interested in engineering and applied science. Deirdre and I attended college in different cities but maintained our relationship. Overall, we dated for about seven years, then got married. We have been married for almost seventeen years.

Like Deirdre, I grew up in St. Louis, Missouri, in the inner city. For some time my family lived near an infamous housing project. The area was crime-ridden—a classic ghetto setting. We were very poor, but our home was never broken. My mom worked as a registered nurse, and my dad, a decorated World War II veteran, worked at the post office. With seven siblings, our family was large and our needs were great. The overriding cause of our impoverished lifestyle was the disappointing fact that my father abused alcohol. He ended his postal career early, retiring on disability based on his war injuries. Health concerns and the closing of Homer Phillips Hospital in St. Louis led my mom to retire early as well. After that we lived on a fixed income. I was still young, as were several of my siblings. When I was eight years old, fire destroyed our old house, and we moved into a house near Deirdre's neighborhood.

I fell in love with Deirdre when I was trying to fix up a good friend who had a serious crush on her. After I realized what a good catch she was, I forgot about fixing him up and focused instead on introducing myself to Deirdre. It was a classic tale of two teenage boys. I was the charming and gregarious athlete—the boy who was not afraid to talk to girls. My friend was a nice guy, but very reserved and shy. He did not feel comfortable talking to Deirdre for himself, and that is how he lost out.

Deirdre attended college in Washington, D.C., and I went to school near Chicago. We were both very blessed. I learned some things in school that she didn't teach me, and she learned some things in school that I didn't teach her, but overall, our relationship stayed good. We never stopped loving each other. She was there for me during the tough times, 100 percent. And hopefully, she would say that I was there for her. After graduation, we both moved back to St.

Louis. We were in love, and I knew she was the one, so I asked her to marry me. The funny part of this story is that Deirdre first said she wanted to wait a few more years before getting married, yet the minute I popped the ring, she said yes. I thank God daily for my wonderful wife.

I was an athlete in both high school and college. When considering college options, I was not interested in Southern living. The South was out of the question, I thought. This was the early 1980s, and in my young mind, I thought I would not be welcome south of the Mason-Dixon. My dad was originally from Corinth, Mississippi, and though my mom was born and raised in St. Louis, I had heard tales about the South—stories that left me believing that black people were not treated fairly, had substandard living conditions, and feared for their safety. I had even heard that blacks needed to be careful when eating in certain restaurants. Some of this was misinformation, but it spread within predominantly black neighborhoods and instilled in me a fear of living in the South. Each school I attended was 100 percent black, except for my last year in high school, when the St. Louis public school system was forced by court order to desegregate.

Years later, when a job opportunity came up in Atlanta, I weighed my options in light of my largely unfounded trepidation. I had good friends in Atlanta who helped convince me to fully consider relocating there. I came down for a visit and really liked it. I love Chicago myself, but Deirdre was not keen on moving to a climate even colder than Detroit. The real paradigm shift about living in the South occurred when some friends I had met in graduate school relocated from Chicago to Atlanta and were extolling its virtues. I was ready to make a change, and though it was in the South, Atlanta seemed like a place where my family and I could progress and prosper.

Atlanta has many churches and faithful people. We had no problem quickly finding a church home within our neighborhood. The opportunities for African Americans to move upward in Atlanta's corporate culture are noteworthy to me. I am a midlevel executive at a midsize public utilities company. I manage approximately ninety employees in a region that covers about 760 square miles. The bureaucracy I faced within corporate America in the North was structured differently. In the North, there seemed to be a strong focus on degrees and professional experience. These credentials weigh heavily in Atlanta as well. However, taking time to build solid relationships with others seems to yield advantages in many circumstances.

As a whole, I think Atlanta is pretty well integrated. Of course, there are still incidents of racism. Personally, I have not witnessed any overt racism or directly condescending attitudes. Most people have been open, honest, and accepting.

Why is it puzzling to some that African-American families would strive for the same things that other middle-class families seek? The chance to prosper should have no relationship to one's color. Most times, housing integration consists of minority races moving into majority neighborhoods. Very seldom do you see whites moving into black neighborhoods, unless there is an orchestrated gentrification of a part of the inner city whereby whites come in to "reclaim the city," as they put it. The expectation is that the black people will eventually move out because they will not be able to afford to stay.

Why some white people prefer never to live around black people is unclear to me. However, I believe that everyone should have the right to choose where to live. My neighborhood in Atlanta is virtually all black. I would not mind at all if whites moved in. I just want good neighbors. I honestly believe that if a white family chose to move into our neighborhood, they would be welcome. On the other hand, if whites do not wish to live around me, I have no complaint. Our neighborhood is open to anyone who has the income to purchase the homes that are for sale. I believe Dr. King would have loved to see a black neighborhood like the one we live in, because he would have observed the prosperity and the progress and would have been very proud. If I am not mistaken, Dr. King also lived in a black community. Dr. King advocated for integration, but it seems likely he would have agreed that blacks should be free to live wherever they choose.

Separate but equal is an interesting analogy. But the difference is in the choosing. We choose whether to live in a predominantly black community, a predominantly white community, or a community that is fully diverse. Under the old separate but equal laws, people had no choice. Barriers existed that said no to both blacks and whites. FOR WHITES ONLY and FOR COLOREDS ONLY signs gave clear directives to individuals. In those days, mixing of the races was not tolerated. Separate but equal laws no longer exist, but at the same time, people can choose to live where they are most comfortable. Many choose to live among people who look like them. Many others prefer a diverse community, and that choice should be equally available. I believe it is these choices that Dr. King and others fought so hard to create and that we value today.

LURA AND CHRIS

Color-Blind

Lura and Chris, a biracial couple living in Birmingham, talked to me about their life together in a city once notorious for its antiblack racism. "There are moments when I wonder," Chris said, "have I taken a step that my family could pay a price for? But the answer tends to be that Lura is worth the risk and my child is worth the risk." Lura told me, "Whether I have a conversation with a concerned family member who has questions, or walk by a person on the street who wants to stare, I'm still coming home, and I'm still happy when I get home."

Lura

My mother grew up in the 1950s through the 1970s in North Carolina. Her senior year in high school, in 1969, was spent in a small town on the coast. There was a big Ku Klux Klan presence in the town. The Black Panthers were coming to power nationally. The town had been integrated a year. On their way to class one day, the principal directed the students to go to the auditorium, instead of class, for a memorial to Martin Luther King. She remembers there was a student speaker. A few minutes into his speech, several white boys came down the aisle carrying a Rebel flag and mouthing off. Fighting ensued, and a white boy next to her—the sheriff's son—helped her get out the side exit, where they found that bedlam had enveloped the school.

A wheelbarrow full of empty soda bottles had been abandoned and became ammunition for the angry crowd. Someone threw a bottle at my mother and the sheriff's son pushed her out of the way, taking the bottle in the face. She dragged him, moaning and bleeding, with fighting all around, to the teachers' lounge for help and went to search for her younger sister. No one had seen her sister, and it was not safe to go into the classrooms. Black girls were in the hallways with razor blades between their fingers, slapping and hitting white girls. Black boys were wielding chains and knives. There was screaming and crying, and sirens were wailing. The state police had been called in to deal with the melee.

They later found her sister. The students had been locked in their class-room without explanation by the teacher. Black boys had started climbing in through the windows, attacking the white students. A boy had lunged at my mom with a knife, and a friend of hers, a black boy, shoved her over, desk and all. She escaped through a window, bruised but unharmed. Many students were hurt seriously, and many were scarred for life.

It was later learned that the rioting was incited by nonstudents. The par-ents—black and white—in these small towns were still afraid of integration. There were a lot of outsiders on the school campus the day of the riot. Whether they handed out the weapons is unknown. To this day, nobody who's talking knows the answers.

This story is one of the very first life lessons I remember getting from my mom. Her family moved all over the United States, and she was raised in parochial schools with very liberal views. But in the town where she lived for her senior year in high school, race was a big deal no matter what she thought.

I'm grateful that I didn't grow up then. I do not have to always look over my shoulder and wonder who will help me. The stares I get when I'm with Chris are nothing compared to what my mom went through.

My mom told me another story, this one about her eighteenth birthday. She was having a few friends over to celebrate, and she had also invited her family's parish priest. He was very active with the youth at the church and highly respected by her family. It turned out to be a very nice evening com-plete with cake, ice cream, and even some dancing.

The next day, her father approached her and asked her what had she been thinking. She did not have a clue what he was talking about. As the conversa-tion continued, he made it clear he was upset that my mom had invited their priest to the house. This made no sense to her. Her dad continued, pointing out that their priest was biracial and that blacks were not welcome in their neighborhood. She argued that what their neighbors thought was not right and she didn't see how it affected them. Her dad pointed out that not only did they have to continue to live in the neighborhood, but that she may have put the priest in harm's way by inviting him to their home, and it might even have an effect on her father's business. Her parents taught her to be "color-blind" and then told her that the rest of our society wasn't—and that she had to accept it.

Thirty years ago, everybody had a completely different idea or perspective.

I'm grateful for finding my true love and for being born in a time when we can live openly and free. It is sad to think of how many great loves were lost or never given a chance because of the color of someone's skin.

I tend to think there are no 100 percent black people or 100 percent white people, or very few. Chris may be black and I may be white, but within us are many colors, races, and nationalities. Being racist usually means denying a part of yourself. Somewhere in everyone's history is someone different and often someone we might not approve of, but you cannot deny your history. When the census comes around, I mark "other" before I mark "white." I pray that in ten, fifteen, or maybe a hundred years, you're not even going to be able to tell the difference, so we might as well start getting used to it.

Our daughter, Aria, is never going to have to worry about a tan and she's never going to be too pale. Her hair is not too kinky or too straight. She's smart. She has the best of both worlds. On Aria's first Christmas, Chris's grandmother sent us books about Kwanza. The most I knew about Kwanza was that in high school the one black teacher we had put Kwanza decorations on her door during Christmas. Now I'm a little bit more educated. Hopefully, I'll learn from Chris and he'll learn from me, because I don't believe that either race is better, only different. God made people different for a reason. How could we possibly learn or improve if everyone was exactly the same?

I usually shrink from confrontation. I walk away and figure, whatever you want to be mad about, you be mad about it in your corner and I'm going to be happy in my corner. I am happy when I go home. Whether I have a conversation with a concerned family member who has questions, or walk by a person on the street who wants to stare, I'm still coming home, and I'm still happy when I get home. I don't have to worry about what the rest of the world thinks. If I stay right with God, then he will lead me, and the world I come in contact with, on the right path.

Chris and I are getting married soon, on August 3. In Alabama, you can get married at seventeen without a parent's consent, but it is still illegal, on the books, for a black man to marry a white woman. I've asked a teacher why they won't change the law. They call it "dead law" or something like that. Another law has overridden it, so the legislature considers it a waste of time to repeal the written law. Within the past year or two, they brought the issue to a vote. There was an initiative to get the law off the books altogether. But not enough people voted to get rid of it. I wasn't old enough to vote then. I'd like to know who wrote the law and who voted against taking it off. I am getting married!

It will be technically legal; the state will see us as married. It's just that the statute remains on the books. By being a biracial couple in a state where most of the people refused to strike down an antimiscegenation law, I believe that Chris and I are making a statement about civil rights. I don't care what it says on a piece of paper. Love is love and love is blind, even if justice is not.

Chris's black girlfriends gave me a hard time in the beginning. They didn't say to me, how can you steal a good black man from us? But that was the feeling. They were mad at him for leaving behind all the great black women he grew up with, as if it was a slam against them. I think I was fairly ignorant until that happened. I didn't know how to take it, but I was almost as upset with him as I was with the girls, because they were still friends of his. I did not understand how he could like somebody that has such a racial opinion about me. Some of the girls after a while got to know me for who I am and said, okay, she really isn't that bad a girl. I'm not out to steal black men in America. I just found my soulmate and was not going to let anyone keep me from him.

My parents didn't care that we were dating. They knew I liked him, so they gave him the chance they would give any decent person. After some of my skeptical friends got to know Chris, they realized he's a great guy. He wasn't the stereotypical bad black boy in the neighborhood they grew up hearing about in the South. My parents said, just be aware that some people aren't going to agree with your decision. I'm aware of that more than I used to be, but I don't let it bother me.

The worst experience I've encountered with racism occurred in high school, when I was dating a biracial guy named Daniel. He and I went to get gas in a rural part of Birmingham. The man at the gas station was a tall old white guy with a long beard, overalls, and a shotgun by his side—straight from a classic country movie. We saw a truck get gas and leave, then pulled up to the tank. "Our pump's not working," the old man said. But I had watched the trucker. There was only one pump, and the old guy hadn't been pumping air. Daniel was afraid for his life and sank down in his seat. I was still ignorant then. I was sixteen and didn't understand why, in the year 2000, someone would refuse to fill my car with gas because a biracial friend was sitting next to me in the front seat.

Well, I got a little scared because we were twenty minutes from the highway with no gas in our car. We rode around and eventually found a Texaco, a more modern place, and got gas with no trouble. Up the street from the gas station, we pulled off to the side of the road and a white man pulled over next to us.

That's the first time I think I was scared at the sight of a white person. But he pulled over to say do you need help? Not everybody on the same block has the same attitude.

When Chris and I are out together, we get stares from both white and black people. It's the same uneducated, scared-of-change look from both sides. I grew up in a mostly white society. I always went to private Catholic schools. In high school I was active in an organization called the National Coalition Building Institute—NCBI. We would go into predominantly black and predominantly white high schools and teach students how to confront racist questions and comments. The group was a way of recognizing and conquering that bit of racism in all of us.

I don't know if you could say my family was against it when I got pregnant, but it wasn't their favorite thing; not because Chris is black, but because I was twenty years old and in college. Some people think we are doing our daughter a disservice because she is biracial. I think that as long as we raise her the same way I was raised about race, she'll be okay. Race is not an issue in your life choices. Chris and I were both raised with good values that will help us raise Aria. Chris's mother is a wonderful woman. I love her to death, but honestly, a white woman was not her first choice for her son. But she put aside her views and her history, opened her heart, and was willing to get to know me. Now she loves me!

When I'm out with the baby, most people just say she's beautiful. I've only had one person ask, is her father black? That was a nurse, when Aria was getting her shots. She was a black nurse. She didn't ask in a derogatory way, but she's the only person that asked in a straightforward way: her dad must be black, right? Yep, he is. Others will point out that Aria is darker than me, as if that's a negative thing. The fact that Aria is black does not hurt my feelings, and the question doesn't hurt my feelings. I am proud of all of her history.

We made a conscious decision not to raise our children in Birmingham, mainly because of the school system. I want to live where my children will get a good education, whether I'm making a lot of money or not at the time. Money for the school system comes from the tax base in the community, and the resources in all-black or predominantly black schools don't match the resources in the white schools. You can say it has to do more with class than race, but in Birmingham, class is race. The white man is assumed to be rich and the black man poor. Ideally, when Chris and I have to pick a school for our little girl, the resources in all schools will be equal.

Chris and I hope we are contributing to a color-blind society. I think the key to having a successful life is how you bring up your children. If we raise our child in a bad way and she grows up to be racist, no matter what else we've accomplished, we've done something wrong. We have to find a way to keep our daughter color-blind. Kids will play with kids regardless of race unless the adults around them push the other way. Whether it's in the South or not, we'll keep Aria where she's wanted, because I don't think she should have to fight for her friends. I don't want her to grow up deciding, okay, I'm black, or I'm white. Being the best black or white girl she can be will not be good enough. I want her to grow up deciding it's okay to just be Aria. She doesn't have to choose a side. There are no sides in America, or there shouldn't be!

It seems to me that interracial couples are pretty common here in Birmingham. I wonder if that is true or if I am only more aware as I get older. We have a biracial couple a block away. They walk by the house every day and they're friendly as can be. But I don't know many biracial couples personally.

I want to work at a school with underprivileged kids, whether they're white or black. I am ready for the day when someone will ask, why do you want to go on this "black" school and make it perfect? I just want to give these kids what nobody else will or can give them; that's going to be my goal. If someone stands in my way and despite all my efforts I can't get there, then I'm not meant to be there, and I'll go somewhere else where they want me to make a difference. There is a place for everyone to make a mark, and I will make mine.

I think it's possible that within our lifetime race won't matter. I'm sure Martin Luther King, Jr., hoped that day would come. Most people hope for world peace, but if people don't take steps to make it happen, it's not going to come any closer. Everyone can take small steps toward that goal. When I started dating Chris, he got me into gospel music. I didn't have the grades or the time for sorority, but I wanted to do something fun and important in college. So I thought to myself, I'm a singer. I can join the gospel choir. But I was afraid that everybody would wonder what I was doing there. It was a low point in my life when I almost let race keep me from doing something I love.

I think some people did have race on their mind when I went to sign up. But people came over to me and asked me my name and what I was studying in school. I told them, I'm a music major. I like to sing. I love Jesus and that's why I'm here.

The first semester I was in the choir, I sang a duet. It was the most rewarding part of my singing career so far. If I hadn't joined the choir, I bet you the rest of my life I would have gone on thinking they wouldn't let me in, and that since I was white I might as well not even try. I didn't join the gospel choir to make a statement. I was just doing what I wanted to do. More white people have joined the choir since then. Maybe that's because they saw me up there. I took an opportunity to sing for God, and in return I was blessed.

Chris played saxophone at an all-black church once when we were looking for a church to join, and I said, why don't we join there? He had to tell me he didn't think they wanted us there. We weren't looking to make an issue. We wanted to sit in church and do what we wanted to do. Chris thought that joining wouldn't necessarily be bad from our point of view, because by and large nobody was going to come up and tell me, you don't belong here. It was almost for the benefit of the other parishioners that we didn't join. Chris felt he didn't want anybody to be distracted because we were there.

Chris isn't the best black saxophone player of Montevallo; he's *the* best. The teachers call on him, the staff calls on him. He's a performer. He takes pride and I take pride in his talent. There's not anybody in front of him, and that's what matters. When he was going to a church in Montevallo and playing the saxophone down there, a guy came to church with his white girlfriend and it was disruptive. Everybody was talking about it. We felt that even if nobody was bothering us directly, we would just feel uncomfortable with the whispers and the stares. I guess that in time, they'd be all right with me. But we'd rather start out on a better foot than that.

When we did find a church to join, I was a pregnant, unmarried girl in an interracial relationship. Right before Aria was born, the entire church threw us a baby shower. We were so blessed. It was great to feel welcomed, especially in a Baptist church. I grew up believing that Baptists thought Catholics are going to hell. But in South Side Baptist Church, we don't have to worry about being judged. Finding our place in it was another lesson in acceptance. If only others could close their eyes and open their hearts!

Chris

I grew up in a predominantly black community and learned about the history and struggles of African Americans and about the Civil Rights Movement. I felt fortunate to have experiences that taught me a person doesn't necessarily love me because they're black. And I had other experiences that taught me a person doesn't necessarily hate me because they're white. So it's humbling to think that once upon a time, someone would have come and gotten me and dragged me out of my house and lynched me for living with a white woman. What offsets that is knowing that even today if I'm in the wrong black neighborhood, I might be dragged out of my house or out of my car, whether I'm by myself or with someone. So I tend not to get into that argument about race.

What does get to me is that at times I don't think we're very far removed from that mind-set. When I was in college, before I met Lura, there was an older woman, a white woman, who had come back to school to finish her degree. She had a daughter about my age. The woman and I were in the hallway and I made some comment about her daughter, like, she sure is pretty; I wonder if she'd like to go out sometime. When I mentioned that, the woman's whole mood changed. This woman had never had one ugly word to say to me, but now all of a sudden she had a different perspective. And this was the year 2000. She looked at me and said, why would you do that to yourself? From her perspective, she was giving me motherly advice by saying, don't do that to yourself. Why would you put yourself in a position for your family to be hated, and for your children to catch a tough time because they're biracial? Why would you do that to my daughter and me, when you could just as easily stay with your own kind and find somebody and be as happy as a bump on a log?

This was a person whom in all other instances I had a lot of respect for. That conversation let me know we're not that far removed from the days of lynching, because if she thinks that, then she probably has a husband at home who thinks the same thing, or a young son or a nephew or an uncle who thinks the same thing. As much as I would like to think that no one would bury a cross in my yard and set it on fire in these times, every so often you hear of somebody getting dragged down the highway chained to the back of a car. Or some policeman is beating someone shitless for seemingly no reason. I'm not going to dwell on it. There are moments when I wonder, have I taken a step that my family could pay a price for? But the answer tends to be that Lura is worth the risk and my child is worth the risk.

It's difficult to say why people get upset, black and white, when they see Lura and me together. It seems to go back to tradition, to people's heritage. People keep going back to what Grandma or Granddaddy told them. I realize that twenty or thirty years ago, Lura would have paid a big price by allowing herself to fall in love with me. She would probably have been disowned by her family and even by her race in some quarters. I've read books about people being disowned, seen TV movies about it, and heard the stories. I have an appreciation and a feel for it, but it's a hard reality to grasp, not ever having had to face it myself.

Black women friends of mine asked me, why would you date a white girl when there are so many perfectly good black girls to date? I tried to explain to them that when I met Lura and developed feelings for her, I didn't have a grocery list of things I was looking for in a woman. We met; we became friends; we developed a relationship. I feel very strongly about her, and she's a regular person, just as much a wonderful young lady as you are. I let them know, I'm sorry if you don't agree. You may as well come out from under that veil of ignorance that old Booker T. always talked about and get with it.

There are things you can't govern, and love is one of them. If two people are going to love each other, they're going to do it, and if it's illegal, they'll do it anyway. If state statutes dictate that I can't legally marry Lura, I can still give her a ring and we can have our ceremony and we're still going to be in love. I hope our daughter, Aria, is going to grow up to be just as loving as we are and to have the same ideal about love that we have. No one can govern who our daughter will love.

I wouldn't say that Lura and I don't experience racism. We've never had a person come up to us while we were out together and make a racist comment. But you tend to feel the things that people aren't saying. You feel people checking you out. Once in a while if I'm by myself with our baby, I can see the look of concern on someone's face, either a black person or a white person. They'll look at Aria and look at me and notice enough resemblance to think she's my daughter, but I can see them wondering, is her mother white? In most instances, they will keep whatever they think about it to themselves, but they're definitely interested, and I find that peculiar. I would like to think that the time has come when my little existence and the color of my wife or child are not of concern to other people. I'd like to think that people have enough going on in their lives that they wouldn't get angry or upset over these things.

We happen to be in a neighborhood and a college and a church where people tolerate our being a biracial couple even if they have a problem with it. So our experiences have been reasonably good, except for a few friends of mine who were critical and who let me know they didn't like my relationship with Lura. And even in those instances, once people meet Lura and get to know her, and they see the smile on my face and the smile on her face, they realize there's nothing wrong with this situation. Eventually, they all come around. The same girl who gave us the hardest time has been calling me and asking, where's my wedding invitation? I didn't get it. Aren't you sending it? Are you upset with me? I want to be there.

When people do ask nosy questions, they always try to be politically correct about it. If Lura is out with the baby, they might comment that Aria has really dark skin. But if the baby's with me, they'll say, oh, she has really light skin. There's always a question behind the comment about the race of the other parent. Sometimes people just come out and ask me if her mother is white. Yes, ma'am, or yes, sir, she is, I say. And then I look at them as if to say, next question? Or, what about that do you want to know?

There are still issues that black America has to deal with. But in terms of Dr. King's dream of a color-blind society, I want to concentrate on being Chris McMillan, and I want my daughter to concentrate on being Aria. I don't always want to have to qualify my race or prove myself on the basis of race. The goals I've wanted to achieve and the jobs I've applied for don't have the word "black" as qualifiers. MTV has awards and BET has them and Soul Train has them, but everybody wants the Grammy. If you win the Grammy, you are not just the best "black" artist, you are the best artist, period.

I recognize that I'm going to have to prove to someone in some way that I'm a good enough musician and teacher even though I'm black, and get my foot in the door that way. It's one of those things that you deal with. But I feel like I'm not doing Dr. King's dream a service if I make it more of an issue than anybody else does. I want to be treated fairly, but I'm not necessarily going to ask for a black student union to be built at the college. I just want to be able to hang out at the student union and be treated like anyone else.

We haven't decided whether we'll have our daughter attend school in the South. In most any school in the South, there's a predominance of black or white students, and that's still hurting race relations. I have a friend whose only experience with a white person is a boss she had when she was a gas station attendant. He treated her very abusively, so in her mind, that's white people. Even though her experience with white people is not far-reaching, it's almost understandable that she developed a sense of enmity toward them. She would never admit she's a racist or that she hates white people, but relations with white people have a negative connotation because of that one experience at the gas station.

When people stick predominantly with their own race, they have very little experience of another race to go on. And when the few experiences they have are in line with the stereotypes, then even when there's not hatred, there's definitely a fear. You don't know if this white person is going to turn out to be that devil that they always talked about. Or you don't know if this black person is going to turn out to be that thug they always talked about. So I would love to get Aria out of the South, to some area where there's a little bit more diversity.

When I get my degree and get ready to teach, I will definitely want to go to the inner city or a lower-income community. I'd like to teach in a poor black high school and try to make a difference for those kids. But when it comes to music, there's a part of me that just wants to be a great musician, and whether it's a band full of Chinese kids or Latino kids, I want to have a great group of musicians and make some great music. Do I owe it to my community to go back to Tuskegee and make a difference there? Do I owe it to myself to just do the best job I can? I wish I didn't have to think along those lines. I wish I could shake it off and just be a human being.

PART THREE

Black Hollywood

Until recently, Hollywood screen icons were mostly white. Today they come in Technicolor. In 2002, for the first time in the same year, two African Americans even received the top Oscar awards—and a third received an honorary Oscar for a lifetime of achievement in film—forcing many of us to wonder if racism in Hollywood is a relic of the past. Halle Berry's widely quoted acceptance speech declared that Hollywood, one of the most contentious battlefields in the Civil Rights Movement, had at long last opened its doors to people of color. Hollywood is famously surreal, a million miles away from Harvard, where I teach. I'm here to discover what it's like on the inside, for black people: as an A-list film star, a top director, a struggling actress, and whether or not Halle's and Denzel's recent Oscars do spell equal opportunity for black people in Hollywood. Where does fantasy end and reality begin?

I have to confess that Los Angeles has grown on me. It's like a sprawling F. A. O. Schwarz for adults: the sun always seems to shine, it never rains, and everyone is dressed to kill. The people here wear the faces of America's future: black, caramel, sepia, beige, white—multicultural eye candy.

It's so easy to fool yourself into thinking that you've left the East Coast's hierarchy of race and class behind, that it's different here. In Los Angeles, people tell you over and over: the only color that matters is green . . . it's money, not race, that powers the machine.

Is Hollywood like the U.S. Army, color-blind in its pursuit of excellence and, in this case, profit?

My first appointment was with a man whose enormous success is certainly a sign that some things have changed. I met Chris Tucker, the star of *Rush Hour*. When the film grossed $241 million, comedian Chris Rock called Tucker "the biggest star in the world." Chris moved smoothly from the regional black comedy circuit to Hollywood's A-list. He has what executives call crossover appeal—his movies are as popular with suburban whites as they are with blacks. From humble beginnings in Atlanta, Chris now inhabits a very different world.

I spoke with Chris in his home in an exclusive gated community in the San Fernando Valley. "Do you think we're on the verge of a renaissance for black people in Hollywood . . . is it wide open?" I asked him.

"There's a broader audience now for black people in Hollywood. But Hollywood is still a tight niche. You flip in through the door to get a movie, and then getting a hit movie is like trying to get into heaven . . . That's why there's only a few black comedians you can name, a few black actresses you can name. You can name a few white actors at the top who are really making a whole bunch of money, really doing good."

Had he experienced racism before making it onto the A-list—or since?

"When you make films in Hollywood, you experience everything . . . Whatever you do, there's gonna always be somebody who don't like you or somebody saying you ain't good enough, or we want to do this or we want to use you for that . . . My thing is to just maneuver right around and step right over whatever it is and keep going."

Does he feel a special responsibility to his black audience?

"I definitely see myself as having a particular responsibility for black people out there," answered Chris. "I've got a responsibility and I'm real hard on myself, harder than anybody. We are blessed here in America, but that brings a lot of responsibility. If you're blessed, you have to help others."

Chris is as levelheaded as he is talented and ambitious. You certainly need to be grounded to survive in this town. He makes no secret of the fact that his religious faith keeps him anchored, and he invited me to attend his church with him one Sunday morning in South Central. This being Los Angeles, I should have known that other stars would worship here as well.

I thought I was hallucinating when I got there—Stevie Wonder *and* Ali Ollie Woodson of the Temptations performing a duet in a black church in the ghetto. And they were just the warm-up act. If Stevie Wonder and Ollie didn't do it, Bishop Jones's spellbinding sermon made me almost get the Holy Ghost. But for most people in Los Angeles, the new religion is not found in places like this; it's about money.

California is the world's fifth largest economy, and Los Angeles is its showcase. Here, conspicuous consumption reigns supreme. Through homes and cars, clothes and jewelry, wherever you look, people display their success . . . or the illusion of it. But what role do blacks play in a city that appears at first glance to be a giant ATM? Hollywood is not long on history, so I wanted to get the perspective of a veteran of the business, someone who has witnessed and participated in change over the past three decades. One of the most talented actors in Hollywood today, and one of my cinematic heroes, is Samuel L. Jackson. He's fitted me into a busy day in a voice-over studio in Santa Monica.

"In Hollywood, many individuals are very liberal without a doubt . . . but is there institutional racism?" I asked.

"There are many ways to answer the question whether Hollywood is racist," said Jackson. "The direct and honest answer, I guess, is yes, only because Hollywood is anti anything that's not green . . . Hollywood can be perceived as racist and sexist, because that's what audiences have said to them they will pay their money to come see."

"There's now a critical mass of black actors. That's unprecedented, isn't it?"

"For a very long time, the people that were in power were white men," Jackson said. "As we get younger producers and younger people in the studios, we have a generation, or several generations, of people who have lived in a society where they have black friends. They have Asian friends. They have Hispanic friends . . . So all of a sudden you see a different look in the movies, as they reflect the way this younger generation of producers and studio executives live their lives."

To be successful, a big-budget film has to gross as much money as the GNP of a small African country, and that's just one film! Every decision a producer or director makes—from who stars to the number of car crashes—affects the difference between profit and loss. A film like *Daredevil* has a production budget of $80 million. So, according to Hollywood accounting, it needs to gross $225 million just to turn a profit. How do producers make these decisions? What role does race play in the process? Why can't even one African American green-light a film? I decided to ask a man who can.

I went to Malibu to meet the man who green-lit *Daredevil*—the head of New Regency Productions, Arnon Milchan. As one of the film industry's most powerful producers, Milchan has a seat at Hollywood's high table. And he was comfortably honest with me about how the numbers work.

"What percentage of films are profitable?" I asked.

"In a good company—one that stays alive—maybe three out of ten films are profitable, maybe three or four break even, and three or four lose money. That's what you need to stay alive and build. If you have a better track record than that, better than three out of ten, you're a genius for a day. And if you have less, you're dead."

"Of the A-list actors, what percentage are superstars?"

"Of the white actors in Hollywood, there are a few guys and a couple of girls—probably five or six actors—that are on the A-list, if we define that as anyone who makes over $10 million on a film . . . Out of those who make $20 million, I would say probably 5 percent, 10 percent, are really superstars . . . I guess all combined, there are maybe ten people, twelve people, that I would say yes to anything they want."

"Right now, the black superstars are who?"

"Denzel Washington, Whoopi Goldberg, Will Smith, Sam Jackson, Halle Berry, Chris Tucker, Martin Lawrence, Eddie Murphy, Chris Rock. Oprah Winfrey *was* a superstar."

"Wow, when I hear you talk, it sounds like Hollywood is all black!" I said. "So why do so many people say Hollywood is racist?"

"I found a lot of French actors who say that Hollywood is racist because practically no Frenchman can get a part on account of their accent," Milchan answered. "I've found that, with the exception of Arnold Schwarzenegger, nobody with a German accent can get a part. It's an endless thing. But how far do we want to take this? . . . Of course there is racial discrimination. I am Jewish; I know there are problems."

"But the average black person would say that Hollywood is closed to black people, for the most part," I said.

"Some people talk like Oliver Stone, as if there's a conspiracy," Milchan replied. "They say the studio system is a closed white boys' club. But it's actually about money. Someone is making $200 million if they can afford to pay Denzel or Chris Tucker $20 million, so who wants to share that? I would say, first of all, people are too selfish here, so they don't have time to have a conspiracy . . . Maybe it's about African Americans and whites not hanging out in the evenings, so maybe that dinner, or that party at the beach, or a long weekend where you'd kind of drink and watch the Lakers or something, is very white or very black, or very whatever. Like Wall Street used to be . . .

"There are a lot of gray areas," Milchan continued. "The issue is not so much worrying about audience perception and racism; it's worrying about the credibility of the story . . . Audiences are changing their views now, with several black superstars on the A-list."

Without what Hollywood thinks of as a universal sort of light-skin beauty— "light and bright and damn near white," as they used to say—it can be a rocky road in the film industry for black women. How does Hollywood decide who's got this look and who hasn't? I was invited to lunch with Matt Rochester and a group of struggling young actors and actresses to discuss one of Hollywood's darkest secrets: the color line within the race.

"In Hollywood, when you're talking about playing opposite your leading males, I call it color coding," said one of the actresses.

"Is it white people who are making these decisions?" I asked.

"It's both. It's the industry. I've experienced it more with black people."

"I was eighteen years old in 1968, the year of 'Black Is Beautiful,'" I said, "and I never dreamed that in the year 2002, if I were still alive, we would be sitting around in somebody's living room, in a place like Hollywood, talking about the whole industry being color-struck."

"But who said black is beautiful?" said one of the actresses. "Black people say that. Who's running Hollywood? Not black people!"

"Do you think that black people are as color-conscious in Hollywood as white people?" I asked.

"Yes," said another, "because they have to follow the rules; they're not the ones who make the ultimate decision."

"And it all rolls back down to money," said a third actress, "to who's got the money and the power."

"How do you know when it's a matter of race, and when it's a matter of your own lack of talent?"

"When you see a TV show, or when you see a commercial that you went out and read for, and you see that on TV and you look at the person they chose, and you look at yourself and you know what you did in that audition— that's when you know."

"You're not kidding yourself?"

"Are all of us kidding ourselves? Can you see this woman who's sitting here—black men looking at her would say she is beautiful—can you see her playing opposite Sean Connery? A white woman the same age, not as attractive as her, would get that part, purely because of the color of her skin and for no other reason."

So black is not beautiful in Hollywood. I can't believe that in the twenty-first century, such small variations in skin tone can make or break a black woman's career. Despite all the progress we've made, it's as if dark complexions are not universal, or not beautiful. That light-complexioned ideal goes all the way back to the twenties and thirties, starting with Fredi Washington, Lena Horne, and Dorothy Dandridge, and extending all the way to Halle Berry and even Alicia Keys. Their great talent notwithstanding, their beige color certainly helped their careers. "If you're black, get back; if you're brown, stick around; if you're light, you're all right." I guess that old black saying still holds true.

I met Nia Long, star of the hit black movies *Boyz N the Hood* and *Love Jones*. I wanted to find out if the superstar roles—and salaries—remain elusive for black women even when they have enjoyed box office success.

"The A-list, the mythical A-list," I said, "seems to have more black men on it than black women."

"Whether you're black, white, purple, or yellow, it's harder for women," said Nia. "Men can be gray and balding and they're seen as being just sexier . . . There are very few movies where you see an older woman with a younger man. The minute a woman goes into menopause it's like, oh well, you can only play a grandma now. Women have a shorter time span in their career to get in there and hit it good."

"So with the same career that you've had, had you been white, how much more would you be making?" I asked.

"If I were a white woman with the amount of blockbuster success films I've starred in, I'd probably be making at least $4 million more per film. And I don't get paid $1 million a movie, so let's be real about that too."

"Do you think that you have to be light-complexioned?"

"Black women are probably the most intimidating species that God has ever created . . . We are beautiful, we are smart, we are strong, and we can appear threatening when we speak our minds. We are also vulnerable, compassionate, and sensitive. Maybe this is why dark-complexioned black women have a harder time making it in Hollywood than light-complexioned black women do. Most white people can identify across the color line with that light-complexioned black woman."

"Do you think you have suffered more because of race or because of sex?" I asked.

"Black women are discriminated against more because of race than because of gender, in my opinion . . . When Matt Damon has a love interest, they don't go, oh, let's bring in Nia Long—we really like her work. They might say, well, sure, we'll see her. They don't want to say no, because they don't want to feel like, oh my God, we said no to the black girl.

"I think their racism is totally unconscious," Nia continued. "I understand the machine. I understand that it might make more sense to put Cameron Diaz in a part for *Charlie's Angels*. I think with the mind of a producer. All I ask as an artist is that we be given a chance, not as a favor or a mercy meeting or on account of a guilty conscience, but just so the game is fair."

Who can disagree with Nia Long that actors should be judged only on talent and that factors such as race or color should be irrelevant? But will that ever be the case? I went to Venice Beach to meet Don Cheadle. Many say he is the most talented and versatile black actor to emerge since Samuel Jackson.

"Do you think that black actors and directors sometimes use race as a cover, as an excuse? Or are they right when they say the place is racist?" I asked him.

"If we were talking about equality of opportunity, or even reciprocity—if we were talking about the way America really looks, rather than the way movies look—then there would be more work for black actors, directors, and producers in Hollywood, and for others of color as well," said Cheadle. "Of course, there are myriad reasons why one actor doesn't get a certain part. If we believe union numbers, there are many more white actors who don't get parts than black actors. If I get turned down for a part, I can't attribute it solely to the fact that I'm black. But it's obvious that I am, so I'm sure that's always a factor in any thought process about whether I get hired."

"But does it help when politics enter? When the NAACP comes in?" I asked.

"Acting isn't bricklaying," he replied. "If you have a skill for laying bricks, you can do it no matter what you look like—if they hire you . . . When it comes to casting, you can't just say, you have to hire these five black people or these four Asian women, because not everybody can do it . . . Yes, we do need more numbers, but if the stories aren't intriguing, engaging, and entertaining, and if it doesn't hold together as a whole, then just sticking a bunch of people in a product that's ultimately not going to be that good doesn't help either. In fact, it does just the opposite . . . Most movies are not very good; most pieces of art are not very good; most CEOs of companies are not very good. That's why, when they *are* very good, they're exemplary, and we go, oh my God. They're lauded because mediocrity is what's rampant. Excellence is rare."

Behind the energy and sunny optimism of Los Angeles is a hard-bitten, take-no-prisoners ruthlessness. Compared to the perils of being an actor, the life of a professor is a piece of cake. Actors can be picked up or dropped on a whim, and their success is continually dependent on fickle audiences. Talk about constant heartburn! For all of the appeal of the camera and the glamorous life of successful actors, the power to effect long-term change in Hollywood lies behind the camera. If we can't green-light films yet, when will we be able to? How much influence *do* black people have behind the scenes?

One person who has blazed so many trails for African Americans in the music and film industries is my dear friend Quincy Jones. Quincy arrived in Hollywood as a well-respected musician, composer, and arranger. He was the first black person to compose scores for films. Since then, he's built a powerful empire embracing film, TV, and music. No black person has more power than Quincy Jones. He's building a marvelous home in Bel Air. Although he's recovering from a shoulder surgery, he's as animated and as sharp as ever. Despite his success, Quincy vividly recalls a time when black people in Hollywood were as rare as rain in Southern California.

"Quincy, what was Hollywood like in the sixties when you started making films?"

"Well, you know it's usually precedent. If you don't see too many black composers, people assume there are no black composers. At the time, the spawning ground for composers was Universal Pictures. They didn't even have blacks in the kitchen. I'm serious! We're talking about the early 1960s."

"If we came back in a time machine, fifty years from now, how will Hollywood have changed? Will we be green-lighting? Will we be studio executives?"

"I think all that's going to happen. The young kids always ask me what I recommend, and I say, want more! Dream more! Don't get hung up on this little jive lame dream down here. Get a big one! And if you get halfway there, you're still okay! But make the dream big."

Quincy has been smart enough to analyze the system and talented enough to master it. He's a role model for a whole new generation of black artists. But is it still harder to realize your ambitions—all things being equal—if you are black? Does race still matter the way it did when Quincy arrived in Hollywood in the early sixties?

Reginald Hudlin is the director of two of the most profitable black films in the history of Hollywood—*House Party* and *Boomerang*. He is also a keen analyst of Hollywood's racial politics today.

"There are no black people who can green-light," I began. "When's that going to change?"

"The studio system—the permanent government of Hollywood, the agents, the managers, the studio executives—is a hard business for black folk to break into, because the skill set that is required to do that is very complicated," said Reggie. "On the one hand, you have to hang out with these agents and drink and go white-water rafting and do all this kind of assimilationist activity, where you have to feel sincerely comfortable in that mix. At the same time, you have to have a level of aggressiveness that is required to make it in the business, period. Black or white, you have to be a shit starter, a driving personality. And that kind of aggressive personality, when executed by a black person, can be very scary and intimidating to white people. But without that, you're not going to make it.

"As if balancing those two weren't enough," he continued, "you'd better be on top of the current trends and personalities in black culture, because your white bosses expect you to have all that down cold. But if you have all this assimilationist skill with whites, then you aren't necessarily listening to the new Wu-Tang record. And the black cultural landscape is so vast! You've got to have the kind of bohemian black thing covered; you've got to have the ghetto black thing covered; and stay up on all the white stuff that all your white colleagues know. So balancing those three things is really, really hard."

"If it's about color, is it green?" I asked.

"Usually a film's profitability is decided when the movie is green-lit, meaning, we're only going to spend money on these kinds of stars, we're only going to spend this much on production value—which means that they're only going to spend so much on marketing . . . If you look at the top ten most successful films of all time, they tend to be science fiction films like *Star Wars* or *Titanic*, where they had a big production budget. It bears repeating: scared money don't make money. So until black filmmakers have access to that kind of production budget, it's gonna be tough to rack up those kinds of numbers."

"Hollywood is quoted as saying that black films don't have crossover appeal," I said. "What does that mean?"

"Let's take a step back from the phrase 'black movies,'" Reggie answered. "What does it mean? In Hollywood, 'black' is only used in the negative. Eddie Murphy isn't considered a black star. He's just a movie star, the same way Egypt isn't part of Africa. So black only counts in the negative. Look at *Training Day*—black director, black star. Is that a black film? I would argue it is."

"What about the idea, entrenched in Hollywood, that black movies don't sell overseas?" I asked.

"Today hip-hop rules in Japan, Germany, and Sweden. So the idea that they're buying all this black culture in every other medium overseas, but somehow in films it won't work, is absurd. The cultural gatekeepers are the problem. The distributors, the marketers on the international level, do not know how to take this product and sell it to these particular markets.

"A lot of times it's not about racism at all," Reggie continued. "It's laziness, because when you have a new product and a new idea, someone's got to come up with a new marketing plan. Now, they've got four marketing plans. So when you come up with something else, they've got to come up with a new plan. That means they've got to work late. They may have to skip lunch. Nobody wants to work late and skip lunch. I'm not saying everything's some evil racial plot with people rubbing their hands together. Sometimes it's just people who are lazy, who don't want to do anything they're not accustomed to doing."

I love the color and rhythms of Crenshaw; for me, this is the soul of Los Angeles. It's a haven for black musicians, artists, and filmmakers who want to remain in touch with their roots. Crenshaw is also the neighborhood that director John Singleton depicted in *Boyz N the Hood,* one of the most profitable black-themed films in the history of Hollywood. Despite his phenomenal success, Singleton still lives in nearby Baldwin Hills and keeps his office there. He shot *Boyz N the Hood* for $6 million. Twelve years later, he makes films with budgets ten times that.

I wanted to ask John how he manages to strike a balance between a desire for commercial success and maintaining his integrity—in other words, how he makes a profit while keeping it real. "You've broken through the glass ceiling," I said to him. "You can make any film you want. How does it work?"

"I always say that if you make a film that is even moderately successful, it allows you to make another film, and if you make a film that is wildly successful, that means you'll be able to make three other movies."

"Where are you in that food chain?" I queried.

"I've been directing just twelve years and I'm going into my seventh film.

I started directing when I was twenty-two years old, and I'm thirty-four, so I'm a veteran at a young age still. I'm cool now . . . For me, it's been a level playing field. I would say differently if I could have any type of personal dissatisfaction with opportunities that have been made for me. But I can't say that. And I haven't had to kiss nobody's pale ass to do it . . .

"This business is not about just expressing yourself and your culture and everything, and then hey, you know, we'll throw $30 million to the wind," he said. "All that stuff about personal feelings and getting culture out and being able to say something, you have to sneak that into your movie. I don't go into somebody's office and say, I want to make this movie 'cause I really want black folks to know this. I don't go in there and say all that BS. I go in there and say, hey, this is what it is—people will want to go see this movie because of this and this, and this is what they're feeling, and this is what's going on on the street. Believe me, this is going to sell 700,000 copies on DVD and video and it'll only be made for this amount, and I think it'll turn a profit of about $50 million. That's what it's about. It's not about all that other stuff. It *is* about all that other stuff, but you can't come on like that."

Like all Hollywood players, John certainly stays busy. As I was departing, he had already started to plot storyboards for his next movie, *2 Fast 2 Furious*. I wonder if John or Reggie Hudlin will continue to move up Hollywood's food chain and eventually be eligible to green-light?

Before I leave Hollywood, there is another director I want to meet. Neither a megastar nor a power broker, he's one of many talented young filmmakers working for their big break.

His name is Reggie Rock Bythewood, and he is in the midst of a struggle with the studios that speaks volumes about race.

"I was sitting in a room with the head of a studio, on a project that I had assembled a superlative cast for—amazing African-American actors whom a lot of people know," he explained. "These are people who are willing to be in a film that I put together, and an executive went through it and said, but here's a black face, here's a black face, here's a black face, here's a black face. The frustration on his part was that there were not more white faces in the film."

"Does he want you to rewrite it and put more white faces in it?" I asked.

"It's basically, 'Reggie, don't take this personally, but to make this film, we have to make the lead white.' And I didn't take it personally, because I've been prepped. My entire career has prepared me to understand that that's how it works a lot."

"What did you say?"

"I said no. That wasn't the film I was going to make . . . My motivation was I'm gonna do a movie where you're not going to hear the word 'nigger'; you're not going to have people running around with guns; you're not going to see brothers with bottles of forties in their hand. This is going to be a hot film. But make it white? Well, go ahead, then. But that's not why I'm here . . . We got set up at Fox Searchlight Pictures. Ironically, this will be one of their biggest films, if we do it. They gave us four weeks to put the film together."

Can commercial success still be equated with the number of black faces on-screen? When will a film be just a film—not pigeonholed as "black" or "Hispanic" or even "white"? When will scripts be peopled with the best actors, their color or complexion incidental or irrelevant?

The growing number of smart, sophisticated black actors and directors is bringing this day much closer. Scene by scene, film by film, they are changing the industry from the inside, using the only language Hollywood seems to understand—box office success. But even they would admit that we still have a very long way to go.

Because of these pioneers, I have no doubt there will one day soon be a black studio executive with the power to green-light a film. I am confident of that. But will he or she force Hollywood's old habits about race to change? Or be seduced by the lure of all the glitter and keep things essentially the way they are? I wonder . . .

CHRIS TUCKER

Different Stories

Actor and comedian Chris Tucker told me he wants to see new stories about black successes in movie theaters. "You got people like Dick Parsons, president of AOL Time Warner, the biggest media company in the world. That's a great story . . . There are lots of billionaires you'd never know about. There are so many different stories, success stories that we should tell. And the more black entertainment there is, the more black writers, the more different stories will be told."

I was the youngest of six children. My mother, Mary Tucker, is a missionary at a church. She's been a missionary all her life, helping people. My father, Norris Tucker, has a cleaning business. I've always been a business-minded person, because I watched my father run his own business, and before coming to California, I only worked for my father. That was it; I never had another job in my life before I went out to L.A. and started doin' comedy.

I was just a kid with a dream and a vision. I loved entertainment. I loved movies. I used to go see all the old movies with my daddy—like *Stir Crazy* with Richard Pryor. On the weekend my daddy would take us one of two places. We'd either go to the high school football game and go to McDonald's afterwards, or we'd go to the movies and then get some pizza.

We always saw the black movies. Every Eddie Murphy movie, every Richard Pryor movie, every black movie, we'd go see. I would sit in the movie theater and be fascinated and just feel so good. I used to look at the screen and say, I'm gonna do that one day—I'm gonna be up on that screen. I used to go home and sleep and dream about being in movies. So from a young age, I had a passion for entertainment and movies.

People know what's funny. When I'm in a movie, I'm a comedian before anything else. I know people, all people, and I make sure I can relate to everybody. I thought about this throughout my career. I said, I don't want to be a comedian that just gears toward black people or just gears toward white people. I want to be a universal comedian. I want to take my comedy and make it broad so everybody'll laugh and I'll never be just in a box. I thought about it when I was young. And to this day I say, when I do a movie, I want everybody to be able to enjoy it. I don't know how I do it, but it's part of my consciousness when I work.

I like a lot of comedians. Eddie Murphy is a genius. He can just laugh and be funny. One of my favorite movies is *48 Hrs.* 'cause he was real; he didn't do slapstick. That's my whole thing. I never wanted to be slapstick. Eddie Murphy wasn't slapstick; he was just straight funny. He was naturally funny, and that's what I always wanted to be. I modeled myself a lot watching Eddie Murphy, just the way he did it. You could feel that he was real. You thought you'd go out of the movies and he'd be standin' right there.

When you make films in Hollywood, you experience everything. I prepared myself for it and I maneuvered around it. Whatever you do, there's gonna always be somebody who don't like you or somebody saying you ain't good enough, or we want to do this or we want to use you for that. My whole thing is, try not to get caught into it. If you spend too much time in it, that means they got you. My thing is to just maneuver right around and step right over whatever it is and keep going, because you're gonna experience a little bit of everything, whatever you do, and not just in Hollywood.

You have to separate this entertainment business from your real life, because if you don't have your life right, and if you're not together, then it's gonna be real difficult to be creative and to make that creativity go over into movies. I knew from the start that when you get successful, when you get famous, you sometimes get unfocused. A lot of new people come into your life, a lot of big decisions. My thing was, okay, I knew it was gonna happen, so let me prepare myself for it. Let me separate myself so I can keep my creativity, so I can keep fresh ideas, keep my vision, keep renewing myself. So I live out of town, outside the star system. If you soak yourself all over in the Hollywood thing, then you just do whatever, because you listen to everybody. Especially because I'm younger, I knew I had to do something to keep myself focused.

I gotta thank God for my parents, because I've always been around spiritual people. My mother's very spiritual, and my father is very spiritual. My spirituality comes from my upbringing, and from Atlanta, Georgia. It comes from being raised in the church. Even though I was sleeping in the church half the time when I was young, it's still there in some way. It's a part of me, just who I am. I've met a lot of people in my life who come to me because I could tell them something, because I've been raised a certain way and can say, when times get hard, get on your knees and pray. I think before anything—before church and everything—you've gotta be spiritual and have a relationship with God. The higher you go, you're gonna have more decisions and bigger decisions to make.

What motivates me is people. I think that's why I know people, and I know what makes them tick. I know what makes them laugh, I know what makes them chuckle, and I love people. That's my thing, my shtick. I study a person in a minute. When I go to the movies, I don't watch the movie. I look to the side. I watch people and see what makes them laugh and what bores them. When they're bored, I say, well, I know I ain't gonna ever do that! And when they start laughing, I say, I can do that; I could take that to another level when I do a movie. I watch people, I listen to people, and then I just do it. People are my thing.

If I look at something and I know it ain't cool, because of the way my mama and daddy raised me, it hurts me more than I think it hurts other people, 'cause people just want to see me do movies. They're just like, do a movie! Do a movie! Do a movie! But I gotta think about the little kids—about all kids, 'cause I got little white kids come up to me, and Chinese kids, everybody comes up to me, and they're my fans, and I don't want to mislead them, no matter what. I don't think a movie is that important compared to these kids. I think movies are good. I love them. They're fun and they're entertaining. But I want to do something that's gonna motivate, and maybe even change people's lives. My expectations are big. I want to go to the next level. I don't just want to make movies. I want to do movies that change people's lives—movies that affect even my life, learning and traveling around the world. I'm always excited about the next thing I'm gonna do. Lots of times I don't know what the next thing is, and that's the good thing about it. That's the point of being alive: don't know.

The movie companies have seen what works, so they keep doing it. What people gotta realize is—and I understand it, and it's fine—movie companies want to make a lot of money. People gotta understand, the studio heads can get fired. Any day! If they make a wrong move—make two, three bad moves—they're fired. Then they gotta go to another studio, or if that don't happen, they might not have work. So they're saying, okay, what works? If Chris Tucker opens big, get Chris Tucker. And they offer me anything, a movie doin' anything. They just want to know it's gonna open, it's gonna make money, and they're gonna look good on the balance sheets. And then there they go; they keep their job. They're fighting for their job, and we're fighting for our job.

Seriously, I definitely see myself as having a particular responsibility for black people out there. I've got a responsibility and I'm real hard on myself, harder than anybody. We are blessed here in America, but that brings a lot of responsibility. If you're blessed, you have to help others. That's why we're put here on this earth—to help others, not just to be well off and not help others and say, that's not my problem. It is our problem, if that's our brothers and sisters. If we know about it, then we need to do what we can to help. Going to Africa changed my life, and it motivated me, 'cause it's more than just doing movies—more than just going to get an award. It's people.

When I went to South Africa, that was special, but nothing like my trip to Ethiopia and Uganda, because I saw real Africa! Especially Ethiopia, because it was spiritual ground, the home of ancient history. The Ethiopian people claim descent from King Solomon and the Queen of Sheba, and Menelik was the Ethiopian son of King Solomon and the Queen of Sheba. There were originally lots of Jewish people in Ethiopia, then Muslims and Christians. The Bible was written there, or close by, and I'm like, whoa! That's like big, you know.

People looked up to me in Ethiopia like I never dreamed of. They thought I was Menelik comin' back home or something. The people I met are very spiritual, and they have dignity. Everybody there is royal—royal people. Be broke on the street, still royal! When I was in Ethiopia, they treated me like royalty, so I think I got some Ethiopian in me. I think it's my Ethiopian eyes. It was like, we just loving you all, keep doin' what you're doin'! And I felt that, 'cause in America we can get a little materialistic sometimes because we're a rich country, and that happens. In Ethiopia you could see that they were a loving people, but there was a lot of poverty. Fortunately, there isn't that level of poverty here in America. But the Ethiopians are just nice people, and they don't care too much about all that stuff. They care about other stuff because they have to live life, survive it. They're not materialistic people, 'cause there ain't too much material over there! It changed my life, seeing it.

They've watched my movies out there, and mostly all of them said, I love you, Chris Tucker—with passion. In America most people come up and say, you funny, man, you funny! Rarely somebody says, I love you. Everybody in Ethiopia, that's just a natural thing—I love you. I love you, Chris Tucker. And I was like, man, these people are just nice, beautiful people, and the movie means the world to them; my coming there meant the world to them. It really affected me, 'cause they couldn't care less about me being a star; they just appreciated the fact that I was over there.

I was invited to go to Ethiopia and Uganda by Bono, who's a big activist on poverty and AIDS in Africa. We met in D.C. through a mutual friend. He said he was setting up a special trip with Treasury Secretary Paul O'Neill to look at poverty and AIDS in Ethiopia and Uganda and help publicize these problems to kids and grown-ups in America so more can be done to help. And I said to him, I would love to go when you get it set up.

So I went with the treasury secretary and Bono and a couple of college students. We toured villages; we went to people's homes and to hospitals where kids were being treated for AIDS and to orphanages with little babies left behind when their parents died of AIDS. We traveled in motorcades everywhere. We visited a lot of schools and we visited places where they were producing coffee, cotton, sugar, and other things they grow for export and for themselves. Paul O'Neill wanted to see what was making the economy so bad and why they weren't capitalizing off their natural resources.

We saw a lot of bad stuff, a lot of sad stuff that I'll never forget, a lot of deep stuff. It changed my life, because it showed me not to take nothing for granted. I've seen a total difference from America. I've seen poverty at its worst, but I also saw a beautiful country. I saw beautiful people. Traveling to Africa let me get another outlook on life, another perspective. Everything ain't just glitz and glamour, and we take a lot for granted, like water and other basics.

I don't know that we're on the verge of great things happening for black people in Hollywood, though I'd like it to be so. For people who make it big, the paychecks keep getting bigger. And there's a broader audience now for black people in Hollywood. But Hollywood is still a tight niche. You flip in through the door to get a movie, and then getting a hit movie is like trying to get into heaven. Even to this day, I see movies that I would've liked to get. I sort of wonder, why didn't I hear about that? Maybe it just wasn't right for me; they didn't think about li'l old me. You gotta be faster and quicker and maneuver better, I guess, 'cause it's real narrow. That's why there's only a few black comedians you can name, a few black actresses you can name. You can name a few white actors at the top who are really making a whole bunch of money, really doing good. It's just tight, tight, tight, so you gotta be the best at what you do, and you gotta know exactly what you want to do.

It's hard for everyone but it's harder if you're black, 'cause there aren't that many good movies being offered. There's a lot of creative black stories out there, but it's hard to get to the studios. It's hard for the studios too 'cause they have to decide, is this gonna make money? That's a great story, but it's kind of sad, they'll say. But it's a true story, and it's uplifting and it's powerful. Well, yeah, we don't know, it might not make money. So it never gets done. And we never see it; the actors never see it. I put myself on the other side, on both sides. I'd like to be in a position where somebody could bring me a script and if it's good and I can do it, I would get it done, or take it to the studios and get it done. But it's hard.

We depend too much on the studios to bring us what we want. We've gotta start opening doors; we gotta open them for ourselves. But to begin with, you gotta get through a narrow door. Some of the black women here in Hollywood say that if you're black and female, you gotta look like Halle Berry to get a good part, but black men can be dark or have medium brown skin or be light-complexioned and still get a part. They're right! Hollywood likes certain looks and they only go with what works. But my thing is, people give Hollywood too much credit. Hollywood and the movie studios are made up of business-men. There's a couple of creative people up top, and you have a lot of creative studio-head people. People who want to make it here have gotta understand, Hollywood is looking for *us* to be creative and for us to open those doors and to break through. We have to bring more ideas to the studios, or do it inde-pendent to get it out there, because we just can't look to the studios to produce projects for different-type people. The studios go with what works. People around the world like Halle Berry. She works. But we gotta stop depending on the studios.

It's time for us to look forward and start inspiring ourselves to greater heights—but never forget. We need to tell the stories from back then, but don't just tell the stories where we got lynched and we got killed. We know that hap-pened—we know that. The movies have been done. Tell the story of Frederick Douglass. The guy came from nowhere and was one of the most brilliant minds of all time—became a great speaker and wrote his best-seller and became the most famous black man on the face of the earth. Put it on the big screen. Mo-tivate me.

You got people like Dick Parsons, president of AOL Time Warner, the biggest media company in the world. That's a great story. You got Bob John-son. He started BET, and a lot of people think he's the first black billionaire, but I heard he's not. I heard there's a lot of other black billionaires. They just don't say anything 'cause they don't want anybody messin' with them, asking them for money. They don't want to get in no trouble. Oh, man! There are lots of billionaires you'd never know about. There's so many different stories, success stories that we should tell. And the more black entertainment there is, the more black writers, the more different stories will be told.

Sadness and grief are part of our history. We've seen too much tragedy and sadness. Sometimes black people don't go to see a movie like *One True Thing* because it's too sad! It's time to move on, though not to forget. Without Martin Luther King and other heroes putting their lives on the line, we wouldn't have the opportunity to become an actor or a comedian.

The first time I ever watched the Academy Awards was when Halle Berry and Denzel Washington both won, and the only reason I watched was because they had been nominated. They're great actors, and there'd been a lot of political pressure about them getting the awards. I was surprised they both won, and I was happy for them. But I don't think that Halle and Denzel getting the Academy Award means anything significant has changed in Hollywood for our people. Maybe that's 'cause I don't judge awards to be giving you credibility. I think your fans give you credibility. I think your peers give you credibility. And I think when people come up to you and say, you changed my life, and man, I loved that movie—it was something, that one little thing you did, it made me think about something when I walked out and I'm still thinkin' about it—right there, that's the award you want. It don't matter how prestigious the award is. An Academy Award would be nice, but I'll take that other award too. That's the main award I want.

In the future of black America, and the future of black Hollywood, there's gonna be bigger and better stories. The story of Gettysburg, the story of the American Revolution, the stories of men like Frederick Douglass. There's gonna be black stories. We want to see the biblical stories of black people instead of just slavery, like that's all our history. That ain't all black history. History—black history—goes back thousands and thousands of years, and I think black America is gonna tell stories like those, stories that are on another level. We have a culture of our own here in America that's bigger than just doin' a cookout.

SAMUEL L. JACKSON

In Character

Actor-producer Samuel L. Jackson is convinced that the broader social circles of today's younger-generation producers and studio executives will translate into more and better parts for African Americans. "When the studio heads look at a script now, they can see their friend Juan or they can see their friend Kwong or they can see their friend Rashan," he told me. "We've been successful in roles as doctors, lawyers, teachers, policemen, detectives, spies, monsters—anything that we have been able to portray on-screen in a very realistic way that made audiences say, I believe that."

I've been very fortunate. All my films have been moderately to wildly successful. I've been lucky enough to be in films like *Star Wars* and *Jurassic Park*. So when studio heads start totaling up my box office figures, I can go, hey, man, I'm in *Star Wars II*. And they go, yeah, but that's a George Lucas film. And I say, yeah, but I can guarantee you a lot of people came to that movie to see me. I have a whole new fan base now. It's totally cool to walk the street and see little kids go, "Mace Windu!" People call me and tell me their kids want my action figure. They're glad their kids now have somebody to emulate in another kind of way. The kids come home and put pillowcases on and become Jedi Knights and say they're Mace Windu. It's a good feeling to be the guy they want to emulate, because when I was a kid, I went home and wanted to be Roy Rogers and Gene Autry and Errol Flynn. All of a sudden kids want to go home and be me. It's like, right on. Totally.

It never occurs to me now to think about whether parts are race neutral, because my managers and my agents know they can send me anything and I think I'm capable of doing it. Unless it says a character is specifically not black, then it's fine for me to do it. I've chased things that were written as other ethnic groups because I guessed the people that wrote them thought in terms of those ethnic groups or the producers hadn't made up their minds what the character was. Most times when people read things, they read them in the mind-set of the culture they're part of. When I read parts, the character automatically becomes black, but that's not an issue for me. It's just a fact that if I want to be that character, then we assume the character is black and everybody's dealing with that fact. In terms of *The Red Violin*, François Girard had always perceived my character as African American. The only reason I got the part was 'cause Morgan Freeman didn't want to do it. So after Morgan, Girard came to me, and I was so honored he put me in the same sentence with Morgan that I just couldn't refuse doing it. Not to mention the script, which is gorgeous.

I'm not going to stop being black and start being famous, because I'm a famous black person. I can walk in someplace and be six different people on any given day. I could be Morgan, I could be Fish, I've been Wesley sometimes, I've been called everybody, Eddie Murphy, I could be a lot of different people on any given day. So I'm always black and I'm always famous. I'm one of them. There's no separation there. Sometimes being black and famous allows me to get away with things that other people can't get away with. If I'm sitting in a restaurant eating and three sisters come to my table and go, oh, we just love you; can we get your autograph? And I go, do I have to put my fork down right now, or are you gonna wait for me to do it later? They go, oh, I'm sorry. It's like, you got home training, right? I can get away with that. If a white actor does it, he's arrogant. I don't have bodyguards and I don't have any of those things around me, because I've been black a long time and I've been taking care of myself. I know how to treat people and I know how to back people off me. If you come at me the wrong way, then I look at you like Jules Winnfield or Ordell, and people back away. See, Ordell is really who I am. That's who I really wanted to be when I was growing up in Chattanooga, Tennessee. I was perceived as Ordell. I was that kind of guy. I was that kind of likable but that kind of dangerous.

I can still be that guy. I'm very used to being that guy from riding the subways late at night in New York, coming from Brooklyn to go back to Harlem from the Billie Holiday Theatre. It still happens on the train. Guys get on the train; they size you up. You're reading a book. There's something about people with books, even though people in New York read. But if you're black and you're reading a book, you might be soft. So if somebody stops and they look at you, you close the book and you just look back at them and it's kind of like, oh, all right, I can go back to my book now. Not to mention the fact that there's an open knife at the side of the book.

I think it's significant for the growth of the business that a black actor like me is being cast in race-neutral parts when twenty years ago I wouldn't have been. It's significant for young actors who have aspirations to be things other than criminals and drug dealers and victims and whatever rap artist they have to be to get into a film. The things I've done and Morgan's done and Denzel's done, that Fish has done, that Wesley's done, everybody's done, have allowed us to achieve a level of success as other kinds of people. We've been successful in roles as doctors, lawyers, teachers, policemen, detectives, spies, monsters—anything that we have been able to portray on-screen in a very realistic way that made audiences say, I believe that, and that brought them into the theaters to see us do it. This has allowed young black actors the opportunity to become different kinds of characters in the cinematic milieu we're a part of.

Before, I used to pick up scripts and I was criminal number two and I looked to see what page I died on. We've now demonstrated a level of expertise, in terms of the care we give to our characters and in terms of our professionalism—showing up to work on time, knowing our lines, and bringing something to the job beyond the lines and basic characterizations. Through our accomplishments and the expertise we have shown, studios know there is a talent pool out there that wants to be like us, and hopefully, these young actors will take care to do the things we did.

I choose characters that are interesting, that give me the chance to delve into aspects of myself I haven't explored and to grab hold of observations I've made about people that I've always wanted to use and incorporate into a character. Or I find traits that make a character interesting. I read the script and see that well, this character feels this way and therefore he must do this. I make up a lot of things about characters that I bring to the role. Acting is an experiment that allows me to do things Sam doesn't normally do. That guy can be brave where Sam wouldn't be brave, or that guy can be angry where Sam would be kind of introspective, or that guy can take a risk where Sam wouldn't take a risk. Or that guy can kill somebody in the trunk of a car when Sam wouldn't do it because Sam loves his freedom.

Luckily for me, when I left Atlanta and got to New York, there was a great pool of actors there. I used to sit around and watch Morgan and watch Adolph Caesar, watch the Robert Christians of the world. What they were doing made me understand there was something deeper to what I wanted to do. I could recite lines and do the right facial expressions. But there was something else there that allowed you to forget you knew them as those individuals, that allowed them to become those characters. And there are kids out there who are still doing those things. I was at the Actors Studio recently, and there are all these bright young faces out there waiting to come into this world we're in. We were lucky enough to get in the door and create the opportunity for ourselves to do all the things we've done. Now these young people are sitting there trying to figure out how to get in there, and they're going about it in the right way. They're in acting school. They're sacrificing a lot of their time to learn stage left, stage right, upstage, downstage, characterizations, dramatic beats here, there, and everywhere. And they're being usurped by guys who do bad poetry to music, only because people who produce movies want a sound track and an audience that's already built in to what they're trying to do. All these rappers are getting the opportunities these kids should be getting, because of economics. And I told the kids, it's just something you have to overcome.

There was a time when I was trying to figure out if I needed to get a stand-up comedy routine so I could get discovered. All the comedians were getting all the acting jobs I wanted, so I figured I'd better get funny and then they'll realize I'm serious. But instead of getting funny, I got lucky. I did *Jungle Fever* right in the middle of my thoughts about stand-up, when I was about to have somebody write a comedy routine for me, even though I think I have a pretty sharp wit myself.

Acting is a matter of craft, first and foremost, for me. There was a time when I totally lost sight of this. When I first started, I was in movie theaters all the time, watching movies and wishing I could be on-screen. The ultimate goal of every actor is to be a movie star. You get to that point where it's the pinnacle. That's where the money is, that's where the fame is, and that's where the work is. But the time came when I realized, okay, I'm getting a little older; maybe I need to focus on getting a TV series. And then when that doesn't happen you say to yourself, maybe I better get on one of those soaps. At least I'd get paid every week. Then when that doesn't happen, you say to yourself, what I need is a good national beer commercial—something that gets a residual check coming in regularly.

But as I continued to work in New York with the Negro Ensemble Company, I ended up in Charles Fuller's *A Soldier's Play*, which won the Pulitzer Prize. I was with a great ensemble of people that included Denzel and Adolph Caesar and James Pickins and Brent Jennings, just a wonderful group of people, Eugene Lee and all those guys. And it became about the work. When I left NEC, I went to the Yale Repertory Theater to do August Wilson's *Piano Lesson*, which also won a Pulitzer. I was the original Boy Willie in *Piano Lesson*, produced by Lloyd Richards. I worked with Lloyd for almost the next two years, through *Piano Lesson* and *Two Trains Running*. The focus was on the work and the characterizations, to the point that I wasn't going to movie auditions and I wasn't going to television auditions; I was just doing these plays and grabbing hold of the work every day. I left there and went back to NEC and did Charles Fuller's series on African Americans before and after the emancipation of slaves, and it was about the work, the work, the work, the work. I was getting better and better at my characterization, and better at grabbing hold of the keys in the language, at making the language sing for an audience so they would understand what I was saying and be into the characters in another kind of way.

By the time *Jungle Fever* happened, in 1991, I had a whole new way of working, through what I'd done onstage and in *Coming to America* and other films, and I was able to go inside Gator in another way. Not to mention I had already done all the research for Gator in my personal life. I was focusing on my approach to the work, and on doing the work, and I forgot about being a movie star. Becoming a movie star was just a by-product of all the preparation and things I had done to get there.

The mechanical things come first, and all the artistic things come later. There is no such thing as a natural. Movie acting is so much easier than theater, only because you don't have the suspension of belief. The set's there. Everything's there. They do close-ups. In the theater, you have to make the person in the back row believe you're in the Wild West on a blank stage, and it takes a lot of work to do that. It's body language; it's vocal inflection; it's co-operation with the people who are onstage, which is another thing you don't have to learn to do in movies. You don't have to learn ensemble play. In film, I've worked with actors who constantly ask the director, what size is this? Are we right in here? It's like, so what are you going to do, change your performance because the cameras are moving closer? And they do. It kind of makes me wonder, hm-mm, what are we doing here?

I use every take as a rehearsal. I do the same thing over and over and over again. It makes it easier for the editor and easier for the director. It makes it easier for the sound guy. It makes it easier for everybody. I'm used to doing that, because when I got into theater, I was told it was a collaborative effort between us all, even though a theater is a dictatorship. The director runs the ship, but you have to work with that actor over there, and you've got to work with the guy in the lighting booth who's calling the cues. You got to be in the right place so that when the lights come on, the audience can see you. You got to be over here so that when an actor comes out, he can present himself to the audience even though he's talking to you. There are lots of things that are integral to what you're doing and that you have to be conscious of in the midst of doing this artistic thing that people claim they get lost in. You can't really walk around in character all day, because it's a job. There are certain things you have to do in the midst of that job that don't allow you to lose yourself in that character, and one of them is hitting your mark. So when people say they get lost in a character, I just say, yeah, yeah. You're not crafty; you're lying about what you're doing.

There was a time when black actors went into predominantly white institutions, into drama departments where they ended up being spear-bearers and they weren't going to play Hamlet. There was no way they were going to end up being the lead in *Streetcar* or be able to do a Chekhov play. We do *Othello,* you got a shot. So that was that. But there have always been a number of places in New York where you could go and learn stagecraft, 'cause that's what it is. You have to learn the mechanics of what you're doing out there. It's a craft, like everything else. There are certain things you have to learn to do to build a bookcase. You've got to know how to use a saw. You've got to know how to use a hammer and nails. You got to know how to go stage left, stage right; you got to know how to countercross. You've got to know how to listen actively so the audience knows that you're listening to that person over there and their attention goes that way. There are certain mechanical things you have to be able to do, along with the artistic act of creating a character that's believable and enjoyable and compelling.

As the fabric of our society changes in certain ways, the fabric of the cinematic world changes in the same ways. For a very long time, the people that were in power were white men. They tended to hire other white men, and when they saw a story, the people in those stories were white men or specific kinds of white women. As we get younger producers and younger people in the studios, we have a generation, or several generations, of people who have lived in a society where they have black friends. They have Asian friends. They have Hispanic friends who do a wide variety of jobs, who went into a wide variety of vocations. When the studio heads look at a script now, they can see their friend Juan or they can see their friend Kwong or they can see their friend Rashan. So all of a sudden you see a different look in the movies, as they reflect the way this younger generation of producers and studio executives live their lives. And consequently, through the worldwide network of cinema, you meet other top-quality actors from other cultures. Like Chow Yun-Fat. I really admire his work. We communicate all the time through notes, or he'll send me a poster, I'll send him a poster; he'll send me a book, I'll send him something. He's the biggest star in Asia. And Jackie Chan. Through that whole evolution, Jackie Chan's become what he's become. And there's Stellen Skarsgard, a huge actor in Sweden; he's come over here to work. The world of cinema brings us all together. And we've started to cast films in a whole other way that reflects the way we live and the pattern of our society. Outside of *Spider-Man,* all the big action heroes now seem to be ethnic. The new Arnold Schwarzenegger is The Rock, and the new Bruce Willis is about to be Vin Diesel. So we're doing something right. But it's difficult to do a film that's of a serious nature and that does not have guns, sex, and explosions in it if it's ethnic.

There are many ways to answer the question whether Hollywood is racist. The direct and honest answer, I guess, is yes, only because Hollywood is anti anything that's not green. If something doesn't make money, they don't want to be bothered with it. Therefore, it's still difficult to get a movie about Hispanics made; it's difficult to get a movie about blacks made that doesn't have to do with hip-hop, drugs, and sex. You can get a black comedy made. Eddie Murphy's funny, Will Smith is funny, Martin Lawrence is funny. We have huge black comics. But getting a film like *Eve's Bayou* made is practically impossible. For five years, nobody knew what that movie was. Like, what is it? It's a family drama. Yeah, but how do we market that? Nobody wanted to be bothered with it. Or *Caveman's Valentine.* What is it? It's a mystery, a murder mystery. But it's a black murder mystery. No, there's white people in it; it just happens that a black person is the lead. So Hollywood is racist in its ideas about what can make money and what won't make money. They'll make Asian movies about people who jump across buildings and use swords and swing in trees, like *Crouching Tiger,* but we can't sell an Asian family drama. What do we do with that? Or if we're going to have Asian people in the film, they've got to be like the tong, or they're selling drugs and they got some guns and it's young gang members. It's got to be that. And Hollywood is sexist in its ideals about which women are appealing and which women aren't. It's a young woman's game. Women have got to be either real old or real young to be successful. If they're in the middle, it's like, what do we do with her? Put her in kids' movies, you know, with some kids.

Hollywood can be perceived as racist and sexist, because that's what audiences have said to them they will pay their money to come see. It's difficult to break that cycle, because it's a moneymaking business and it costs money to make films. Hollywood tends to copy things that make lots of money. The first thing they want to know is how many car chases are there and what's blowing up. They're over the how-many-people-die thing, because of 9/11. Now it's like, how many people can we kill and get away with it? We can't blow up anything right now unless it's in the right context. We can blow something up over there, and the bad guy can be a guy with a turban. So there's all kinds of things that go into what people say about Hollywood being racist. There have been times I had to go in a room and convince people I'm the right person for their script and the fact that I'm black will not impact on the script in a negative way. I've had to explain that my being black won't change the dynamics of the interaction; it won't change the dynamics of the story in terms of my character's interaction with the other characters. I'll just happen to be a black guy who's in that story doing those things.

I used to think that a person of my skill level should be paid more money to do what I do because there are other people who make more money for doing what they do who aren't as good. But they still bring more people into the theater, for whatever reason. I don't profess to know the reason, but I do understand the business a lot better now. When somebody's got a specific amount of box office clout, okay, they get $20 million for the part because they're going to open big and the movie's going to make $100 million. All A-list stars are not created equal. If I show up in a place, okay, I'll get treated a specific kind of way, and that's very cool. But if Eddie Murphy comes in the door behind me, he's gonna get treated a little better. If Tom Hanks comes in the door behind him, he's gonna get treated a little better, and if Will Smith comes in the door behind him, he's gonna get treated a little better. And then if Tom Cruise comes in, then everybody, fuck, gets kind of pushed to the side. So it works out. This is not the kind of job where you work your way up from the mail room and you may become president. There's a pecking order. But it's tied to the box office. It's not tied to anything else.

There's this whole theory about Denzel and Halle and Sidney all receiving awards from the Academy in 2002; it's like, usher out the old and usher in the new. Fortunately, Denzel did a role that was so different from anything he'd ever done, and he did it so well, that he won an Academy Award for it. It was the best and most compelling performance of the year. I have four criteria for the Academy Award. First, the role is totally different from anything you've seen this actor do before. Second, the character is compelling and interesting, frightening even; you talk about the character when you leave the theater. Third, the character is an integral part of the story; the story would not work if this character were not in it. And fourth, you know that the actor poured their heart and soul into it. Denzel did all those things, and that was the best performance of the year. Out of all the women who were nominated, Halle's performance was a good performance for her. It was something the audience had never seen her do before, and it was compelling and kind of awesome, even shocking in terms of the intensity of what happened on the screen.

So they were well-deserved awards. But there have been years when other African Americans won Academy Awards. Just because Denzel's and Halle's were the two most high profile awards, the year 2002 was viewed as a watershed when it really wasn't. It's what it should be. I look forward to the year when somebody's going, well, where are the white nominees? The year that all the performances that are nominated are ones by African Americans or Asian Americans or Hispanic Americans. And that can happen. There have been years where we won for sound and for best documentary, best short; we won for all kinds of things, but people don't recognize those individuals. I know brothers that have two and three Oscars at home, soundmen, and people don't even know who they are. Getting an Academy Award is important no matter what category you win it in. It's an event. It means something. It means you're going to make more money, for sure.

It also means more black people are gonna get Academy Awards sooner or later, because these guys did it. They have other people behind them that are their protégés. There were young girls sitting at home in Polk City, Iowa, somewhere, looking at Halle Berry, and they ran into the bathroom and picked up their toothbrush and made their Academy Award acceptance speech. I used to do it every year. I used to stand in front of the mirror and thank my mom and my teachers and everybody I knew, and it was great. That's something to aspire to. The first time my wife and I went to the Academy Awards, we were calling people in Atlanta, people in New York, everybody we had acted with, and telling them, we're in a limo on our way to the Academy Awards. Make sure you're watching the red carpet! Check it out! Now it's like, do we have to go? Oh, man, get dressed at two o'clock, get in the car, you know, *argghh*. But you still want to do it because it's a celebration of what we do, and it's important that young ethnic actors sitting at home see us there, whether we win, whether we present, or whether we're just in the audience. Because they know we're an important part of this business; we are recognized as part of it. That's why we're there. Because not everybody can go.

Will Smith and Halle Berry, in a romantic comedy, $100 million—that might happen in our lifetime. Or Denzel. I think Will and Halle would be an event. People would go see that, even Martin Lawrence and Halle Berry, Chris Tucker and Halle, we're talking about event guys now, $20-million players. Eddie, Will, Chris, Martin, event players, with Halle, yeah, that might happen. *Down to Earth,* Chris Rock's 2001 remake of *Heaven Can Wait,* didn't work too well, but there's a romantic comedy out there somewhere. People are starting to remake everything now. I'm sure there could be some interesting ethnic remakes of some of the films we knew and loved from yesteryear that they're starting to bring back out again. I don't think there's anything inherent in the audience that would keep them from identifying with two characters who are falling in love, both of whom are black. In a lot of people's minds, Halle is just a beautiful girl who happens to be black, and Will is an incredibly funny and handsome, intriguing guy. He's kind of like Jim Carey. People want to see Will be funny and charming and all the things they fell in love with in Will as the Fresh Prince. They don't want to see Will bloodied and bulked up and being Ali.

People know who they want to see. They know what Will Smith they want to see, they know what Harrison Ford they want to see, they know what Eddie Murphy they want to see, they know what Tom Cruise they want to see, they know what Tom Hanks they want to see. With me, part of the game when people come to my movies is seeing how different I'm going to be. But those guys have made a reputation on being a specific thing that audiences bought into. It's like, hey, I bought into this. I didn't ask you to change your hair, change your face, do nothing. That other guy, I pay to see him do that, 'cause he's always doing that to himself, so we're used to it. But when we come to see Will, we want to see Will Smith's face. I don't want to see scars on it. I don't want to see a different kind of hair. I want to see him being jolly. I want him talking like Will Smith. We want him being that guy we know and love. That's just a fact.

I don't know if we should present our stories differently. I think there are enough skilled writers and enough skilled directors and definitely enough skilled actors that we could effectively tell whatever story we want to tell. It all goes back to who's willing to put up the money so that these stories can be told effectively. I go back to *Eve's Bayou.* We had one budget for it and everybody kept telling us it had to be done at another budget. But people bought into our belief in it, so they did things for less money or as a labor of love. The local people in New Orleans showed up. We didn't have enough people to fix hair period-style, so we called hairdressers in New Orleans and it was like, well, child, we'd love to come help you. It became a big collaborative effort. You've got to be able to do that and be willing to sacrifice in certain ways to get things done, because nobody's going to give you what you think you deserve to get them done. The people doing it have to believe in what you are doing. You start working too hard, and you run your crew down working overtime. They got to believe as hard as you believe so you can get an independent film done. That's the only way independent films get done.

I've been on studio pictures that should have ended in December and didn't end till March and nobody said a word. But you could never do that on an independent film, because when the money runs out, the money's out. We were begging them for one more day on *Eve's Bayou* and they were like, we just can't do it; we just can't. Just a day, one day so we can—no, we don't have it. And the movie did fine. I was just a little country doctor doing his thing. A little country doctor like we all know. The movie is still doing well in the world. In fact, I just got a check for the worldwide sales. There were places that movie never opened. People in London kept waiting for it and waiting for it, and we finally got over there with it. People in Germany were hearing about it, and hearing about it, and they never got it. Now it's kind of moving into video over there, so they're getting it. But it did relatively well for the amount of money it was made for. It made the studio's money back, and people are now sharing in the profits. We all had to say, we've got to wait. This is five, six years later and we're just getting into the money, but some money's coming.

The reason our people didn't go to see *Beloved* is because it was bad. It's a hard book to read, although Toni Morrison won the Pulitzer for it. And then your friends tell you, wait a minute, child, don't go and see that. This is black people saying, I can't wait to see *Beloved*, and somebody who's already seen it goes, well, you know, you might want to wait on the video. And then they'll call you later: child, you were right about that *Beloved*. I'm sorry, it was just not an event. We wanted it to be something. I was at the premiere, and it's difficult to know what to say to the people who were in it. It's one of those things.

One more NAACP boycott doesn't seem like the answer to me. In fact, why don't the NAACP leave all of us alone? Every time they get involved in Hollywood, something strange happens. When they were protesting *The Color Purple*, it was like, what the hell is Steven Spielberg doing directing *The Color Purple*? All right, and then everybody was like, well, he paid for it, so he can direct it. Then all of a sudden it was like, well, why didn't nobody from *The Color Purple* win an Academy Award? Well, number one, you said Steven Spielberg shouldn't even have been messing with it, so why you talking about that now? Why weren't there any black people nominated for Academy Awards for *The Color Purple*? Well, let me see, we had *Booty Call* in 1996; who you want nominated for *Booty Call*? Which actor? Who you want? It's, get over it, leave us alone, let us do our thing.

We need to produce our own films. Black money is not widely known for going into an artistic endeavor, especially a film. Film's a crapshoot. Films can be made for varying amounts of money, and there are a lot of black people with a lot of money that won't invest in a movie but they'll buy stock that might die tomorrow. You can put that money in a movie and you can get a constant return, because the movie's going to make X amount of dollars when it goes to video; it's going to make X amount of dollars when it goes foreign. It's going to make more money then, depending on who's in it, because your foreign cachet is an important part of actors getting paid. If you don't have foreign cachet, it ain't happening.

I go to Europe as often as I can, or Asia, so people can see me and see that I'm concerned about my fans and I care about them liking the film I'm in and liking me. They used to say, we can't cast you because you won't play in Japan, but that's not true. I've counteracted that. In fact, I was walking down the street with this guy from a studio in Japan and I was asking him about black actors in Japan. He goes, well, they only know Sidney Poitier, Eddie Murphy, and Will Smith. And as we were walking—it was rush hour—all these people were looking at us and pointing at me and talking to each other. So I asked him, what are they saying? And he's like, oh, they know you. It just so happened that *Die Hard* had been out and was the highest-grossing film in Japan that year. It was the highest-grossing film worldwide. People knew who I was. People in Paris were camped outside the hotel. It's crazy. I was like, oh, okay, so I'm getting somewhere with this.

We need to own our own theaters in addition to producing our own films. The more theaters we own, the sooner we can have our own distribution chain. So when you can't get in that distributor thing that goes on out there and you've got nowhere to play your movie, we would have our own network of theaters. I learned when *Star Wars* was about to come out how many screens there are in America. You always think in terms of maybe 10,000 or 12,000 theaters. But there's more cities than that, and you find out there's over 35,000 screens. So you look and you say, with *Spider-Man* and *Star Wars* on most of the screens, how many are left? They've got all the screens. It's a matter of us having that kind of network, so when we do make small films that we want to distribute to a specific group of people or to a wider audience, we're able to do it. *Caveman's Valentine* was never in more than fifty theaters because they didn't know what to do with it. And Spike Lee was never able to compete with the big films. *Do the Right Thing* and *Fever* and all the Spike Lee films could never be number one at the box office because they were never in enough theaters to compete with the big films that were out at the time. The big films always have the highest per-screen average. That translates to only so many screens that could show Spike's films, so people had to line up and wait to see them. All kinds of things dictate how much money a film makes: the length of the film, how many screens it's on, how many times you can play it during the day, how many prints you have out there, and the advertising budget so people are aware of that particular film.

I'm sure I can do what I'm doing for a long time. It's not like digging ditches. I don't need my back that much. I can act in a wheelchair. I can act until I drop over. I started late, and maybe that's part of the reason I tend to work a lot. I wish I could have been doing this when I was twenty years old, but hey, I had to do what I had to do to get here, and I wouldn't trade those experiences for anything. I think it's great that some people are going to have forty-year careers—not a lot, but some people start out at twenty. I've had a twenty- to thirty-year career, and I'm closing in on a hundred movies. So I'm doing okay. I also know that I need to work so the people around me can take care of themselves and their responsibilities. I care about them and their families. I haven't changed in that way, because I care about people. I want to be able to produce films for friends of mine who haven't had the opportunity to be seen in the way I've been seen. They're good at what they do, and they deserve an opportunity to be seen by a greater public.

I continue to try to find things that allow me to grow as an actor and as a person. I'm not as political as I used to be. I don't espouse my political positions to the masses or even to people who listen to me. I do still feel very responsible to a lot of people, especially people who are around me and who work with me. I know I make an enormous amount of money that allows me not to work in ways that most people do, but the people I love and care about, who do things for me, work like normal people. So when people say to me, why do you work all the time, well, I work because I have a work ethic. I grew up in a house full of people that went to work every day, and they had two weeks of vacation a year, maybe, and that's how I know people go to work. And when I was doing theater, that's how I worked. I was rehearsing a play, doing a play, and auditioning for a play all the time. People who work for me can go work for other people when I'm not working, but I'd rather have them around me because I enjoy their company, and hopefully they enjoy mine.

My tastes in certain things have changed. I still like fried chicken and turnip greens, but I like caviar too. I know what a blini is now; it's a little buckwheat pancake served with smoked salmon or sour cream and caviar. I still like to dress well. My mom taught me how to take care of my clothes when I was growing up. I tend to wear fine clothes now, finer clothes, and I take care of them. When I get tired of them, I give them to my friends; they like them too. But I like to think of myself as the same guy. I have the same friends I had when I was jumping the turnstile in New York because I couldn't afford to ride the subway to get to work. We pooled our money and bought one sandwich or four glazed papaya hot dogs. I still have those same friends. I play golf with those guys. I take care of their kids and they take care of mine, and we get together and eat and talk and ride together. We are the same group of people who were actors together in New York and who just happened to relocate out here.

When I go back to New York, I still hook up with those same people. I still tend to gravitate to Narcotics Anonymous meetings uptown, because that's where I got clean and that's where I found out I was not what I used to refer to as chronically unique. That's where I found out there were people who had bigger addictive habits than I did, who were in worse-off condition than I was, who did things I would never dream of doing, and who made me believe that I never had to use again and that I could still be a human being and have fun in my life. I tend to go back to those places and recharge my battery when I'm in New York. It helps me make sure my feet are still on the ground, and that what people there said is real, about being able to stay clean and have a life after what you thought you were doing when you were using was having a good time and having a life. When I got there, I had no time in the program clean, and they had ten years. Now they have twenty-two years and I have twelve, so it means a lot to me to be able to go back in there and see those people and know that they're taking care of themselves the way I'm taking care of myself.

ARNON MILCHAN

Changing Minds, Breaking Even

"It could be there is an assumption that Hollywood is closed to the black community," producer Arnon Milchan said to me, "and the assumption could be wrong. Maybe the club door is closed, but not by conspiracy. Maybe it's by disassociation socially . . . unless you get into that room, you don't have access. But if we hang out, we talk, and if we talk, we do business."

In a good company—one that stays alive—maybe three out of ten films are profitable, maybe three or four break even, and three or four lose money. That's what you need to stay alive and build. If you have a better track record than that, better than three out of ten, you're a genius for a day. And if you have less, you're dead. It's almost impossible to really be profitable. It's like real estate. You have to build and build. You have to recycle whatever you make into your next movie, and the production keeps growing up and up and up.

Let's say you want to do an art movie. If you also own *Star Wars* or *Spider-Man,* you can get the right theaters. You can say to the theater owners, if you want *Star Wars* you have to also accommodate this movie. You have to do a kind of trade-off with the guys who own the theaters. Otherwise, you can have a great movie and then sit there and wait for word of mouth to advertise it. And you can get wiped out in two weeks.

Of the white actors in Hollywood, there are a few guys and a couple of girls—probably five or six actors—that are on the A-list, if we define that as anyone who makes over $10 million on a film: Tom Cruise, Tom Hanks, Russell Crowe, Cameron Diaz, and Julia Roberts. Certain actors or actresses have become highly bankable not only because they are stars, but because their choices of what to do, when they take their $20 million, are smart commercially. Tom Hanks will put himself in what looks like a risky thing—he would do *Philadelphia,* or he would do *Apollo,* and he's great, but he's the guy next door. He's very smart about how he picks his roles and marries them with a director—with the right director. Julia Roberts is very smart. If you call smart being a star. Some people don't care. Brad Pitt doesn't care. He wants to do what he wants to do, and he tries not to be a star. I think Leonardo DiCaprio is looking for challenges. Among the black superstars, I think Denzel Washington is not looking for the easy way. With some of his choices, like the last one, he won the Academy Award. Denzel is in a position where he can take almost anything he wants. He turned me down a few times.

Out of those who make $20 million, I would say probably 5 percent, 10 percent, are really superstars. The black film superstars are Denzel, Whoopi Goldberg, Will Smith, Sam Jackson, Halle Berry, Chris Tucker, Martin Lawrence, Eddie Murphy, Chris Rock. Oprah Winfrey *was* a superstar. How come there are only two superstar girls? There are more African-American stars than women stars combined. We don't hate women in Hollywood, but somehow more stories are written for men. The women ask why; maybe it's because men write them. I've done so many movies with women, from *City of Angels* to *Sommersby* to just now *Life, Or Something Like It,* but I'm in a minority in that way, because most studios want the guy movies—blow up some buildings and cars and do hocus-pocus and special effects. So black women have the feeling that there is both a thing against women here and a racial thing against them.

I guess all combined, there are maybe ten people, twelve people, that I would say yes to anything they want. Will Smith is one of them. I have a story about Will. Many years ago, a movie was presented to us with Debra Winger, and I think they wanted Jack Nicholson at the time. It was about artificial insemination, and I said, hmm, interesting. A girl wants to know who her father is 'cause her mom tells her she was conceived through artificial insemination. I thought it would be cool to do that with an African-American woman and a white guy. And we called Whoopi Goldberg and did a movie called *Made in America.* There was a kid in it called Will Smith. I had met him when he was doing a scene from *Fresh Prince of Bel-Air,* with Quincy Jones. I walked over to Will and I said, God, I like you—I don't know you, but I like you. And I said, you're gonna be a movie star one day. A few months later, Fred Schepisi called me and said, there is a movie I wanna do so badly—it's a play I just saw, called *Six Degrees of Separation.* And I said, on one condition—Will Smith is gonna star; otherwise, we're gonna lose money. He said, who is Will Smith? I said, I'm gonna introduce you. But you should know before, I'm not writing a check unless Will is in the movie. And Will established right off the bat that he can act. He was fantastic. After that, he could do *Independence Day* and *Men in Black* and anything he wants. But I didn't think to myself, oh, I'm talking to an African-American actor. For me it was, oh, I like this guy. Most people I know think this way in our business—they think about the part before they think about whether someone is white or black.

For example, with *Made in America,* I was thinking, wouldn't it be cool if a black girl finds that her father is white, and wouldn't it be funny if the mother said, what? Like, white? I don't want white like we see in the movies. Like, *how* white? So it was so funny; cool. I did a movie called *Power of One* against apartheid and a movie I'm very proud of with Morgan Freeman and Ashley Judd, called *High Crimes.* They'd probably never allow this one in South Africa, but it's okay. We had to make the decision should it be a black guy or a white guy? No, we thought; it's about who is a good actor, who could be a good cool thing to be with Ashley.

I was going to do a movie called *The Negotiator.* So we get the screenplay, and Sylvester Stallone is attached. We liked F. Gary Gray. I think he did only two movies before that. Anyway, we liked Gary and Stallone. Stallone wanted the other guy, the negotiator, to be a girl, and didn't like the director, and I thought, hmm, we have to make a decision. We decided instead of Stallone to hire Samuel Jackson, and instead of the girl to hire Kevin Spacey, and Gary Gray directed it.

To my surprise, at the outset there was friction between Sam and Gary Gray. And I said, I can't believe it. It's two African Americans. One is directing and one is acting. What's wrong with them? So I tell them, the other day two friends of mine were fighting on a tennis court and they're both Israelis, and I said, what are you doing? What a bleeping Israeli thing you're doing to me. So I went to Samuel Jackson and I said, what's going on here? He said, oh, he doesn't listen to me, he's too da-da-da. And I went to Gary and said, what's going on? Is that like a black thing you're doing, or a Jewish thing, or what is going on? It's a territorial thing. Now, the territorial thing was between actors; it wasn't about black and white. One was Jackson and one was just getting his way, was not asking for advice. So even when I was playful, it never dawned on me, there was never a thought of black and white. Never a thought. When I did *A Time to Kill,* with Sam Jackson, it wasn't just about a black man; it was about a father who wants to avenge the rape of his daughter. The movie was shot because it was written by John Grisham and it had an African-American background. So again, it wasn't a racial thing. In that scene in court at the end—five minutes of twenty years of my work—there's the line "Do they deserve to die?" And Carl Lee Hailey, Sam's character, says,

"Yes, they deserve to die. I hope they burn in hell!" That was the highlight of my product reel.

Many black people say Hollywood is racist, but why is it that when we did *Power of One*, which is a very good movie, it didn't do well in this country and it did some good business in other countries? Someone said, oh, the Americans. They only care about the blacks in their country; they couldn't care less what happened in Africa; the African Americans in America are racist against blah, blah, blah. The movie tested fantastic in America, but I couldn't get anybody to come to the theaters.

I'm not defending Hollywood. But I found a lot of French actors who say that Hollywood is racist because practically no Frenchman can get a part on account of their accent. I've found that, with the exception of Arnold Schwarzenegger, nobody with a German accent can get a part. It's an endless thing. But how far do we want to take this? Isn't Dick Parsons the head of the greatest conglo, AOL Time Warner? Isn't Colin Powell secretary of state? I think when people are upset that they're not doing well, they find a million reasons. Do I think that socially there is no discrimination? No. I think there is. Of course there is racial discrimination. I am Jewish; I know there are problems.

When Sam Jackson was cast in the leading role of *The Negotiator*, I was thinking of him first as an actor, not as a black man. When Morgan Freeman was cast in the lead in *High Crimes*, I wasn't thinking of him as a black man. And the great Whoopi Goldberg actually fell in love and went to bed with Ted Danson, not only in *Made in America* but in real life. I'm not saying there is no racism. I'm not even the man, but I think it's not a black and white thing; there are a lot of gray areas. The issue is not so much worrying about audience perception and racism; it's worrying about the credibility of the story.

Here's an example. We're doing a movie called *Runaway Jury*. Will Smith was disapproved by Grisham. A lot of people say, well, Grisham is racist. No, Grisham is the same guy who wrote *A Time to Kill*. He's not racist at all, but what he said was, if you put Will Smith in that role, you would open an undertone of association, of what the writer's intentions were about the man against the big corporation. You would think, oh, it's the black guy, or the African-American little guy who's screwed by the corporation. And then the interpretation would be all because he's not white. And the thing is, no, it's not white or black, it's because he is just a guy and they are the big corporation. So the reason not every lead goes to bed with his leading lady is because when we get a screenplay that is finished, the writer has already boxed us in to a story. It's not like I'm saying, okay, we're having a nice day, I'm writing a story. If I wrote it, believe me, everybody would be sleeping with everybody.

In art, if somebody looks like a star, I don't care if they're white or black, I'll go, come here; I have a contract for you. Well, thank you; I'll sign mine in a little bit. We all like the scent of what might be a big market. We did a movie with Martin Lawrence called *Black Knight,* where we're making fun of the Middle Ages. But when it comes to the accountants, to the chief financial officers, to the people who are sitting on the cash machine, that's where the problem is. The Hollywood business community is white; the moguls and the people with the yachts and the G4s are white. I think you would find very few Hollywood executives who are African American. I feel the studio execs kind of look at me like *I'm* a foreigner.

I go to France a lot, and they ask me about American movies and what is this invasion of the French culture with American movies and American wine. I'm sitting there saying, how are we going to invade the French culture? Why don't you think you can ship as much French wine to America? You know what, your people want to see American movies and your people want to drink red wine. If you want to compete with Napa Valley, they're trying their best to make better wine than da-da-da. What I was saying is that it's all about what consumers want, and where the consumption is.

I'm building a company that does movies, does television, does sports. We own Puma, so I see this young girl, Serena Williams, and meet her father, Richard, and we build a whole agenda around Puma sponsoring her clothing. We built this thing around a young black girl who's just rising, and we backed her up. She went to play at the French Open in the colors of the Cameroon team. Now she's on the cover of *Time* magazine. She's a superstar. The Williams sisters are cool girls, and their father is very interesting and very educated. That sounds racist, and I don't mean it that way at all—saying the Williams are very educated, and like, why not? But when I used the word "educated," I was thinking of the stereotype for athletes, for young tennis players. The Williams girls study and they write poems and they're multilingual. Oh, they're phenomenal girls. I can sit there and talk to these girls and it's beautiful.

Some people talk like Oliver Stone, as if there's a conspiracy. They say the studio system is a closed white boys' club. But it's actually about money. Someone is making $200 million if they can afford to pay Denzel or Chris Tucker $20 million, so who wants to share that? I would say, first of all, people are too selfish here, so they don't have time to have a conspiracy. They're too arrogant for a conspiracy. It's not like they're meeting to share anything, so the arrogance is key.

I can refer to a meeting I had many years ago with Robert Redford. I was young, and Redford said to me, I'm not getting any scripts, and I said, really? You? No kidding. Height of his career. And I found out most people assumed that Redford is so busy, why even bother. We would always talk about movies without even thinking about him. I'm not saying that race is as simple, but it could be there is an assumption that Hollywood is closed to the black community, and the assumption could be wrong. Maybe the club door is closed, but not by conspiracy. Maybe it's by disassociation socially. Maybe it's about African Americans and whites not hanging out in the evenings, so maybe that dinner, or that party at the beach, or a long weekend where you'd kind of drink and watch the Lakers or something, is very white or very black, or very whatever. Like Wall Street used to be. And it's possible that last Sunday, when we were a bunch of white guys watching the Lakers' Sacramento game, what we were talking about businesswise were the opportunities between white people. And it's true: unless you get into that room, you don't have access. But if we hang out, we talk, and if we talk, we do business.

I was flying one day from Bora-Bora and I stood in the wrong line, and finally somebody was screaming at me and searching me and terrorizing me. Then it was an African-American officer who just said, you come here, and he did his duty with dignity, with gentleness. He asked me the same horrible questions, but he was kind; he was not screaming. And when I drove out of the airport, I said, this is a man who represented his country without anger, who did his job well. I called the airport and found out who he was, and I went to see his kids and his family and we became friends. It was just a gesture; it's only a personal story. But it's contact.

Will blacks be executive film producers in our lifetime? Will we see peace in the Middle East in our lifetime? I hope; I really hope. Would I have thought that Denzel Washington and Halle Berry would be standing there and we would be cheering for them? Would I ever think that Russell Crowe and Nicole Kidman would not win almost *because* they're white? I believe that we are on the right path. In 1991, I received a humanitarian of the year award. The Scud missiles were flying, and I remember two people came to sing "Hava Nagila" for me, Sidney Poitier and Harry Belafonte together, and the whole place was rocking. It was a very moving evening. I couldn't believe

that all these white guys are gonna sing with Sidney Poitier and Harry Belafonte. And I was thinking about Marvin Davis and the Carousel of Hope
Ball, which raises money for childhood diabetes; they're honoring Sidney
Poitier this year, and Halle Berry will present the award to him. I think a lot
is possible in our lifetime. It's not like we're surrounded by wholesome people who never did anything to get in the club; it's not like white people came
with a suit and tie and stood in line and didn't step on anybody. So blacks
will be part of the club soon. There's no question.

It is very important that Denzel and Halle, two black people, won the Academy Award in 2002. Never in a million years, when we say we need some A-list
names, would the name Halle Berry have come in the same breath as Julia
Roberts. Never would you have heard, Halle Berry's a star. And now she's a superstar, and the superstars transcend any kind of designation.

Audiences are changing their views now, with several black superstars on
the A-list. People didn't go to see them much before. We have to make money,
and we're only going to put these people in roles if they draw in the crowds.
If they don't draw in the crowds, you have to face it: it's business. That's when
I'm going to use the word "black." When a black man and a white man—or
a black man and a white woman—when black and white are having a good
time, like in *Lethal Weapon* or *Trading Places,* everybody loves those movies.
Everybody. It's big. If the movie is fun, it's also very interesting culture-wise
and language-wise if you have a white guy with a black neighbor, the *Meet the
Parents* type thing. It's not only about De Niro and Ben Stiller; you can do it
in any configuration. So I think the audiences, as time goes by, from *Lethal
Weapon* to *Trading Places* to all those Martin Lawrence movies, to Will Smith,
will be more and more open to these movies.

What are people actually looking for in movies? They're looking for five basic emotions. It's sadness or laughter or fear or compassion or a mix, or to be
dazzled with fireworks. The easiest thing to do is with the guy or girl next door.
In the minds of the moviegoers, the guy or the girl next door is blond and blue-
eyed. They are definitely not Mexican; they're definitely not African American;
they don't have accents. They're kind of cheerleaders, all-American. So when
you give me a screenplay with a black actor, say *Independence Day* with Will
Smith, I think, hmmm, should we do it? I think, well, are there enough fireworks and it's not da-da-da so people won't think it's only about a black guy?

So, yes, there are issues of race in films. But it's not because people are bad
or good. It's because there is not the deep-rooted kind of work done to open

the world, to open the consumer. The problem is educating the consumer. If they want to buy black and black and red and yellow, sure, we have it. There was a time when the consumer wouldn't even go to see Lena Horne at the Cotton Club.

How do we educate the consumer? That's a good question, and an important question. I think that maybe if Richard Gere feels he has responsibility for the Dalai Lama, maybe we should feel that we have also some responsibility, because we are all very wealthy, fortunate, privileged people, and we should think, yes, it's important to help the sick and the elderly and the deceased, but it's also very important to help the healthy and the living and the future and the kids. Maybe we should have a fund, a low percentage of our profits, to encourage filmmakers to make movies that don't have racial barriers or to solve business issues connected to racial problems. If I could find a couple of people to work with me, I would go for that. It would be a good thing to do. Let's fund some of these movies, and let's show that we can make money and do well with them.

I think Hollywood itself is a bunch of cowards about fighting things like anti-Semitism or antiblack racism. I think Hollywood has this righteous thing about honoring people every five minutes to raise money. Everyone has his charity or her charity, and I don't think they get their hands dirty in any issues. When they come into an event and take a stand, I don't see anybody sustaining or staying with a cause when the cameras are not on and nobody heard that you did a good thing. I don't see anybody giving something anonymously that would never be found out so that you could say anonymously, yeah, she gave. I think they're not my kind of people. I don't socialize much here. People here love gaining the respect of all of our friends. Everybody comes to nice events, from Michael Jackson to Liza Minnelli, da-da-da. That's good, but we have to do more than that. I mean, really, really.

I can't change the system, myself alone, no. If there was a place, a way to do something about it, yes, absolutely, I would be part of it, because I come from a place where Jews and Palestinians are shooting and killing one another and I want that to end. I want people to eventually be happy neighbors. I feel as sad as anyone does about this. It makes me think—and I'm not being sarcastic—maybe with all these organizations for helping people with different illnesses, from AIDS to multiple sclerosis to depression, there could be a charity to help whites and blacks to work and socialize together. Why not?

We get more right than wrong, so we stay in business. I want to challenge the idea that to stay in business, you can't challenge the formula. I'll tell you what I'm going to do. You go under the radar. You give them *Six Degrees of Separation,* you give them *Free Willy, Made in America,* something challenging like *Tigerland* or *Mambo Kings,* something outside the box like *Out of Sight.* And you yoke them together. So either the theater has to take them, or your partners are heavyweights enough to forgive you for losing money from time to time because it balances; the bottom line is cool. It's from the periphery that you can start to change. That's where I'm talking about that fund for independents. I wish I could start it. I'd like to say to a director, your next job is a love story and it's the next Halle Berry and the next Denzel. The butler is white. And the profit is green.

REGINALD HUDLIN

Independent Means

Director, producer, and writer Reginald Hudlin told me that "there's no one approach, clearly, to how the next level of change is going to happen in Hollywood . . . We always have to support efforts outside of the system because that's what spurs quantum leaps. But the institutional autonomy I'm suggesting doesn't necessarily mean turning away from all the advantages Hollywood has to offer."

Before I came on the scene, my brother, Warrington Hudlin, had made independent films that were aesthetically and financially separate from Hollywood. So I knew there were alternatives besides working within the belly of the beast. Not only did he make films, he addressed the problem from an institutional level with an organization he founded called the Black Filmmaker Foundation. For ten years he had been supporting independent film, before it was even called independent film, back when it was underground cinema. He and the BFF would literally drive around from borough to borough in the Bronx or Staten Island or wherever and throw up a sheet on a brick wall and just show a movie. So you would have these kids or adults in the neighborhood who would suddenly be seeing black films by black filmmakers for the first time in their life. That kind of grassroots work got bigger every year and helped create an environment for people like Spike Lee and myself to finally gain entrée—to gather the resources, the funding from grant organizations, and so on, to put together our early films.

I look at *Sweet Sweetback's Badasssss Song,* in 1971, as sort of the atomic bomb that signaled the start of the modern black film movement. And from that explosion, there were shock waves going in two different directions. The most obvious direction was the blaxploitation era in Hollywood—films like *Shaft, Superfly,* and *The Legend of Nigger Charley.* But then you had another movement happening underneath. You had Warrington Hudlin, Haile Gerima, Charles Burnett, Julie Dash—all these independent filmmakers, East Coast, West Coast—and they were all making really amazing films. The general public wasn't seeing these films, but they were important; they were creating a canon of their own.

Then the two strains crossed in 1986 with *She's Gotta Have It*. That was the pivotal crossover film, where the underground broke above ground. What was important about that film was that it was made outside of Hollywood and it made a lot of money. So Hollywood said, wait a minute. This is a movie that didn't cost a lot and that made a lot of money, and we could never make anything like that. The profit motive then demanded that these folks had to *deal* with black filmmakers. *Sweet Sweetback* had the same effect in the seventies, but they had successfully pimped that movement into extinction. They no longer hired the directors; instead, they only worked with two or three black stars. But now there was a new style of filmmaking that white filmmakers couldn't reproduce. So Hollywood goes, we have to buy these guys. Suddenly, there was opportunity in Hollywood. And I got one of those opportunities.

When *She's Gotta Have It* came out, I had graduated from college, where I had done a short film called *House Party*. It was my senior thesis, a twenty-minute short, and it's essentially the same premise as the feature, just kind of shrunk down. I had done a couple of other short independent films. I had done all kinds of jobs: I had taught at the University of Wisconsin at Milwaukee; I had worked in advertising; any job that would give me access to equipment so I could keep making small independent films. Then *She's Gotta Have It* came out, and it was, we're on!

I remember very clearly a party at Nelson George's house around that time. Nelson George has been the hub of black culture since the 1980s, whether it was black music, black film, or black comedy. For example, Nelson gave Spike the money needed to get his movie out of the lab when he didn't have enough money to finish it and Du Art was just going to throw the negative onto the street. Nelson went to the ATM, pulled out a bunch of money, and gave Spike a list of names of other guys, like the musician Mtume, and said, here are some other people who may give you money too. So Nelson George was a very, very pivotal character.

Nelson was also hanging out at this time with Russell Simmons at the Disco Fever in the South Bronx, at the beginning of hip-hop. A few years after that, Chris Rock contacted Nelson and said, I want to write a script but I really don't know how; would you help me? So all these movements were happening through Nelson. Nelson George is like Alain Locke in the Harlem Renaissance. Even today, he's still tracking the cutting edge of black pop culture.

So there was a party at Nelson's apartment in Brooklyn. Spike was there with this script—it was the Otis Redding story—and he said, I met with the studio, and I don't want to do it, but I told them about you, Reggie. You should give them a call. I said, yes! "Sittin' on the Dock of the Bay." I'm with it! I've got no problems with it. Now, Russell Simmons was at the same party. Russell was getting ready to do *Tougher Than Leather,* the second Run-D.M.C. movie, and I was sweating Russell to direct *Tougher Than Leather.* He was saying, no, no, no, my partner's going to direct it; I'm sorry. Now, I'm sure that Russell was looking at me, a Harvard-educated guy, not from New York, and thinking I couldn't have any real understanding of hip-hop. At the time, New York *was* hip-hop. There wasn't even a West Coast scene, let alone a midwestern guy like Nelly to point to . . . so I didn't look like the man for the job.

I called the studio about the Otis Redding job on Sunday. I couldn't wait till Monday. When I finally reached them, they go, oh no, we're not going to do the Otis Redding story. We want to do a movie with Janet Jackson and The Time. Now I'm *really* hyped. Sign me up! We did a deal for that and I wrote a script—my first professional script, so I was being paid to learn. The movie ended up not getting made, but it was okay, because I got paid enough money from that job to buy my own computer.

Back in those days, a computer was an expensive item—you could buy a car or you could buy a computer. I figured, if I buy the computer, it's an investment that will make more money because I can use it to write. And since the Janet Jackson/The Time movie had fallen apart, I decided to write a movie that I could make independently. So I wrote a feature-length version of the *House Party* script.

I thought I could make the movie in the *She's Gotta Have It* $300,000 range. You do it for whatever you can do it for. You beg, borrow, and steal. I had done that for the past ten years making short movies, so I was used to begging. I ain't too proud to beg.

Then I got a call from New Line Cinema. A black executive there, a junior executive, had heard about my short film and about my brother's work with the Black Filmmaker Foundation. We went in, pitched the movie, and they said yes. It was an extraordinary thing. Suddenly there was this huge opportunity. And we went off and made *House Party* for $2.5 million. The movie grossed $27 million domestically, not to mention international sales, three sequels, and other ancillaries.

Even more than any of Spike Lee's films—though Spike Lee really kicked the door open—what *House Party* said to Hollywood was, you can make a black coming-of-age genre movie like *Risky Business, American Graffiti,* or *Animal House.* The studio executives said, great! We *get* that!

House Party is based on my experiences growing up in East St. Louis, Illinois. I grew up in the ghet-*to*. If you go back and look at *House Party* today, it's like, wow, that's a very progressive film, compared to the kind of nihilism you see in a lot of hip-hop today. It's actually a movie about safe sex. That was the original impulse behind it. But it only reveals itself two-thirds or three-quarters into the movie, when Kid's alone with the girl and says, I don't have a condom, and they choose not to have sex. At that point, you don't think, oh, so that's the driving premise behind the story. You're having so much fun that you take it in as part of a movie that's entertaining.

The success of *House Party* meant a green light for *New Jack City*. That was the domino effect. Every black movie had to hit, because the success of one movie meant the green-lighting of another movie.

After *House Party* debuted at Sundance, we won two awards, and they added extra screenings; it was a huge success, and I literally had offers from every studio in town. We signed a deal and developed a bunch of projects, but the project I ended up doing next wasn't the movie I had planned on making. I planned on making a big science fiction epic, because my role model was George Lucas. The same way he made *American Graffiti,* I made *House Party*. His next film after *American Graffiti* was *Star Wars*. So I'm on the George Lucas plan! We presented our big sci-fi movie, and the studio was like, whoa! This is expensive. This is going to cost $30 million. We'll only spend $15 million because it won't make any money foreign.

We asked if we could shop the foreign rights for $15 million, and the studio said, sure. Forty-eight hours later, we had a foreign partner who would put up the $15 million. Then the studio said, we're not going to give away the foreign; this could be a hit!

Then we get a call from Eddie Murphy, who says, boy, that *House Party* was really funny. We should make a movie together. Never in my wildest dreams did I think I'd ever work with Eddie Murphy, because even though Eddie and I are the same age, he was on TV when I was a little kid. I don't understand that to this day. Why did he always seem grown even when I was little?

So there I am in a meeting with Eddie, and we're throwing ideas back and forth. A while later, he called and said, okay, I've got the script; this is the movie we're gonna do. He sent over the script for *Boomerang,* and I thought, great.

This is exactly what people want to see. It's a fun romantic comedy, no different from *His Girl Friday* or a Rock Hudson/Doris Day movie.

Boomerang gave people a chance to see a new side of Eddie, and that was sort of my master plan. Eddie is such an amazing personality, and he was clearly bored with doing Axel Foley over and over again. His success from *Beverly Hills Cop* and *48 Hrs.* had put him in a box where he was playing variations of the same character. When you're around him, you see not only the broadness of his range but the depth of his talent, and suddenly you get intimidated, like, oh my God, how can we get the entire iceberg on-screen, because we're only seeing a small piece of what he is. I wanted to build on what people love about him but expand what he can do on-screen. That way, he could have the kinds of choices that Tom Hanks has. I don't see anything that Eddie *can't* do, but you have to bring the public along with that notion movie by movie. So with *Boomerang* came an opportunity for Eddie to expand, to change.

We had a budget of $40 million for *Boomerang*. That's the joy of having one of the world's biggest movie stars as the lead. We got to have everyone we wanted in the cast. I remember one of the producers was like, hmmmm, this Martin Lawrence, this David Alan Grier, you think these guys are the guys? I said, yes, yes, I'm absolutely certain these are the guys. There were a lot of questions about Halle Berry, about Robin Givens, Chris Rock, all these people. And I said, one day people will look back and not believe that all these people were in the same movie. And they went, ahhh, you're trippin' on some black stuff now. Not those exact words, of course. But it went on to be a real milestone film. We made $130 million worldwide.

House Party and *Boomerang* are both beloved films, but for black people, *Boomerang* is the favorite, because it is our first aspirational film. It's a movie that says you can have it all. Most films about middle-class black people work on the proposition that you can be successful and corny or you can be poor and hip. But most people I know don't have to make that choice at all. We have no problem going from Bach to James Brown to Eric B. and Rakim. So let's have a movie about me and my friends. And that's what people wanted to see. People were really happy to see the full range of black lifestyles on-screen.

Now, if you make black people that happy, then white people are going to be incredibly shocked. They said, this is not like *Good Times*. This isn't like *The Jeffersons*. What the hell are you doing here? What the hell are you saying here? There were a lot of interesting reviews. *Hollywood Reporter* said, this is like a science fiction view of black life. I didn't think I was making a political movie. I was thinking, I'm making a fun movie, and later on I'll make my own *Battle of Algiers*. Little did I know that *Boomerang* was the most revolutionary film I could make. I showed black people who weren't spending their lives reacting to white people. They were completely comfortable and happy, not walking about complaining about the white man. They have a self-contained black world in the film, and white people were offstage. I think it shocked and offended the studio executives on levels they did not understand. Turns out some white people would rather be despised than ignored.

But it didn't shock the general audience. While it was not one of Eddie's biggest movies, it was still very successful, especially given the bold new direction for Eddie. The movie had enormous crossover appeal. It continues to be an incredibly successful rental. We're getting ready to come out with a deluxe DVD with commentary and extra scenes.

I'd love to make five more movies like *Boomerang*. But when you try to make that kind of movie in Hollywood, they don't want to make it. They go, there's no market for that, or you can make it, but for $6 million. And you say, look. I'm not trying to make a movie that's going to gross $20 million. I'm trying to make a movie that's going to make $100 million, so you need to put resources behind me. And you know what? I'm not a first-time filmmaker. You need to pay me what my white counterparts get. And they go, well, but it's just one of those black movies, and to them it doesn't make a difference whether you're a first-time filmmaker or you've been making movies for ten years, because they don't understand the subtle nuances in how you show that culture.

I make movies for a living, which is something very few people on the planet get a chance to do. On top of that, I get to make the movies I want to make. Even in a privileged class, I'm in an especially privileged position. So when I say that of course I've experienced racism in Hollywood, I say that within the context of a very comfortable life. Not that my comfort negates the inequities I've experienced, but I realize that others before me have suffered police dogs and fire hoses to afford me my success.

I guess the most tangible way of measuring racism is if you are denied opportunities because of your race. Am I given the same opportunities as my white peers? If you measure it by that standard, then, yes, I have encountered prejudice—less racism, more prejudice. It's unfortunate that the word "prejudice" has kind of gone out of style, because it's such a really good, specific word.

Racism is the old-fashioned Klansman: "I hate you niggers!" That's just cornball. That kind of old-fashioned racism is slowly being wiped out in this country. There will always be pockets of ignorance, whether in Boston or down South. Those people are those people. But prejudice means you don't necessarily hate black people. You may have black friends. You may have no particular feeling one way or the other toward the ethnic group as a whole. But when it comes to having two people interviewing for a job, and they're both equally unqualified, let's just say—which is more likely the case, particularly in Hollywood—and you say, which unqualified person do I hire? If you go, I've just got a feeling about this guy, 'cause I'm going with my gut, well, that refers to comfort level. And lots of times what makes up your consciousness of comfort falls back on things that aren't necessarily grounded in reality. That's where prejudice kicks in.

The studio system—the permanent government of Hollywood, the agents, the managers, the studio executives—is a hard business for black folk to break into, because the skill set that is required to do that is very complicated. On the one hand, you have to hang out with these agents and drink and go whitewater rafting and do all this kind of assimilationist activity, where you have to feel sincerely comfortable in that mix. At the same time, you have to have a level of aggressiveness that is required to make it in the business, period. Black or white, you have to be a shit starter, a driving personality. And that kind of aggressive personality, when executed by a black person, can be very scary and intimidating to white people. But without that, you're not going to make it.

As if balancing those two weren't enough, you'd better be on top of the current trends and personalities in black culture, because your white bosses expect you to have all that down cold. But if you have all this assimilationist skill with whites, then you aren't necessarily listening to the new Wu Tang record. And the black cultural landscape is so vast! You've got to have the kind of bohemian black thing covered; you've got to have the ghetto black thing covered; and stay up on all the white stuff that all your white colleagues know. So balancing those three things is really, really hard.

To top it all off, to get "into" Hollywood, you usually take a free job. You take an internship. You work in a mail room at a talent agency. So you're graduating from a very expensive school, you've got all these loans, maybe you have a law degree, and you're going to start in a mail room? Your mama and daddy are going, what? *What?* I don't *think* so.

Other ethnicities in Hollywood had the option of assimilating into Wasp culture. That's part of the whole appeal of California to the American imagination. What America represents to the rest of the world is what Los Angeles is to America. It's a place where you can remake yourself and make dreams come true. But black people don't have the racial mobility that comes from getting a nose job, a name change, and passing—although many have tried. We've got to plant our flag where we stand and make it work.

It's unfortunate that we don't have a *Trading Places*–type situation where we take drug dealers and hustlers and put them in Hollywood. I think they would charm everybody. A lot of these guys are very charismatic, and they're brilliant entrepreneurs. They know how to go with their gut; they know how to make quick decisions; they know how to be ruthless. I think they'd do great in Hollywood. I think we're missing out on a tremendous talent pool that is just made for this place.

In Hollywood, the worst thing you can do is be first. People would much rather be second than be first. In fact, they'd rather pay twice as much to be second. When you come with an original idea, you're just causing problems. They don't know how to market it. How much do you spend making an original idea if you're not sure of the market?

It's easier if you just make the same movie over and over again. It's not a racial thing; it's a genre thing. I'm still scheming to get a proper budget for that science fiction film. I'd love to make an action movie. But I'm pegged as the funny guy. They have no idea how much violence is in me! I can't wait to blow something up. Please!

The next evolutionary step in black film will occur when black filmmakers, or black film executives or entrepreneurs, put together a bunch of money and start green-lighting movies on their own. Hollywood didn't wake up and say, hey, we should make black films. The success of movies like *She's Gotta Have It* and *Hollywood Shuffle* inspired them to move into that arena. In the same way, black film as a business won't be taken seriously until we show and prove that it is a smart business move. We have to do it on our own, and then Hollywood will follow. That's the nature of how the town works. The money can come from anywhere, but it's on us. There's nothing in the nature of the system to make that kind of radical change on its own.

But if someone says investing in the movie business is a crazy thing to do, I can't say, oh no, it makes sense. It *is* a crazy thing to do. If someone says, I'd rather do real estate, I go, you know what? I'm doing real estate too. Money you invest in the movie business is money you're willing to lose and never see again. It's like Vegas. Don't bet what you can't kiss good-bye and never care twice about. Unlike the record business, which has relatively cheap barriers of entry, the film business has very high barriers of entry. And the vertical integration of the movie business in the last ten years makes it foreboding for that kind of wildcatter entrepreneurship.

Today you have people who own movie theaters who also own movie studios who also own the home video chains who also own networks who also own cable stations, so they make a piece of product and they can exploit it at every point on the food chain. They make money no matter what. Look at a company like DreamWorks, which is extremely well financed. Then magazine articles speculate about whether DreamWorks can make it if it's just a movie studio. Gee whiz! I'm not worried about DreamWorks; they're clearly doing great. But that's the kind of financial environment we live in, where it can be very scary for that kind of seat-of-your-pants, roll-of-the-dice investment. That said, scared money don't make money. And clearly, there's a huge opportunity waiting for someone to exploit. There is the right business approach to doing that kind of entrepreneurship, where you can win big. I am certain, because I've been working on it myself.

There is a lot of cash out here. The trick is to put together the right plan with the right people. And it's hard to do, because my full-time job is very demanding. I've got movie projects, I have television projects; I'm doing lots of things as a creative person. At the same time, I can't just be a creative person. I have to have my business hat on too—not just in what I do, making sure I make movies that are going to be profitable, but also building an institution. I can't keep asking permission. So I have to do two things. I just sleep less.

For me, a black film is a film by a black filmmaker. In other words, a film with an all-black cast with a white filmmaker is a white film because it's defined by a white sensibility. Conversely, my movie *Serving Sara,* which stars Matthew Perry and Elizabeth Hurley, is a black movie because it's my view on those characters in that world. I think black folk have some interesting things to say about white people too, and people need to hear it. It's very healthy.

There are white directors whose work I admire who have made films about a black subject and it's the worst movie they ever made. Despite the fact that they're enormously gifted filmmakers, they weren't the right person for the job. Ironically, it's easier for a black filmmaker to do a film on a white subject, because we live in the white world all the time. We know *your* stuff. But it's rare that the white filmmaker has enough knowledge of black society, of black culture, to successfully make the most out of that film.

The ideal is when films are judged by their content *and* profitability. Is it a good or a bad movie? That's all that matters. "Black film" isn't really even a genre, like horror or romance. Race itself is a social construct. And the more people realize that and just let it go, the healthier we'll all be. It could take a hundred years. Derek Bell says race will never go away. He may be right.

The success of Halle Berry and Denzel Washington certainly helps black actors, which is great, because ultimately Hollywood is driven by star power. When Halle and Denzel won, we as a people hadn't felt that good since Joe Louis beat Max Schmeling. Obviously, Denzel had been denied for way, way too long. Julia Roberts said it very well: he should have two or three Oscars by now. And if you look at the month after Halle and Denzel won the Academy Award, you see a very interesting phenomenon. That night, you had three black actors get Oscars—Sidney, Halle, and Denzel. But that same weekend, *Blade 2* opened, with Wesley Snipes. Number one, $33 million. Just him on the poster. The following month, every weekend, the number one movie had a black costar. You had *Panic Room,* with Forest Whitaker costarring with Jodie Foster; *High Crimes,* with Morgan Freeman and Ashley Judd; and *Changing Lanes,* with Sam Jackson and Ben Affleck.

For the black director, though, the question is, will we get access to these stars who in many cases got their start in black films that we directed? Everyone wants Scorsese and De Niro to work together—oh, that's a perfect pair; whenever they're together, magic happens. But unlike white teams, it's hard for black directors to keep working with black stars, because when that black star becomes successful, the studio executives, the agents who are managing all these people, advise them not to.

This is a town that is driven by fear and insecurity. The town plays on that, and if you're just getting some real money in your pocket, while your white peers have been getting paid and performing great parts for years, you don't want to blow it. Maybe you have the enlightened self-interest to say, but this person is going to make the best movie for me. But then you have all these forces around that say, no, that's *not* the best choice for you. They tell you that if you have a black director, you're going to have a smaller production budget, which means you're not going to get your usual fee and you're going to have a smaller marketing budget, which means the film is going to fail. You're going to go backward. It's not your fault, they tell you; it's not anyone's fault. It's the invisible hand of capitalism at work. So it's hard for people to take that risk. It's hard for them to see that this risk is not an act of charity but is the best thing for their career. And it's hard for them, even if seeing that, to step out there and say, okay, I'm going to bet on this person despite the advice of everyone around me. It's a very scary thing.

Eddie Murphy did that for me with *Boomerang*. Samuel L. Jackson did it for me with *The Great White Hype*. Sam has done it for a lot of people. Whether it's John Singleton or Kasi Lemmons, Sam's willingness to support black film is just incredibly laudable. For Denzel to back Antoine Fuqua in *Training Day* was an amazing thing. Look at the results: a film that got two Academy Award nominations for its two stars, the black and the white star. That's extraordinary, and it was a great break for Antoine, who did a fantastic job with the visuals and performances in the film.

One great model in some ways is Ang Lee, who did all these wonderful films about the Asian-American experience as an independent in Hollywood. He made a wide variety of films, like *The Ice Storm,* which is a mesmerizing movie about white suburbanites in Connecticut. And then he came back with the hard-core red, black, and green equivalent movie about Asian culture, *Crouching Tiger, Hidden Dragon*—a movie that makes no intellectual or cultural compromise and still took in $120 million in the United States alone. So maybe that's one approach.

So often Hollywood "experts" claim that black films don't have crossover appeal. It's ridiculous. What does that mean? Do Merchant Ivory films have crossover appeal? They appeal to a very specific niche audience. The fact is, probably if you look at the profitability, black films make more money than Merchant Ivory films. I'm glad that Merchant Ivory films exist, and I'm glad that "black movies" exist. But let's take a step back from the phrase "black movies." What does it mean? In Hollywood, "black" is only used in the negative. Eddie Murphy isn't considered a black star. He's just a movie star, the same way Egypt isn't part of Africa.

So black only counts in the negative. Look at *Training Day*—black director, black star. Is that a black film? I would argue it is. Definitions of what's black and what's not are very convenient for making self-fulfilling prophecies. Usually a film's profitability is decided when the movie is green-lit, meaning, we're only going to spend money on these kinds of stars, we're only going to spend this much on production value—which means that they're only going to spend so much on marketing. If you only spend $6 million on making the movie, that means you're probably only going to spend $3 million to $5 million on marketing the movie, so yes, you're going to end up making $20 million. There are no surprises there. That is a formula. And it's a profitable formula. But it's hard to exceed expectations with it.

If you look at the top ten most successful films of all time, they tend to be science fiction films like *Star Wars* or *Titanic,* where they had a big production budget. It bears repeating: scared money don't make money. So until black filmmakers have access to that kind of production budget, it's gonna be tough to rack up those kinds of numbers.

About once a year I have a get-together at my house of all the black directors in Hollywood—no agenda, no spouses, no hangers-on, no documentation; just us. It usually goes from seven in the evening to four in the morning because once we're together, all these issues come out, and people who didn't know each other, or didn't like someone else's films, suddenly get to know each other as people and go, oh wow. You're really cool. It's a very healthy, exciting thing. The nature of directing is that you kind of have built these camps around yourself and you don't necessarily talk to one another. So again, whether it's a Black Filmmaker Foundation event or just an informal gathering at your home, finally you have situations where folks get together and talk.

Berry Gordy transformed the music industry, made movies, and made extraordinary breakthroughs in so many fields. While our generation has achieved a lot, what we're doing is coming *up* to what Berry Gordy did. I don't feel that we've doubled his lead. Quincy Jones is another great example. You look at Quincy Jones's career, as an artist, as a humanitarian, as a businessperson. It's unbelievable what he has achieved in his life. Or go back further, to Adam Clayton Powell, who was an extraordinary minister, legislator, and civil rights leader. One of the many great things he did was help start the National Endowment for the Arts. Many black filmmakers, including myself, have gotten their money from the NEA. He helped make my career possible. I look at the achievements of the previous generations and realize I'm just messing around. I need to step up my game.

I want race to disappear as a barrier, as a stigma, but I want to retain all the flavor that race and culture confer. Look at Italian culture in America. Whether it's their cuisine or the Mafia or *Moonstruck,* people love the unique ethnic flavor of Italian-American culture. But at the same time, there are no barriers to Italian-American advancement in any aspect of American life.

Black Americans have the unique legacy of slavery. Even when we finally started making some money by the turn of the century, they bombed us. I'm speaking of Rosewood, Oklahoma, East St. Louis, and other places in our history where incredible crimes have been committed against us. That is the tragic hidden history of African Americans. Every time black folks really did get successful, there was a vicious backlash. So it takes a generation, as with the old slave revolts, to forget the horror of what happened last time and get up the heart to go for it again.

Black folk have so much history we've got to cover. But the problem is that the black audience won't see period black films, because for them, anything in the past is literally pain. There's nothing back there that has any kind of positive association. That explains why *Beloved* and *Rosewood* didn't do better. Now, the kind of period film that black folks did go see? *The Legend of Nigger Charlie*. Why? Guaranteed foot to ass in *The Legend of Nigger Charlie*. For every crack of the whip, there are two white people getting their ass whooped. You have to *promise* the black audience that you will get payback twenty times over for them to go see a movie like that. People work hard all week, then go to the movies to escape all that for two hours. What do they want to go see? They catch a beat down all week; they don't want to pay to see a beat down there too. They want to be shown how to whoop somebody's ass. They want blueprints for living. You've got to show people how to win, how to overcome. It's not like they don't want to deal with real issues. They just want to be entertained too. That's what I've tried to do with my career. How do I embed the message enough so no matter how entertaining you make it, the message is still there?

There's only been one great movie about slavery—*Spartacus*. And until we as black people make our own *Spartacus*, that subject won't succeed. I want to do it. The question is, who is going to finance it? This is why we have to stop asking permission in Hollywood. Hollywood makes decisions based on precedent. Most executives don't have any actual black friends, so they make decisions based on black product they've seen. This is why you keep seeing variations of *The Jeffersons* and *Good Times*—because that's what they know. If we're not going to get black executives in decision-making positions, we at least need to get better black shows on TV so that the white executives who will be making decisions will grow up watching these new shows and have better taste.

The New South, so to speak, is international. In the 1950s, it was thought that a black actor would not be acceptable down South. So you had movies like *Ski Party*, where you've got Frankie Avalon at the ski lodge, and then the door opens and James Brown comes in, does his thing, and slides out, and the door closes and the movie starts again. They did it that way so they could take that movie down South and they could cut James Brown out and it wouldn't affect the plot.

No one thinks like that today. Instead they will say, your movie won't sell overseas; they won't buy it in Germany; all the Japanese hate black folk. Again, it's the bogeyman of the international market. For years, up-and-coming black artists in the music industry, like Jimi Hendrix, have gone overseas, become famous, then come back to America. Today hip-hop rules in Japan, Germany, and Sweden. So the idea that they're buying all this black culture in every other medium overseas, but somehow in films it won't work, is absurd. The cultural gatekeepers are the problem. The distributors, the marketers on the international level, do not know how to take this product and sell it to these particular markets.

A lot of times it's not about racism at all. It's laziness, because when you have a new product and a new idea, someone's got to come up with a new marketing plan. Now, they've got four marketing plans. So when you come up with something else, they've got to come up with a new plan. That means they've got to work late. They may have to skip lunch. Nobody wants to work late and skip lunch. I'm not saying everything's some evil racial plot with people rubbing their hands together. Sometimes it's just people who are lazy, who don't want to do anything they're not accustomed to doing.

There's a studio executive who gave me a great story. Disney used to distribute its films through Warner Brothers International. Then Disney decided to start its own international division. The last film under the old deal was *Sister Act,* and the people at Warner Brothers International said, there is just no way we can sell this film internationally. Disney's new international division, the Buena Vista people, were like, come on; this was a big hit in America. Oh, no, no, there's no market for that internationally; you can't sell that film, the Warner people said. So the Buena Vista people said, fine. Instead of it being the last film in your deal, we'll make it the first movie that we put out.

The Buena Vista people believed in *Sister Act,* and it was a huge hit internationally because they were not closed to the idea that a movie like this could sell internationally. That's what I mean. I'm not speaking in a blue-sky way. The fact is, historically speaking, the idea that black films won't sell internationally is ridiculous. It's disproved all the time. And the fact that people hang on to notions like that, even though there is clear evidence to the contrary, is where prejudice comes in. That's where the institutional racism of Hollywood comes in, because that notion runs counter to the facts.

There's no one approach, clearly, to how the next level of change is going to happen in Hollywood. I think the important thing to remember is that the reason we had big change in Hollywood is that we went outside of the system, and we always have to support efforts outside of the system because that's what spurs quantum leaps.

But the institutional autonomy I'm suggesting doesn't necessarily mean turning away from all the advantages Hollywood has to offer. I think there are ways you can work with the system but still have a far greater degree of autonomy than we currently have in Hollywood—for example, the way George Lucas makes movies essentially independently. He's the world's biggest independent filmmaker. He takes that product through the studio system and takes advantage of everything good about it, but is free to make the movie he wants to make. So George Lucas is still my hero.

When you test a movie, you break it into quadrants. You've got older men, older women, younger men, younger women, blacks, whites, "other ethnicities." So you can divide a film's audience up a lot of different ways, beyond simply black or white. Male or female is as important a distinction as race. Older/younger is as big a distinction as race, sometimes bigger. What is happening in Hollywood is they are realizing that young people today have grown up without an Elvis, and that's a big, big deal. Until the hip-hop era, there was always a white interpreter of black musical culture, whether it was Benny Goodman, Elvis Presley, or Led Zeppelin. People "got" black culture, but they got it through a white interpreter. But with hip-hop, if you go to an Ice Cube concert, the audience is 50 or 60 percent white. If you go to see Snoop, there are all these white kids who know every line. Yes, Eminem's a big star, but Eminem isn't their only source of black culture. And Eminem is only cool because he's with Dr. Dre. For Eminem to have the proper credibility, Dr. Dre has to cosign him, even among white kids. White kids want their funk uncut in this generation. They have no problem going to see a movie with a black star, whether it is Denzel or Method Man. Even in Hollywood you have junior executives who get that. Not a lot of them. But over time there's a slow attrition of the old guard, and in ten years today's junior executives will be running things.

This is the hip-hop era, just as the 1920s were the swing era, or the eighties were the disco era. The negative side of the hip-hop era we're in is that the subject matter of most hip-hop lyrics right now slides back and forth between shallow materialism and utter nihilism, and neither of those two ideas is anything to build on.

There is a confusion between Afrocentricity and ghettocentricity, which is very unhealthy for black culture. Gangsterism is okay, kinda; it's just a stand-in for machismo and raw dog capitalism for these kids. But when you have gangsterism and it always ends with some kind of spectacular death, that's like, come on; you can't even dream about winning? Kids traded *The Godfather* for *Scarface*. And when your role model goes from Michael Corleone to Tony Montana, that's a problem. Michael Corleone wiped out his family to preserve it, but Tony Montana just got shot up. And that's what kids are into. Tony Montana. And Tony Montana's not a winner. He's a loser.

Until we get off that plateau and move toward other subject matter and get people to thinking about other things, we really can't move forward. But when hip-hop got bought out by the music industry, it quickly stagnated. So there needs to be a deeper social shift to move the art in hip-hop to the next level.

Too many kids don't get that there's a bigger win out there. But I understand how that kind of gangsterism thing comes about. These kids are Reagan's children. They are the product of budget cuts, diminished opportunities, and the glorification of wealth. When you cut funding to schools so you don't have school music programs, and kids don't learn how to play instruments but they still want to make music, what do they do? They take a turntable and go er-uh-er-uh, screw this disco beat—I'm going to manipulate it. I'm going to take the part I like about the record and I'm going to change it; I'm going to put my own words on top of it. That is black invention at work—the same invention that took the saxophone and said, we're not going to play a polka with it, *um-pah-pah-pah*, we're going to go, *bee-boo-o-o-o-o-op!*

These kids did that and then some—they made a turntable an instrument. They made an instrument where there isn't an instrument, like steel drums. It's black genius again, hallelujah, doing its own thing when resources are taken away.

At the same time that this innovation in music occurred, there was an explosion of crack in the marketplace. There are a lot of reasons why there's all this crack readily available; some of it, I think, has to do with the U.S. government. And these kids are going, gee whiz, you mean after all that marching, after all that integration, we still aren't equal? We still aren't having the same opportunities? Then what's the point? What's the point of getting that college degree? What's the point of all that? Because things still aren't fair. So if it's just a money game, if it's just about Ivan Boesky "greed is good," then fine. I'm going to be about greed is good too. I'm going to make a lot of money selling drugs. And that's what they did. They just followed popular American trends, in the ways that were available to them. Now, was it the smart play? No. Because when you sell crack, there are higher sentences for that than there are for selling cocaine, but if you steal from Wall Street, you won't go to jail at all. They're stealing in the wrong way from the wrong people in the wrong places. But I understand.

The dream really did die in the sixties. When they killed Malcolm, Martin, and the Kennedys, the idea of systemic change went away. People's hearts didn't shrink. People still want to make things better, and they make tremendous efforts with charity, whether it's Big Brother programs or donating to 9/11 or other things. People still want to give. But the idea that you can change the fundamental unfairness of the world has gone away, and I think that's really tragic, because if you can't even dream that things can get better, then things definitely won't get better. So we have to be willing to at least imagine it.

ALICIA KEYS

How It's Done

Alicia Keys knows how to get things done. "This world was based on racism . . . There's a lot of 'isms' I've experienced, but it doesn't stop me. And it won't stop me . . . I'm not into perpetuating stereotypes. I think we can break those stereotypes," she told me.

I have ambitions to do a lot of things. I have ambitions to be successful behind the scenes as well as onstage and in the recording studio. I started my recording career as a producer and a writer, like Quincy Jones. He's an idol of mine. My visions for my future include writing scores for movies and the theater, and producing films—doing things that might be beyond the obvious next move. I'm open to a lot of possibilities. I would love to produce a film about Angela Davis or Lena Horne, or star in a film about Lena Horne. I like Lena Horne very much. She's a goddess.

The people behind the camera tend to have the control. I'm not a puppet. I want to have control, especially over my own career and decisions about the people I work with. I've always claimed control over my creative work. I want to learn and know about everything that's going on.

I think Hollywood is more open now to our people, in terms of making it. In certain circumstances, opportunity is always open to us. If you're a ballplayer, hey, you can make it. If you're a singer, hey, you can make it. Now, if you want to be a doctor, hmmm, maybe. If you want to be a politician, maybe. But I feel that Hollywood is definitely becoming more open. And I think it's up to us to make sure that Hollywood continues to open the spectrum of possibilities to our people.

This world was based on racism. It's also always been a part of Hollywood and it's not easy to negate it, although it's diminishing some. Black people are definitely becoming more accepted. We're fighting harder and we're in better positions. But there are more fights to be fought. We haven't even scratched the surface.

In my career I've experienced racism, I've experienced sexism, I've experienced ageism. There's a lot of "isms" I've experienced, but it doesn't stop me. And it won't stop me.

In certain circumstances, for some reason, people tend to go toward a lighter-skinned kind of thing, and that's almost thought of as natural beauty. But I personally disagree. There is so much beauty and richness in dark skin. I don't know if some people get that. The bias toward lighter-skinned women is a form of racism in the industry. It does exist. I feel it does. I don't think that's how it has to be, and I will not accept that, no. Black men of all different shades have become superstars. I'm not into perpetuating stereotypes. I think we can break those stereotypes.

NIA LONG

Life Purpose

Actress Nia Long tells it like it is. "Black people generate enormous amounts of money for the American economy. The crux of the matter, when it comes to sports, entertainment, and music, is that we bring the culture to America . . . We don't know what the Midwest will come out to see, after all, and I'm sick of playing it safe."

I was born in Brooklyn. My dad is a poet, an educator, and a historian. He's a deep brother. He loves black people; he loves being part of the crusade. My mom is a painter and an educator. She wanted me to have the freedom to do whatever I wanted, whenever I wanted to do it—to explore the things that made me happy.

The word "Nia" in Swahili means "life purpose." It means recognizing that each of us possesses a divine purpose and that we are responsible for developing our potential. It's heavy to walk around with that consciousness, but both my parents were committed to raising a daughter who was aware.

When I was two years old, my parents divorced. When I was four, my mom and I moved to Iowa City so she could enter a master's program in fine arts at the University of Iowa. We lived in Iowa City until I was seven. I had dashikis and a huge Angela Davis Afro, and my mom was such a hippie. I was able to go with what was in my heart, explore acting, and deal with the rejection when I didn't get the part. I knew that when I got home it would be cool, because my mother wasn't putting the pressure on me to achieve greatness. She just said to me, if this is what you love, then go for it. It was all about being who we were in this midwestern white corn country, and it was great. I have good memories of that time. I should make a movie about it and play the Fresh Princess of Iowa City.

We left Iowa for Los Angeles because my mom was planning to marry her boyfriend there. She dumped the guy but we ended up staying. When we got to South Central L.A., our new home, I was like, wow, we're in the ghetto. It was actually a lower-middle-class neighborhood, on 54th Street and St. Andrews Place. A lot of the gangs are based over there, east of Crenshaw.

I could deal with South Central L.A., but fitting in was a different matter. I didn't fit in with the girls whose big brother might have been a gangster or drug dealer or living the street life. I didn't fit in with the light-skinned girls that were more mulatto-looking, because I didn't have long hair, I didn't have straight hair, and I didn't have light skin. I'm a black woman. Both of my parents are very culturally conscious. I come from a huge, mixed ancestry; my great-grandfather was white. But looking at me, you go, oh, she's a black woman. You don't go, oh, one of her parents must be white, the way you would with a mulatto. It was difficult for me through high school because I couldn't really grasp who I was. I used to end up fighting all the time. The girls would pick on me because I was not afraid to speak my mind, and I probably spoke up too much at times.

It just got to a point where I discovered myself as an artist. After that, I was able to represent so many brown-skinned women who never before had someone they could look to and say, that's my life, that's my voice; God, I'm kind of like her. I know what she's talking about, because I'm not a hard-core street girl but I'm also not a flighty, ditzy girl. These women know I'm going to tell it like it is. I'm going to call it like I see it. And if it gets me in trouble, then I have to deal with the consequences. But I'm never going to sacrifice myself for anyone else or for this business.

Black women are probably the most intimidating species that God has ever created. We have so much historical baggage that it's become innate. It's in us. It's who we are. It's our essence. We are beautiful, we are smart, we are strong, and we can appear threatening when we speak our minds. We are also vulnerable, compassionate, and sensitive. Maybe this is why dark-complexioned black women have a harder time making it in Hollywood than light-complexioned black women do. Most white people can identify across the color line with that light-complexioned black woman.

The same imbalance holds between dark-complexioned black men and really black women in the availability of roles. Either the parts black men get are written for them, or whoever is producing or writing the movie says from the start, that's who we want. There are many white women in Hollywood with the authority to say, put him in the movie. Perhaps black women have less of a mystique in the white culture than black men, who are still the white woman's forbidden fruit.

Each black man who is a star has a unique position in Hollywood. There's one Wesley Snipes, one Denzel Washington, one Laurence Fishburne. And I don't want to say it's easier for Chris Tucker, Bernie Mac, and Cedric the Entertainer because they're comedians. They all bring something different to the table. But in reality, the black movies making $100 million are mostly comedies.

Chris Tucker and I go back a ways. I remember when we were making *Friday* and were driving to work. He had a beat-up Jetta with a piece of plastic on a broken window. I had a nice little BMW because I had been working for years, and he goes, girl, one day I'm going to be just like you; I'm going to have a car just like yours. And now he's done it. Made $20 million, and I say good for him.

There's a myth out there about opportunities for both female and male black actors, particularly in movies that aren't necessarily comedies or action films. There might be a few who are allowed in—Denzel Washington and Halle Berry and Sidney Poitier—and how long ago did Sidney Poitier deserve a second Oscar or even an honorary one? He was the first black actor to win an Oscar, for *Lilies of the Field* in 1963. But he's made more than seventy movies, including other classics and Oscar worthies, like *Blackboard Jungle, To Sir with Love, A Raisin in the Sun,* and *Guess Who's Coming to Dinner?* Halle, Denzel, Sidney Poitier, all honored at the Academy Awards. Thank God. It's a wonderful thing. It's a great moment of celebration for them, and very well deserved. But I don't see how that alone will change anything.

The people who are my friends, who I adore, whose work I support, we've sort of grown up in this game together, from Halle Berry to Regina King to Vivica Fox and others. I remember when we were very young, seventeen, and we'd all be at the same auditions going up for the same jobs. As you grow and you start to see everyone taking their places, it's a beautiful thing, but it's hard to all be going for the same roles at the same time. Whether you're black, white, purple, or yellow, it's harder for women. I am a true believer in that.

Men can be gray and balding and they're seen as being just sexier. In that sense, I do understand why there are more leading men than leading women on the so-called A-list. Older men can have younger women, and it's totally fine; it's sexy to a lot of people. There are very few movies where you see an older woman with a younger man. The minute a woman goes into menopause it's like, oh well, you can only play a grandma now. Women have a shorter time span in their career to get in there and hit it good.

But as important as age is in determining opportunity for women in Hollywood, black women are discriminated against more because of race than because of gender, in my opinion. Ben Affleck just did a film with Jennifer Lopez, and she's a woman of color. But black women are not immediately considered for those roles. When Matt Damon has a love interest, they don't go, oh, let's bring in Nia Long—we really like her work. They might say, well, sure, we'll see her. They don't want to say no, because they don't want to feel like, oh my God, we said no to the black girl. So it's like, oh, that's a great idea, yeah, bring her in, because saying no from the start would weigh too heavy on their conscience.

I think their racism is totally unconscious. I understand how it works. I understand the machine. I understand that it might make more sense to put Cameron Diaz in a part for *Charlie's Angels*. I think with the mind of a producer. All I ask as an artist is that we be given a chance, not as a favor or a mercy meeting or on account of a guilty conscience, but just so the game is fair. We don't know what the Midwest will come out to see, after all, and I'm sick of playing it safe. Why do we have to play it safe? Why do the studios give us only $8-million budgets when they know these movies are still going to bring home the money? Why don't we get the $40-, $50-, $100-million budgets for our films when they've been proven to score at the box office over and over?

People in Hollywood may say it's about money, not race; that they're not going to put black people in leads when they aren't going to bring in $200 million. It is about the money. But very few black people are given the same level of opportunities that white artists are. Most blacks in Hollywood are exploited, making films with a budget of $10 million and being paid less than $1 million per lead while our white counterparts are making films for over $100 million.

I feel like there's a committee that goes, all right, we're going to let these couple of people in; yeah, let them go in. I wouldn't call it a conspiracy, because it's not organized on a conscious level. The way I have to swallow it is just to know it's a subconscious thing; it comes from the historical events that directly tie into the color line issue. It's the one-nigger syndrome. It used to be the scourge of black writers, and it still afflicts the black film industry. The studio lets one in and someone else is dead; their career is over.

I'm a hardworking woman, and if I were a white woman with the amount of blockbuster success films I've starred in, I'd probably be making at least $4 million more per film. And I don't get paid $1 million a movie, so let's be real about that too. I think black actors get paid less because our value is deemed lower than it would be if we had our own artistic independence. We don't have studios. We are not running companies. We are producing our own movies on a certain scale; we have amazing directors and amazingly talented people. But we haven't pulled together to really be in charge from top to bottom.

If black people could green-light films—$100-million romantic films with two black leads—a lot of the problems stemming from race could be solved. There are so many intelligent black people that haven't had a chance to showcase their work, be they writers, actors, producers, or directors. We are the most diverse group of people on earth. We're storytellers from all over the world. It's about who we are in our entirety, not just about black people in America. We have black people from Africa, black people from the islands, black people from South America. We have black people mixed with Chinese coming over from Jamaica, but they're still black. They have a whole other recipe for soul food to share with us.

The creation of a black studio would make room for black voices everywhere. It will take finding the right person—someone who is educated, has leadership qualities, isn't racist, and knows how to deal with all types of people. I don't think it's a matter of having a black studio for only black people, where nobody white can work. That would be just as bad as what we have right now. We need to find a way to coexist in this society with equal amounts of respect and the same levels of opportunity.

Short of having a black studio as a point of embarkation, black actors can begin to change the system by saying no to really bad films. I know people have bills to pay. I know we have families to feed. A lot of us help our parents. I understand all that. But to be a responsible player in this business, you have to say no and hope that God blesses you with a big yes the next time around. If enough of us refuse to work in bad films, we might eventually be offered better-quality films.

There are those few people who are chosen to lead the crusade at certain moments, and they pass on the baton to the next person. But there's always a juncture in that relay where it's like, okay, stop; you're done right now. We're going to take over from here because we don't want to lose our jobs. And when I say "we," I'm talking about white people. The people who green-light the movies. I'm not prejudiced against white folks; I don't have a problem. But I'm speaking the truth about the system.

Black people generate enormous amounts of money for the American economy. The crux of the matter, when it comes to sports, entertainment, and music, is that we bring the culture to America. There's no longer pop music versus

R&B music. We are R&B and we are pop. We are everything. We have crossed over. And it has crossed over to us. That's what it boils down to, because our culture has been stolen from us and modified to be sort of the American culture, but it really has always been ours.

Being used in the Hollywood system is different if you're black than if you're white. In the last five years, I'd say, this industry has changed tremendously. You have the hip-hop world and you have the world of show business, or rather the world of Hollywood actors. And now we are all one thing. We are all commodities to white Hollywood. They know that if they put a rap star in the lead of a film, they're going to get not just that rap audience, but also the sales on the sound track. I'm not knocking the rapper who can act. What I don't like is the system. I don't like the way it's designed, because it's no longer about how talented you are, what you've done, or how you've proven yourself.

What happens here to people is profound. I've had a successful career and I'm thankful for it. But it wasn't easy getting there. The good thing about taking time off and stepping away is that I've been able to see clearly. When you're in it, you can go around in the same cycle and just be there and be there and be there, and grow only a little as an artist. Then one day you look up and you go, God, I was used all these years, and I haven't even reached my potential.

You've got to really believe in yourself and be able to cool yourself out and re-create yourself and come back stronger and better. You have to be centered. Otherwise, you can end up feeling like you've put in all that work and you have nothing. I try to continue to do the things that are good for me and the things I truly believe in. And then you go, well, damn, there's five other girls that haven't done half as much work as I've done, but we're all being considered for the same part because we're interchangeable. Oh yeah, Nia Long, she does great work. But if we hired X over here, we don't have to pay her quite as much and then we're also not putting Nia Long on a pedestal. She's still fair game; she's in the pool. And guess what. I'm not in the pool. I'm sitting on the side of the pool and I'm waiting till I find the right thing.

In 1997, I starred with Larenz Tate in *Love Jones,* a film I thought was ahead of its time. To me, it represented the artistic, bohemian, in many ways European culture of black love. It portrayed very educated, sophisticated black folk that we don't always get a chance to see on-screen. I think that if *Love Jones* had come out now, with more advertising and more merchandising behind it—the same big hoopla they give other mainstream love stories—we would not have disappointed anyone. The studio tried to rerelease it when they realized how great the sound track was.

What happens with a film like *Love Jones* is the studio executives go, okay, this is a great script, a love story; we're going to take a chance on this one. We're going to make it as low-budget as we possibly can, and we're going to put it out there and step back and hope that it sticks. But not only did *Love Jones* stick, it did great numbers. Had it been given better distribution, it would have been a bigger success. But when they do these films, they give us 50 percent of the distribution they're going to give *When Harry Met Sally*. It's almost as if the studio heads are setting us up for failure but giving us just enough success so we want more.

The reason Whoopi Goldberg has been able to break through lots of barriers is that she's beyond color. Whoopi is Whoopi. I can't imagine there ever being another Whoopi. I did my second film with her, *Made in America*, in 1993. They were torn between me and Thandy Newton, the black Englishwoman who was in *Beloved*. We're both good actresses, but Thandy looks more mulatto, so it seemed more believable that she and Ted Danson would have had a more mulatto-looking daughter. They hired Thandy, but she couldn't get rid of her British accent. So in the end I got the role, thanks to Reuben Cannon, the film's amazing black casting director.

I am here because God put me here; put this passion in my heart to do good work. If I'm just one of the torch throwers, then let it be. I'd love to be super superfamous and have projects coming to me left and right, but there are very few people who get those opportunities. I would love to be one of them, but if I'm not, I'm okay with it. We have to continue to lift each other up and be there for each other and support one another and really try. Even if we don't agree with the choices that we make, we are black people. We have to give each other love and not be so critical and not tear each other down and not be envious, even though this industry is set up for people to act that way.

I love what I do so much when it's good. I love what happens between "Action!" and "Cut!" They can put the political side of Hollywood on a ship and send it so far out of here that I never see it again.

Right now I think the key for me is to just be still, continue to read, continue to try to find things I like. For the first time in my life, I can do whatever I want. I get to lie in bed all day if I want to. I took the time to have my child and be with my family and focus in on what's important to me. I allowed myself the space and the distance from the business to get a better perspective on things, and I don't want to rush it.

I've always been the type of person to hibernate and then come back out. I'm not the type of person who's always visible. I don't want to be the flavor of the week. That's what happens to a lot of girls in Hollywood. They might get a couple of good hits and then it's over. In this business, as with any other, the only way to get higher pay or more recognition is to take the next step in a logical sequence; to work hard to get to that next place.

My girlfriends and I have often discussed the fact that as black people, we are not raised and trained for success. We are raised and trained to know how to survive. So we're coming from a place of, how can I get in here and make this work for myself? How can I get my hustle on? This isn't all bad, because it means we can overcome obstacles—and we have proven throughout history that we can prevail. But at the same time, when we have our first small success, the first thing we do is go buy a car and nice clothes. You walk down the street in L.A. and everyone's about their hair, their nails, their clothes, what kind of car they drive. If you're not careful, you can get caught up in that.

I love like nice things. I'm the first person to admit it. But I've made preparations for my future, for my retirement, for my son's education. My purpose is to make sure my son is inspired to reach a higher level of success. I'll be happy with that. I want my son to realize that he can do whatever he wants to do but you have to be smart during the process. You can't just go and spend all your money. The parents of white kids always have a stash for their kids. And they pull it out right when that child is either getting married or graduating from college. So it gives them a head start with life.

If my son says to me someday, Mama, I've decided to be a movie actor, I'm going to say, God bless you, babe, but you know what, you're going to college first. I didn't have a chance to finish school. I want to finish school; it's one of the things I most want to do. I want my son to have that, because everybody has the right to have an education. And college teaches you how to socialize with people. It's like life, but in a small, isolated community. There's a lot to be said for that.

Education gives you confidence, and we need that, especially for our black men. I think black men have had a hard road. My son is only eighteen months old, and every night we read and he speaks and understands Spanish. I'm trying to do the right thing. When he was still an infant, I took him to Trinidad. That's where my roots are, on the islands. Many of my relatives are getting old, and I wanted them to meet my son. He was too little to really know what was going on, but I just felt like he was blessed, like he had the kiss and we could go on again.

I hope someday to be a producer. You have much more power behind the camera than in front of it. But I'm happy with the sequence of events that has led me to where I am today. I couldn't have planned my career any better. For now, I'm working with writers, trying to find roles I believe in. And once I find a script I'm passionate about, I will capitalize on the relationships I've already established and get the movie made. I just recently finished my first screenplay, called *Purple*, with my writing partner Avery Williams. Look out. Here I come.

DON CHEADLE

Excellence

Movie casting is about "timing and opportunity," actor-writer Don Cheadle told me. It's about "who at the studio level holds the stick at the time and what are they willing to risk, because it's always a risk . . . I would like to see people instead of trying to make one movie for $100 million that makes upwards of $100 mil, make ten movies each for $10 mil that each make upwards of $10 mil," he said. "That way, you can still have some sort of content. If we give people the content, they will go see the movie."

The status of black movies and black actors in America is a microcosm of the country as a whole. The people who run the studios are predominantly not women and predominantly not black, or anything other than white. Most of the stories they connect to, and most of the ideas they can understand, are not from a perspective that is other than where they come from.

The definition of racism, for me anyway, keeps moving and changing. In a general sense, everyone in this country is a victim of racism—white, black, Chinese, whoever. While the effects may be more subtle for some than for others, I don't think it's any less hurtful, culturally, for people not to know about each other than it is for some of us to be cut out of something. Obviously, what goes on in Hollywood casting is different from the kind of racism we had at the country's inception. We're talking about an institutionalized ideology now. Today there's a pervasive attitude that black movies don't sell. I know people who have tried to set up independent movies with overseas financing. Often what we hear over here is that black movies don't perform overseas. But I also know that when producers go into their meetings and they have a briefcase and they have four movies, they don't even pitch the black movie. A producer who's nonblack told me that. He told me that when they go in these rooms with German bankers and French bankers and Italian investors, they don't even get into discussing how the black movie can sell. So then they come back and the numbers support the view that black movies don't sell. It becomes a self-fulfilling prophecy.

People don't want to take risks on movies they don't think are going to make money. They need everything to be a home run. Everything. There's this idea now of vertical integration, where they want the sound track, they want the video, the cups, the T-shirt. They want to saturate every market. It's basic greed.

I heard a very successful producer—on the $100-million level—say to a director on a film I was doing, see, the difference between you and me is, you want to make good movies that make $100 million, and I just want to make movies that make $100 million—and I'm going to be here longer than you! That's the prevailing philosophy. Get paid. Make the money.

Nothing sells itself. And if you're already thinking, well, it's not going to sell because the last black movie that you didn't try to push didn't sell, then you're not going to be behind it trying to push it. Everybody wants to do *Spider-Man* now. Everybody wants to produce in the rearview mirror. Nobody really wants to take a chance.

Now we come to the real crux of moviemaking, which is how to sell a movie. Again, we're talking about people who are for the most part not black, not representative of anything other than white males or white females, and who are instructed to target the demographic of fourteen- to thirty-five-year-olds.

If I spent $40 million on something, I would want to see a return. I can't get mad at people not wanting to spend $40 million on a movie that's not going to make a return. But I'd back it up even further in time. I'd say that America's huge conglomerates sprung out of companies whose profit base traces all the way back to the slave-based economy that established this nation's prosperity. So if we were talking about equality of opportunity, or even reciprocity—if we were talking about the way America really looks, rather than the way movies look—then there would be more work for black actors, directors, and producers in Hollywood, and for others of color as well.

Of course, there are myriad reasons why one actor doesn't get a certain part. If we believe union numbers, there are many more white actors who don't get parts than black actors. If I get turned down for a part, I can't attribute it solely to the fact that I'm black. But it's obvious that I am, so I'm sure that's always a factor in any thought process about whether I get hired. If they put me in a lead in a big-budget movie, they're most likely going to have to get me a white costar. It's got to be a buddy film, unless it's Will Smith and Martin Lawrence. Where they have a huge audience from their first film, they gamble on putting those two together and getting box office results.

I don't think that Hollywood is as color-struck for men as for women. It's very hard for black actresses. Dark-skinned actresses don't fit the classic beauty standard, so they're often overlooked. Light-skinned actresses are too light to be thought of as black, but they're not quite white. It's even harder for an Asian woman than it is for a black woman to be a movie star; it's difficult for most Americans to name even one. It's hard for women, period.

In terms of who has the power to green-light a movie, there are still no black executives who are running a studio and who therefore have their hands on the checkbook. And I know of only a couple of women who can write the checks. Now, if Will Smith or Denzel Washington or Eddie Murphy wants to do your film, you have the clout to go to those people who write the checks and it becomes a negotiation whether your film will get made, depending on the size of the budget, the genre, and other factors. Granted, there are only about five or six white actors who have the same kind of clout. So does racism play a part in that? You have to look at it in a more comprehensive sense. Sure, there's some progress in that three black actors have a level of say that's new. But when blackness does become green, it's comedies and black and white buddy films that get done, not a broader range of genre.

I think the two areas where racism is most apparent in Hollywood are opportunity and timing. White actors are subject to cultural stereotypes, but to a lesser degree than black actors. Historically, the stereotypes that have characterized blacks in this country and, by extension, black actors and actresses, have been far more limiting and unacceptable. As a corollary, good white actors have the luxury of being able to fail—or being in a movie that fails to make money—and still get hired for many more films with budgets higher than the one for the film that just tanked. That's not the case for many black actors. But again, it depends. If you were to be in a huge blockbuster and it was perceived that you were the main reason for its success, you'd probably get a few more at bats—black or white. As far as timing goes, it's approaching close to a century since the beginning of film in this country and it's only in the past few years that moviegoers have had the chance to become familiar with a handful of leading black actors whose films aren't spaced apart by years. It's timing and opportunity—who at the studio level holds the stick at the time and what are they willing to risk, because it's always a risk.

I guess that whether there's such a thing as a "raceless" role in Hollywood depends on your understanding of the word. My role as Cash in *Family Man* could be viewed as one of those roles if you were to look purely at how the character needed to function in the story. But Brett Ratner, the director, decided to inform the part with my race. The fact that Cash comes in the store and the guy automatically assumes he's pulling a scam, instead of thinking that his lotto ticket could be real, was based purely on the racist element. I did Luke Graham in *Mission to Mars,* and that character could have been any color. Yet, unless we progress very far from where we are now, a big issue would be made of the fact that the first person to go to Mars is a black man.

Not every scene in a movie lends itself to exploring the issue of race. For one thing, as a writer, you sometimes start to factor something into a script and then the story goes left, and it's like you have a whole other movie. I think there are roles, more and more, where the person's race unfortunately doesn't necessarily have anything to do with their function in the film. The issue of race per se is not a talking point in mainstream movies. You might want to write race into a person's role in the film, but mainstream moviemaking really is not about art or consciousness-raising. It's about generating money.

There's got to be a story. The need for a good story supersedes issues of race, white or black. That's just a fact for everyone who pays to see a movie. From three years of age or younger, that's what you get turned on by. Once upon a time, this happened. Oh! Then what? There was intrigue, oh, then he succeeded, oh, then he failed. Oh, oh, then he did this and that. That's a story, and we can follow that. We don't want to hear, "Now I'm going to give you a lesson for thirty or forty-five minutes and then I'll give you five minutes of entertainment."

I think Carl Franklin put it best. We were doing an interview for a BBC program and he said, this is still about dreams and illusions and fantasies: "In my dreams, *I'm* slayin' all the dragons. *I'm* the one who's rescuing everybody. The hero looks like me." Dig that. We're all at the center of our own stories and imagined epics.

And when it comes to casting, it's hard to get the right people, because good movies are about craft, art form, *and* storytelling. A good movie—and good isn't always successful—but a good movie needs to ring true with the fantasy that moviegoers bring to the experience.

Acting isn't bricklaying. If you have a skill for laying bricks, you can do it no matter what you look like—if they hire you. You can plumb a brick and put it on the mortar, and then boom, do it. When it comes to casting, you can't just say, you have to hire these five black people or these four Asian women, because not everybody can do it. Not everybody is right for every role.

It's not as simple as saying, we need more numbers of blacks or Asians. Yes, we do need more numbers, but if the stories aren't intriguing, engaging, and entertaining, and if it doesn't hold together as a whole, then just sticking a bunch of people in a product that's ultimately not going to be that good doesn't help either. In fact, it does just the opposite.

It's possible for black actors and directors to sometimes cover for individual shortcomings by blaming racism. It's an easy crutch for black actors and directors to rest on because it's there. It's not like we made it up; racism is a real, tangible thing. But you can't always pinpoint it as the reason why something doesn't get made, or why something's bad or something doesn't get supported. A lot of so-called black movies are junk. But so what? Most movies are not very good; most pieces of art are not very good; most CEOs of companies are not very good. That's why, when they *are* very good, they're exemplary, and we go, oh my God. They're lauded, because mediocrity is what's rampant. Excellence is rare.

Everybody in Hollywood needs to hire a no-man. Everybody in life needs a no-woman or a no-man—somebody who will sit there and when you go, yeah, they go, no, do it over again. It has to be someone you can't fire—someone you can't get rid of. You have to have your no-man.

As for the role that the writer might play in changing the racial balance in Hollywood, I'm also experiencing now how the writer is low man on the totem pole. They treat writers like garbage out here. There are going to be ten more of them on the script anyway. Unless you're one of the A-list writers who has some sort of control, and who they have some sort of reverence for, you're just there to get the first couple of drafts done and then they're going to change everything and your words don't mean anything to them anyway. It's very difficult once you get to a position where a movie is being made and they have to cast people and they have to think about how they're going to sell this thing. I don't know any writers who write into their script, "He holds up a can of Pepsi toward the camera and takes a drink." The scripts are just the templates—loose blueprints—and I see them get gutted very quickly.

The power, in my opinion, lies with the producers—the handful of guys who run Hollywood. The writers put their best foot forward; they write the best script they can. They can people it with whoever they want to people it with, all shades. Once it gets to actually casting the thing, then it becomes about "Who is available?" "Do they open a movie?" "How can we market this?" You green-light from what you know, and from the experience at the box office. And all of those things together don't equal more black movies or more roles in films for black actors.

I would like to see people instead of trying to make one movie for $100 million that makes upwards of $100 mil, make ten movies each for $10 mil that each make upwards of $10 mil. That way, you can still have some sort of content. If we give people the content, they will go see the movie. I don't think people go to see bad movies because they want to see bad movies. It's the dirty water, clean water analogy. People want something to go see, so they'll go see that movie that maybe ain't that good and they'll justify it and make it make sense, and if they get laid at the end of the night, then hey, that was a good night. But if people were to see movies that are interesting and thought-provoking and engaging and that aren't just popcorn and fluff, I think they'd appreciate it.

JOHN SINGLETON

Living in the Community

Director, writer, producer, and actor John Singleton says that his new film, 2 Fast 2 Furious, is a whole new thing. It's all about making money at the box office, he told me. "I wouldn't be in the position I'm in if my films weren't profitable. Every film that I make pretty much has been profitable. The bottom line is the difference between a film that is a commercial film—that can be shown in two thousand or three thousand theaters—and a film that is only going to get a limited amount of people who are going to go see it."

I call myself the first black film brat because I was able to come out of school saying, I'm not going to let you guys have this script because you people make bad movies all the time and I'm going to do it myself. If you don't want to make it, I'm going to make it myself. They were like, oh wow, oh wow, he must have something. And I did *Boyz N the Hood.* It made $60 million and it was made for nothing, for $6 million. With the success of that, I was able to do all these other films and was able to not have to kowtow or ask for anything. I was like, this is the way it's going to be, boom, boom, boom. But that could not have happened five or ten years previous to me doing *Boyz N the Hood.* If it wasn't for Spike Lee coming up and making a name and making successful films, or Eddie Murphy coming up making films that were wildly successful—films that made billions of dollars—I wouldn't have been in the position I was in. They kept the machine going. That's what all this is about, is keeping that machine going. And once you come out of favor, no matter who you are, you're out of here.

There's plenty of people that get in this business that come from different cultural backgrounds and that want to change. They don't realize what's special about themselves culturally that they can bring to the medium of film. If you realize what's special about you culturally, you can channel that into your films in a commercial way that makes everybody want to see it. Even if there are white characters in it, it's not much different; that's the thing. But a lot of people say, well, what does Hollywood want? What do they want? Well, who the hell is "they," you know? There is no "they."

Everybody talks about the five guys who run Hollywood. Well there *are* about five guys that run Hollywood, but they really don't. They're running scared anyway, about the next two films that come out. They could be out of here tomorrow. Those five guys that run Hollywood could be five new guys six months from now. It changes just like that. The whole business is about new blood; it's about new, new, new. Oh yeah, that's cool, you made us $200 million last week; what you got now? Oh yeah, you did? You made a movie that made $100 million? So can you do it again? Show me the money. That's what it's about.

I don't want to sound like I'm some conservative or whatever, 'cause I'm not. I ain't no Clarence Thomas. But I go on the old adage my grandmother said, that if you're black, you've got to be three, four, five, six times better than anybody else in what you do. Ten times better. There was a time in which you were ten times better at anything you did and the response was, we don't care. It didn't matter. You were a ten-times-better basketball player, and we still ain't going to let you play in the NBA. Now you're ten times better in your subject and you can excel in this country.

I knew—not to sound high horse or whatever—that I was the best writer in my class at the University of Southern California, and I knew that whatever I wrote was going to get made. I wrote *Boyz N the Hood*, and I said in the class, I deserve an A for this and I don't need to come to class, 'cause I did my senior thesis and this movie's going to get made. The teacher gave me an A, and I made the movie within a year. You have to have the attitude, but you have to be able to put the work in to back it up. My saying is that the black man in this country has no power, whether financially or anything else in America, but all the black man has in this country, if he can keep his balls, is his ego. But you have to have the know-how and you have to have the patience to be able to back that up with hard work. If Muhammad Ali said he was going to knock somebody out, he knocked them out. He would call the round. If you are about something, whatever discipline it is, whether or not it's filmmaking, whether or not it's literature, whatever is your thing, you have to be able to do the work and the blood, sweat, and tears, be able to back it up, be the best you could. That's a lifelong lesson. It's like that whole thing where the guy gets a new toy and says, I want to play with it, but he doesn't sit back and follow the instructions to put it together. I think there's a whole lot of people that are living their lives like that. They're not sitting down and following the instructions.

In my business, to get a movie made, you have to be able to have it on the page, but you have to be able also to verbally tell it and excite the people who are in a position to say, hey, we need to give him $20 million or $60 million to do this. And you got to be able to tell it in less than two minutes. You got to be able to say it in two sentences and then get somebody hot to do your movie. I won't say I've mastered doing this, but throughout the years I've been able to get down to like, hey, this is what this movie is about, and hey, if you want to do it, cool, and if you don't, somebody else is going to want to do it. You have to make it just so that the person, they have to think twice, you know, wow, they feel left out if they don't do it. You know, this whole thing is about what's hip. It's like you're hip one minute and you're square and L7 the next. That's what it is. It's like, give me something new. It's that attention-deficit society. You got to be new and you got to be fresh. We make Hollywood what it is and we feed it, and it feeds upon us, and that's how it works. So much money is at stake that it's a corporate decision what gets made, and so a lot of the big features suck.

After ten years of doing different types of movies, trying to establish myself with some type of respect as a filmmaker, I figured I want to do some films just for fun. Not every movie has to be serious or topical, 'cause it's much more difficult to get a film like *Rosewood* made than a popcorn movie that everyone in the world is going to see. If I continue to just try to make films like *Rosewood*, I wouldn't make any movies, 'cause those kinds of films are not necessarily commercial. But they're important and need to be made, so I have to use two sides of my brain as a filmmaker. I have to entertain as well as do things that I'm interested in. Financially, *Rosewood* didn't do well at all, but it was probably one of the films I'm most respected for.

I've been directing just twelve years and I'm going into my seventh film. I started directing when I was twenty-two years old, and I'm thirty-four, so I'm a veteran at a young age still. I'm cool now. Hopefully, I'll be able to do this for the next twenty or thirty years. My second career, I want to be a photographer, follow in the steps of Mr. Gordon Parks.

As a filmmaker I've helped people to escape, but I've put harsh reality in people's faces too, as a function of entertainment, with films like *Boyz N the Hood* and *Rosewood*. I love movies, man; I just love movies. In the sense that I'm going to try to do just basically fun films for the moment, *2 Fast 2 Furious* signals a dramatic shift in my career. If I find something that I'm really passionate about that says something, then I'll go ahead and shoot it. But I grew up going to movies as an escape, and I'm a big comic book fan, so it's important for me to try to do some things that are really close to my heart, that don't necessarily have to be based in reality.

There's a moment during the first race in *Fast and Furious* that's just an adrenaline rush. They're going at 140 miles an hour on a straightaway. In *2 Fast 2 Furious,* we don't use cars just as cars. We use them like spaceships almost. Every kid wants to be Luke Skywalker in a spaceship, but it's more accessible to get like a Celica with some hot rims, not with knots, and to be able to drive that fast, man. The way they shot the cars in this movie, they made street racing even more sexy to the kids. This is a genre of filmmaking that has been seen over and over and over again and that *Fast and Furious* put a new spin on. My mantra is, I don't want to do anything from *Fast and Furious* that the audience will know in *2 Fast 2 Furious.* It's a brand-new spin, a whole new thing. *Fast and Furious* was drag racing straightforward. We have twists, we have turns; you've got gravity to contend with, with cars hitting turns at 80 miles an hour and fishtailing. Thank God for computers. We can do all the amazing stuff we want. Still, what I'm going to rely on in the film are the basic cinematic elements of editing and the juxtaposition of certain shots to create speed and to create different levels of tension.

Every Friday and Saturday night, we screen new movies—art films, commercial films, everything. Posters of some of my favorite films are up on the wall in my little screening room. Like *Sanjuro,* a film by Akira Kurosawa starring Toshiro Mifune. And of course, *The Good, the Bad and the Ugly,* directed by Sergio Leone. I have the Italian-issue poster. One film real close to my heart is François Truffaut's *The Four Hundred Blows* (Les Quatre Cent Coups). This film is very significant for me. It was one of the films that influenced *Boyz N the Hood,* and it was one of the first films of the French New Wave, or La Nouvelle Vague. A lot of what I've done can be seen as having a foundation in the French New Wave movement. All these French film directors, from François Truffaut to Claude Chabrol to Jean-Luc Godard, Eric Rohmer, and later Louis Malle and others, were critical of the kind of conventional, formulaic movies that had come out of the French studio system in the 1940s and 1950s. They revolted against that system. They wanted to have more control, to be innovative and authentic. They carried lightweight cameras that gave them lots more flexibility in the way that scenes were shot. And even though they challenged the stereotypes of Hollywood films, they knew you have to tell a story to hold the audience.

The stories these directors told through their films often had autobiographical elements, had personal meaning for them, just as *Boyz N the Hood,* for instance, does for me. And the ideas of the French existentialist movement that had a huge impact on them are a part of my philosophy as well—individuals exercising their free will to make choices and taking responsibility for their own actions and behaviors. The way we talk about and analyze and theorize about film today owes a lot to the French New Wave directors. They gave film a new theoretical framework, gave us a way to talk about film.

The Four Hundred Blows is one of the first big films of the French New Wave, and it's always been close to my heart. I likened my life to François Truffaut's, because he used to say that the cinema kept him from delinquency. Movies became his passion, and they kept him from being a criminal, and the same thing is true for me. Movies were my escape from the environment in my neighborhood in South Central L.A. If I had problems with school, with kids or in the streets or whatever, I'd go running to the theater and I could just escape. Mentally, I could just go to another plane; I could visit other people's lives. And look where I am now.

I can make pretty much any film that I want now. Almost any film. There's a few subject matters that would be more difficult than others to get made. I do want to make something on the African slave trade and on slave revolts, as well as just that period of time, but I want to do it in my way. Many people have come along and done it and the films haven't made any money, so it's going to be more difficult for me to get something like that done. But that doesn't mean I'm not going to try to do it anyway.

A number of factors explain why black people didn't come to see *Rosewood* in the same way that they came to see *Boyz N the Hood*. I think that African Americans on the whole do not actively think about how history affects them in a contemporary way. There are a lot of different people who for whatever reasons are successful in American society and who continue to be knowledgeable of their history, whether they're Chinese immigrants, whether they're Italian immigrants, Irish, whatever. African Americans didn't have the benefit of making a choice to come here. We were brought here, and now they say that if you actively know your history, then you can feel empowered. You can draw power from that.

This isn't the generation that came out of the 1960s, all new, where everybody who was black discovered themselves. The sixties were the first time people were, oh yeah, I'm not Negro, I'm Black, and I'm proud to be Black. They made it hip, like, oh wow, you proud to be Black? Oh wow, that's kind of hip; I'll go with it. But it's not about being hip to know your culture; that's just the way you have to be. And I think that this generation kind of turns a blind eye to that. So it's much easier for a film that is right in and of the contemporary, like *Baby Boy* or *Boyz N the Hood*, to succeed. People can see those films and just walk along, look across the street and say, yeah, I can identify with what I saw in that movie, personally as well as culturally. They don't want to identify with what happened seventy-five or eighty years ago because they don't think that that's a part of their lives. But it is.

I had the benefits of coming along after Spike made a career for himself, after Gordon Parks did what he did, after Eddie Murphy made $3 billion or $4 billion for the Hollywood studios. I've had the benefit of all of these successful black people coming before, so that I could come right out of school and a month later at age twenty-two be shooting my first movie, *Boyz N the Hood*. I'm so happy that I went to USC. I was so young in the sense that I was having to try to prove myself as to why as a young black man I had a right to say what I had to say, and what stories I had to say, in the context of all these people who weren't black giving me a look that said, why are you here, even though they weren't saying it out loud. And my attitude was because none of my stories have been told, and my people come up with everything hip that goes on in this country anyway. So that was my attitude.

They would call me on campus a black supremacist because I would play NWA and Public Enemy in the middle of the campus and everybody would look at me crazy, but I enjoyed that energy, like, yeah, what the fuck are you looking at? Whatever. Excuse my French. I think that the fallacy that a lot of people, black or otherwise, make within American culture is to try to be American. If you're here and you're doing something productive, then you're part of the American dream. What is being American? Being American is you being American. It's the Egyptian guy that has the laundry. It's the Jewish guy up the street that runs the deli. All of that is American. It's the dude who runs the barbecue joint. That's American. It's so funny that it took me a long time to come to that conclusion, but I always was on that path. That's okay. If I'm admired and I understand myself culturally, and I understand where I'm from and I appreciate where I'm from, I can also appreciate and understand where other people are from without giving up myself, because that adds to me and I add to them. And a lot of people don't really get that, man.

Hollywood is racist, but America is racist. Hollywood is an institution. Let's put it this way. Corporate America is white-male-dominated. So anyone who might be female, or any other ethnicity or group besides white males, will all fall to the wayside unless you can make the machine continue to function and be well oiled and continue to grow. Unless you can make the machine grow and continue to function, then you're a cog in the machine. That holds for the film industry or any other industry. If you're not in this thing and you can't draw people and make people want to pay money to see your creative endeavors, then it's not the industry for you. That's how it works. Straight up. For studio heads it's like, my job's on the line, so we don't want to really like this movie because we don't think it's going to make any money. That happens for black people as well as anybody else in this business on a regular basis. It's the nature of the industry.

I think it's all about you making money at the box office, rather than a matter of race. I wouldn't be in the position I'm in if my films weren't profitable. Every film that I make pretty much has been profitable. The bottom line is the difference between a film that is a commercial film—that can be shown in two thousand or three thousand theaters—and a film that is only going to get a limited amount of people who are going to go see it. That's how Hollywood is ruled.

Not all of my films have opened at two thousand theaters. Some of them opened at nine hundred theaters, fifteen hundred, two thousand, but they make millions and millions of dollars. So I always say that if you make a film that is even moderately successful, it allows you to make another film, and if you make a film that is wildly successful, that means you'll be able to make three other movies.

In this sense, Hollywood's not any different for black people than for anybody else. It's a level playing field. I see this phenomenon now where there are more young black directors working than ever before, doing different types of films. You hire a young black man to direct a film, you get a much different vision than you would with Joe Blow from the Valley, who grew up with nothing but white people. It's hip-hop culture, and black culture fuels all pop culture, so the people that are in and of black culture, if they have their sense of the pulse and the rhythm of what is hip and what is pop culture, they'll always prosper. All the way down to the beginnings of syncopated music, blacks have always been on the cusp of what is hip and cool in this country, and Hollywood is no different.

If I had gone to film school for four years and never got a movie made, okay. But I'm not that kind of person. For me, it's been a level playing field. I would say differently if I could have any type of personal dissatisfaction with opportunities that have been made for me. But I can't say that. And I haven't had to kiss nobody's pale ass to do it.

I think this is the beginning of a great business period for blacks in Hollywood, 'cause in terms of artistic sensibility, there are black people making films, working behind the camera, directing, whatever. Still, black filmmakers are doing themselves more of a disservice than anything else because most of the films being made are just big commercial comedies. There's not enough people coming in saying, hey, we got to do this for the people. There's not enough of them. But you got to find a way to do it so the film has not necessarily got a message, 'cause as soon as you declare a message, people lose interest. You have to have a film that has a passion for the subject matter, and the political import has to be buried in. And the only way I can get that message out to other black filmmakers is by making films I want to make, like *Baby Boy* or *Rosewood* or *2 Fast 2 Furious.*

I was there the night Halle Berry and Denzel Washington got Academy Awards and Sidney Poitier was honored for a lifetime of achievement. This means that something has changed. It doesn't mean that Hollywood is just automatically going to change all the way over and be totally different. White America still has a problem with black sexuality as a whole, for one thing. It's like a fascination and a revulsion at the same time. That duality of attitude kept sexual innuendo down in *Shaft* —kept sexual content out—and on the other hand, that fascination got Halle her Oscar. Hollywood wants to appeal to the widest possible demographic. So they say, it can't offend anybody. We don't want to offend this group or that group, and that kind of homogenizes a lot of the product that gets out when it's done on a big-budget basis.

But I'll tell you one thing, that you're going to see change in terms of the modern films coming up, and I always talk about this. Most commercial films in Hollywood now are not all lily-white movies. They're multiethnic films. When they make a lot of money, $200 million, $300 million, they're multiethnic now. In *Rush Hour,* you had Chris Tucker and Jackie Chan. In *The Fast and the Furious,* you had Vin Diesel, Paul Walker, Jordana Brewster, and all these different types of people within one film. I think that American films are becoming more American, for the very reason that the American studios want to appeal to the widest possible demographic; they want to get everybody to come to the movies. And to do that, you increasingly have to have a mixture of people within every film, 'cause that means you're hitting all the different demographics within one piece.

Behind the camera is a whole other thing. You have a few people directing, but you don't have a lot of other people who realize that Hollywood is like a steel town. There's work in all disciplines, from sound to camera to just even clerical positions. People always say, I want to be an actor, I want to be an actor, I want to be a director. They're thinking about the glitz and the glamour and the stars in their eyes and the shine and everything. They don't realize that the nuts-and-bolts people always work.

When people in the industry say they won't green-light black films because they won't do well abroad, they're talking about a film that is all black and is a drama and has no action element in it. Is *Rush Hour* a black film? Chris Tucker is one of the leads. Is an Eddie Murphy movie a black film? Is any movie with Denzel Washington a black film? Yes, they are. What makes them different is that in each one of those films there's different cultural elements. They may have a black star, but there's all types of different cultural elements, which makes it a trip. It's so subjective as to what is a black film and what isn't a black film. To me, a black film is a film that is made by black people and that has an all-black cast in it. But that is becoming more and more of a hard prospect to get done, because when you do a film that just has a black cast in it, then basically you're targeting it just toward a black audience. And black folks are fickle. One week they'll like something and then the next week they're like, well, I'll see it on the bootleg or I'll steal a copy.

Boyz N the Hood crossed over, but that was at a certain time, in which hip-hop culture was coming into prominence within pop culture even more. Black people discovered *Boyz N the Hood,* but then a whole other audience discovered it, because it was a window on a world they hadn't seen. And now they've seen that world. They hear it in the music, and they see it in every rip-off of *Boyz N the Hood.* So I always say that you have to change. You have to change and evolve, especially within the entertainment industry.

Black people can green-light a film now. You don't have to make a movie for $60 million. You can make a movie for nothing. You can get your camcorder and your best friends can act in it. You can edit it off on a Cut Pro and you can make it for your rent money. I think black people will be able to green-light

Hollywood studio big-time stuff in our lifetime. It's possible. But by that time, it won't even matter.

I think the audience is ready for a black love story, for passion on the screen, with Denzel Washington and Halle Berry as the leads, but I think it'd be a limited amount of people that would see it, depending on the subject matter. It could be a profitable film, though I don't know just how profitable. If they would just fall in love and they were like yadda, yadda, yadda, with the dinner scenes and the romance and everything, then I don't know how many people would go see it. But if they were falling in love and going in the car and shooting at the bad guys and then they hop on a spaceship and everything, then it would probably make a lot of money. Tom Cruise and Halle Berry, the same film, whatever the plot, would bring in twice as much money. Julia Roberts and Denzel Washington, same film, even more money. But Tom Cruise and Halle Berry with the dinner scene, the yadda, yadda, yadda, no cars, no spaceship, you ain't making no money. Denzel finds his own rhythm and what he wants to do and what he doesn't want to do. He has his own way. He's manufactured the way that he wants to appear. Whether he gets the girl or makes love to the girl might be a decision he's made personally.

The pressure from people in the black community to make a film that helps our people is amusing, 'cause I walk on the street and people tell me, hey, you need to make movies, man, let me tell you what movie you need to make. You need to make a movie about Cleopatra and whoever Cleopatra was with at that time, not Anthony, not the Roman dude; no, he needs to be a black man. Cleopatra and a black man; that's the kind of movie you need to make. And I'm like, oh, man, you know, okay. No, but you really need to do it, and I got the script in my car. I hear that all the time. I do lectures on this, and I always talk about what is known as the oral tradition of African storytelling. Everyone has in their family an uncle, an aunt, a grandfather, a grandmother who can weave a story, who can weave a verbal yarn that can make you laugh, make you cry, that's steeped in history, and that goes all the way back to Africa.

But this business is not about just expressing yourself and your culture and everything, and then hey, you know, we'll throw $30 million to the wind. All that stuff about personal feelings and getting culture out and being able to say something, you have to sneak that into your movie. I don't go into somebody's office and say, I want to make this movie 'cause I really want black folks to know this. I don't go in there and say all that BS. I go in there and say, hey, this is what it is—people will want to go see this movie because of this and this, and this is what they're feeling, and this is what's going on on the street. Believe me, this is going to sell 700,000 copies on DVD and video and it'll only be made for this amount, and I think it'll turn a profit of about $50 million. That's what it's about. It's not about all that other stuff. It *is* about all that other stuff, but you can't come on like that.

There's the idea that a black studio will solve all our problems. But you know what? It's not true. If you gave anybody black, no matter who—even me—$500 million and said, okay, you can make any movies you want to make, a slate of movies, ten movies, they would have the same dilemma that each corporate conglomerate has with any other films. And that dilemma is the question whether or not each project they're doing has the potential to make a profit.

It's not my responsibility professionally to change society, but personally, I aspire to greatness, and it's something that I deal with all the time, the question of whether or not the personal aspirations I have for the material far exceed what the audience wants. That's something I've been dealing with ever since I was twenty years old—questions like, am I preaching too much? Am I trying to say too much? Sometimes I don't want to say anything. Sometimes I just want to make a movie and be like John Huston. You know, this movie takes me to Africa, this movie takes me to Europe, this movie takes me to New York, and I can party, whatever. I want to do that. I don't want the crutch of being the black kid that makes movies. I want to just make movies and be a maverick filmmaker, in that I say what I want to do and I do it, not because this is what I should be doing.

Let's imagine the NAACP says, John, you have a social responsibility to our people, uplift the race. To which I'd give them the finger. I'd be like, no, I don't. I have a responsibility to tell it like it is and make people on an individual basis make the decisions for themselves. And even then I have a moral responsibility to entertain, because if I don't entertain, my kids don't go to private school next week. But I don't want to do anything that will glorify violent acts—that will glorify negative social activities, like, yeah, it's cool to shoot heroin. I'm not about that personally at all, and I wouldn't be about that professionally at all.

REGGIE BYTHEWOOD

Action

Reggie Rock Bythewood began his career in the theater as an actor before going on to write, produce, and direct. But he is energized by a new role, he told me. "I never saw myself as a businessman before. Shame on me!"

I did a lot of acting as a kid. I thought I wanted to be an actor, and I went to the High School of Performing Arts in New York. But every time I pursued something I wanted, I realized there was a different goal to pursue. So after acting the goal became writing, then producing, and then directing.

When I began working in the film industry, I had a strong perception that as African-American filmmakers we've got to change the world. We have to use this industry, I thought, to open doors and change perspectives across the world about who we are and what we're about. I call it the Film Rights Movement. But I've revised my own perspective; now I say, what *I'm* about, not what *we're* about. We're as diverse as any other people. If some other black filmmaker wants to make people laugh at any cost to make a lot of money, that's on them. I'm not going to dis anybody for their source of inspiration. What inspires me is the desire to reveal our diversity and to tell stories that bust through the stereotypes.

The first screenplay I wrote that got made was *Get on the Bus,* and I loved it. It wasn't a situation where we could pitch to the studio, hey, we want to make this movie dealing with experiences in the Million Man March. When I went to the Million Man March in October of 1995, I had no idea I'd be writing a film about it. But it turned out to be a unique experience, and very educational, in terms of taking control of your destiny as an artist. We raised money—fifteen African-American men—and I put in every dime I had and we made the film. It cost about two and a quarter million, so it was very reasonable. Everybody got their money back and made money. It was a great experience and a great thing to have as my introduction as a screenwriter.

I tried to make the story very human. It could have been all about the politics of the march, but it was about love and devotion and loyalty and the passing of time and fraternity. I think a lot of people are tired of political stories, both white people and African. Even political stories need to be told in a better, more compelling way. The challenge I find, though, is going to the Hollywood system and getting different stories made.

Prior to *Get on the Bus,* back in my acting days, I had a small role in 1984 in *The Brother from Another Planet,* kind of a slave narrative in science fiction. I sat down with John Sayles, and he said that what he did at the time was write screenplays, then take that money and make the film he wanted to make. I was like, cool, and it always stuck with me. So I eagerly invested in *Get on the Bus.* It was empowering to put money into the film and even more empowering to see the film get made and get my money back.

We had a similar situation with *Dancing in September.* We raised a million dollars and made an independent film. Then we sold it to HBO and made more than twice the money we spent. Everybody made better money than they would have made on Wall Street. What I learned was that an independent film is great because essentially you are making the film you want to make. The problem is that at the end of the day you're shopping it around. You're back to Hollywood, saying, okay, I didn't ask you for the money to hire my cast and write the film and direct the film, but now I have to ask you to distribute the film. I was glad I had gone through trying to make sure everybody got their money back and made money, but it was challenging, man, it was a very hard process to go door-to-door-to-door-to-door seeing who would give me distribution. That was the process that really made me say, oh, now I get it! It's about being the studio.

There is a point of view in the Hollywood system that you have to tell stories that black people can relate to, but the people who are making the decisions on what stories black people relate to are not black. So, for example, in many ways it's a lot easier to sell a derogatory or stereotypical gangster story and have a bunch of brothers with forty-ounce bottles of beer in their hands and carrying guns. It's a lot easier to get that pushed through. It's easier to get a political or civil rights story told on the air or in the movie theaters than to say, there's something else; there are different experiences. That's the real challenge.

As challenging as it's been, and as frustrating as it's been, I think one of the blessings of the situation is that it motivates me to try to just push through and make these things happen. A recent experience provides a good example. I was sitting in a room with the head of a studio, on a project that I had assembled a superlative cast for—amazing African-American actors whom a lot of people know. These are people who are willing to be in a film that I put together, and an executive went through it and said, but here's a black face, here's a black face, here's a black face, here's a black face. The frustration on his part was that there were not more white faces in the film. This is a predominant point of view in Hollywood, and it's interesting that there's a perception of Hollywood that it's one of the more liberal places in the country, that they're progressive and wide open and all these sorts of myths. Hollywood has really become more and more co-optive.

So the executive goes through my script and says, black face, black face, black face, and he wants me to rewrite the script and put more white faces in. Initially, I had presented the script and people really felt strongly about it, and we attracted a lot of talent. It was very high-budget for what you would call a black film, but not high-budget for an action film. It got to be $25 million, then $30 million, because they wanted it bigger. And I'm telling my wife, man, they're really digging this script; they want to put more money in it. Then it gets to be around $35 million and I'm saying, okay, cool. I'll make a big-ass action film.

So then you get in the room and it's basically, "Reggie, don't take this personally, but to make this film, we have to make the lead white." And I didn't take it personally, because I've been prepped. My entire career has prepared me to understand that that's how it works a lot. My career could really use that sort of boost—to do a big action film like that. It would have been only the second film that I directed, and one of the few times a black director had directed two white leads. From some people's point of view, I would have made history if I had directed a film with two white leads. To some people, it even would have been a great civil rights victory for African Americans. But not from my point of view.

I have a need that stands outside of my career, and that need is to have a cause bigger than myself. What would be a victory, for me, is for this to be an action film with two African-American leads. Don't make it black; don't make it anything. Make it what it is. Make it an action film. And let's make this film hot. Let's make it all the things we want an action film to be. The film I'm talking about has a lot a substance as well. But the film they were talking about felt wrong. It felt like I would be saying, I agree with you; this is the way it has to work. And I don't think that's the way it has to work.

So I'm sitting there and they go, essentially, Reggie, we've got good news and bad news. The good news is that we're gonna give you $30 million. The bad news is that your black film is now a white film! And I said no. That wasn't the film I was going to make. I said to the studio heads, you already took away my motivation for why I wanted to do this specific project. My motivation was I'm gonna do a movie where you're not going to hear the word "nigger"; you're not going to have people running around with guns; you're not going to see brothers with bottles of forties in their hand. This is going to be a hot film. But make it white? Well, go ahead, then. But that's not why I'm here.

People who know me well are aware it's not a big deal for me to say no. Many times I've said, I'm not going to do this or I'm not going to do that. Some people who don't know me say, wow, you said *that* to the studio! But really what I'm trying to get to is a place where I can say, hey, man, I've got to maintain my integrity in this situation and still get the film made.

It's important to understand that from their point of view, the studio heads are not being racist. From their point of view, they are operating within a Hollywood formula, and a script either works or doesn't work within that formula. I'm operating from the point of view that I want to change the formula. Five, six years ago, there would have been a shouting match. I've had my share of those in these rooms. But basically what I said was, that's not what I want to do. I was very up-front and told them, while we were all in the room, what motivated me to do this film. So what we did is we just sat there for a while and nothing was going to happen, and it was like they sort of passed on the project. I think the way it went was, it was a Friday that I had the meeting; the Academy Awards came on the following Monday, and Denzel won and Halle won, and the next day they passed on the project. They said no.

So it wasn't happening, but what they did allow was for me to take the project and shop it elsewhere. We went throughout Hollywood, and everybody had the same point of view. Everybody wanted us to make it white. And we said, you know what, the Hollywood formula is that this is not a safe investment to make, a film starring African Americans for this amount of money. So instead of saying let's make it white, we said, okay, let's take it upon ourselves to make it for half the money. We started telling people we could make this movie for $15 million. Then people were interested, and we were like, how are we going to make it for fifteen?

We started figuring it out and we got set up at Fox Searchlight Pictures. Ironically, this will be one of their biggest films, if we do it. They gave us four weeks to put the film together. We got an amazing crew and put together an amazing cast, and then presented everything we had put together in the four weeks.

A lot of people knew the history of the project. And when you're going into a meeting and you have a crew that you've hired, you start feeling obligated. You want to make sure everybody here has a job. One of the people I had hired pulled me aside and said, Reggie, do me a favor. You know I'm here to protect your vision, and I appreciate what you've done and what you can do in this project. That's why I'm here. Don't walk into that room if you can't walk out and say no. Now, this is from a sister that needed a job.

We're heading out—myself and the other producers—to do our presentation for the studio, and everybody in the production office just stops and claps for us. The night before, everyone stayed up till two A.M. helping us pull some things together, and nobody was getting overtime. It wasn't just about keeping a job. They wouldn't have done it—they told me this—if they didn't believe in what we were doing.

I think the presentation we gave exceeded everyone's expectations. We did more than was required because we didn't want to give anyone an excuse to say no. So if they do say no, it's not based on our merit. Creatively, the film was tight, and it has a clear and specific vision. We have the top crew people assembled and we're paying them hardly any money. This is low-budget, and these are people that do big, big films.

Everyone sent us off with a round of applause and we went out there and did the presentation. I think we did a great job. When we came back to the office, everyone clapped again. All along, they validated our commitment to maintaining our integrity.

It would be attractive to be hot, to be the man, the guy. And really, if that was my agenda, I would have gone an easier route; this is not the only film that was offered to me. What I need to be able to do is make a successful film the way I want to make it, let the studio make a profit, then go to the business community and say, here it is.

I don't know how much a $15-million film is going to have to make for me to have a command of the marketplace, or how compelling it needs to be so people will say, Reggie, we trust your vision; here's the money to make more films. I don't know if it's $100 million, which would be great, or really what that number has to be. At the end of the day, the money is not going in my pocket. First off I have to make a good film, one that I can be proud of; and second, the film has to be marketable. I have to be clear on this. I want to be able to say, hey, I did it—not just that I made a film that was marketable, but that I held on to my vision. I want to be able to say I made a film with African-American leads and it's marketable.

If I am successful, it won't just be that the film made $100 million, $200 million. If I'm successful, some other filmmakers are going to be like, man, Reggie did it, so I'm holding on to my vision too. They did it, so why can't I do the same thing? *That*'ll make me the man!

It hasn't happened yet. People sort of know who I am. Some people think I'm crazy, and some people are cool. It's not like I go up in a room and I'm jumping on people's desks and cursing them out. I'm a professional; I know what it's about. I don't think I'm known as a troublemaker—maybe not till this documentary comes out anyway. And if I am, so be it. I've certainly had my share of arguments with people, but I think, if anything, people know that nine times out of ten I work harder than the next guy. It would be a lot easier in many ways to chase the money, because the money's out there and it's attainable, and all you have to do is follow the formula they set up and there it is. But everything has sort of been frustrating. Everything that's made me ask myself why I bother is the same thing that makes me get up the next day twice as motivated.

We have more black A-list actors right now than we've had in the hundred years of Hollywood history put together. And I've got many of them for this film—people that have been nominated for Academy Awards. So I'm saying to the studio, what's up? I got 'em! And for like no money, but just because they get it; they know what it's about. These are people that don't need to do this film; they don't need to help me out. But they want to do it.

If I was the person green-lighting this film, I would tell everybody working on it, roll up your sleeves and market this as an action film. If I hear anybody in the room saying it's a black film, you're off the project. It's an action film. If it's a weak script, then we have problems. But nobody's going to say it's a weak script. If it was weak, we wouldn't be attracting the people we're attracting. So you have a good story; you have a clear vision. Don't be limited by the fact that they are African Americans in these roles.

If a white film doesn't work, you don't look at it and say, white films don't work. You say, *this* film didn't work. I think the perception, when a black film doesn't work or when a black TV show doesn't work, is that black films and black TV shows don't work. This is a real dilemma. If there's a belief that black dramas don't work, then it seems to follow that blacks have to all be in comedic situations.

I don't buy that. I think that people respond to good work. At the time when *The Cosby Show* came on the air, the sitcom industry was kind of dead; it was really all about dramas at that time. *The Cosby Show* helped revitalize NBC. But if you put another sitcom on the air right now, on NBC, and it failed, they might take the view that black sitcoms don't work. So they'd be judging the whole from one part. For every black film that they say was not successful, you could find three times as many white films that weren't successful. White films flop all the time, but we're not real about that.

The challenge that a lot of African-American filmmakers face—I'm not just speaking for myself—is how to make a film that will be perceived as something that can cross over. There is a perception that if you make a film with people of color in it, particularly with black people, it can't sell well overseas and it can't even cross over in this country. It's interesting, because if you point out that there were two people of color starring in *Rush Hour,* it doesn't matter, because that's Chris Tucker, so the perception is that it's not a black film. But what the perception should be is that if it's a drama, if it's an action film, if it's a comedy, market it as an action film. It doesn't matter if the leads are people of color; it's still an action film. But it has to start at the studio level, because if the studio sees it as a film that will not go outside of a black market, they are not going to be able to sell it to other people and say, this is a film that can cross over.

The answer to changing the system really lies on the other side of the table, where the guys who make the decisions sit. I have no interest in complaining anymore. I'm tired of it; I'm tired of hearing people complain. When I was younger and thought I wanted to be an actor, I would audition for stuff that didn't feel right and I said, man, I need to be a writer; that way I can control my destiny. Then you write stuff you believe in and you say, yeah, this is where it's at, and then it's like, no, I've got to be a producer, and then I realize I've got to be a director, and you know what, that isn't really where it's at either.

To make the significant change we need to make, we need to be on the other side of the table running the studio. Otherwise, we are going to continue to be in a position where we are complaining and saying, they won't do this for us and they won't do that. So certainly, my motivation now and my goal even in doing this project is to facilitate getting myself to that position. It's the film rights movement, and it starts with us and it's gonna end with us.

I sort of got spoiled when I first became a writer, because my first gig was writing for *A Different World.* I loved it prior to getting on the show; it was my favorite series at the time. So I got hired to write in the show. Debbie Allen became producer and director in 1988, and it was a mixed writing staff. You never had to explain to anybody, hey, this is derogatory. People asked for your point of view, like your point of view mattered.

After that, I worked on a short-lived show called *South of Sunset* that nobody saw and that was totally night and day colorwise compared to *A Different World*. Basically, I was the only black writer on the staff, and some of these guys were writing some really offensive stuff for this black character. I was cool to one of the white writers and I'd say, damn, man, every day I got to tell these other guys how offensive this is, and the white writer was sympathetic with me. I'd say to him, I feel like I'm like the black police on the show, man, and I hate that. I just want to be a writer. And he'd say, yeah, yeah. He agreed with me.

The next day we're all in the writing room and we're going through the script, and then a totally other writer, like the head writer of the show, turns to me and says, so is that okay with the black police? I was really pissed off by that. But what I decided then and there was I'd rather them look at me that way than look at me as a brother who's scared to say, hey, that's not cool.

So I think that with any show I've worked on, or any situation I've been part of, no one will ever say that I sat back and let things like that slide. I'd rather not have to be in the position of needing to call people on things. But I've learned that things are going to change if we are inspired enough to make them change. I've learned it through situations like *South of Sunset*, and by waiting to see if the studio executives will green-light my film, and even through people applauding as I was walking out of the room on my way to the presentation.

After Denzel and Halle both won an Academy Award, so many articles were written asking whether things have changed. I think things will change if we determine and demand that they change. Personally, I don't think they'll change by us boycotting or picketing studios. We should look to ourselves and hold ourselves accountable. If there is going to be some change, it will be because black filmmakers say, I want more, I want to do better, then go through the system and break down a formula or say, I'm going to start my own system where we can green-light our own films.

Everybody—black and white people—saw *Blade,* with Wesley Snipes, and *Bad Boys*, starring Will Smith and Martin Lawrence. But those actors are perceived more as stars than as black. Black audiences stayed away from Carl Franklin's film *Devil in a Blue Dress*. You can say that maybe that film did not have the right marketing. People didn't flock to see it, but they flocked to see

Waiting to Exhale, for whatever reason; and *What's Love Got to Do with It* was successful. Maybe people don't want to see pieces on slavery, and maybe kids don't want to see a film on blacks settling the Great Frontier after the Civil War, if it's told as a drama. Maybe that's not the way it should be, but I think action films do better than dramas across the board now. Maybe settling the Great Frontier could be told as an action-drama.

The question is, how do we get from this side of the table to that side? Well, I'm learning. I never saw myself as a businessman before. Shame on me! We've been in talks with people and we're learning. We started from the black community, and in the process met white people in the business community. I don't have any reservations about who gives us money if they want to get behind this vision and behind a market that's been under-served. In Hollywood, I go through a few things, like I say. I wrote *Get on the Bus,* I produced *New York Undercover,* and I wrote, directed, and produced *Dancing in September,* and my wife directed *Love and Basketball* and they say, okay, cool. But it's interesting—we've been finding that the business community has been paying a lot more attention to us than the Hollywood community has been.

I think it's not individual racism; it's institutional racism, at the level of the production, the green-light people, the people who are making the final decision. That's where the bottleneck is. I think we'll open it up eventually; we'll squeeze through. But what is the incentive for a white studio executive? Why should they have to take that chance, and why would they? The onus is on us. Our job is to make a film as marketable as possible. I can't come in the door and say, hey, man, I'm Jackie Robinson and you're Branch Rickey. That's not what it's about. We've got to go in and say, look, you can make money and this is why, and then hope that they can see beyond their perception.

I guess I'm trying to do for Hollywood, through this film and films like it, what *The Cosby Show* did for sitcoms on TV. *The Cosby Show* was about black people ostensibly, but it was not a black TV show. It was about a father and a mother and their growing children, and that's why everybody in the world watched it. Bill Cosby did a great job because he is really funny, but it wasn't a sociological study of the Negro family.

It's taken me a while to get that paradigm, because the people I admire most are not people in the film industry. My wife and I were in South Africa for our honeymoon, and we saw Nelson Mandela's home. You look at somebody like that and say, well, he stood up for what he believed in. But he didn't just stand up for what he believed in, he also succeeded. He became president and helped end apartheid. I'm not saying I want to be locked up for twenty-seven years. But it's not just about being in *Variety* and making lots of money and being that kind of success; it's bigger than that. And I believe deep down that the world is not as racist as some studio executives perceive it to be.

If there had been a point of view about *The Cosby Show* that it was just a black series, that only black people would come to it, maybe they would have put it on anyway. They didn't have UPN at the time, but if the show were just coming on today, it might just be on UPN and only go after a specific audience. Sometimes it's really hard to see whether we're making progress. Even prior to *The Cosby Show* there was *Roots*, and I was a kid at that time, but I remember everyone in the world watched *Roots*. At the time, it was like the NBA play-offs were going on. We went to school the next day talking about *Roots*, and when I was a kid, I went to an interracial school. It was predominantly white, and all the kids were talking about *Roots*. That show went beyond specific characters, specific nationalities, to the deeper human emotions. That's what art does. Just as *Othello* is not about an interracial marriage; it's about jealousy between two men, and using the woman as a pawn.

We need to be able to tell a good story that goes beyond sociology. And a lot of the onus also has to be on executives who are intelligent enough to know when there's a good story and when there's not, and who are willing to be innovative instead of just repeating something that was already successful. But ultimately, it comes back to getting to the other side of the table. And when I'm on the other side, I'm not going to be the guy saying, black face, black face, black face.

I don't know if everyone has the same agenda that I have, and I don't know if everybody needs to. Whether or not our agendas are the same, it's actors like Denzel and Sam Jackson and Chris Tucker and Laurence Fishburne and Will Smith and Halle Berry and Angie Bassett who have been making it possible for people like me to even be in a room to fight for these projects. The biggest contribution that African-American actors can make is to do good work. The biggest contribution African-American audiences can make is to ensure that their good work makes money.

It's possible to tell stories about black people in a new way, an authentic way, and be profitable. I think that's what people want. We need to change our frame of reference for who we are. Slavery was a very important part of our history, but I'm tired of being offered slavery projects, and I think people are tired of seeing the gangster thing. The sixties were another highly relevant time in our history, but we're not supposed to be doing the same thing we did then—because if we are, then what was the point of doing it in the sixties? This is the twenty-first century. We have to move with the times or we'll get left behind.

We have to be very committed to sitting down on the other side of the table. If we don't do it and I'm asked about our progress ten years from now, I'll be saying the same thing, and that's not cool. We need a black studio to be the Motown of the film industry, and it will come, without a doubt. If the studio heads want to start a black studio and say, hey, Reggie, we want you in there, I'm like, cool, I'm there. But the stand we need to make is to start our own studio. If I figure it out for us, that's great, and if somebody else figures it out for us, that's great too, as long as we figure it out.

DARNELL HUNT

The Buddy

Professor Darnell Hunt of the University of Southern California told me that in earlier days of television and film, African Americans "weren't quite equipped" to pull off roles as doctors or nurses, or roles of similar status, and as a result they "bumbled and fumbled." Now it is less a problem with competence than with taking the lead. Whether in action films or TV sitcoms, African Americans are typically relegated to the role of "buddy."

Imagine a tourist unfamiliar with American culture deciding to spend just one day learning who the African American people are. He might stop in Los Angeles and divide his time between the American Film Institute and the Museum of Television and Radio, studying blacks in movies and on television from the 1950s to today. Our visitor would receive a very limited view of the people he was trying to understand. There are comedic images—he would find lots of those, from the early days of television straight through to today. He would find images of African Americans that show them as somewhat secondary in terms of status relative to whites, because most of the roles we see, with a few exceptions, are African Americans playing the buddy to the central white character. This is true in all the buddy cop films and in many situation comedies and dramas on television.

Even though African Americans have roles as series regulars, much of the research shows that not all series regulars are equal. More "marquee" series regulars, typically the white ones, garner most of the screen time. And it is these regulars, rather than the others, whose families are represented on television. Lots of African-American characters are presented as atomized, as just being there, again at the pleasure of the white characters, going back as far as the 1965 inaugural season of *I Spy* with Bill Cosby and Robert Culp.

I think our visitor would also find an overrepresentation of black men relative to women. We tend to see black men much more frequently on television than we do black women, and I think the same is true for film. In early periods, we'd find black Americans shown in roles that weren't exactly considered to be high-status, and people were very concerned about this, going back to the days of *Amos 'n' Andy*. Even when African Americans were extensively seen in roles as doctors or nurses or in roles of similar status, they weren't quite equipped to pull it off, and as a result they bumbled and fumbled. And this was at a time when America was moving toward integration.

The main character of Calhoun the Lawyer, for example, in *Amos 'n' Andy* was not a high-status role. It certainly did not reflect African Americans as they wanted to see themselves, at a time when they were trying to become full-fledged citizens of this country. As time progressed, at least we saw more respectable images, for example in the sixties with shows like *I Spy* and *Julia*. But then the problem was that these characters were completely disconnected from the realities of what was happening with the rest of black America—the turmoil of the sixties, the uprisings and protests. All those goings-on were just completely erased from escapist television.

I think the thing to remember is that television is, and has been really, our major cultural form, even more than film. A lot of work has been done on the creation of the concept of nation around mass media, and television in particular, giving people the sense of participating in the same phenomena at the same time over wide expanses of space. And when television provides these images—particularly when people don't have face-to-face contact, or when most of what they know is through these images—it plays a major role in shaping the way race relations have unfolded in this country.

A great deal of research, again with respect to mainstreaming, indicates that television views of the world become the views people embrace when they watch lots of television. I don't think race is immune from that. In fact, I think race probably is more susceptible to that than most other things. So I would think that much of what Americans know, or think they know, about African Americans comes from televised images. In other words, the largest part of society in America, particularly white people—not just foreign visitors—learn who African Americans are by watching them on TV and at the movies.

BERNIE MAC

The Chameleon

Born Bernard Jeffrey McCullough in 1957 in Chicago, Bernie Mac has been extraordinarily successful in Hollywood. "But what got me here," he told me, "definitely wasn't Hollywood and it definitely wasn't whites. Blacks got me here. When they filled those rooms up for me, when they filled those shows up, seven-thousand-, five-thousand-seaters, it was black . . . All those people that came and saw me in places where no one ever bought tickets—Meridian, Mississippi; Graysville and Harrison, Alabama—I went to places where a lot of cats never wanted to go because there's blacks there. It made me."

My focus, man, right now is, and has always been for a long period of time, on the essence of what I do: the humor—the story. I'm a storyteller. I love reinventing myself, especially today, because a lot of people really are just not tuning in to Bernie Mac. They thought Bernie Mac was something, was potent like them, these little things I've done. They haven't even got a fourth of Bernie Mac, and that's where my focus lies right now. It's really tuning America more in to that man, to the message.

My message is, I deal with the truth. I try to find humor in the most inopportune places and times. My humor comes from pain, to be able to laugh at your misfortune, to really laugh at your struggle, to really laugh at the trials and tribulations that occur in everyone's life. It tells the tale about an individual, and I learnt that from my grandmother.

I used to think something was wrong with me because I never understood that I was poor. I never understood that I was having to struggle, because the way I thought, I really wasn't. I thought I had it all. I was so much at peace and I was so much into the total surroundings of my family, my grandparents, my mother, and the true love, the true essence of the word "love." I didn't know what all that other stuff was until they passed. I was twenty-six when my grandmother passed, and I was fifteen when my mother passed. When they left, I saw what this thing, what we call life, is all about. I saw the downside of it and tried to be able to tell the story so many of us live. So many of us, we try to put it on the back burner and block it out from reality. That's why so many people are really in pain struggle. Being able to find humor in those places, that's really where my focus is.

Now, what you put on me, that's your own perspective. But I know what got me here, and it definitely wasn't Hollywood and it definitely wasn't whites. Blacks got me here. When they filled those rooms up for me, when they filled those shows up, seven-thousand-, five-thousand-seaters, it was black. When you set up and they ran up and down that aisle and I told stories about what the white folk didn't understand, they were black. When they sat there, when the television show came up, I was ready. I was seasoned. I was over the campaign. All those people that came and saw me in places where no one ever bought tickets—Meridian, Mississippi; Graysville and Harrison, Alabama—I went to places where a lot of cats never wanted to go because there's blacks there. It made me. Now I get white people too. I've got the biggest crossover program on television. They call that growth. You go from point A to Z, you don't go from M to Z. I brought the people from Meridian, Mississippi; Detroit, Michigan; Savannah, Georgia—all those places—with me. When they put *that* me on television, the old people knew me. I did the groundwork, and that's what made the show successful. The audience just travels over.

I think anytime there's change, it frightens people. Especially in Hollywood, because they're experts; they're the geniuses. They want to be responsible for your existence. They want to be able to say, I created that. And when I came in with the story for *The Bernie Mac Show,* with the outline, it really shocked them, for number one, that I had that. They want to be in control of you. They want to be in control of your existence.

They wanted to be able to say, well, this is what we see and we'll put your name on it. That satisfies most people. We'll pat you on the knee doggone, that's what. We're going to have a little girl here, she's gonna talk back and she's gonna shake her head and all that old stereotypical stuff and I was saying, no, we ain't having that. *This* is what the story is about. I wanted to go back to basics. I wanted to show, hey, it's time out. It stops with us. A kid is going to be a kid. I'm gonna tell the truth; I'm gonna say what Americans only wish they could say. And you know what, it fit. I took the laugh track out, because I didn't want to insult my audience. I got tired of that old fictitious, phony-assed ha, ha, ha, telling you when to laugh and how to laugh. I really truly thought that was an insult. I thought, America, it's time. It's time for us to go back to basics.

I can't take credit totally for the success of the show, because it's so many combinations that are involved. It's the story, it's the writing, it's the acting, it's the style, it's the look, it's the titles. It's the love; it's the warmth. It's innovative; it's a breath of fresh air; it's all that. All that combined in one. And I have to give credit to all the people before me that set the precedent for me— from Harrison, Alabama, and all of that. And the word of mouth and how they say, you better watch this guy; this is the guy I was telling you about, and how it was like a snowball effect. And now, when they tap in, the people who did know me, the white audience, the Asians, everyone, they see the Iranian; they see all the different cultures on the show; and they see how that's real life. It's real life, man.

My uncle used to come over to the house, and we used to love this cat to come over because he was real. He would turn and say something unexpected, offensive, maybe rude, but he got it. He knew what was happening. It wasn't so much what he said as how he said it. But he told the truth, even when he lied. He'd be sitting out at the table with his fork in his hand and he'd be like, now you pray for that. Do you want me to feel sorry? I'm not feeling sorry for a goddamn thing. If you went there with him, you kept on getting nothing. And he used to just sit there.

He only came once, twice a year, but he knew what everybody did wrong. He knew and he told it. My grandmother would sit there and she would go, that's right, that's right, I keep telling them. But when you heard it from somebody else, it registered, versus coming from her, because she was too close.

My auntie, she was so phony and everything. She would go, don't say that. Because she always worried about what other people thought, what other people said, and how they feel about it. My grandmother and my uncle, they were what you call real. My grandmother could always tell you the truth as she saw it, even when she was wrong. She could say, I apologize for that. She'd say, when you're wrong, you've got to stand up and look the person in the eye and tell them you're wrong. She could say, I didn't use good judgment on that, but because I didn't use good judgment doesn't mean you do the same. She always broke it down like a fraction. She was always honest, and that was unusual for adults in those days.

And I had my brother. I used to watch my brother. He was my role model. He was one of the first blacks at First National Bank of Chicago. I was so proud. He was a hell of an athlete, and I watched how, man, everybody kept trying to put us under here, his standard. We had to mimic what Mitch did.

Mitch was this, Mitch was that, he was, oh, the academic, while I was thinking, I can't follow those shoes, man. And I saw how he got a little bit cocky. He was a hell of a baseball player. He went to the St. Louis Cardinal farm system and he got cocky. I saw how his head got big and I saw how all his hard work just dropped, because he got too much into the moment, and I said, I'm not going to do that.

I watched how my sister was the queen of Chicago, how she used to sing all the radio jingles, and how she'd sing in the background with Aretha Franklin. She found out who the real queen is, and she had to come back home with her head between her legs. And I said to myself, I'm not going to do that. I saw how you go from one level to the next, and how you do things for the wrong reasons, and how you lose everything overnight. You never know. We don't know what tomorrow brings. That's why I can't get excited about what's happening, because I'm not done. When I've done thirty years in the business and I've done exactly what I wanted and I set a look, a tone for the thing, and I can reflect back and hopefully in my old age sit somewhere with grandkids around, then I can say, thank you, Lord. That's when I've done something. I ain't done nothing.

In our show, people are incidentally black. I mean they're black, but people can identify. We bring out their humanness. It's 2002. I'm trying, baby. We have done it, almost to death. We have killed it. I want to show the human side of us, man. It's good to be upper middle class. We are that now, would you know; and we still got our roots. There's a time and a place for everything. My grandmother, she was great, man. That's something we don't have today— manners. What you talk—yes, ma'am, yes, ma'am—and we sat there, me and my brother, and she would sit there, and we get in the car. I'm kicking your ass a bit. You know damn better than that, embarrassing me in front of those people. What the heck's wrong with you? I'm gonna tear your behind off. You're doggone right; she didn't play with you. We grew up on manners. I miss that. We had manners; we don't have that anymore. And if I'm wrong, you tell me.

Our mentality, and not just blacks, but a lot of minorities, has fallen. It has fallen from where we were. The spiritual guidance has gone and left us, for number one, and that's a very dangerous thing. And the mentality in terms of microwaves has risen. We want things overnight. It's a fast-food, instant-gratification, efficiency-not-quality society. We hate ourselves. Oh yes, we hate ourselves. We hate anything that has uplift in it. It's just constructed that way and I see it in everyday life as I talk to the schools. I see it in our young people. I see it more and more in our society, whereas our desire to be more and to be better has just disappeared.

It's the fault of the individuals and it's the fault of the system. It's a combination. You can't blame one without the other. We've just gotten away, man, from the spirituality part, which is really the main focus. It's gone. I mean, that's what kept me safe. I knew God; I know him. I don't want to say "knew" in the past tense. I know him, and that kept me out of a lot of things. Big Mama, man, she is still there. I had a tight family unit, a network, and oh man, oh man, respect. Respect is on the back burner now. We're just a selfish society now. No deferred gratification; just give me, give me. He got it, I want it. Doggone, I'm better than him; how come I can't have it? I had no mother, man, my father left me. You're forty-seven. Let it go.

And don't forget slavery. Oh, man, we were slaves. I heard something that kind of flipped me out and I had to really just shake it off. A lady said, God paid New York back because slaves was traded on Wall Street and they built the trade buildings on top of a black cemetery. We put the Lord in it. This is 2002, man. You know, we still talk in the same old, same old way.

I'll give you a perfect example. If I were to tell you how tight I was in 1974—that's the year I was a junior in high school and that's the year my mother died. Man, I had women; I had, excuse my French, the bitches. First thing you would tell me, man, is let that old shit go. Am I right or wrong? I mean, get away from that old antique stuff; nobody wants to hear that no more. But we constantly keep on. I know it, I get it, I understand it. I know what we were about, but here we are right now; what are we going to do about right now?

Another thing is that we think we're the only ones that have suffered. We think we're the only one that has struggled; we think we're the only one that has been dealt a bad hand. We think we're the only one that is perfect people, you know, but yet sometimes we come off as the most prejudiced.

If you say that, people get mad, but it's true. It is very true. And we do a lot of stuff that's responsible for our own repression, no question. We don't want to get the noose off our own neck, because we're not comfortable. It feels good. Because if you take it off from around your neck, you feel naked, you know? Where's my noose? We say that. You get mad, but see, I learned from a very wise woman, Mary McCullough, my grandmother. She taught me how to deal with the truth, and I was symbolic of that stigma too. Don't say that, don't say that, Mama, don't know what you mean, like that. I used to get tight. And she taught me how to deal with what was in front of me and analyze it for what it is. I mean, the world don't mean nothing. Every day, every day under the struggle, you know what? If I reflect back to my childhood from one of the rough days that I thought was rough, I ate every day. I might not ate what I desired, but I ate every day. When I looked to that beer, or I said the lights seemed ready to go off, or that gas was kind of hot, you know what? For some kind of reason, my father got paid. I don't know how, but he got paid.

And I'm here. I made it; always found a way. All of us have experienced, man, I don't know what I'm going to do tomorrow, I don't know what the heck, and you go to the mailbox and you got a surprise check there from somebody. What the—but you still don't appreciate. You were gratified for that second, that moment. And then we always go back to that old, same old messed-up ways. It's like the doctors tell you something and all of a sudden you're meek now, but as soon as you get better, you start back the same old, same old ways. Yeah, I'm all right now. I'm okay, I'm okay. You know what, man? My blood sugar's good. I'm going to have the bacon now.

I'm still in the appreciative stage, and I'm still glad that I never left that. I don't want to leave that. And if I don't, maybe I'll continue to be successful. That's why I stay where I am, because I have a life. Everybody say, well, you know, you're doing so well now, you're doing this. I've always been doing well. Now the only thing that's different, for me, from my perspective, is I'm doing what I really choose to do. And that, right there, is of the elite. You take away all the material things, I'm doing what I set out to do. From Wonder bread to here. Oh yeah, all those humble beginnings, man. And I think that's something I don't ever want to lose. I don't want to lose the appreciative stage I'm in. I don't want to lose that.

LARRY WILMORE

The Bonus

Writer Larry Wilmore told me he was inspired to create the pilot for *The Bernie Mac Show* by a desire to do something different, to make a statement. "We don't have to live for somebody else. We can do it ourselves, which is the most powerful thing in the world, as far as I'm concerned," he said. "I always wanted to show people more as they really are than as stock characters on TV . . . there was a very conscious decision to work against not so much racial stereotypes as against television stereotypes."

I became a writer kind of by accident. I was doing stand-up comedy. I always wanted to be a comedian when I was younger. And you just have to write because you need an act. So I would write, but I never considered myself a writer. I studied theater in school, and I studied playwriting and the classics. But still I didn't think it was something that I was doing, even though I was doing it all the time. And the more I did—the more I wrote—the more ideas I got that really didn't fit into stand-up, that were either movie ideas or sketch ideas or more about depicting a character, and I just thought I needed to go further with it and do more.

A lot of it is being in the right position to do things. I always felt if I had the opportunity to do it, why not try to do something different and original? I remember someone asked me once, "Larry, how come there's no black Seinfeld?" and I said, "Because you haven't written it yet!" I said, "Write it! You know, let's do it. I'll do it with you!"

When I was developing the pilot for *The Bernie Mac Show*, there were a couple of things I was looking for. I wanted to use Bernie as he really is—a successful comedian—and I wanted him to be unapologetic about his success. I didn't want him to be a fish out of water, like, I'm black and I'm rich, but somehow I don't believe I should be here, so I'm gonna act like it's not for me. Like Fresh Prince, maybe—him, not the family. Or even his family. We didn't buy them as authentic in some ways—maybe the mom. In some ways, they weren't comfortable with their identity and their social situation. But we were supposed to look up to them; they were comic foils for Will Smith, who was the real deal in our eyes. Fundamentally, I wanted to do something a little different, like Bernie should be our role model—he's comfortable being rich; he's unapologetic. "This is my shit—don't touch it!" That's his point of view. "I earned it and I deserve it. And I'm comfortable with it." Bernie and I were, like, we don't have to apologize for any of this stuff. I deserve to be here—get yours! Join me! House comin' up for sale next door. Move on in! And it really is Bernie's point of view too: Be proud of what you have and work hard for it. It's the work ethic. That's Bernie's parents' generation.

It's that ethic, and it's something that has lost a little bit. Not completely, because I think those things go in cycles too, and I think a lot of young kids have a lot of that ethic now, which is great. We don't have to live for somebody else. We can do it ourselves, which is the most powerful thing in the world, as far as I'm concerned. But some of it got kind of lost, and that's part of Bernie's humor too and part of Chris Rock's too. What is that joke he did where he said, "I take care of my kids!" "Niggers, you're supposed to take care of your kids! What are you bragging for?" "I put food on the table!" "You are supposed to put food on the table! What are you boastin' about it for?" It's that kind of thing, where Bernie and I consciously wanted the show to be unapologetic about his standing. And it is. He belongs in that neighborhood. The fact that the kids are the kids of a drug addict, that's about, this is family. It's about emotion. In fact, Bernie is in the same class with them; he just has a different checkbook. He hasn't changed classes at all, he's just changed addresses. But he's very successful and very comfortable.

I'm from Los Angeles. To me, Los Angeles is so diverse I don't view the show in terms of black and white. It's almost like Bernie and the rest of the world, and everybody makes up that. So here you're gonna see Asian, you're gonna see Hispanic, you're gonna see white. You're gonna see all kinds of things because that's what Los Angeles is. It's never really been black or white. If the show took place in the South, it'd probably be more black characters than white characters. But I always wanted to show people more as they really are than as stock characters on TV. So you're not gonna see the white guy coming in like on *The Jeffersons* with "Well, Mr. J.," or being a real stiff or that kind of thing. They're just people. The conflict, the tension in the story, would be about how they're gonna interact and how they're gonna react to what happens, or how Bernie relates to them, and that type of thing.

I wrote the pilot at a time when I just wanted to do something different. I wanted to make a statement. I'd been inspired by a lot of people who had come before, people who have always taken a chance and a risk, like Sidney Poitier. They just honored him with the Academy Award. He was one of my early heroes. He was out there by himself, doing it. I remember watching Sammy Davis, Jr., as a kid. Flip Wilson was the first guy to have a variety show that worked. I've been inspired by a lot of people who went out on their own and did things—just did them. And that's what I wanted to do with *The Bernie Mac Show*.

I saw the *Cosby* reunion show, and it made me remember what was really funny about it. I think *The Bernie Mac Show* and *The Cosby Show* are the left hand–right hand. They're both big crossover shows. They're different, but I think the way they're the same is more significant. *The Cosby Show* traces back to Bill Cosby's stand-up act, which is ironic because I started with Bernie's stand-up act. In that act it was about parenting, just how hard it is. It's such a universal thing, and how he feels like he wants to kill those kids.

There's a line Cosby has: "I brought you into this world, boy, and I can take you right out of it." It's what all of our parents said, not just black parents. Everybody feels that way. That was the universal appeal that *The Cosby Show* had too. It was: I'm your father, I'm gonna tell you what to do, and you're gonna do it. I think that's what people responded to more than anything else. Plus the star power of Bill Cosby was huge and I think was underestimated at the time. And sitcoms were dead. *The Cosby Show* came around when sitcoms weren't doing anything, and it just skyrocketed through the roof. It was so fresh, and when you look at the pilot, it still feels fresh. So in that way we're very similar. Bernie talks about how hard it is to raise these kids, even though they're not his kids, and that's what makes it a little more contemporary. They're brought in because of a drug problem, which is completely different from Cosby, but it's the exact same attitude. "Boy, I will bust your head"—I mean, he's frustrated, and that's the thing that everybody responds to, is that frustration as a parent.

What's also coupled on top of that, which is a little different these days, is how political correctness plays a part in parenting, which is a lot different than in Cosby's day. Cosby probably could whup one of those kids on TV and we would have thought nothing of it. But today Bernie can barely talk about it and we'd get in trouble. And stylistically is where the shows are really different. *Cosby* was a very traditional show in front of an audience, with a multicamera format. I wanted to tell stories in a different way; that was one of the goals of the show. I wanted us to be drawn in to who Bernie is as a person, and I couldn't do that in front of an audience. If I put Bernie in front of an audience, I'd be competing with the Bernie Mac in *The Original Kings of Comedy*—the one who's up there saying "you mother" and all that stuff. I didn't want to compete with that. I wanted to show America the Bernie Mac who I talked to and I met.

I went to Chicago and talked to Bernie personally, talked about his childhood, heard the kind of guy he is. I wanted to introduce that person to America, Bernard Jeffrey McCullough instead of Bernie Mac. And I knew that with the single-camera format I could introduce that person. I could tell stories that are a little quieter, that have some drama in them but not always a joke. Sometimes, when he talks to us directly, we can see things played out. It feels like we're eavesdropping on the action, instead of the action being presented to us. We had an episode where he was just getting the kids out to school, and it was like we had hidden cameras set up because there was no plot. He just had to get the kids out of the house, but it was very engaging because we saw his struggle the whole time. Those are the kinds of stories I really like to tell.

When I pitched this show three years ago, they said I was crazy. They thought I was too hard; they thought I was too blue; they thought the audience wasn't ready. I pitched it to ABC and they didn't even buy a script—they weren't interested at all. And I'm pitchin' it with Bernie Mac sittin' right there. I mean, at the least, you want Bernie Mac on your network, surely? But they wanted an old, traditional sitcom.

Fox believed in the show immediately and bought it right in the room, in fact. They were excited about it from the beginning. What they weren't sure about was the style of it. They weren't quite sure it was gonna work because it was so different. But believe it or not, they always did believe in Bernie, and thought he was a huge star and thought the idea of the show was a really good idea. I give Fox credit for going out of their way first most of the time. Whenever you see something different, it's usually on Fox. They did *In Living Color*. They did shows like *The Simpsons*. They've always taken creative chances.

The question people should be asking is, how come NBC doesn't have a show like that on? I don't know the answers, but I think that's the right question. If someone asks me how many black writers I have, or whether I have black writers, I'm not offended by the question. We had a really small staff last year, of about five writers. Three were black, so we had a majority black staff. And if you count me, that's four. I was the main writer, supervising the script, and I wrote the pilot. I wrote it at a time when I felt like I had nothing to lose, and I was kind of fed up with a lot of stuff on television. We try to keep it real here. But they should be asking *Friends* that question, not me! They should call those people up and ask. Ask Seinfeld, how many black writers did you have?

Bernie Mac says things as a character that other people think and want to say. We might have these liberal white people say, he shouldn't say that. But everybody thinks it.

Bernie Mac is a comedian who happens to be black. And I feel that black is the bonus. Because it means that Bernie views the world through a very comic-centered point of view. And it has some of the best parts of classic comedy, where there's some tragedy underneath it all, or some sadness. That's where we empathize with him. We know he came from a hard life, like the sister situation and all that, but we know he's gonna make us laugh, and that's why we love him. The bonus is that Bernie's life has been colored from his cultural perspective, and those are the things he can share with the audience that may not be familiar with his perspective. What he's doing is from a point of view that is very familiar emotionally, but it's in the context of a black lifestyle, which I think is fantastic. I'm really proud of that, as opposed to the black being first and the experience being second, which to me is a little more superficial.

I think when the show was being put together, I was reacting to different ways of representing black people on sitcoms before this program. Especially in the last ten years, it seemed to me that a lot of black sitcoms just became kind of the same thing. They were more, I think, about hip-hop, more than it was black. Like, you had to, in fact, have a codebook to know what people were saying half the time. And that was considered the real thing. In some ways—and I shouldn't generalize—but many seemed to be marginalized by a certain style, and a certain type of put-down humor that was very much the same. It was who could put down who the best. I saw that as a bit negative and I wanted to get away from that. Also, I wanted to do characters that were just more real, more three-dimensional, and had more depth to them—real relationships between a husband and wife or father and kids, that sort of thing. Because I have a theater background, I'm just more interested in that type of thing anyway.

So there was a very conscious decision to work against not so much racial stereotypes as against television stereotypes. You know, what are the stock characters in television? Let's get 'em out! In fact, one of the reasons why Bernie talks to the audience, there's a stock character in television called the best friend, and this is a friend who comes over and you tell the exposition to. You know, they sit down and you say, so yeah, my wife's gonna leave me, and oh, man! I'm gonna get canned at my job, and all that stuff. I said, that is a stock character! I said, let's get rid of that character. What if we made America that character? So Bernie talks to the camera. He tells us, these kids are doin' this to me and they're doin' that and they're doin' that. We're that stock character now, so we don't need that character in the show. I figured, the people on the show can just be who they are. Bernie will tell us the information we need to know, when we need to know it. The hope was that it would pull us in, invite people in. You never know if it's gonna work, but luckily it did.

We have a pretty wide demographic. Culturally, the show reaches across racial lines, both black and white. My goal was to represent the generational tensions of a family, not the generational tensions of a black man. On the other hand, I love the fact that it's from a black perspective and that it's seasoned with that underneath it, because to me that's what gives it the richness and the texture. And it's funny—it reaches across generational lines, which I'm really the most proud of. Old people love our show. We get white-haired Jewish women from Palm Beach talking about it as well as young urban kids, and the black audience is really huge. What I love about the feeling from the black audience is that there's a sense of pride about the show, which is great. People are proud to say, oh, yeah, *The Bernie Mac Show*, yeah! That's nice; it's a nice feeling. And yet, just from the mainstream audience too, they really respond to the fact that it is different and that it has the universal theme about parenting and how hard it is. People really love to laugh at Bernie too—he's so relatable. When he puts the weight of the world on his shoulders, that's the funniest thing—"America, you know what I'm talking about . . . y'all wanna beat those kids too." I channel Bernie. That's how I write. I just try to think like him.

This whole segregation in television is a really recent phenomenon. Shows like *Good Times* had no problem crossing over. *The Jeffersons* had no problem because they were on the major networks. When the shows are on the major networks, they have no problem crossing over. *Fresh Prince of Bel-Air* is the most recent example. But it was on NBC. If you're on a big channel and you don't cross over, you don't stay. If a show's on some channel that's like sixty-eight and a half in some markets, and people try to find it, most people are just gonna watch the big channels. Now I always joke, the black people are still gonna find the black shows: Honey, we gonna find some niggers on TV tonight! Keep clickin'. There's a Burger King commercial. Wait! Wait! So you'll seek it out if that's what you want, but if you have to work to find it, what's the point? If I was Japanese and I knew there was a Japanese show on Channel 38, I'd look for it because I know it's there, but otherwise I'm just gonna watch what's in front of me. TV's a passive medium. People turn it on, they're tired. They've eaten, they're almost half asleep, and then, uh, hey, look at that! Uh, funny—huh! *Simpsons!* Huh. Funny! I think that's how people watch TV, basically.

I guess sociologically, you could say Bernie is first generation. If he had kids, they would be a lot different than he is. And in some ways, his wife is a little bit in the middle there. Her parents were probably very successful and passed that on to her. She's very subtle, very particular. She's confident with what she is. She doesn't have to prove anything, which was also a very important trait. I wanted a black couple that were supportive of each other and didn't bicker. You know, that when they had conflicts, they were real conflicts, and they loved each other and they were best friends. I really wanted that. It was very important to me. That's Bernie's relationship with his wife—they've been together for twenty-six years or so, and they're best friends. I put a lot of thought into all that stuff; all of it was very important to me. But the kids thing was more of an emotional thing, more than a social commentary—absolutely.

In our show, people are incidentally black. I mean they're black, but people can identify. We bring out their humanness. It's 2002. I'm trying, baby. We have done it, almost to death. We have killed it. I want to show the human side of us, man. It's good to be upper middle class. We are that now, would you know; we still got our rooks. There's a time and a place for everything.

I'm really proud of the set, the inner sanctum. I wanted a set that felt like another character. I wanted the house to really be a character too. I didn't want that typical sitcom house that had the two stories and was flat. I was searching for something where we could move the camera in the space, because I always imagine Bernie chasing the kids down a long hall and the camera being at different angles and watching it. And I also wanted the house to have a real warm feeling, more earth tones and that kind of stuff, and for that to jump off the screen and to seem like it was Bernie and Wanda's, like, married single house. And like the stuff they had in there was from being married for years, and collecting stuff from around the world. Even the room the kids are in feels more like a bed and breakfast than a kids' room. I mean, it's not set up for kids to be in it, which helps the conflict, the theme of the show, to be real.

We have a whole area of the set we call the basement. It was supposed to be a parking garage or something, but since we're a single-camera show, we don't need to bring an audience in, so we can use all of this space. So it's Bernie on the bottom. See how they do us, man! Always putting the black people in the basement! Put us down here. We got ducks—anybody else got ducks down here? And the white people are upstairs, right above us! For us, it was kind of our escape. We felt like, fine, we're down here, we'll get away with things! And we built sets all over the basement. We did a lot of the Chicago episode down there—we didn't even go to Chicago. In fact, we used the neighbor's façade there for the Chicago episode. And our little girl on the show, played by Dee Dee Davis, her schoolroom is there too. We have costumes there. It's full of life. If you're down there when we're doing it, there's so much going on—it's just amazing.

I hope the success of the program will help black people in Hollywood. That'd be great, especially in terms of just being able to do original things, and being able to do anything. I hope more black writers get jobs on more mainstream shows. That's more important than just hoping a show like this comes out so they can get a job. I would hope that other shows would say, hey, you know, there are some really good black writers. Let's put 'em on *Raymond* or *Friends* or *Frasier*, and all those shows.

It reminds me of that Godfrey Cambridge joke. He said that if we ever redo *Birth of a Nation,* y'all gonna have a job again! Oh boy. We can't wait! Godfrey Cambridge was very funny. Bernie and I—I speak for Bernie in this sense—we both know what came before. We can talk about Godfrey Cambridge, Skillet Leroy, people like that, as well as Redd Foxx. All those people. We have a respect for it, we really have a healthy respect for it. We know what came before, so we know where we wanna go and where we wanna take it. We respect all those performers, black and white. We're both fans of Jack Benny and Groucho Marx and Buster Keaton. Bernie's a huge Red Skelton fan too. He had great timing and a great face. He'd do funny faces, and that's what Bernie does too—he makes all those faces. In fact, he went to clown college, I think, or something like that. He was a clown for a while, and that's how he makes all those kind of clown faces. But I almost see Bernie as a silent comedian, like Buster Keaton. I always say, if you can turn down the sound and still laugh, then that's great. I think Bernie would have been a classic comedian in any area, you know.

The thing is, I think what you are makes you what you are. I mean, those great Jewish comedians are great because they had a Jewish point of view. They were outsiders, they were immigrants, and they brought that to their sense of humor. I think that's part of what makes you funny. It's being an outsider; you have that point of view. It's part of what Jewish comedy and black comedy really share, more than anything else, is the outsider commenting on everything else. That's why they always said, write Yiddish, cast British. It's like, write it from that point of view, but let's put Robert Redford in the role! We don't want it too Jewish.

Too black—now that's a little different, because it's hard to write black and cast something else. I don't know if that's so much anymore. I think people don't know what they really mean when they say "too black." I think they mean too specific, maybe, like too much hip-hop. And people have to realize that hip-hop's just one part of a culture. It's not the whole thing. But sometimes people think it is, because of popular culture, like black culture *is* hip-hop culture—ghetto culture, street culture. And it's just not true. The culture of our people is much more complex. And I think that's what makes it rich. It would be a shame to all be the same! You know, it would be a crime. That's why people need to go back and read James Baldwin and read all the great black writers, as well as great white ones too, and broaden your horizons a bit, you know. That kind of thing.

If somebody says, Larry, do you know who so-and-so is? And I say, I never heard of 'em. And they say, you never heard of 'em? What's wrong with you? I say, well, did Martin Luther King say, yo, wassup, man? He wasn't like that. But it doesn't matter. You don't have to be ensconced in a certain popular culture to add something of value to the culture, or to value the culture or where you came from.

PART FOUR

Streets of Heaven: Chicago's South Side

The city of Chicago is tearing down the largest black community in the country. It's not just bricks and mortar that the city wants to destroy, but the negative aspects of the culture that the Robert Taylor Homes represent for too many people. It is a culture that, for most Americans, is synonymous with poverty, crime, hopelessness, and despair, in which one in five black men in their twenties is in jail or prison or on parole; in which 69 percent of all black children are raised in single-parent households; in which the average life span for an African-American man is fifty-nine; and in which only 45 percent of black adults are working in a given week.

These statistics call to mind a Third World country, not a neighborhood in America. How could this have happened? If the million-dollar mansions rising in Atlanta's new black neighborhoods are today's equivalent of the Big House, the Robert Taylor Homes in Chicago's South Side are the equivalent of the slave quarters.

Chicago's sublime skyline symbolizes the wealth and stability of America's midwestern city. The lure of this property has drawn African Americans to Chicago since the beginning of the twentieth century. Three decades ago—when Dr. King was killed—most blacks in America were poor, the middle class tiny. Since then, the middle class has tripled. But like a parallel universe, extreme black poverty persists, seething in the shadows. The Taylor Homes highrises, a world away from downtown on the city's South Side, were home to many of the African Americans in Chicago, 29 percent of whom officially live below the poverty line. How could this be?

Scholars on the left say that the system is to blame: a legacy grandfathered by slavery, fathered by Jim Crow racism, and nurtured by de facto segregation and job discrimination. Scholars on the right say it's their own fault: they are too dependent on government handouts; they are lazy and irresponsible and have no self-reliance. They have decided to be poor. Stay in school, get a job, go to work. Stop blaming the white man.

Neither argument satisfies me. Both ignore the human face and voice of poverty that lie behind the statistics we all know too well. I wanted to find some answers from the people who live here. I want to learn from them about the difficult choices their environment forces them to make, and the irresponsible choices they make themselves.

I began my journey at 4946 South State Street, one of the few remaining high-rises of the infamous Robert Taylor Homes. This is one of the poorest neighborhoods in the United States, a microcosm of the worst social ills of America's urban poor. Unable to fix it, the city has decided to tear it down. On my way to visit a resident, I encounter some graffiti—gang signs, children tell me. A six-pointed star and upward-pointing pitchforks mark the turf of the Gangster Disciples. In this community, gangs are a law unto themselves, instilling terror and controlling the drug trade and even a few legitimate businesses.

Two elevators serve about a thousand people. One of them has been down for several weeks. We have no choice but to wait. With temperatures in the high nineties, it's like standing in a crowded oven. I'm claustrophobic in elevators anyway. After fifteen minutes, thinking about the heat inside the electric casket, I head for the stairs. I'd rather walk up eleven flights of stairs than get trapped in that thing. This is routine for people here. The views from the eleventh floor would be priceless . . . if you could see past the heavy-gauged wire balcony, installed after some teenagers dropped a five-year-old boy off the fourteenth floor.

I visited the home of Mrs. Carolyn Massenberg, who has lived here since the seventies with her daughter, Patrice, and now resides here with her grandchildren. What's life like for these three generations?

No statistics can convey Mrs. Massenberg's pain, the poignancy of her awareness of her dilemma, her sensitive articulation of it, her powerlessness in the face of so many forces that keep life from being normal, despite all her good intentions and hard work.

"My oldest grandson was killed six years ago by a gunshot wound to the head. He was seventeen years old," she told me. "Violence is everywhere, but it's congested in the projects. There are people on top of one another. Drugs have turned a lot of good people I knew into someone you don't even want in your house anymore, one of the reasons being they take items, money, and so on. They get so they don't care about their children—whether they eat, have clothing, or just being there for them. These kids are left to raise themselves and are at the mercy of the situation. It's unthinkable unless you've heard it before."

It's hard for Mrs. Massenberg to keep optimism alive in this looking-glass nightmare of fear and instability, this vertigo of constantly shifting ground. The challenges that the Massenbergs face are the norm, despite their best efforts. In the coming years, tens of thousands of South Side residents like them will be rehoused in new buildings all over the city. But the doubts linger. Where will the guns, the drugs, and the gangs go? Will our families be any safer?

Home is our last refuge from the world, the place where we feel safe. Which is worse—coping with the living conditions inside or with the social chaos of the streets outside? As the spiritual says, "Went down to the rock to hide my face, the rock yells out 'No hiding place.'"

I next visited the Ida B. Wells Homes, named for a famous black journalist and completed in 1941. Built for black Southern migrants searching for the Promised Land during the Depression, these homes were once a model of public housing, worthy of Ida B. Wells's great name. Streets were swept clean, gardens well tended. People here worked and were poor, but they didn't know they were poor. Today it's more of a war zone than a neighborhood.

Twenty-year-old Lyndell Newman has lived here most of his life, but he's determined to escape. I wondered about his chances, especially after he told me he's making $600 a month in a restaurant when he could be making $6,000 a day selling drugs. "You can't get a better job?" I asked him.

"It's hard. Most of the jobs I see, you got to have training already."

"Have you ever sold drugs?" I asked.

"Yes."

"Okay, why did you get out? How did you get out? Took the $6,000, banked it, invested in the stock market?"

"No. It just wasn't me. Selling drugs didn't click with me. It wasn't something I wanted to do. I don't like quick cash basically. I like to work hard for my money."

I recognize this ethic. I grew up in Piedmont, West Virginia, in the 1950s. My father worked two jobs to support my mother, my brother, and me. I guess you could call us members of the working poor, but the *country* working poor, not the *city* working poor. The difference is huge, which I realized only after visiting my parents' friends in a Pittsburgh ghetto in 1957. Crime—city crime—simply didn't exist where we lived. We were poor but safe. We also attended school, and most of my father's friends had jobs; those who didn't were supported fairly adequately by the welfare system. I couldn't imagine why anyone in their right mind would want to live poor in a city like Pittsburgh, in crowded, hot, stifling tenements, surrounded by the constant threat of crime. Or so it seemed to me. Had my same family been transported whole to these tenements, even with all of my parents' energy and determination I do not know if I would have made it. My parents' friends migrated north for economic opportunities; what they encountered instead was largely a cycle of despair.

What happened to the city of refuge my grandfather's generation sought in the North—the North, where "the streets of Heaven were paved with gold"? What happened to this street in Chicago which St. Clair Drake and Horace Clayton in *Black Metropolis* once called Little Harlem: "Around you swirls a continuous eddy of faces—black, brown, olive, yellow and white— in most of the . . . stores there are colored salespeople . . . In the offices around you, colored doctors, dentists and lawyers . . . There is continuous and colorful movement . . ."

The roots of Chicago's decline can be traced to the Great Migration of the 1920s and 1930s. Fleeing poverty and the repression of white racism and Jim Crow, blacks from the South flocked to Chicago. They built homes, claimed entire neighborhoods, and constructed businesses. Hope was palpable. A new Black America was born, a new culture, a rural Southern and urban Northern blend reflected in Chicago's blues and jazz . . . and in the modern urban ghetto.

City historian and activist Timuel D. Black knows this story firsthand. These first migrants, like Mr. Black's family, aspired to a middle-class life, pursuing education and adapting well to Chicago's dynamic clash of cultures and ethnicities. But division *within* the black community began to appear when a new wave of migrants arrived during World War II.

Class trumped race. The old Negroes and these newer Negroes were as different as black and white. And when housing began to be desegregated in the late 1940s, many in the black middle class saw their chance to escape the cramped confines of the ghetto. The newcomers were rural blacks: "In the rural South, where most of these young people's families came from, children were considered part of a responsibility," Timuel Black explained. "They could slop the hogs and they could milk the cows and gather the eggs and pick cotton. They were an asset there. They were a liability here."

Those who blame the poor for their own poverty always point to the exceptions. And, indeed, strong leaders and positive role models have always been found here. Elaine Rhodes was raised in the Robert Taylor Homes. She became a teacher and a community activist, and she stayed in the neighborhood. In 1972, she started teaching baton twirling to young black girls who later named their troupe the Twirling Elainers, which still performs at church functions, family reunions, graduations, and other events in the community.

Elaine's goal was to instill discipline and generate pride within a group much more likely than not to be single parents and poor. The building in which Elaine grew up is already a casualty of the demolition team. Now she lives about three miles away. I did my best to help her cook lunch for the hungry twirlers. It's almost like Sunday dinner with friends, including a huge, delicious peach cobbler—until the conversations turn to the past, to stories of loss buried in the bricks and mortar of the Robert Taylor Homes.

"Dr. William Glasser talks about the basic things people need in life—love, fun, power, freedom, and belonging," said Elaine. "People need to feel that someone loves them and that they belong. I make other people feel that way, and they have given that back to me. And my creativity has allowed me to think outside the environment I'm in. Love and creativity have sustained me. I really do believe that."

Life is fast-forwarded here. Mothers bear children when they are children themselves. Tammie Cathery, whose nickname is Pooh-Pooh, bore her first child at seventeen. She's hoping her children have a different experience, she tells me.

"My eldest daughter is thirteen," Tammie told me. "I keep her in the house a lot. I cannot always do that, but I try to talk to her. She's not more mature like I was when I was thirteen. I was more experienced back then than how the kids are now. I try to talk to them and get them to understand life, what life is all about, and what I've been through—my mistakes, my wrongdoing. I try to tell them my wrongdoing. I don't hide nothing from my kids. I tell them everything I think they won't know. I don't hide nothing."

Many young women like Tammie are struggling to make better lives, for themselves and their children, but in households in which black men scarcely feature. Where are the young black men? One in three of these women's husbands and lovers is likely to be in prison or on probation or parole. For many of them, the first stop is the Cook County Jail.

If you are arrested in Chicago, the Cook County Jail is where you are held until your trial date is set. It's bigger than many Illinois towns, with more than eleven thousand inmates, three-quarters, around 70 percent, of them black. It's almost as black as Chicago's South Side, which is 78 percent black—a perverse vocational school replacing the public school system.

When I visit the jail, Officer Clark Clemons is my guide, a mild-mannered Virgil escorting me through Hades. He takes me to see a typical medium-security block, housing 120 inmates. Most of them have been there before and will be back again.

"Fifty percent of the men who are here are doomed to be in this jail or in a prison for the rest of their lives. They're here till they check out. One circumstance or another they'll be here or they'll come back. And that's sad," Officer Clemons tells me, but "the state has a problem too. When a person commits a crime, we the public are the first ones to say, put them in jail."

If this is not cruel and unusual punishment, then I don't know what is. The clang of the cell door must trigger a living nightmare for these men. And most people stay here between two and eight years, often "graduating" to prison to do more time. Even if released, many end up back here, starting the process all over again. Why would anyone do anything to return to this hellhole? I asked to talk to one of the inmates. Officer Clemons introduced me to thirty-six-year-old Kalais Chiron Hunt, alias Eric Edwards.

"It's hell in here," Kalais tells me, "but you have to understand something. I was always intelligent; I just didn't use the intelligence that God gave me."

Why not? I wonder. It's a question of role models, he tells me.

"If I was seeing like, let's say, a fireman every day, then that could be a role model. I'm not saying there wasn't firemen, but they wasn't around in my neighborhood; they didn't actually live in my neighborhood. If a fire broke out, the firemen would come from a station that's not in my neighborhood to put the fire out. If the ambulance driver come to my neighborhood, he would come from another place; he wouldn't actually live in my neighborhood. I wouldn't wake up in the morning and come outside to play and see a fireman on his way to work or see a policeman on his way to work. I'd see a drug dealer. I'd see someone stealing something."

Kalais is sharp and quick and witty: in another world, he could have been a successful entrepreneur, a lawyer, or a doctor. Instead, he has been in and out of jail for the better part of his life.

It may be too late for Kalais, but some young men, all juvenile offenders, are being given a second chance. I visited the Evening Reporting Center at the Westside Association for Community Action. Instead of going to jail, these teenagers have been sentenced to the Pretrial Service Program in the Department of Probation and Court Services of the Cook County Division of Juvenile Justice. After three weeks they will be reassessed. Gang rivalries disappear here, replaced by counseling, homework with tutoring, recreation, socializing, nurturing. It's three times cheaper to keep a young man on this program than to send him to jail, and it has a 91 percent success rate.

Seventeen-year-old Jason Smith entered the program after being arrested for possession of a loaded semiautomatic handgun. First arrested at the age of twelve, he had been a member of a gang and dealing since he was thirteen, and had quickly climbed the drug hierarchy. Around the time he turned fifteen, he was given his own "set." I asked him what that meant.

"A set is a street, sometimes by a school, sometimes by a neighbor's house, where a person's spot to sell drugs is designated by gang members. I was out there on the set with three or four guys I had grown up with," he said. "By the time I was sixteen years old, we were making about $10,000 a week from the crack house in Evanston, between the ten of us. Sometimes I'd go home with $1,000 a day. I started buying clothes and spending money on girls and more expensive cars. I helped my family with the rent and continued buying drugs to sell."

Jason feared he would probably end up shot or in jail before long, but instead, he ended up before a judge who sentenced him to the Pretrial Service Program. There, something "buried within" helped him turn his life around—to the extent that he is now completing a bachelor's degree in business and works as a probation officer with the Illinois Circuit Court of Cook County.

Gangs, drugs, teenage pregnancy, the breakdown of the family, white racism, lack of role models, bad choices, nihilism, instant gratification: these are the explanations that the people from the South Side themselves give for the causes of a seemingly inescapable downward spiral of hopelessness that has become synonymous in America with the inner city, despite the fact that most people here are decent, hardworking, responsible—fighting against odds that would have crushed me. It is intolerable—or it should be—that anyone lives like this in America in the twenty-first century. How do we change this?

My generation was raised to seek freedom through education, to use the schools and literacy to "beat the white man at his own game," as our parents put it. Now, with segregation outlawed, with more equal opportunity in education available than we could scarcely dream of, whose fault is it? The ethos of education and self-help that was drummed into my generation sometimes seems as far away from here as the mass migration of hundreds of thousands of poor southerners that turned this part of Chicago into a black metropolis. A concerted assault on *all* of these problems is the only way to stop the rot in our inner cities. But welfare and other social safety-net programs have been cut dramatically in the last few years. And without federally and state-funded support programs, especially job training, these residents have very little chance of escaping the cycle of poverty.

No one has done more in the past thirty years to generate hope and aspiration among inner-city citizens than the Reverend Jesse Jackson. Jesse's message is filtering through. Hope *is* alive, even here. But the problem, he laments, is that "people who are living with low roofs on their dreams develop lifestyles to match."

I attended graduation ceremonies at Chicago's famous black Du Sable High School. The students come from some of the most deprived backgrounds in America, but they have thrived. This is more than a commencement: it is a victory in a war against terror. Armed with diplomas, the students have embraced Frederick Douglass's message that the road from slavery to freedom is paved with education—that education is the blackest thing one can do.

Walking through Du Sable's Hall of Fame, I saw politicians, scientists, entertainers, and community leaders—even Nat King Cole went to school here. So did Mayor Harold Washington. A small, determined minority will always transcend their environment, against the odds, with a strength of will that few of us in more privileged backgrounds can imagine.

But how much hope do today's students feel about their future? Dr. Emiel Hamberlin, a teacher at Du Sable for thirty-six years, expresses hope tempered with realism.

"I suppose I could get very upset about finding out that a student has dropped out because she's pregnant or another is in the Cook County Jail because he's busted for selling drugs," Dr. Hamberlin told me. "But then I look at the students as they're walking through the hall, as they're sitting in the cafeteria and in my classroom, and I wonder, if I was in this community, which one of them would I be? Just which one would I be? If I was dealt a hand of an environment that is so negative, that draws so much energy away, that actually reinforces their negativity so well, and they are successful being negative, then how can I offset it with being positive?"

The bricks and mortar at the Robert Taylor Homes are coming down, a housing project so horrendous that only its destruction could fix it. But can a healthy culture grow on this fallow ground? Racism, economic discrimination, poor medical facilities, substandard schools, drugs, crime, violence: beyond the bricks and mortar, these are the forces still alive and well in the ghetto. In the end, our lives are determined by the choices we make. No white racist forces you to get pregnant at sixteen, or to sell or use drugs. What separates the graduates at Du Sable from the "vocational students" at the Cook County Jail? When we figure that out, can we bottle and sell it? Can a different culture flourish here, where the hopes and dreams of each individual have a chance to grow? Only if we as a society at long last destroy the structural forces of racism and job discrimination that curtail the choices and possibilities of the people who live here. Our people have always had to fight against and conquer tremendous forces arranged against us. We have done so through sheer willpower and an almost naïve belief in the power of education and in the principles upon which this democracy was founded, believing—against the odds—in the promise of an unfettered future. Only if each person here embraces the best of the *black* tradition, and takes refuge from this culture of chaos through education, deferred gratification, and hard work, can we, too, claim our stake in the American dream. For in the end—despite all of the various explanations—there can be no other way.

JESSE L. JACKSON

Restitution, Reinvestment

The Reverend Jesse L. Jackson, Sr., shared a story with me involving a young Chicago man from a big housing project who earned a degree from Eastern Illinois University and "escaped his environment. His wife is a doctor, he has six children, and he has nine hundred employees. He has an outstanding janitorial firm. The city of Chicago owes him $1.9 million for work his company has completed. This sort of business phenomenon is true in more places than we tend to realize. Many of our cities, counties, and states are behind four and five months in paying workers."

Today we view slavery as a kind of blur in the history of this country. Yet America is too young for the memory of slavery to be so old. The existence of slavery is too close to be thought of as so far away. When one considers the economic origin of America, it was Africa and her people who subsidized America's development. After all, two hundred years without wages is an African subsidy to America, redefining what party is "creditor," and which is "debtor," in the African-American relationship.

In telling the story of America, we focus on Ellis Island and on the immigrants who traveled here seeking economic liberation—far more than religious freedom, I might add. But we cannot understand Ellis Island in New York unless we understand Gorée Island in Senegal, because it was the wealth derived from the African slave trade that enabled America to become strong enough to attract immigrants.

Unlike other groups who came to America as immigrants, Africans were brought here and enslaved and exploited for economic ends, with the support of a national legal system. In other words, the exploitation of African Americans has been built into the political, legal, economic, social, and cultural structure of America. One cannot simply evolve out of an exploitative status that is so thoroughly structured into the institutions, laws, and culture of a nation.

It is true that immigrants were exploited, but they were able, based upon their skin color, to move beyond it and take on new identities. But because there was such degradation around the issue of race, America was built for two hundred years on African people having no rights that whites were bound to respect, and on whites being able to make full use of Africans for economic advantage. Thus, slavery was about both race and class, because while race was the ideology, greed was the driving force.

We are taught that whites basically came here looking for religious freedom. It's not really true. Some did, but there were notices posted in Europe that said, if you will go to America, we will give you one hundred acres of free land, and free laborers. The promise of America was both free land and free labor. Europeans may have been scholars, prisoners, entrepreneurs, or oppressed— none of that mattered. No matter what the status may have been in Europe, they came here, in the main, for the promise of free land and free labor.

The existence of slavery was woven into the fabric of the country. It was woven into religion, because slavery could be rationalized as having been or- dained by God. It became part of the country's sociology, part of our schol- arly institutions, our politics, our culture, our literature. Race is a deep matter. And each time there's been some law to change the equation politi- cally, it has never had an economic application. Two hundred years after slav- ery was instituted in America, it was made illegal, but no one changed any of the economic assumptions, or any of the educational assumptions, of the sys- tem that put it in place.

As Frederick Douglass said, ". . . we became free, but then we were free to starve, free without land, free without education, free without compensation, free without reparations; just free." Those who were "supreme," who were "seven-fifths human," lost nothing economically. Those who were considered three-fifths human gained nothing economically. The law changed, but the economic infrastructure did not change. People on the American political left say that poverty is a problem of the economic system. People on the Ameri- can political right say it's a problem of individual initiative. What all of those persons fail to do is deal with the matter of historical continuity. Since God started making days, not a single day has been missed. And all things there- fore are connected.

Let's look, for example, at the matter of insurance. When our forebears were enslaved, the slave owners took out insurance policies on them. If a parent died or escaped, the slave owners collected. Insurance companies collected as well, and in turn invested the money in the burgeoning American infrastructure of the 1800s, such as railroads and cities. When American slavery was abolished legally, what did insurance companies do? Those insurance companies that would sell insurance to African Americans—and many of them would not—established race-based premiums, logged on two sets of books, one for "Colored" and one for "White." African Americans and people of color were forced to pay more for the same insurance policies than those for whites, and more for the policy than it was worth. Consequently, insurance companies developed a system to deny or "redline" access to capital for people of color.

There is continuity between slave-era exploitation by insurance companies and present-day exploitation of African Americans by insurance companies. Therefore, a critical issue of our time is, state by state, which insurance companies maintained slavery-based policies, and which—an even larger number—had race-based policies? How much money did they make on the original premiums, and on any investments they made on that capital? These are very real questions. An analysis of the current disparities in wealth, health, education, and access to capital between African Americans and European Americans rests on historic economic exploitation of people of color in America, particularly African Americans. Thus, America must address its legal history of inequities in order that her creed of equal protection under the law and equal opportunity carries a resonance of reality.

To do so, each state legislature must conduct research to identify exploitative companies, and proceed with legislation to recover what amounts to stolen assets. Recovery is separate from reparations, and relates to stolen property. While the process for reparations may coincide with recovery, each must be viewed distinctly. For example, based on the investments that were made with that stolen property, reparations deal with injury over time and opportunity lost. If today I were to take $50,000 from you and hold it for twenty years, you would lose your house, you would lose your property, you would be unable to send your child to school, and your world would come apart. If you catch me twenty years later, I cannot just pay you; there must be recovery and restitution for the robbery. That is a real issue for African-American people, and it must now take on the dignity, if you will, of legislative action. It cannot just be seen as something that the mad people on the margin talk about. The fight for research, recovery, restitution, and reparations must be systematized, as was the process which robbed so many for so long. The process must be mainstreamed.

Another example of historical continuity is the connection between the

Revolutionary War fought by enslaved Africans in St. Domingue and the expansion of America. In 1799, the French general Napoleon ordered an army to St. Domingue to put down a rebellion by colonized slaves. Waging and winning a war of attrition over several years, the enslaved Africans eventually established the first republic in the Western Hemisphere and named it Haiti. We now know that the defeat of the French armies in St. Domingue, Napoleon's most prized possession overseas, was a major factor in his decision to sell the Louisiana territory to the United States.

The land from this purchase, extending from New Orleans up to Montana, doubled America in size. Without the Louisiana Purchase, America would not have been able to expand westward. Likewise, railroads would never have been built. Later, the U.S. government, under the Railroad Act, gave away all railroad properties—thousands of acres, six miles extending on either side of the tracks—to whites only. Consequently, the prosperity of the South, the settling of the West, the building of the railroads, all were triggered by the work and deeds of Africans and Chinese, whether they were coming from Africa or from the Caribbean or China. Thus, the exploitation of race has been a huge factor in the development of America.

In many ways, the tentacles of oppression that suck the blood and energy of African Americans are still real though less obvious. For example, every day, the media projects African Americans as less intelligent than we are, less hardworking, less patriotic, and more violent. In some sense it helps set a certain negative, limited parameter of our human value. We speak of the humiliation of police profiling, but the more basic profiling for the masses of our people is much more humiliating. African-American people, like me, pay more for insurance. We pay more for our home mortgages, we pay more for bank loans, and we pay more for our automobile financing. Predatory exploitation is a multibillion-dollar industry driven by race. In some cases, entire zip codes are used to exclude; sometimes they use other schemes, such as "payday loans." But if we pay more for less, and get fewer services, and live in stress, then we do not live as long.

If I were writing a *Freedom Symphony* in four movements, the first movement—the dominant movement—would reflect the abolition of slavery as an institution, by law, although we had no educational rights and no economic rights. The second movement would be about the end of legalized racial segregation, which was another phase of economic exploitation. The third movement would be about access to the right to vote for all citizens, a movement and struggle unto itself. But one can be out of slavery, out of legal segregation, have the right to vote, and still starve to death, because none of those movements dealt with the economic infrastructure. They were all about our legal status; about changes to the law. None of them put forward any plan for economic recovery or economic restitution or economic restructuring.

American "apartheid" was ended as a matter of law, but unless one has some plan to offset the economic denial and exploitation, then the racial denial continues. Therefore, the fourth movement of the *Freedom Symphony* is the quest for economic restructuring, restitution, and recovery. It is the mastery of the financial system under which we live. By and large, the wealth of this country is within the private sector, which represents 80 percent of all jobs. That is why in the fourth movement of the symphony, we must now become shareholders and not just sharecroppers.

Being a shareholder in America's growth and development requires personal responsibility. Personal initiative and discipline, punctuality, a thirst for educational excellence, valuing preparation over pregnancy, and abstinence from mind-altering drugs have to do with will. However, the structural crisis afflicting African Americans cannot be ameliorated exclusively through the agency of individual will. For example, if you have a size 9 foot and a size 8 shoe, individual initiative and manipulation of your toes will not keep you from damaging your feet. There's a structural context for your individual efforts, and in time, walking with a size 9 foot in a size 8 shoe will increase your pain so much that you will give up; you will just stop walking. You'll spend your time trying to anesthetize your pain, whether with drugs or other forms of gratification. You will figure that since you cannot change the structural context, short-term fun is easier than preparing for your future. For the economically exploited and oppressed, life is not worth fighting all the time. Some rationalize they will never possess a size 9 shoe for their size 9 foot, and relinquish hope.

The real struggle has to be about structural change. Why are we so good as African-American people in golf, football, basketball, baseball, track, and tennis? These sports require the most of any human being in terms of correlating more than cognitive skills. To be a professional athlete, you must be the best in the whole world, exceeding others of whatever race, class, or religion anywhere. Why are we so good in these endeavors? Some would say because African Americans have an athletic genetic superiority. The answer is rooted in the structure of American society. Whenever the playing field is even and the rules are public and the goals are clear, we can advance to the next level. Who becomes the best basketball player in Boston is determined by objective criteria: who gets the most rebounds, shoots the most points, makes the most assists, and plays the best defense. Who becomes president of Harvard University is very subjective. Anyone who watches a basketball game can see how the players handle the ball. The president of Harvard is chosen behind closed doors.

African Americans do not do as well in situations where decisions subject to cultural influence are made in private. We do better when the playing field is even. In some sense, we are making more progress in the army than in the society as a whole, because at least if you have more stripes than the other person, they must respect status that is born out of the structure of stripes and bars and leaves.

The mission of the Rainbow/PUSH Coalition is to defend, protect, and gain civil rights, by leveling the playing field in every aspect of American life and spreading peace around the world. The point, it seems to me, is that America has too quickly defined the civil rights struggle as having ended back in the days of civil rights protest and activism. What is Rainbow's objective? It is to even the playing field. Is there even access to medicine? No. Is there even access to who may be a judge? No. Is there even access in who may run for governor? No. Is there even access in who will receive construction contracts? No. Most of the field in America is yet uneven. Where the field is uneven defines our agenda.

The most basic step within the goal of economic restructuring is access to education, because strong minds bring strong change. Think about the slavery system. The slave owner had the right to rape the woman on his property, anytime he wanted. Had the right to hang the black man for trying to escape brutal work conditions, or for striking a white man, or for lying with a white woman. African Americans lived under degrading conditions and under the slave owner's rights. Wouldn't let you go to church, his rights. If a slave master were caught teaching you to read or write, even he could be punished, because even in slavery, they knew that strong minds break strong chains.

Maybe the most disappointing aspect of our struggle today is that there is a generation of young African Americans who no longer see getting an education as defiance, as rebellion—who no longer understand that the right to learn is a revolutionary act. To learn is an act of defiance, because there is so much strength in education. To the extent that we accept mediocrity and do less than our best academically, while exceeding the norm in athletics, we are accepting an equation we cannot settle for if we are to catch up to other Americans.

If you compare Neuqua Valley High School in the suburbs of Chicago, Illinois, to a high school on the South Side of Chicago, for example, you view the imbalance in the American public school system. Neuqua Valley High is forty-five minutes outside Chicago, in a suburb called Naperville. It has a 14:1 student–teacher/staff ratio. It has a Library Media Center with more than twelve thousand books. The library has thirty-six networked computers. The school has cushioned carpets. It has a pool and several gyms. Some of the veteran teachers earn $72,000. Real estate brokers refer to the school in newspaper ads. On Sundays, local churches rent space in the school and the community sponsors programs using the gymnasia and one of two Olympic-sized pools. In other words, what you have is a school industrial complex, as opposed to a jail industrial complex. In that environment, students tend to rise to expectations.

People with education take the roof off of their dreams. They say, "Why can't I be president of Harvard? If Bill Clinton or Jimmy Carter can be president of the United States, why can't I be? Why can't I be a U.S. senator?" The people who are the most educated are the most likely to raise those questions. Not always, but most often. Giving up on education is a mind-flipping process. That is why I try to lay out the movements of the *Freedom Symphony* and their impact on the oppressed and the oppressor. If one stage is to end slavery, that is the movement as the oppressed defined it. That was not "the thing" for the slave masters; that was the thing for the oppressed. If the movement was to end legal segregation, that was not the movement for the segregator; that was our movement. If the thing was to get the right to vote, oppressors were not in agreement. Today there must be a movement for access to capital, industry, technology, and economic recovery. If that becomes the thing to do, then we begin to raise economic questions having to do with historical continuity. The militant thing to do today is to find out how much pension monies there are in each state, and whether common people may share in those monies. The militant thing to do today is to find out which insurance companies had race-based premiums and how much do they make and in what do they invest. The militant thing to do today is to fight for our share of education, because education is one of our strongest weapons. Let us not forget that if we are going to even the playing field, those most likely to even that field are those who have the equipment to do so.

People who are living with low roofs on their dreams develop lifestyles to match. We hear about how many black women get pregnant and get abortions. We do not hear as much discussion about how many white women get pregnant and get abortions. This type of focus always assumes that something is wrong with the behavior of black people. Many poor people smoke cigarettes. Most poor people have poor dietary habits. Most poor folk do not take regular exercise. The things that middle-class people do, most poor people, who are black, do not do. There is a culture of poverty. The more that people are educationally and financially liberated, the more their behavior changes. That is why the movement of getting access to capital, industry, technology, and economic recovery has become the big challenge.

I grew up in Greenville, South Carolina, living in legal segregation, but I did have an infrastructure of support. I had parents and teachers with high expectations, because in segregation there was the sense that we had to prove we could win against those odds. My family moved "up to the projects," and we bought a car at the same time—private transportation. My father purchased a 1948 Hudson in 1957. But it was *our* car. The point of it was, we moved to the "other side" of town.

I remember Mrs. Sara Valena Shelton, one of my favorite teachers. I shall never forget her. When we moved, we came to her class, the middle class. Children do not quite know what teachers to avoid once their family lives on the new side of town. There were two sixth-grade classes, and one was very overcrowded, with maybe seventy students. One had maybe five students, maybe six. So this was logical to me: I should sit where there are a lot of seats. I did not know why those who had been there the year before had gone to another class. I did not know there was a class where the teacher was less likely to challenge them. Other students avoided Mrs. Shelton's class. So Mrs. White, who was our principal, came and evened the classes out.

One day Mrs. Shelton walked in with a certain military rigidity and she said, "Good morning." And we said, "Good morning, Mrs. Shelton." And we sat upright. She started writing long words on the board, and we thought she thought it was the eighth grade, because they were big words to the class. Suddenly she turned and said, "I know this is the sixth grade, not the eighth, and these are no longer big words; these are polysyllabic terms. Over there is a dictionary and there is something called *Roget's Thesaurus,* and beyond that toilet there is something called the Dewey decimal classification system in the library. And furthermore, I will not teach down to you. One of you little brats might run for president or governor one day, and I do not want to be made ashamed, so listen to me intently."

When I ran for the presidential nomination in 1984, Mrs. Shelton had retired from teaching. In 1985, running on the Democratic ticket, she became one of a very few African-American members of the House of Representatives in South Carolina in the last century. The teacher who said she would not "teach down" to us was on the same party ticket as one of her former students. There was that sense of the quality of the teacher. These same teachers, I might add, who taught us on Monday through Friday also shopped at the same grocery store with our parents. They went to the same church. Even if your parents missed a PTA meeting, Mrs. Shelton would see your mother at church, and your mother would know if you were acting up at school.

Individuals dream past their reality to survive. They can stand up and say, "I am somebody!" If you have self-affirmation, you keep fighting back. If you have self-affirmation, then you define yourself as "free," much like the enslaved Dred Scott did in 1857. If you have self-esteem, you can be a Rosa Parks, you can be a Martin King. Keep pushing forward. If you stop asserting yourself, then you will not change the structure of the laws under which you live, and that is the tension between individual will and the structural crisis. If the structure is bad, you do not change it by surrendering. You change it by acts of defiance and acts of assertion. And people who are the most likely to do that are the ones whose ambition has been cultivated by education.

We do ourselves a disservice when we underestimate lack of access to equal education, lack of access to equal insurance, lack of access to equal employment, lack of access to capital, lack of access to universities. So let's not underestimate those things. On the other hand, I say that we all have the burden of doing our best against the odds. That is why coaches are so successful, because they cut it real hard in terms of what you must do to win. Recently, I was speaking at a school in Newark with about two thousand kids. I said to a basketball player standing near the equipment shed, can anybody dunk? Oh, we can dunk. So I said, how many hours do you practice a day? They said, about three and a half. I said, what time? Six to nine-thirty. That's homework time; they had some superintendents sitting there. Six to nine-thirty. How many days a week? Six. I said, well, do you ever have any radios in practice? Oh no. A TV in practice? No. I said, well, suppose you were running and you get real tired, can you sit down? No. What do you do? You have to suck it up. I said, wait a minute, six days a week, four hours a day, no radio, no TV, no telephone. You're good. You're good at what you work at. That's why we excel in football, basketball, baseball, and track, because we work at it.

Given how the culture is, if one says to a white suburban coach, this year you must coach at a predominantly black inner-city school, he doesn't like that; he considers that to be punishment. It is the same thing if I want the physics and math teachers to go to that school. They say no, or, I am going down there but I am not sure they can learn; I am not sure their parents will help. I am not sure they have enough equipment. I am not sure I can park my car. Their cultural bias kicks in. But I submit to you that in poor and under-served neighborhoods, the same place where the athletes come from and musicians come from, scientists come from the same area, and scholars come from that same area, but the athletic entertainment dimensions are more exploitable; they are the more commercial "cotton pickers." Therefore, there are more ways out as athlete and as singer than as scholar. There are more young black men getting scholarships who play basketball or football than there are young black men getting scholarships in medicine.

The result of what I would call the system in crisis is that there are now nearly 1 million African-American men in jail and more than 2 million black men in the criminal justice system, including those on probation and parole. There are only 625,000 African-American men in college. More young black men in jail than college. In 2002, there was a daily average of 11,200 inmates compared to about 10,000 beds in the Cook County Jail in Chicago. Most of the young black inmates there are high school dropouts. Forty percent of these young men are in jail on nonviolent drug charges. If those who are at Cook County Jail and other jails on a nonviolent drug charge were let out with an ankle or wrist bracelet and monitored, conditional upon their mastering some trade or getting a GED, America would then have more young black men in college than in jail.

All the data show that most drug users and pushers are white. In 2001, 86 percent of all the rural arrests were white; 71 percent of all urban arrests were white. Yet about 54 percent of American men in jail in 2002 were black and about 19 percent were Hispanic. The majority of those in jail now are black and brown, and poor, without adequate legal representation. Once you are caught in that system, it tends to recycle itself, because that system is the epicenter of HIV/AIDS, and it is the epicenter of drugs. You leave there slicker, because you learn the science of the system. You leave there slicker and sicker. You get more drugs in than out, so you leave there slicker and sicker and you return quicker. If we broke up recidivism alone in jails, you'd have to close down half of that industry today.

It would mean losing a lot of jobs. We would have to turn that institution into a library. The Cook County Jail budget today is bigger than any Historically Black College or University in America, including Howard, Morehouse, or Florida A&M. None of those schools have a budget as big as the Cook County Jail budget. It is ridiculous, but it is real. In the last ten years, half of all public housing built has been jails, mainly for black men committing nonviolent drug-related crimes.

That is why I am saying that it is simplest to study harder while young. We have also got to study harder on the structural forces that are undercutting spiritual opportunity. When the right wing could not reverse the Supreme Court decisions on education, they started planning to undercut the educational system. When I was growing up in Greenville, South Carolina, you had your black high school, Sterling High, and you had your two high schools for whites, Parker and Greenville. The right wing could not stop the *Brown* v. *Board of Education* decision, but they started taking big churches and turning them into white, private Christian day academies. That became a way to keep black and white education separated. Then they went from there to various formulas and charter schools, and as they began to take teachers away and students away, they reached a stage where they want to take funding away through vouchers. Those who opposed desegregation contend that race is not currently a factor in segregated schools, rather property real estate tax formulas. Either way, the result is the same: a tale of two schools.

You have a terrible imbalance based upon the real estate tax base, and it ends up being separation by mostly race and class. The gap between the all-black high schools of the 1950s and the all-white high schools of that period was not as great as the gap between today's high schools in poor neighborhoods and those in more affluent neighborhoods. Then, the all-black school received books three years after the all-white school did, but basically the same books. There was a kind of parallel. But the new vertical class-race gap based upon real estate funding is wider than the old horizontal race gap was a little more than fifty years ago. Now it has the indignity of not only race exploitation but class exploitation, and rural white youth as well as black inner-city youth suffer from lack of an equal funding formula. The children of Appalachia are suffering from lack of an equal funding formula, but it does not make it any less unfair that in addition to blacks, and in addition to Hispanics, rural whites and Appalachian whites are not getting a fair deal. It just means that they, too, are getting less than the promise of the American dream.

Life is some combination of nature and environment. There is nothing wrong with our nature, but there is something wrong with our environment, and we tend to underestimate environmental opportunity. The fact is that in America the black and brown youth have less access to equal education today, less access to health insurance today, less access to a job today, less access to promotions today, less access to mortgage lending at a fair price today, and less access to risk capital to go into business today. We must not underestimate the structural forces that impinge upon our nature and upon the way we behave.

For example, in Chicago, there is a young man from a big housing project who graduated from Eastern Illinois University and escaped his environment. His wife is a doctor, he has six children, and he has nine hundred employees. He has an outstanding janitorial firm. The city of Chicago owes him $1.9 million for work his company has completed. This sort of business phenomenon is true in more places than we tend to realize. Many of our cities, counties, and states are behind four and five months in paying workers.

So this young man is "floating" money to the city. As a result of the lack of payment by the city, his employees' union takes legal action to attach his bank accounts because he is not paying his union dues on time, and they charge him a 15 percent penalty. The government is on his back because he is not paying his taxes on time. He cannot get a "bridge loan" from the bank because he has bad credit. He had to fight to get the contract in the first place, and now he has to fight to get the money for the completed contract. Even when he gets the money, the government penalty for paying his taxes late has wiped out his profit margins. The penalty for paying the labor union dues late has wiped out his profit. Again that's structural; that is not something wrong with him. City, county, and state governments are notorious for paying people late. When you pay them late, you pay a penalty, but when they pay you late, you're lucky. You just suck it up.

The class divide between poor and middle-class blacks was not created by African-American people or by Hispanic people. The fact is, without the banning of discrimination in places of public accommodation that was part of the Civil Rights Act of 1964, without the right to vote, without affirmative action, even African Americans who are in the middle class would be living in poverty. And most of those in the new African-American middle class are government employees in one form or another. They are firemen, they are police, they are teachers, they run for state government, they run for the federal government, they get contracts from city, county, and state governments. Most of the black middle class is heavily dependent upon government.

Dr. King did not die so that we have two classes of black people. But he did make it clear in his last campaign, the Poor People's Campaign, that America cannot lift one ethnic group out of poverty without working to lift all of them out. We have been amazingly successful, over continuing odds. We do have more doctors today. We do have more lawyers. We do have more businesses. We have more of all of that, and the increase in these areas has been in proportion to the extent that equal protection under the law was enforced. The lack of more blacks coming up from the bottom, the lack of more poor Appalachian whites having insurance, is not the brewing of the black employed class, the government-employed black middle class. No. That's what must be destroyed, the notion that somehow because blacks have finally got a job teaching or a government job they have the power to end structural dislocation. The idea is an insult to our intelligence.

Teaching is a noble profession. Black men and women can leave their humble conditions in getting an education and end up teaching at Harvard or some other Ivy League school, but they will not make enough to lift the masses. The government-driven middle class has tried to lift itself. They at best will get their own family up. The young man in Chicago who has nine hundred employees, many of whom are ex-convicts who otherwise could not get a job, is about to lose his business because the city owes him money and because those nine hundred employees have families. And they have home mortgages. Again there is yet another trap, because he is lifting as he climbs, but if he cannot climb, he cannot lift.

I do not want to make any excuse for people who do less than their best to reinvest. Even honeybees have reinvestment sense, and a honeybee doesn't have a human brain. There are no Harvard-graduate bees, there are no doctor honeybees, and there are no trainer honeybees. Yet a brainless honeybee, driven by buzz or instinct or whatever honeybees are driven by, gets its nectar from a flower and doesn't just fly away and say, I am satisfied. Even the honeybee has enough sense or instinct to drop pollen where it picked up nectar and then fly away. It knows that at one point its supply will become empty. And if it flies back and didn't drop pollen and the flower's dead, the honeybee dies. The honeybee understands the law of regeneration, or of reinvestment.

There are a significant number of African-American churches today that are getting into community development and reinvestment. They are purchasing property, or they are building life centers; they are teaching economic literacy classes; they are forming partnerships with the private sector and with other nonprofits to revitalize inner-city neighborhoods and create thriving communities. African-American churches comprise the single largest purchaser of land in black America today, and the largest builder of houses.

This is what you see happening with the Abyssinian Baptist Church in New York City. The new 64,000-foot shopping center is a church-driven CDC (community development corporation). Likewise, what one sees with the work and with the congregations of Reverend James Meeks of the Salem Baptist Church of Chicago and Reverend Jeremiah Wright of the Trinity United Church of Christ in Chicago and Bishop Eddie Long of New Birth in Georgia and others is emblematic of a newly emerging African-American middle class, through its church structure buying land and engaging in entrepreneurial activities. Entrepreneurship can reduce the poverty among 40 percent of black children only when the system works with the entrepreneur, not against him.

Just as it takes a village to raise a child, sick villages will raise sick children. Connected villages raise connected children, and disconnected villages raise disconnected children. I would think that another of the big challenges today is the issue of churches retreating from their duty to even the playing field. The Scriptures say that "faith without works is dead." Faith is a substance that things hope for, and evidence of things unseen. Dr. King's tradition was in effect saying that we live in our faith, our belief system, but we live under the law. People of faith must fight the law. Our theology must be about changing public policy as well as private habits. We had faith and religion in slavery. But until the law changed, the shackles wouldn't come off. We had religion at the back of the bus, but there was also a sign up front that said coloreds sit in the rear and whites up front and those who are violent will be punished by law. People of faith must fight for public policy. Faith cannot just be internal, personal, and private.

Moses marching to Canaan was a public policy march. Joshua marching round the walls of Jericho was a public policy march. Jesus challenging Rome was a public policy struggle. Daniel resisting Nebuchadnezzar was a public policy struggle. So our churches must not just admire Dr. King; they must follow him. They must revive a theology that inspires the quest for equal opportunity through shared economic security and empowerment.

TIMUEL D. BLACK

Looking Back, Looking Up

Tim Black's family has lived in Chicago since 1919. They were part of
the first Great Migration north, preferring the dangers of Chicago race
riots to the terror they left behind. He talked to me about three generations of African Americans, from the "self-contained colored world" of
the first migration to an era of vulnerability, in which African Americans
lost "the protection or the wisdom and support of those who had left the
old community."

I'll be eighty-four years old next December. When I was a kid, I hung out in
the streets, with my mama nagging me every night. Sometimes I'd come
home drunk and stay out there with people like Redd Foxx. I knew him well.
You'd have to be out on the street with Redd to really know how bright and
quick he was. Redd was a Du Sable High School graduate. He played the
dozens on the street. Now if you were foolish enough to play the dozens with
Redd, you were gonna get crucified. You were gonna have to hit him, because
he was so quick and so colorful and so artistic that when he could get to talking about your mama, that was just the beginning. He could take your whole
ancestry. Guys like Billy Eckstine hung out on the same streets. They knew I
was dumb, so they wouldn't ask me to do anything wrong. In fact, they would
stop me from doing anything wrong. They liked me, and they'd say, Shorty,
I've got something for you if you want it. They weren't looking down on us;
they were just appreciative of us.

I briefly went to Xavier University in New Orleans on a basketball scholarship. I saw all those pretty girls, and I knew I wasn't going to be serious about
school. So I came back home. After I returned from World War II, I went to
Roosevelt University. I was in the social sciences. I was concentrating primarily on cultural anthropology and sociology, but I found that even after ob-
taining my master's degree from the University of Chicago, it was hard to find
a job as a black anthropologist or sociologist. That master's was intended to
prepare people to teach at least at a two-year college level, from where they'd

hopefully go on to teach at a four-year college. I was in the master's program from 1952 to 1954 and the doctoral program from 1954 to 1956.

I got caught up in the Civil Rights Movement, and I've never regretted it. Professor Allison Davis, my adviser in the doctoral program, used to call me up every week because I was the only black guy in the program, and he'd ask, "When are you coming back here to finish?" I did what many people do. I finished everything but the dissertation. I tried for three years to do that. But when I was teaching in Gary, Indiana, and saw Dr. King on television, I said, ain't no place for me to be but Montgomery. I jumped on a plane and went there. From that point on, I was suckered in. I went back to the university and I got enough history to teach at the high school level and continued in that vein till we broke the racial barriers in the community colleges. There were then two of us who were qualified teachers of anthropology and sociology as well as history. So I had three preparations. And my classes filled up.

I was born in Birmingham. My father, who was born in Jacksonville, Alabama, worked in the steel mills in Bessemer, outside Birmingham. My mother was born in Florence, Alabama, also the birthplace of W.C. Handy. But she met my father in Birmingham.

Many people of that period were leaving the South like refugees. They were running away from fear. They were running away from a lack of equal opportunity. And they were running away from the terror. So they came to Chicago as part of the first Great Migration.

My family arrived in Chicago in August of 1919, right after the race riot of July 1919. It gives some idea about what they feared. They feared staying in the South more than they feared coming to Chicago. They had riots going on all the time in Birmingham. My aunt met us in Chicago and we moved to the South Side. My grandmother was here, on my mother's side, and we had other relatives and many friends who were already here. In actual fact, I can walk from where I live now to every house where I've ever lived, including the lots that are vacant now.

It was community, and I mean that definitively in terms of the spirit and the feeling of the people toward one another, though we lived in a ghetto. By that I mean we were bound by boundaries and restrictive covenants and agreements that no landlord or landowner would rent or sell to people of color at all. And so we were literally on the South Side, restricted, from about 26th Street on the north, at that time, to about 43rd Street on the south. The black population when we came to Chicago in 1919 was under 100,000, but by 1920, it was about 123,000. It had almost doubled since 1915. We all lived in this compact area, but many of the people were from the same hometowns: Birmingham, Nashville, Memphis, Little Rock, Atlanta, New Orleans, primarily the middle part of the Southern area. They had family connections and a social network. So there was a feeling of safety. The most important thing, I would say, is that they had a feeling of hope, particularly a dream of the future for their children. Parents watched their children's behavior very closely, and were very concerned about how their children were doing in school. They felt, as my mother said, that if you stayed out of trouble and you prayed and you worked hard in school, God would take care of you and everything would be all right.

So the optimism led us to not worry about the poverty that might exist, or the hard times. Of course in the 1920s, they were still pretty good times. My sister and brother joined us, and we were growing up during that period when there was quite a bit of prosperity on the South Side of Chicago. There was no great need to go outside the community, because even though it might cost more to stay there, particularly as it related to residences, everything else was available—not all owned by blacks, but some of it.

It was really a socially, politically, and in some ways economically self-contained world. All of the classes were represented within the black community. There were four class distinctions. And this was not to be ignored. One was pigmentation. Another was income. Another was where you worked, and a fourth was where you lived in the black community.

If you lived in the north end of the Black Belt, that was considered the lower class, even though you might have more money than someone who lived on the far end of the South Side. There were the prosperous people, like the Earl B. Dickersons and the Stratfords. Earl Dickerson came to Chicago in 1908. He was a very prominent lawyer. The Stratfords came later, after the race riot in Tulsa in 1923. Mr. Stratford was an attorney. His father had been an attorney. They were literally burned out in Tulsa. If you hung around with their children and that group, it didn't matter whether you were of the same class. My brother was allowed to hang out with them, and I could hang in there, but I got annoyed at times with many of them.

Having money, of course, meant that you were in business, like the Dickersons, who were in the insurance business, or the Motleys, in the art business. Archibald Motley was an artist, born in New Orleans, who settled in Chicago around 1914. His nephew was Willard Motley, the writer. If you were in that class, you were considered well off. If you had a stable job, like in the post office, you were considered kind of prestigious. If you lived in a kitchenette, which there were plenty of, that was not considered so hot, because then you couldn't have your friends over too easily, since you were living in cramped quarters. But that didn't cause any disrespect of you. They knew why you were living in that kitchenette. You might be living in an apartment that was split up into three rather than one. And where there had been six families living in a building, you might have as many as twenty families living in that same building. You were caught by the restrictive covenants that determined where you could and couldn't live, and so you had to make an adjustment. If you were fortunate enough to live on Michigan Avenue, for example, or Grand Boulevard—later renamed South Park—you were considered a little more hoity-toity than if you lived on Prairie or Indiana.

If you had gone to Tuskegee or Fisk or Howard and you were dark and you had some money, then you fitted in. If you were light-skinned, like Earl B. Dickerson and that group of people—in other words, if you looked white—they figured eventually you would struggle into the money. They figured white people didn't have no right to be poor. So we had lawyers and doctors and businesspeople living in the area along with maids and janitors and unemployed people and working-class people. It was a whole self-contained colored world.

In my block there was Dr. Dawson, brother of the late congressman William L. Dawson. There were many others whose names I can't recall. There was Bob Carroll, whose father associated with the big ministers in New York and in Europe, and they would come to his house and we would meet them. I'd be looking at Dr. Dawson and I would say to myself, I can be like that. We played together, Dr. Dawson's son and daughter and all those people. We played basketball and softball, and we were equal.

The change in the character of the community began to come at the beginning of World War II, December 7, 1941, when there was again a need—as there had been during World War I—for cheap labor. The restrictions on certain potential immigrants from Europe then made jobs available for well-trained Southern young men and women of that period. They flocked north because there was very little work for them in the South, given the kind of training they had.

That was the first flood of primarily young African Americans, male and female, and the start of the second Great Migration. As World War II went on, it gave rise to inventions, particularly in the field of agriculture. Agriculture became more mechanized. One example would be the invention of the cotton picker, which meant that the labor of the people who had worked in the fields of Mississippi and Arkansas, in the tobacco fields and other places, was now unnecessary. So the people of the second Great Migration were mostly from the rural agricultural South. They came to Chicago with less training and less motivation. They had been isolated in these areas of the South in the cotton fields and tobacco fields and other large plantation-like places. They'd been denied the opportunity for education, and their reading ability was scanty. The wave of new immigrants, pushed off the land in the South, came north with almost no context. They didn't have relatives already living in the North, and they brought with them a different culture. Many times their hopes and dreams were not that big. They'd heard of the Promised Land of Chicago, where there were plenty of jobs, a diversity of job opportunities. There was a saying during the first migration, when my mother and father came north: if you can't make it Chicago, you can't make it anywhere. That meant that if you got without a job in one place, the stockyards, for example, you'd go to a steel mill or some other place. It was very open to colored labor, to cheap labor.

But even if you were skilled, as my father was, you could not get a job that surpassed that of a white person. And very few colored people could get into the craft unions. Very few of the bricklayers, the painters, and decorators. In fact, I gave testimony on this before Adam Clayton Powell's committee in Washington, D.C., on the issue of the exclusion of blacks from the opportunity to get into apprenticeships. It had to be based on your lineage, on your uncle or your papa or someone in your family. It was very select. And so blacks hadn't got in, even though many of the blacks from the South had experience in the crafts, like the sheet metal workers.

The people in the first migration, though they had been the children of slaves, stopped in places like Birmingham before they came to big cities like Chicago. Many people don't realize that in the first migration, more black people moved from the rural South to the urban South than moved from the South to the North. They were urbanized even though they may not have been urbane. They became urbane through the experiences that were cited to them by the friends they met in the urbanized North. They were pretty sophisticated politically, particularly. It is important for people to know that the first black American to be elected to the U.S. House of Representatives in the twentieth century was Oscar Stanton De Priest, from Chicago, in 1928. He was elected to the Seventy-first Congress and the two succeeding Congresses.

There was a political sensitivity in that group who comprised the first migration. My mother told us that my father would put his gun in his pocket and go vote in Birmingham. He was considered a "crazy nigger." There were a few like that. My mother persuaded my father to leave the South and come to Chicago, because she feared for his safety; she dragged him into the city, practically.

The reason my father got away with his attitude in the South, I was told, is that my family name, Black, derives from the family name of Hugo Black. According to the oral history of my family, all of my grandparents were born in slavery. When I was about six years old, my father told my brother and me that his own father was a slave in the home of Hugo Black's father in Alabama. It was customary in those days for slave masters to impose their family name on their slaves so that people would know who owned them. Thus my father was considered a Hugo Black "nigger." And there was some favoritism toward my grandfather and his family because of the relationship with the Black family— a relationship that was respected by the larger, hostile white community. During their lifetime, my grandfather and my father continued to have communication with Hugo Black and his family in Alabama.

Here's a little sidebar in connection with that story. When Hugo Black was nominated to the Supreme Court in 1937, I went to my dad in anger. I had just graduated from high school and thought I knew something. When I said to my dad—who didn't care for white people at all, particularly white men— "The president has nominated an ex–Ku Klux Klansman," my dad put a cigar in his mouth and said, "He'll be all right." I thought my dad had gone crazy. But Hugo Black turned out to be one of the most liberal Supreme Court justices on all issues. He was a very unusual man.

In 1939, Mr. Carl Hansberry, father of Lorraine Hansberry, the great playwright, went to the Supreme Court of the United States. He had enough money to be able to do that. He wanted the right to move into a restricted white neighborhood. It was the first time such a case had gone that far since *Plessy* v. *Ferguson,* in 1896, when the U.S. Supreme Court upheld the ruling of separate but equal facilities for blacks and whites after Mr. Plessy had objected to separate transportation facilities for blacks in Louisiana.

Mr. Hansberry had the means to carry his case all the way to the Supreme Court, with the help of some other people and of the NAACP, of course. We had a very strong NAACP in Chicago. The case was *Hansberry* v. *Lee,* and Justice Hugo Black read the majority opinion that outlawed restrictive covenants in this one particular white section of Chicago. Those of us whose parents could afford it immediately moved into that section. And that's what we were supposed to do. That was what part of the Civil Rights Movement was about: as soon as you could break it down, you got out of segregation and you integrated the white community.

The white community soon fled these neighborhoods, though the people who came in were better than those who were there, educationally and all kinds of ways, if you want to measure it in those terms. But the white people left, because there are factors called prestige and status that go with living in certain neighborhoods, around certain people. There was an attitude about living around all those colored people, but we didn't care, because we had more space now and we brought our entertainment with us. We brought our jazz and all the good things that went with the life we'd had on the other end. And now we could brag that we lived in the better neighborhood.

In 1948, another case went to the U.S. Supreme Court, *Shelley* v. *Kraemer*. In 1945, Mr. Shelley had purchased a house in St. Louis on a tract of land that was restricted to white occupancy. And in that case the same justice, Hugo Black, read the majority opinion that restrictive covenants were unenforceable anywhere in the United States, which meant now that the second migration had barged in. Stylistically, the two Great Migrations were different, not inferior or superior to each other. Different people. Walked different, talked different. The new migrants brought with them country blues, not city jazz. Country Negroes. That's what we unfortunately labeled those who came with the second migration. We gave them almost no help. The separation was dramatic and complete. The class separation was pronounced right away. If they lived on the West Side, those of us who lived on the South Side already had a snobbish attitude towards them. Still do. I'm the only one who can cross those boundaries. The mother of the person who runs Indigo grew up in Chicago. I asked her, what did she know about the West Side? She said, "What do I know? I don't need to know about the West Side."

A lot of people don't understand that blacks have been divided among ourselves by class for a long, long time. And that separation removed the knowledge, the experience, and much of what we had been given by those who were part of the first Great Migration. You see, the black population at the time of the first migration outvoted the immigrant white population.

And then the new migrants didn't vote. The new black migrants of the 1940s and 1950s plummeted almost immediately. I was teaching school, and I noticed the difference in attitudes towards education. I noticed the difference in the students I was teaching in the early 1950s. By that time, as a result of *Shelley* v. *Kraemer,* the more fortunate had moved to neighborhoods like Hyde Park and Woodlawn. They had begun to move into the South Shore and had created another neighborhood in Chatham, which is still a very stable middle-class black community. They began to move into Beverly and other neighborhoods. It was like two streams that just start to diverge. The rural Southern people in the second migration then went one way and became poor, and the other people went into the middle class.

Then another thing happened. When those in the second Great Migration first arrived, there were quite a few jobs for them. But then the jobs began to go away—they were going to the suburbs, or companies were going out of business and moving somewhere else. The stockyards, for example, began to move to places like Iowa. The steel mills began to send much of their business overseas and other places.

Jobs that could have unskilled labor were no longer available. Even jobs requiring semiskilled labor were no longer available. Now this meant that the woman would apply for welfare, but she could not receive it if there was a male in the house over eighteen years old. So the family began to be immediately affected. The social worker had the right to come into your apartment any time of the day or night and look around. And if she even saw a pair of shoes that belonged to a male, she had a responsibility to cut that person off the welfare list, very much in the same mood as John Ashcroft's attorney general office.

So then the increase in public housing began and the beginning of the demolition of the old housing structures that were dilapidated, the real slum kind of housing. There was no resistance to that, because the people had not learned how to organize. And the idea came up to keep this population contained, to build more public housing. Like the Robert Taylor Homes. The high-rises. That was coming into the 1960s. The concentration of poverty and problems became intensified and greater. And that has continued up until the present.

The separation, psychological and social and certainly economic and cultural, was very pronounced. For a period of time, during Harold Washington's mayoralty—the first black mayor of Chicago, who was also a Du Sable High School graduate—we brought people together. I got money for Mayor Washington's campaign from Ed Gardner, who had a big business, according to black business standards. Ed brought all the black businessmen together because the whites would not finance a black man.

If I had been born in the Robert Taylor Homes in the 1960s, it would have been very much more difficult. There are examples of those who somehow did it and there are some who will do it. They are usually people who have met with a great teacher or a minister or a very strong woman or someone else who has helped them, like a mentor or some kind of role model. Sometimes just Mama, who somehow can see that future that my mother and father saw for their children.

The way to transform the tragedies of that period and those people—the decline from the wonderful self-contained colored world to all the statistics that we know about the Robert Taylor Homes today—is that number one we must provide quality education, the kind of education that will prepare all of the young people for college and for citizenship and for earning a living. We can do that. We must break down the barriers that cause any form of segregation, so that people can make a choice as to where they want to live. And we must create institutions of mentoring that will help those less fortunate people recognize that they must somehow change their style of living if they are to be accepted.

We must also teach them the nature of power. We must help them understand finances, as we understood in my generation. People were taking money that we earned out of the community. I walked my first picket line when I was twelve years old and thought that things would be all right after that. We created a slogan: Don't spend your money where you can't work. We must use our finances much more carefully and we must organize politically. Not exclusively for any party, but so that we can bargain—with our vote, with the power that comes from the black vote—with all of the parties. We can do all these things on the inside, among ourselves. The rest of the society needs to recognize what it promised: freedom, equality, and justice to all people. The larger society must recognize its role and understand that if it does not play its role fairly, the society itself may be in jeopardy in the long run. So there's societal responsibility. There is group responsibility and individual responsibility.

The breakdown of the community, so rapidly as it occurred, left those who were left behind with relatively few resources to survive. That community then was given an opportunity, or maybe it was imposed by outside forces that said, we can help you live. Then those outsiders brought in drugs in great quantities to be delivered to other people and guns to protect the turf. Those people who live in the Robert Taylor Homes do not make the drugs and they don't manufacture the guns. That's an outside industry that is very, very prosperous. The people who do these things and who live in the suburbs or in the more wealthy communities are respected citizens in those communities, while they have exploited these poor people who have no choice if they are to survive.

One reason the people in those conditions were exploitable was that they did not have the protection or the wisdom and support of those who had left the old community. The black middle class had left because of the end of segregation, in housing especially, and because great opportunities in education began to open up. We're talking about the civil rights period again now, in the 1960s particularly, when young people, my children, for example, were able to go to any school they wanted to go to, if they had the qualifications. The old colored middle class moved in with the white middle class.

The breakdown of the family occurred partly because of the poverty and the fact that resources were not available for a full family, particularly if there were males over eighteen years old in the house. Then you had the concentration of this despair and poverty, and you began to get three generations living in the same building or adjacent to one another, feeding on each other's misery. One of the things some of them felt was that to have more children was to get more money from the welfare system. There are great-grandmothers who live in those situations who are not forty-five years old. When I approach some of these young people, where I would ordinarily be the grandfather, say, of a teenager, or maybe even someone in their early twenties, they consider me at the very least a great-grandfather.

In the rural South, where most of these young people's families came from, children were considered part of a responsibility. They could slop the hogs and they could milk the cows and gather the eggs and pick cotton. They were an asset there. They were a liability here. That tradition still exists in the South because it has not been erased. But as a sign of manhood and womanhood in the environment where they now are, girls will say to other girls, this girl has a baby. Something must be wrong with you, honey; you're not pregnant yet. A boy is accused of being something different if he has not fathered a child by the time he's fifteen, sixteen, or seventeen years old. So for them in that group, that's normal. Leon Dash wrote a superb book about this, called *When Children Want Children: An Inside Look at the Crisis in Teenage Parenthood*. And since we haven't broken that cycle, then you're acting out of normalcy. You're acting out of the normal trend in a community to become pregnant or a father at such an early age. And then once a girl has one or two children, she becomes fair game for all the other young men, because they know she has done it. And so they are predators.

I think the only way to change that is we have to break those communities up, just like the people who live across the street from me in the high-rise have to be separated from that background. They may be moved out; the university wants to clear the property. Even though they are not friendly to people like me, I have tried to be friendly with them. I live in a building with middle- and upper-middle-class people. The people who live in the high-rise think I've got something and that I think I'm better than they are. And then the males may think I'm a spy for the police, because I'm almost sure that drug dealing is going on over there. I have approached some of them on occasion, and I find myself being asked by the men, what do you want? I think that's a sign they're suspicious I might be doing undercover work for the police or something of that sort.

We have to find young men and young women who came out of those environments and who are willing to go back and do some mentoring and some lecturing. What I have found, however, is that once most of those young men and women escape that environment, they never want to go back. They've escaped, and they never want to return to that pain. And unfortunately, too many are stuck in that environment.

That's a very dangerous situation for a society that claims equality, justice, and opportunity for everyone, because the enemy, those who are now picking at the United States for its own lack of opportunity, can say, look there. You have a black people there and at least one third of them are living below the poverty line. No child among them under the age of eighteen has much chance of being in a house where there are two parents, a male and a female.

The break has to come within us, and as old as I am, I refuse to give up on them. I continue to go to places like Du Sable High School and Phillips High School to assist, if I get asked. But I'm not going in the Robert Taylor Homes. I used to. I'll go if I have a friend who lives there, because they know how to deal with that situation. But as long as we allow, or force, that population to be concentrated with one another, and we reject them in various ways and do not provide them with an education to prepare them for the new world in which they must live, then we will continue to have the kind of separation of race and class that we have now.

ELAINE RHODES

Twirling for Success

Elaine Rhodes started a baton-twirling troupe for young women more than thirty years ago. "I stepped up to the plate," she told me, "not only by strengthening my whole structure in myself but by beginning to think of those things that made me happy and then asking, what is it that's wrong? I examined myself first, and then I examined the things I observed happening in the community. And I saw that one particular thing was happening over and over and over: I did not see people who liked themselves."

We moved into the Robert Taylor Homes in 1962—my mama and me and my four siblings. I was nine or ten years old. I'm the baby girl of the family, and I have a brother who's younger than me. Ruby L. Rhodes was my mama. She's deceased now. I dedicate this vignette to her, my baton teacher and friend. Mama was active in politics and community activities. She was the founder of the original Henry Horner Home, the Angels of Mercy Twirlers, and the Robert R. Taylor Home Cadettes Baton Twirling Troupe. She stood by me through everything, and she taught me how to stand on my own.

When the Robert Taylor Homes first opened, they were a very positive symbol, not demeaning. We lived in 5322 State, at the corner of 53rd and State, in apartment 501. Then there was 5326 State and 5323 South Federal. Eventually, these three buildings were called the Hole, because they were shaped like the circumference of a U. They were big buildings, 22, 23, and 26, bam, bam, bam.

The windows had Xs on them because they were new. Not all of the buildings had been opened yet. It was just brand-spanking-new. There was a feeling of excitement. You could smell the newness of the tile, and the walls were beautiful. The banisters were shining; the stairwells were well lit. The elevators were shiny. Oh, it was just really great.

There were 10 apartments on a floor, and sixteen floors. So there were 160 apartments. If you had, say, two daughters and a son, you had to have a bedroom for the son. Or if you had two sons and a daughter, you had to have a separate bedroom for the daughter. The family structure would dictate how many rooms you would need for your apartment. The 01 apartments had four bedrooms, and a basic family of maybe six to eight lived in each one. The 02 apartments had two bedrooms; 03 had three bedrooms; 04 had two; 05 had three; 06 had two; 07, two; 08, three; 09, three; and the apartments on 10 had four bedrooms. If you had four bedrooms, you often had more than three or four people in a bedroom. People needed a place to stay, and relatives who weren't officially residents were always staying with families there. People helped out their extended family. It became overcrowded. But everybody took care of their own business in their own way.

At first, we felt safe, because everyone who moved in was excited about their new home. I attended Farren Elementary, down the way on 51st and State. I could walk to school. Then we transferred to Mary Church Terrell Elementary, which is still standing but is closed now.

I remember Red Rooster, the grocery store. We used to have fun with the brand-new red carts. Red Rooster was near the Beasley Elementary School, at 5255 State. And I remember Mr. Berry, a black entrepreneur who owned the Starlight Paper Company and Starlight Supermarket. He helped families that didn't have it. You could shop at his store even if you didn't have money. He gave you credit.

I graduated in 1965 from Du Sable Upper Grade Center, a middle school for sixth through eighth grade. They built the middle school addition in 1964. Before then, Du Sable was just a high school. It opened in the 1930s because the Phillips High School caught fire and the students there didn't have anyplace to go. It's named after Jean Baptiste Pointe du Sable, a black man from Haiti who founded the city of Chicago. The city recognized him as its founder in 1999.

In the early sixties, Du Sable—the Big D, as we called it—was a very good high school. There were a lot of kids there, over four thousand, because of the Robert Taylor Homes. But by the mid-sixties, when I entered the ninth grade, the gangs and the teenage pregnancies made it into a different school. The gangs would try to recruit during school time on the school grounds. People who were seniors started transferring out of the school, to get away from the trouble.

Before things got bad, the 5322, 5323, 5326 residents had a softball team. Mr. J.B., the coach, lived in 5326. We had leagues and tournaments. You couldn't just play one game. People would come out to watch the games. We even messed around and got some uniforms. We used to play softball against the other buildings and against different teams in the community. I held down third base. Nobody came home. Batted left, threw right. The 5322 building and 23 and 26, all of us formed one team. We were the In the Hole Kids.

My mama had a baton-twirling troupe in the 5322 building, and from the time I first performed, I loved it. More than anything else, being a twirler in my mama's troupe gave me tenacity and confidence. I wasn't considered pretty, but I had stamina, and I was an excellent student of my mama's. My marching position was the caller, from the back line. My mama said I couldn't be the leader—it wouldn't be right, she said, me being her daughter, even though I was the best of them all. So I called out routines from the back line up to the front line. We had five lines, marching four across; then a front center mascot; and Mama.

The troupe didn't practice every day, but I did. I practiced hard every day at home, with my mama coaching me harder each time I made up new twirls and dance steps for my partner and line marchers. She let me and the back line, the four of us, march all the way to 39th and Federal, down the fire lane, just to get the routines down. She would take out one line at a time to go over their routines. Then when we had it together, we'd march as a troupe down to 39th and Federal.

Mama's coaching was brutal: Get those legs up! March on your toes! Point those toes! Shoulders back! Stomach in! Chin up! Left hand on your hip, and keep it there till you use both hands to twirl or unless you're using your arms for choreography! Smile! Do not be distracted! Keep in step, breathe, keep going, go right into the next routine, and don't forget the footwork. Let me hear those toe taps on your boots! Now do everything over till you get it right! Turn around and let's go back and try it again!

We would practice for at least three hours at a time, in white, traditional majorette boots. Mama said they were a must! This type of drilling is what developed my performance level. Some of the girls could not keep up and stopped coming to practice, mostly the cute ones in the front line. I didn't quit. I was determined that one day I'd be up front leading.

At Du Sable High, I wanted to be a cheerleader, but they were going with the cute girls with pretty legs. They had majorettes with uniforms who performed for the basketball team—the Du Sable Panthers—but they just danced; they weren't twirling. The team was going downstate to Champaign-Urbana in

1965, my freshman year, to compete in the citywide championship, and they needed the majorettes to go. Well, Ms. Nezelle Bradshaw appointed me captain of the majorettes. It was my job to teach the other girls and to take responsibility for the squad. From then on, it was no more back line. I was the leader. I was following in my mama's footsteps. And I was beginning to understand that I could help others increase their self-esteem and develop their athletic skills through an activity that was part sport, part art. After the citywide championship, we twirled at every Panthers game through my senior year at Du Sable, and I was captain all four years.

Everything I think, feel, and do is generated by what happens inside me. My baton is the tool I use to twirl for spiritual development and self-support. When I pick up the baton—my "stick"—I can create, I can choreograph, I can dance, imagine, feel empowered, and yes, have a damn good time. And fortunately, I can reproduce the same skill and technique in others.

As a young girl living in the Hole at 5322 South State Street, apartment 501, I had a brick-house body with a side of big, beautiful legs and thighs. I had short, "nappy" hair, as they called it, and a dark complexion. More than my siblings, I looked like my mama. People teased me by calling me "Boston Blackie," who was a white detective. It's a good thing that the Black Power Movement came into being, for many reasons. Oh yeah, I was also called "Buckwheat," a nickname given to one of the Little Rascals because of his hair. Ain't that a blip; now that's one of the hairstyles that's been brought back into full circle.

The kids called me ugly too! I took it and dealt with it. I could fight, and I would if I got too mad. I'd beat up the boys and girls. I was a tomboy when I had to be, but I was really a back-line marcher, dancer, strutter, and twirler. Even in the back line, we were powerful as we sang one of the old church hymns, "Holding Up the Blood-Stained Banner." We were jammin' and kickin' ass! You could hear the toe taps of our majorette boots louder than the whole rest of the troupe.

The violence at the Robert Taylor buildings began with the gangs, in the mid-sixties. You could tell when the community changed because we stopped playing softball. Different gangs would come from across town to recruit there, from the Ickes projects on 22nd and State Street and from Stateway Gardens and other projects. Some of the gangs were already started at the Robert Taylor buildings. Some of them began with the baseball teams. Certain teams started protecting themselves by fighting with the other team on the field during an argument, and most of the teams would get into rival fights after the games. Each gang had their own philosophy, their own identity. Part of it was the way they dressed, or danced. If they got one guy to go along with them, they had recruited him. That guy would bring along two or three friends. But it was one or two or three guys that started organizing the gang.

It got so you weren't free to walk with your purse hanging. You could leave your door open just long enough to go knock on your neighbor's door and say, hey, you got a cup of sugar or whatever. At that time, they began to put locks on the stairwell doors for the first time. We had a security system installed. And then we got guards for the elevators.

You began to see a difference then not only in the Robert Taylor buildings themselves, but in the structure of the families living there and the structure of the community within the Homes. Some family members had gone on to meet their maker because of gang violence. Some had been incarcerated. Members of the family were being taken away from the family as a whole, and that weakened the family structure. The sense of community within the Homes began to break down. The community no longer embraced certain families because of the violence.

In my junior year of high school, in 1968, I became pregnant. It was a difficult time for me. I was still living with my mama, and I began to think about taking the initiative to make some important decisions. I knew I was gonna go to school regardless. I didn't consider getting an abortion, nor did I think about giving up my baby for adoption. My mama thought it would be best if I gave the baby up. She knew I had to finish high school and that I wasn't financially ready to support a child. And she was concerned about the Rhodes family image. In our family it was home, church, school. School, church, home. That's the way it was.

I became a teen mother in June of 1968. And as a teen mother, I realized that things had changed not only because I was a parent, but because my living circumstances were about to change. CHA—the Chicago Housing Authority—ran the Robert Taylor Homes and was saying, okay, you have an extra person living there now, so your rent is going up. If you were a child living in Robert Taylor and then you became a parent and your child was there with you, that changed the structure of your lease, because the baby wasn't on the lease. That's when I began to realize it was time to think about making it. And my mother was letting me know I was gonna have to get out on my own. I finished high school living at home with my mama and my baby boy, Edwin. My little brother, Louis, helped baby-sit while I attended day and evening classes in my senior year, and I graduated from the Big D on time with the Class of '69.

In the summer of 1969, I left home to attend Alabama A&M in the town of Normal. I took Edwin with me. My mama was from Alabama, and there was family there who supported me all the way through college. In 1974, I returned to Chicago, and to my mama, with a bachelor's degree.

We were back in apartment 501, and I knew things were bad, but I needed a place to stay. There was a lot of drug dealing going on in the buildings and on the streets. The older guys in the gangs had to handle the drug deals. Everything started getting uglier in the buildings, and most of my siblings had left home. My older sister, Genice, who had graduated as valedictorian of her class at Crane High School, had entered Northern Illinois University. The Baptist Training Union from our church, Greater Harvest, provided some financial assistance for her college education. Genice is the doctor in our family. She was a scholar even at a young age. My sister Peggy had graduated high school and was at the University of Colorado. My older brother, Jesse, was in the army. Louis, my younger brother, was in school. Louis was astute. He was a prominent athlete, but he excelled in academics. My mother sent him away to Amundsen High School on the North Side of the city because of the gang violence. That's how devastating it was at the Robert Taylor Homes. I don't know if it's different now, but back then, she had to go through changes to get him into Amundsen because you couldn't live in one area and go to the school across town.

When Jesse returned home from the army, wearing his uniform, the police beat him at the Greyhound Bus Station, claiming insubordination as the reason. Then when he came back to the 5322 building, a gang beat him with a bat. I got a call from St. Bernard Hospital. I never will forget it. My son was still very young at the time. Jesse has beautiful hands for a man, and he had a scar or something on his hand from the service. That was the only way I could tell it was my brother. To this day Jesse is not the same; he's a disabled vet. A lot of tragedies have happened to families who lived in the Robert Taylor Homes, because of people's mentality, I guess. Some stuff just makes no sense.

After a few months of living with my mama at 5322 State, she told me that Edwin and I would have to leave. I knew that was coming, and I had applied for public assistance and food stamps, using my mama's address, and put Edwin on a waiting list for the preschool in her building. The Centers for New Horizons—CNH—sets up preschools on the South Side of Chicago, and kids who lived in the Hole went to Robert Taylor South Day Care. The Salvation

Army took in Edwin and me while I looked for work and day care. Four months later, Edwin was accepted into the CNH preschool at Robert Taylor South.

There were some dark moments before I got the two-bedroom for Edwin and me at 5041 South Federal. The Salvation Army extended the limit for our stay more than once, but finally, after fourteen months there, we had to leave, and I wasn't employed yet. Just before it was time to leave the Salvation Army, I rented a slum apartment, for which I paid first and last month's rent and a security deposit. It was a third-floor apartment, and the steps leading up to the second-floor outside landing were bad. The apartment was wet and damp, not good for a mother and child who both had asthma. And there was a gas leak. When it got bad, I called the fire department. On his way up the back steps, one of the firemen plunged his foot all the way through the stair and wrote up a report on the spot. The landlady then kicked me out on the spot, and attacked me while I was climbing the stairway with Edwin in my arms to get our belongings.

In 1976, there was an opening at Edwin's preschool for a teacher's aide. I applied for the position and was hired. The Centers for New Horizons had some power to hook up with the Chicago Housing Authority because the preschools were in CHA buildings, and the teachers for the preschools were recruited from those buildings. Once I was hired as a teacher's aide, CNH told the Housing Authority that I needed a two-bedroom apartment at 5041 South Federal. And that's how I got my placement in apartment 407 with my son at the Robert Taylor 5041 building.

It was when Edwin began preschool that my next life transition began. At that time the Centers were using an Afrocentric curriculum because all of the children in their preschools were African American. Edwin began his own cultural educational journey in room C with Mrs. Claude O. Jack. Parents who spent time in the preschool had to do volunteer work and weren't allowed to volunteer in the same room with their children. So I volunteered with other classrooms in 1974 and 1975. I began to embrace the same knowledge and history that my son was learning. And I started teaching twirling to four little girls from room A.

When I began teaching the preschoolers how to twirl, the Centers for New Horizons did not have a teaching methodology for helping the children develop fine and gross motor skills. I saw this as an opportunity to help the children and myself. Not only could baton twirling assist the children in their total development, but teaching them, I knew, would help mend some hurt feelings of my own. I wanted to take the child with or without the pretty Easter model look—the child I could transform and make beautiful, the way I wanted to be as a little girl! If I could sum up the essence of my journey from then till now, I'd say I ain't mad or sad, but I sho am glad that I had a chance in my lifetime to contribute to the world through the lives of children, sharing my God-given gift of talent and creativity.

The children had their first recital in 1975, and a few years later, when they weren't so little anymore, they came up with the name that has stuck to this day: the Twirling Elainers Baton Company. Over the years, we've grown older together, and we've multiplied. Many days I run into someone who says, Ms. Rhodes! Ms. Elaine! Don't you remember me? You used to be my teacher! Or they'll say, didn't you used to be in the Bud Billiken Day Parade? Are you going to be there this year? Do a step when you get to 47th or 51st! You'll probably see us all down by the pool at Washington Park. I'll see ya there! You know y'all be getting down! I just smile and say, okay. I want the world to know that I was always positive in my daily values and that I always tried to model moral behavior—to be a good daughter, sister, aunt, and especially a loving mother to my son. I've been instrumental in the lives of more than six hundred students, throughout the Chicago metro area, in various schools, churches, and parks, in community organizations, annual city special events, and parades. I've taught African dance, fire twirling, acrobatics, aerobic fitness, swimming, cooking, and basic life skills. To this day, my baton is a spiritual and visible force in my life, conversation, and work.

As a mom living with my son in apartment 407, I observed many people in the building who did not like themselves. I could see the connection between this attitude and a lot of negative outcomes. I knew there needed to be a support group or a way of embracing the people who lived at the Robert Taylor Homes—a way of helping them come together. Now that I had my own apartment, I began to work with other residents to organize self-help groups. Next to the laundry room on the second floor was the pram room, where you could store your things. This is where we met to talk about organizing tenants and having floor captains, local advisory councils, presidents of the buildings, and team councils. This was around 1978.

People responded. A similar system had been in place before things changed. Most of the early residents in the Robert Taylor Homes were older. They weren't teenagers. People were screened before they moved in. But later, you had younger adults running the apartments—more teenage moms. I felt that I wanted to extend myself as a tenant, as the head of a family, not just to my own family but to other people. I've always believed that if you're in the community and you want to make it and you don't see anybody else who's doing it, you have to step up to the plate. I believe in myself, and I believe in the seven principles of Nguzo Saba: unity, self-determination, collective work and responsibility, cooperative economics, purpose, creativity, and faith. It's about self-determination and taking initiative.

I stepped up to the plate not only by strengthening my whole structure in myself, but by beginning to think of those things that made me happy and then asking, what is it that's wrong? I examined myself first, and then I examined the things I observed in the community. I saw that one particular thing was happening over and over and over. I did not see people who liked themselves. There was nobody to give praise. I had learned that "praise before opens the door to so much more that all of God's children have in store." There was nothing positive at that time for parents, children, church, or community to do as a collaborative. I began to ask people, what is it that makes you all kill each other? Why don't you like living here? What is the problem? And they began to tell me things like, I was mopping in front of my door and she stepped in front of me, so I hit her. It's silly, but it was real.

The violence and the drugs didn't scare me. Sometimes I would cook for people. I just like people, and they know that. It sustained me to embrace people with kindness, to help them find the support they needed. I used to be on 47th Street, at the Robert Taylor management office, and on 43rd Street at Human Resources looking for ways to help. I was in touch with the city aldermen and with the police department. I was very positive. I knew how to go about finding people who could make a difference.

I took time with other people's children. I invested my life in helping my son and his friends. I think the reason I did okay was I always said to myself, I can't let things get any worse. I have to get better; I have to do better for myself. I try until I can do. I complete tasks. I don't like to boast, but I'm not a quitter. My mother—the head of the house—said to us, you all are going to make it. That was back in the 1950s and the 1960s, when you did as the older siblings instructed you to do; you followed suit. Now, with my two sisters in college and brother Jesse in the army, there was nothing left for me to do but to make it. Out of all of my brothers and sisters, my mama coughed and spit me out. I had to be able to do it.

It wasn't just about myself. I was a parent. I had to be a role model for Edwin, not only for the community. I knew if I didn't save myself, I couldn't save Edwin. Having Edwin has been the most touching thing in my life, but I felt I had to prove myself because I had a child out of wedlock. My mother was really embarrassed about it. I had to show that I could do it.

Dr. William Glasser talks about the basic things people need in life—love, fun, power, freedom, and belonging. People need to feel that someone loves them and that they belong. I make other people feel that way, and they have given that back to me. And my creativity has allowed me to think outside the environment I'm in. Love and creativity have sustained me. I really do believe that.

The Robert Taylor buildings have been coming down for four years. Out of the original thirty-two, there are five buildings left: 4037 South Federal, 4429 South Federal, 4946 South State, 4947 South Federal, and 5135 South Federal. These will be torn down as well. People know it's time for them to up and leave, but many are adopting the attitude that since they have nothing to lose, they might as well stay there till they're kicked out. They're not taking care of themselves. There's still a lot of fighting at a couple of the buildings. People are fighting each other for control of the gangs. When cocaine came back on the scene in the late 1980s, and it got easy to get, the gangs came back big.

The people still living at the Robert Taylor Homes know they're gonna be put out, and they don't have much get-up-and-go. They have been beaten down; they have been told what's gonna happen, and they believe it. They have no creative thought process for getting out. Some people will change. Others won't. And then some people are satisfied with whatever, and that has always been.

When the Robert Taylor Homes were built, it was a criterion for living there that you have nothing, that you be on public aid. That changed in the late 1970s, when you paid rent on the basis of your income. My son and I were on public aid in 1976 when I moved back to the Robert Taylor Homes, though by the early 1980s, I no longer needed the support. Each time I had a salary increase, the rent went up. In Edwin's second year of college, in 1989, he said, Mom, it's time to move. I had waited a long time, because when I moved back in, my two-bedroom apartment was $17.36 a month. I wasn't about to go anywhere. In 1989, when I was working as tutorial program director at the YMCA, the rent was $358 a month. There's another program, and I don't care to say the name, but one of the criteria for being in it is that you don't have a GED. You don't have a high school diploma and you don't have a job, and you're eligible for the program. What kind of a mess is that? You're at the bottom of the heap.

The kids who grew up in the Robert Taylor Homes were raised by young mothers. Now the mothers are in their thirties, and their young kids have babies. When the residents got kicked out of the Robert Taylor Homes, they were given Section 8 vouchers if they were paid up on the rent and their utilities. Lots of them left the city. Lots moved down South. Many that stayed moved to the southeast side of Chicago, in the South Shore, 'cause it was the only place with buildings that had twenty to thirty apartments available, and they accept Section 8 there. It's the only place these people could go. People who had been in the projects their whole lives were now in a different part of the city where it's still predominantly black, though it's more multicultural. The apartments in the South Shore have their own gangs and their own drugs, though it may not be as bad as the Robert Taylor Homes got. Lots of the people who lived in the South Shore apartments before are now moving out.

The Robert Taylor area is ten to fifteen minutes from downtown. You could walk it in thirty or forty minutes. If you go to downtown Chicago and look at the expensive condominiums, you see they have the same structure as the Robert Taylor Homes. Maybe something was slightly restructured or the bathroom or kitchen was a little different, but the buildings are the same. Typical high-rise. And yet that downtown area is so rich. Black and white yuppies live there.

The reason the redevelopers want the Robert Taylor land is that it's right next to public transportation. I remember hearing about the redevelopment plan back in 1997. Most of the people living at the Robert Taylor Homes were scared. They didn't know what to think. At that time, I was working in a community agency that dealt with residents who were going to be displaced. It would have been a good idea to address the problems at the Robert Taylor Homes, not to tear down the buildings.

People wrote a report saying that the Robert Taylor Homes were the murder capital of the world. The report didn't come from the building residents and the police; it came from the people who wrote it. People didn't know how to challenge the report and ask, what facts made you say this is the murder capital of the world? They said it cost more to rehab the buildings than to tear them down. But the redevelopers wanted the land. They're supposed to build townhouses, row houses, like single-family homes, with no more than two families in a single building. The new homes are supposed to have at least 25 percent occupancy by former residents of the Robert Taylor Homes, but they may not pass the screening process. And there will be a one-strike policy: those who violate their lease once will be out.

It's like subliminal advertising. You associate something with something else, and then people start believing it's true. Yes, things got bad. But if problems like gangs and drugs and teen pregnancy persist, there's a way to stop them. The system did not have enough policing to control the gangs. Each building had a booth inside with a couple of trained police officers, but all they could do is put on a Band-Aid. The gangs had more weapons than the police had.

People need to learn to take initiative. The way to reach people who are having babies out of wedlock, or who are doing drugs, is through education. You have to get them to feel what the child is feeling, what's happening with the child that they're having. There's a whole generation gone now, but it's never too late.

With most of the Robert Taylor buildings gone, there are less than nine hundred kids at Du Sable High now, instead of four thousand. There are still fights at school, but fewer. The gangs are still trying to recruit on the school grounds. But Du Sable has one to two computers in every classroom, and it was one of the first high schools in the city of Chicago to get hooked up to the Internet. The library has more than twenty thousand books and a large collection of books about African Americans. If you go to Du Sable High School, you'll see my name and picture posted in the Hall of Fame. I'm noted as a successful student, a parent, a scholar, the director of the Twirling Elainers Baton Company, a provider of social services to community youth and adults—a positive role model, living and working then on the Greater Grand Boulevard.

I often revisit the words of my sister Genice: "Mom has left behind a legacy to be carried on, and so it has been carried on." I live my life serving people young and old. Nowadays, I am the Silhouette Rites of Passage facilitator at the Chicago Area Project. Our program is based on an African frame of reference but serves people without regard to race. We help female and male wards of the state—young people who have been taken from their families by the Department of Children and Family Services. Our goal is to teach them life skills that will prepare them for emancipation from the system and a life of independence.

TAMMIE CATHERY

A Mother's Story

Tammie is a twenty-nine-year-old mother of six, a survivor of the Robert Taylor Homes. She told me that she would run things differently if she had the chance. "If I was in control, what I would do to change the life of our people in the ghetto is I wouldn't give up on you. You see, that's the problem. We give up too quick. First of all, I would have to think about it and map out what I would want to do. I would like to clean up our community . . . I would start with the ones that want to do for themselves. And ask questions, ask about them, what they like, what they wanna do, how they wanna raise their kids, what kind of environment they want to live in."

When I was a kid, I lived on 61st and Marshfield with my mom and went to the grammar school over there, Earle Elementary. I was always doing sports and other activities. I was on the cheerleading team and was the cheerleader captain there.

We moved from over there into the Robert Taylor Homes in 1987, but I didn't go right away with my mom 'cause I didn't want to move into the Robert Taylors. My mom was always telling us that when we were growing up, we were saying, I ain't moving into the ghetto. But eventually I did.

When I moved, I didn't know no one. I knew people, but I was always a loner. I used to always hang by myself. When I graduated that year from Earle Elementary, I wanted to go to Du Sable High School. So I became involved in a lot of things at the high school, 'cause there was problems at home with the drugs and alcohol and it was like destroying a lot of our families over there.

Basically, it was like you were raising your own at the Robert Taylors. It was like there was one big family, everyone in one big home and in different bedrooms. That's how the building was. But in reality there was different apartments, and some people had their head on their shoulders and some didn't. Everybody knew everybody else, and a lot of the people were related to one another. Just like families, they argued sometimes.

Myself, I started off very good. Then I started getting peer pressure and arguing and fighting with my mom. I'd come home, and even if she hadn't been high on drugs or anything, she'd still trip off on me or fuss at me. So it was very hard for me, and I started hanging in the streets. At this time, I was thirteen or fourteen years old. I always thought I was a superstar anyway.

I decided, I'm gonna go up to Du Sable High School and talk to some of the peoples there. So I started hanging out with the high school kids. They knew I had abilities even before I came there, 'cause they heard about them from the grammar school. So when I graduated from Earle and came to Du Sable, I was kind of like a bad kid but I had a lot of good things in me.

They got me hooked on the cheerleader team, and I was very, very good. I was on the volleyball team and the softball team. I was in a mixed choir, and I was volunteering. I used to work with some of the students, some of the basketball team and the football team. There was a lot of things that I started doing.

I grew up around my aunt Rochelle Catherine, who was a cheerleader at Du Sable High School. One of the girls was the cheerleader liner and she had to baby-sit me. I used to get tired of sitting all them hours watching the girls practice. I used to cry and get mad. My candy was gone and I was ready to go home. So I started playing with the batons. My aunt gave me a baton: here, girl, get this baton—we're almost finished; we'll see you later. So my auntie Rochelle, she was like, you should become a cheerleader instead of being always out there fighting, 'cause I was like a tomboy.

So things changed. I was dedicated to twirling. It was like I came home from school, and even going through the trouble I was going through at home, I was doing everything I could so I wouldn't get no punishment, 'cause you can't come to baton practice, the girls would say. Oh, it like breaks our heart. It breaks our heart 'cause we loved it, oh, we loved to twirl, loved to twirl, we did. We did a lot of shows back then. We had Coca-Cola sponsoring us. And we did a show for Mayor Harold Washington. More companies were promoting us, and it kept a lot of us out of trouble.

After that it was like everyone started getting older, becoming teenagers, and we started breaking loose. Some of us kept on. We always kept in contact with someone. We'd jump on a bus and see each other, or we'd visit somewhere; we'd bump into each other. That's when my life went from good to worse. I lived with my grandmother before I had my first child 'cause I couldn't take it no more with me and my mother. I was an A student. I stayed on the honor roll in high school. I didn't finish, 'cause I had so much other stuff going on in my head. I didn't have no one really to back me up, to keep me focused, keep me going. It was like I actually just gave up, so I hung with a street gang.

Once I stopped going to school, started hanging out, it became like a lot of tragedies are happening. A lot of classmates started going to jail, dying; there was so many killings over there at the Robert Taylor Homes. It was a lot like Harlem. One building is one thing, the next building is another. Two different gangs. You step on someone's toe, bump into each other, or one gang member liked the other gang member's girl, or it was just 'cause of something stupid. Someone says something. You have a pair of Jordans, then they take your Jordans. Next thing you know, they coming back with the next building and they all get to fighting. But then it's like always one person come here with a gun, then the next person.

Then that's what became like a big war. So tenant patrol, they come to each building, holler up in the buildings, say, you kids come on down. They pick them up out of each building and walk them to school 'cause some parents are probably hung over or couldn't get it together for some other reason. You get them ready, then you pick them up from each building and walk them to school. The different buildings was doing things together, just to make sure the kids weren't hurt by violence.

It was so bad down there that the U.S. Marshals had to come and escort the kids back and forth to school. We couldn't come outside. If you did, you took a chance. Over there it's like life is based on a chance. You might win, you might lose; you might live and you might not live. It was so bad. They had them close the buildings down, and you had to sign on the first floor to come up. We had to buzz you in, like normal high-rise buildings, but we had police officers. There was a police for each project location—each project had a station in it. They were the CHA Police—Chicago Housing Authority. They called them Chicago Rental Cops, or Robocops, as a joke. They were tough cops.

The Fifty-first Police Station also sent a lot of people to the Robert Taylors, people who knew the area and the residents. Some of the officers they sent were part of the regular force and some were private security officers. So it was very dangerous. You couldn't have a birthday party for the kids downstairs in the playground; that's how terrible it was.

The street gang didn't get me. I gave it up and started hanging out with friends. I never did drugs. I got pregnant, and I had my first child when I was seventeen. And it was like, okay, what am I gonna do now? Public aid. They ain't giving no money to no kids, so you have to go on your mother's grant. I wasn't living with my mom, but she was still in the Robert Taylors and I was still coming over there.

A year passed after I had my baby, and then I got my own apartment. Only if you had a child and you were a certain age could you get an apartment. So most people was like, well, sure, I'm having me a baby to get my own apartment. That's how I was thinking, and I wanted someone to love me and to have for my own. Them years I was thinking that way, but now I know more. I wish I would've took my time and settled down instead of doing a lot of things that I did. I wish I had thought things out before I reacted. It was just so terrible.

You see the guys, the drug dealers, have things that you would like to have, and you get with them. The car, the fashion; it was all about the fashion, really. Selling drugs for fashion. A lot of people did a lot of things for the fashion and appearance and the talk of the town. Selling drugs for the cars, the money, and now you're more important to us in the projects. You have all this money, so we're gonna try to get with you and hang around with you and be your friend. You don't know that wasn't the right way until after you have thought to yourself if that's what you really wanted.

Now I'm twenty-nine, and I have six children. If I could do it over again, I probably would've had them six, but I probably would've been on number one now. If I would've stayed with the YMCA that we had to practice in, and the activities that we had at the time, I would have had more options. The communities would've had more options for the teenagers, which they don't really have now, because everyone is going their way. It's more kids that's out of grammar school now than it was back then, and more kids pregnant by sixteen too, and have more than two children now.

I have three girls and three boys. I kept having babies; they kept coming out. I couldn't stop them; no, I could not stop them. I thought about abortions, but I never had no abortion. My mother she did prefer abortions. She said, well, you get pregnant, you should have taken more of a responsibility, 'cause I'm not gonna keep them. That's what she told me. So why did I go six times? I don't know. I haven't asked myself that. It's just I got pregnant and I had them. With help or not. I had one actually born in the Robert Taylor Homes. I was having it so fast it just came. The baby came on down on my auntie's bed. The birth certificate has it.

I'm a good mama, though. I went through a lot of changes to be the good mom that I am today. I had to learn from my mistakes and experiences to know what to look for.

I went through a lot of things dealing with DCFS—the Department of Children and Family Services. They come to your home, and if there's something wrong, you get reported. They take your children and you have to go through parenting classes, or whatever they ask you to go through; you have to go through it. They took my children away. So much was happening in the Robert Taylors, I mean living the fast life.

There is things that you do have to think about if you have children first of all, if you love them and want them to be with you and grow up with you, and not just with you, but with each other. So it was good they went to my mom. They were in the system but they weren't spread out all over town somewhere and don't know each other.

Oh, but I have them back now. I have certificates and everything. My eldest daughter is thirteen. I keep her in the house a lot. I cannot always do that, but I try to talk to her. She's not more mature like I was when I was thirteen. I was more experienced back then than how the kids are now. I try to talk to them and get them to understand life, what life is all about, and what I've been through—my mistakes, my wrongdoing. I try to tell them my wrongdoing. I don't hide nothing from my kids. I tell them everything I think they won't know. I don't hide nothing.

Some things I tell them straight out. I know how to talk to my children. I know how they will understand me the way I talk to them. Sometimes I come straight out with it, and sometimes you have to not beat around the bush, but put it in a different level for them to understand what you're talking about, trying to explain to them.

My son he been suspended from school before I got them back home with me. I don't have a male in my home right now; none of the kids' fathers are around. I don't see them; I don't have no contact with them. It don't bother me at all. I really don't worry about it. I really don't care, 'cause I've been making it all this time without their help. So I can stay alone.

From my experience at the Robert Taylor Homes, I'd say the trouble was from drugs and meanness. Both. But then sometimes you get some good things going on. Like they had Triple-H. They had summer programs where the children could eat breakfast and lunch. They took the children on trips. There was a lot of good over there too. But it didn't last long, 'cause some of the workers, when they get shown around, didn't want to come over there. So they gave up on our community over that. They gave up, so we had more people to get together, to make a solution, and everyone joined in. See, everyone talks the talk, but a lot of people just don't do the walk. A lot of people they say, well, they should've did this and should've did that, but we don't have peoples, my peoples, black peoples, we don't get together to make a statement and make it last and stick together. We say one thing to the next person, but we don't make no action towards our world, see.

I see a lot of mothers my age now. A lot of them are doing real good. Like one of the twirlers, she's trying to open up her own day-care center for the children. It's things like that we need to be doing, getting together to help other black people. There's some of us out there can be saved if we have the right hand to hold on to, to help us save the communities, the children. Our own children first; we have to start at home. We have to teach our kids not to run down the street twenty years later, be in jail for robbing the lady next door. We need to get them back into these schools and onto these basketball teams and into cheerleading. I don't see a lot of competitions going on anymore. They used to have the Pizza Hut, the small pan pizzas given to them free to read so many books. I don't see that no more in schools. I don't see a lot of trips no more. Not just going to the park, to the zoo, but going to these libraries to pick out books and read. Have them do a report on them as we did. A lot of the kids nowadays, we put them with so much material things that whatever they do they have to get paid for. That's the big problem.

Most of the adults in my neighborhood, a lot of them have jobs. Also they had jobs in the Robert Taylors. The Robert Taylors had a lot of programs for tenants. Janitor, the lunchroom, building presidents, tenant patrols, all of them had a part in the community. You had the porch captains; you had to make sure you kept your own porch swept and mopped. No clothes hanging on the galleries or the gates. It was basically helping us to develop ourselves as a clean environment, helping us keep it clean and be lovely neighbors. Everyone got into it some of the time, but if your children aren't home, you can't teach them about respect and honor, and about honoring other people's things and property. If you could, the neighborhoods wouldn't be so trashy. Over my way, where I live at now, they have garbage cans on each corner. Over at the Robert Taylors you probably would've had but one trash can. You'd probably only see one out of the whole community. Of course people are gonna throw trash on the ground and things and on people's grass.

The reason so many kids at the Robert Taylors went wrong, I guess, was because they was somehow dealing with fashion, with wanting fashion. If we'd stayed in school, we would have had more money to get more fashion later. But we didn't learn that when we was growing up. We see them making money quicker with drugs, so why go to work? This is how I learned things. Why work for three weeks when you get that same amount in five or ten minutes just by selling drugs? So it looked good.

Or there was a group of girls who used to go hang out with the drug dealers. They'd trick off with them and get the cash and get their hair and nails done and an outfit. It's not like standing on a corner for it and getting twenty or thirty dollars. It's like for hundreds and thousands. It depends on how much the guy makes. You get your 5 or 10 percent. You wouldn't be his regular woman; you just need some money, and you gotta look for. You get the money from the guys, get the nails and the hair done, nice little outfits and shoes. House looks a mess, no food, bills not paid, kids look a hot mess too. Terrible.

If I was in control, what I would do to change the life of our people in the ghetto is I wouldn't give up on you. You see, that's the problem. We give up too quick. First of all, I would have to think about it and map out what I would want to do. I would like to clean up our community. You can't put no wall around the whole project, 'cause someone gonna find a way to get over it. Someone gonna leave half a motor and crawl over it. So I would start with the ones that want to do for themselves. And ask questions, ask about them, what they like, what they wanna do, how they wanna raise their kids, what kind of environment they want to live in. I'd go to the source to start making a solution. See what they talk about. See what they aiming for and what they do to set their goals, and see what they need to get to their goals.

I would start with the first group as the ones who know what they gonna do, and help them and see what kind of things I can do. There's organizations now here. You can look in the phone book, in the papers. You can dial information; you can dial 311 and ask them about different things, so there's a lot of connections I do have. There's Section 8 if you don't have no home. There's a lot of things that you can do to help them. What I would do is put my connections that I have to help the ones who want to be helped, 'cause those who don't wanna be helped, you're just not gonna be able to reach them.

Our people who live in ghettos now all across the country, I know they're not gonna live in a project all their life, 'cause they're tearin' them all down.

This is going on right now. My building was torn down. I had just had my last child and come home from the hospital. They were tearin' the building down; it was cold, frozen. There was ice on the door and I couldn't open it. So they put me up right away in a hotel and told me they were gonna give us our emergency housing, which was Section 8.

I'm still leaning on Section 8 now, because some people said it's the last three years. Well, I know it's not three years 'cause I've had it four years now. That's a big change right there, to live someplace that's not a Robert Taylor in the ghetto. You can have a regular apartment for $800 a month rent, but I just pay a small portion 'cause Section 8 pays the majority of it. So it's a lot of chances they are helping us with, and it's on us to go get it.

There's still drug dealers very subtly around the neighborhood I live in now, but no way like there was in the Robert Taylors. It's more quiet. I live in the South Shore area. You don't hear gunshots. You're not scared and terrified to walk the neighborhood, walk the parks, Rainbow Beach. It's better. You have some people who don't want to leave the Robert Taylors; that's why they're still there. I understand 50 percent of them want to stay, because some of them have been there since the homes were first built in the 1930s and 1940s. It's home to them; that's all they know. But the other ones, like me, the 50 percent I was in, we left there; we got out of there.

I don't miss the good old days of the Robert Taylors. I miss the cash, though. That's the truth. I miss the cash. They had to clear all the drug dealers out of the area. I didn't live a working life; I never had to work. That's why I miss that cash. That's fast cash; it's hot cash from the drug dealer. But I hope all the guys who are still there don't try getting it on now with the drugs. One of them is living in Statesville Prison, the father of one of my kids, and I don't know how much time he has to do there.

The kids nowadays, they still look tough out there, but there's not as many drugs, not like there used to be. Eventually, all the drug users are dead, or there's someone don't have no choice but to stop. Hip-hop don't have anything to do with the drugs and alcohol. Them videos, them songs, probably do. I think they just put something together that makes them money. I watch the videos on BET, Channel 75. They have alcohol in the videos, and they have blunts, which is marijuana wrapped in cigar paper.

If you want to teach your kids different from you, why have that environment around them and your home first of all? That's where a lot of kids learnt a lot of stuff from in the Robert Taylors. They looked up to the drug dealers as mentors 'cause their parents weren't around. That was around 1993 and 1994; them was them days.

I can't say 100 percent that my kids are gonna get through their teenage years without getting pregnant. But I can say 100 percent that they're gonna finish school and they're gonna make it. If my daughter came home pregnant, I wouldn't say, okay, we're gonna get an abortion. I feel that no matter how old they are, that's their choice, 'cause it's their body and their life. They can go and get an abortion for the first time and not walk back out of there alive. So I don't take any chances.

I would just talk to my daughters and ask them how they feel about it; ask, do you want it? Whatever they would want with the pregnancy, I will go along with. I would be upset and hurt and mad, 'cause I know what I've been through. But I think it'll be different, because they have me on their side now. I didn't have my mom or no one. I had the streets to go to. I had my aunties, but they had their own life; they couldn't be there 100 percent with me. And I had two younger sisters I was taking care of.

There's so many apartments where I live now, and they're beautiful, like the neighborhood, the neighbors, the stores. Part of it's all black and then it's mixed. It's all cultures over here. There's Jamaicans over here, there's Indians; there's a lot of different people. And it depends on us if we want to keep the neighborhood clean. It's way, way different, and I like it more.

THE MASSENBERGS

Finding Their Way

Carolyn and Patrice Massenberg, mother and daughter, have lived in the Robert Taylor Homes since the 1970s. Their building is one of the few remaining high-rises in the development, once a beacon of hope for African Americans aspiring to a better life, and now a frequently cited symbol of despair.

Carolyn

I moved to the Robert Taylor Homes with my three children in the late 1970s. Like so many other black households, there was no male figure to speak of. My children were thrust into the middle of all this negative activity with no one to watch over them but me. I think they resented me a little for moving here. I wasn't working at the time.

These buildings need to come down. They hold way too much sorrow for a lot of people, including myself. My oldest grandson was killed six years ago by a gunshot wound to the head. He was seventeen years old. Violence is everywhere, but it's congested in the projects. There are people on top of one another. Drugs have turned a lot of good people I knew into someone you don't even want in your house anymore, one of the reasons being they take items, money, and so on. They get so they don't care about their children— whether they eat, have clothing, or just being there for them. These kids are left to raise themselves and are at the mercy of the situation. It's unthinkable unless you've heard it before.

It's not all people that use drugs. And a lot of people on drugs still manage to take care of home and family, hold a job, and lots more. I'm not condoning, just saying there are two sides to a coin.

Don't get me wrong. Not the whole twenty-four years at the Robert Taylor Homes have been bad. We've had some good times, and I've met a lot of good people that I've come to love and respect, young and old. It's not what you do all the time, but more so how you do it.

I know Robert Taylor is one place I won't miss, with having to walk up the stairs all the time because of problem elevators, not to mention all the police brutality and corruption running amuck. Everybody knows it's happening and no one does anything about it. After all, we're just black folks living in the lower development projects. We deserve what we get, right?

Patrice

I see a change for the worse at the Robert Taylor Homes since the 1970s. When I was seven, people were worried, but they wasn't worried as much about their child being in the playground, right in front of their own building, as they are today. Anything can happen. Right now somebody might be down there shooting—gangs shooting gangs, the police shooting gangs, gangs shooting police. It's like the police and the gangs are at war here, and we're caught in the cross fire.

I've kept my kids from getting involved in drugs and gangs by keeping them close to me. They may go downstairs, if I let them go outside. I tell them to come upstairs and check with me maybe every hour or every hour and a half. That way I know they're not across 47th Street. I know they're not down on 51st Street selling drugs and hanging with the wrong people.

Everybody has someone in their family who's been tempted. If they say they haven't, they're lying. It's not something that we hold our head high and be proud about, but it's something that happens. It's life. As a parent, you've got to be strong yourself, first of all, and second of all, the child has to be strong. You've got to be willing to be strong. It don't make no difference how old they are. If they're not willing to be strong, and if doing drugs is the life they've chosen for themselves, sometimes you're not able to do anything but let them go. You've got to let them go.

CLARK CLEMONS

Revolving Door

Clark Clemons is an officer in the Cook County Jail. Most of the inmates, he told me, are either black or Hispanic. "A lot of these kids were brought up in poverty. Their dreams are a guy with a big car and a lot of gold hanging around his neck. That's the only dream . . . If you're a user and all of your violent history, all of your negative history, is coming from using drugs, then we ought to try to solve that drug problem and we might not have an inmate."

I've been working here between thirteen and fifteen years. It's difficult, but I know the violence in the street. I know how it is in the street, and I know how it is in jail. I could use that phrase "somebody has to do it." But I still believe there's hope. Working here has made me more conscious of the youth of today. It's made me more conscious of what's really going on. And me personally, it has taken me to a more spiritual sense of dealing with the youths. I know some of the circumstances that put some of these guys in here were really dreadful. I'm not saying that it's an excuse, but their situation outside is not much better than the situation inside.

For example, a young lady that's been raped at home feels she has nowhere to go and wants to run away. She runs away. A dope dealer says, I'll take care of you, and provides her with clothes, food, and housing. And then before she realizes it, she's in another world with people she thinks care for her but don't. And when she's asked, how did you deal with five years in the streets, she'll say, my situation here is better than it was at home. And then you look at her situation and you say, there should have been somebody there between her and the streets. But her mother didn't speak up, or her father molested her, or something like this happened, and what do you do? They run away. They start taking dope; they start being prostitutes or whatever happens. Life is dealing them a raw hand all the way down. So there's a program here called My Sister's Keeper. They get those battered mothers, those who have been on drugs or have been suffering from abuse, and they try to start them out fresh with a job and an apartment when they get out. The majority go back to the old neighborhood, back with the same friends, back under the same conditions. Those are the ones who'll come back.

The percentage of the prisoners that we see again and again at the jail I would say is an embarrassing 40 to 60 percent, because of the environment they go back to. When they get out, it's not the end; they're not free. They're handicapped to a certain degree by dealing with the same parents or going back to the same neighborhood or back to the same drug dealers. Finding a job is not easy when you have a background like five times in prison, on robbery or drug abuse. Who's gonna hire you? They're scared to hire them when they're back out in the street. So they can't get a job, and eventually, if there's not a program there to help them get established all over again, they will end up doing the same thing they did that brought them to jail in the first place.

Most of the population in the jail is black and Hispanic. Well, you know that breakdown. If you started on an even keel, it would be great, but we know everybody's not starting on an even keel. A lot of these kids were brought up in poverty. Their dreams are a guy with a big car and a lot of gold hanging around his neck. That's the only dream. You can count the people who are living well and can afford to send their kids to college. Those that are on aid, they don't have a shot.

Guys are in here for all sorts of things. Burglary to narcotics, murder. You name it. They're all in here. All of them *seem* like nice guys, and there are some that are. One guy will tell you, I had three hundred tickets and fifty warrants and never answered one, never went to court. I was minding my own business and they stopped me for a traffic violation and found out I had all of these tickets. Now I'm in jail. Another will tell you, I was just standing on the corner minding my own business and they picked me up for no reason at all. I was in a car with a friend of mine; I had no idea he was in narcotics. And I'm arrested. You hear every story that you can imagine you'd hear: I shouldn't be here. I don't know what I'm doing here, really. I don't know why I'm here. You have no idea? No idea.

Sixty or 70 percent of the people who are here are guilty of something. It might not have been today or yesterday; they just got caught today or yesterday. They'll say, well, yesterday I did that and I did this, but today I didn't do nothing, and you got me. There ought to be a law. They'll tell you that in a minute.

Prisoners on the new come in with those who are returning from court. The buses bring them in from morning court and they dump them here. And then we have an evening court that dumps them. They come in from buses and from the coaches, on the new, and down a tunnel into the jail. And then they're put in holding cells. This is the scary part when a guy comes in on the new. The holding cell is a very unstable area, depending on the type of crime that's committed on the outside and whether it's their first time in. In an hour or two, all of the holding cells are full to the ground. These are people who just committed crimes yesterday, last night, night before last, in all the surrounding townships, and the buses bring them to Cook County. Some have seen a judge already; some haven't. Some are sent to jail from the courthouses; some are brought off the street and got a date to meet the judge.

A new prisoner hears that noise in the holding cells; he hears that cursing; he hears guys who have been here before. It's a little fearful coming into a place like this for the first time. And when you see it, it kind of hits you. You're frightened to be here in the first place and are wonderin', what's gonna happen to me? The ones who haven't been here before don't know what to expect of the other inmates, and they hear stories before they get in jail.

You'll hear from conversation those who have been here before, and you hear a different conversation of those who just came in on the new. Those who are returning are a little loud because some have received verdicts of guilty and they know they're going downstate to prison. We put them on buses and ship them to the prisons Monday, Wednesday, and Friday. Some might be convicted of violent crimes or murder and don't know any way out, so their temperament might be real up. When you've been charged with everything, I'm frustrated, I've been sentenced to death, what are you gonna do? I don't know how I'm gonna act. I don't think I needed to be here. I think the sentences were unfair, you know. Sometimes people just are so frustrated they beat up each other.

We try to do everything we can to protect the inmates in here. We're not gonna allow any murders to be committed here in the holding cells, that's for sure. It's a very unstable situation when the new are coming in and those who went to court are returning. We have rules and regulations to try to have them go through a process, to calm them down and give the feeling that we're here to help them get processed and nothing else. They would rather be in prison than to be in this jail, because we stick to the rules and regulations. Once you settle down and make a jail your home and you meet other friends, you can communicate better with them and control certain actions. When you're on the new and you don't have that kind of awareness of who the other people are, everybody's on their own.

Prisoners are taken from the holding cell and see one of the officers here; get processed in. They get fingerprinted. They get their picture taken and go into the computers. They get an ID number. They turn in personal property and are strip-searched for drugs, weapons, money. People rob each other, 'cause you've still got your money with you that you had on the outside. If you don't let anybody know you've got it, you get by and you get a chance to turn in your property. If you are a flasher or they find out you have money, someone will try to steal it from you in jail. It's not unusual. Start an argument and a fight and go in your pockets. That's a common thing there that we have to break up, until the inmates' property is checked and they feel a little bit safer at that point. We ask that those who have a large amount of money on them let us know when they come in here and we'll try to separate them and take their property before anything can happen. But a lot of them want to hide it. And then someone else finds it.

We ask the prisoners for personal information—name, address, next of kin, and gang allegiance—and we try to do what we call an evaluation of what they did and how they did it. We don't put an inmate here on a traffic violation with a murderer. We try to keep traffic violations classified, domestic violence classified, theft classified. The divisions are kind of like a county, a neighborhood. We classify prisoners by age, gender, and type of crime. When they process in the jail and we do a classification of them, we send them to divisions that will fit their crime. Maximum is where you get a good shot at what the prison is. A little more serious than minimum or medium. The people in maximum have done something more serious, like murder, rape, domestic. These are the prisoners you have to watch. You can't let them socialize as much as the others 'cause they're a little bit more violent. Minimum security is no murderers but maybe accidents. You kill a guy with your guy speeding. Maybe you kill a guy and you were drunk, but you wasn't a violent person trying to rob him or that kind of stuff. There are all such a ways that people get killed.

Prisoners on the new or coming back see the medical department, get an X ray for TB and get checked for HIV, high blood pressure, or diabetes. Some come in with their own ailments. They get more interviews if they need special placement. Whatever you got here, you're treated every day for that ailment as long as you're here. And we try not to put prisoners that are HIV positive with other prisoners.

Like anywhere else, sexual contact can happen. We are glad to say it's down to a minimum here in the jail, but you're still in a jail, three people in a room together overnight, and you don't know everything that's happening. That's for sure. And the way they do things in jail is different from in the street. You either pressure or threaten. And if you are threatened, what can you do? If someone makes a complaint about another prisoner, you go through the necessary procedures to see who, what, when, and how, and that person may be charged with another crime while he's in jail. He may be separated from that person, put in a hold in a different part of the jail. You just go through the procedures, investigate just like you would do on the outside. And if he's found guilty, you charge him with sexual harassment.

Not many prisoners bring sexual harassment charges, 'cause there would be consequences. If a person wanted to do something to you and you were bunking with him every day, really there's nothing to prevent him from doing it. You can respond after it's done, but you don't know people's thoughts, when they're gonna take action on something. It'll either happen and you calm it down or separate them, or you lock them up in different parts of the jail, but you can't prevent everything from happening in a jail. Sooner or later everything happens. Nothing you can do about it. That's life.

Ones who have their court dates when they come in here have been given a mittimus paper with their name and charges and the bond amount. It tells us to hold the prisoner until his next court date and see that he shows up in court in front of the judge and nothing should happen to him while he's here. At that time, his case will be discussed and he will be presented with a lawyer. If he doesn't have one, then one will be appointed to him, and he'll have a chance to see what the charges are against him and what his lawyer decides to do at that time. If the lawyer decides to continue the case till he reads up more on the charges, the prisoner is brought back here and that court date will continue. Depending on the extent of the case and evidence, it could be continued for two, three, four, five years. And he'd be here the whole time. The longer it's continued and he's not sentenced, he'll be here. The average stay in the jail is normally up to two years. But we're in a difficult time now where cases in the courts are slowed down to a minimum, and we've had prisoners stay here as long as eight years. We've had some go to court and their time was considered served in the jail before they went to the prison. Case continued, case continued, new lawyer, new evidence, whatever it is to continue your case through the years and keep them here. And more than 250 a day are arriving while he's here.

You wonder what kind of system will hold somebody for four or five years before they sentence him, but then you look at the cases. Look at the reason they were continued. They have night court, holiday court, to try to take the weight, try to expedite the cases. It works in some cases; in some cases it doesn't. In the meantime, we're still taking in a hundred thousand a year on the new. So you can see how quick the jail can get overcrowded.

Right now, due to the overcrowding, there's three to a cell. It's only supposed be two, but there's three in there now. There's not much room. So it is a breeze to get them to leave the cells at night and stretch their legs. The three people are confined in a cell for fifteen hours a day. They're unsupervised in the sense that no one's watching them, but we make tours around the cell doors and we look through the holes to make sure everybody's okay and talking all right. It's a steady monitoring of them when they're in the cell. The officers walk around every cell, looking in, asking questions. If anyone's sleeping and can't be woke up, then the officers go in and shake them, make sure they're all right, and then they go around.

You can go from one to the other and you can tell by some rooms, by the pinups on the walls, they're not interested in the spiritual side. Whatever helps them to pass the day there, I guess. The library tries to provide them with books and magazines, and they're not supposed to cut the pages out but they do. We clean house every so often. If the pinups were in a wing where they were breaking the rules, or where somebody was sexually abused or something like that, none of it would exist. But if the guys are handling themselves in a normal way and there are pinup pictures all around, we might as well cut them some slack.

Prisoners are out in the common areas for two or three hours in the morning and two or three hours in the evening. They have a certain time limit that they let them out and they have to be back in their cell. They're out for breakfast and dinnertime, and they have time to play checkers, chess, watch TV. We program movies and special tapes for them. So as far as the individual prisoners are concerned, you learn daily to work and sleep and eat with others.

These men are in jail. They use the toilet in front of each other. What can you do? These are the things you give up in the street when you commit a crime. You don't have your own room and private bathroom. This is it. If a guy's sick, he's just sick. He throws up. They have to clean up just like you do at home. It's the way it is. Everybody takes care of their own, keeps it halfway clean. We don't mix the old guys with the young guys. We keep a lot of arguments down that way. We figure the elderly can get along better with themselves and the young get along better with themselves.

I've been involved in altercations with prisoners a few times during the time I've worked here. We won't go into numbers, but each time, if you hadn't been able to breathe a little bit or to run a little bit, to keep your cardio up a little bit, it could be ugly. I'll be sixty-seven years old on October 5. You have to stay in shape on this job. The sheriff requests us all to be physically able to handle ourselves in case of an emergency—to be able to run a block or two to an emergency without fainting when you get there. He has a training program that we all participate in. He put training equipment in the jail, and the officers are made to work out. We're told to stay in shape.

The stereotype is that you go into a jail and everybody's got guns. Nobody has a gun. I don't know any prison that would let an officer walk around with guns with criminals. When you watch a film, everybody's got a gun. But that's Hollywood. Hollywood would do anything. But in real life, the consequences are too serious. You wouldn't want to have an inmate grab a gun and go haywire. You can imagine if there was a fight broke out and someone grabbed a gun, what would happen in the jail.

You can't prevent violence or keep prisoners from hurting each other. It's the same in the street. Violence only happens when it happens. You take control then. But before it happens there is no violence. You establish rules and regulations for them to follow. Violence happens when you break the rules and regulations. As long as everybody is on the same keel with the rules and regulations, there's no violence.

It's like anyplace else. I step on your foot, I don't like you, I get mad. We can't solve it verbally, so we'll solve it physically. That sort of thing doesn't happen too often in the jail. We try to separate the different gangs so they won't have confrontations on a daily basis. Where we find problems, we find gang problems.

You could say that socializing new people is done mainly by the gangs. When you first enter the jail, the gangs jump on you to recruit you. Recruit a new one as they walk in the door. They find out in the cell who do you belong to, what side of town do you live on. Are you a Latin King? Or are you a Blackstone Ranger, or a member of the P-Stone Nation or some other gang? There are so many names, they pop up all over. So when they do find out something about who you belong to or you don't belong, if you don't belong then they'll recruit you. You join my gang, not that gang. You ship along with us, the gang will tell you; we are a majority in this jail, and you won't be able to get along peaceful in this jail without our help.

And if you say no, well, they try to convince you that you should join their gang for your own health's sake, for the sake of getting along, especially if you go into a wing where they have the majority of their gang members there. A gang member will explain, it would be easier for you to get along with me if you belong. I wouldn't be responsible for you if you didn't, and I'll put up a good word for you if you do. Well of course I'm scared, first time in jail, so I want somebody to look out after me, put up a good word for me so I won't get my food stole or my money stole, my head bashed in.

In the penitentiary, a prisoner might not see any choice. The odds are so against him there that there's no argument. In the penitentiary I might lie and say, yeah, I'll belong to your gang, 'cause I don't want to get hurt. I don't want to get beat up. But in the jail, I have a shot at getting out and maybe not going to prison with you, so I might act a different way, depending on my circumstances. I might say, I don't want to belong to your gang, and be willing to fight you. Then the gang members might go to the inmates who are not members of a gang and just demand things, like you've got to give me half your toothpaste. You've got to give me half your lunch, or all of it.

So if I want peace in the jail, I need to belong to somebody or I'm left out on my own. I make a mistake, I get reprimanded for it. If I'm a member of a gang, my gang will protect me. To join, you just say okay, I'm a Blackstone Ranger or a Latin King or some other. You commit yourself. They have the rules and regulations what you have to do to join. Say, for instance, one of the rules in a particular gang is to take ten blows to the chest for a minute. That might be the initiation fee. You won't be able to take it, but these are the rules and regulations when you get in. They'd probably knock you out or have you gasping for breath, or you're on the floor by the eighth or ninth blow. And once you're in, it's usually a double procedure to get out. Even maybe death-threatening. Maybe it's twenty blows to get out. Under certain circumstances, you can get out. But usually those circumstances are so dangerous you would be near death with those blows. I don't want to be hurt, so I don't quit. And if I quit, I'm going back with the understanding that I'm ready to take whatever you've got to give me so I can get out, and you do. That's some pretty harsh treatment.

The gangs have meetings every day. Not only meetings, but promotions for people who are doing a great job in leadership and recruiting. Oh yes, you can move up in rank. You can recruit so many on the new in a short period of time that you deserve to be moved up to supervisor. You learn from the ground up and you progress just like you were on the outside. You get in the business, only you might do a few things that's not legal in the business. Unlike Wall Street, of course. But you're in big business. Big benefits, big commissions. You supervise twenty-five guys, and if you have any problems, you report to the captain or the lieutenant or the sergeant. The chief is only approached by his top officers—the lieutenants and the captains. It's a military situation. You know who the head man is for each gang. Everybody knows. And you don't override nobody either. You don't try to go to the chief over the lieutenant. You listen to the lieutenant; you follow rules and regulations. And you get assignments. Someone will say to you, I want you to recruit at least twenty guys this week. It's a must. Twenty guys coming in here in on the new. I want you personally to recruit twenty, and I'll get someone else to recruit twenty. The chief and the lieutenants and the captains exist primarily to take control. And the officers of the jail, we're here to maintain control.

The role of gangs in the prison system is to control. Control their members, their turf, their power, their influence. There are members of gangs here who have referred their members to certain lawyers so they can clear away cases better than the regular lawyers. They've got a referral system. You belong to certain gangs, you can get certain privileges. If I'm a member of a gang and they're getting extra food from other inmates, and you're a lieutenant or captain in that gang, you'll have more food and more toothpaste and more cologne and more of everything you can get.

The gang operates day by day within the prison the same way it does outside. They get telephone calls, and they can make telephone calls out of here every day. They keep up with what's happening on the outside. And just because they're locked up on the inside doesn't mean they're not controlling their members outside to a certain degree. You still walk the same walk, do the same thing; it's just you're confined.

Say somebody wanted to make a telephone call. The gang members would make their phone calls first, and that person would only be able to make theirs when the gang members are through. And you don't have anything to say about it. There's things we can do about it if we find out about it, but half the time we don't find out about it even though we know it's going on. We try to regulate it if we see it, but an inmate would walk up to you, oh, Officer, I don't mind him using the phone in front of me. I don't mind at all. It's okay. Can we go down this way? Okay. After you. The prisoners organize for their own rules and regulations, and the secrecy. If you break the rules, they have their own penalties for what will happen to you. They're a law unto themselves. What can you do? If someone complains, then you can do something about it.

If they're known gang members of particular gangs, we try to separate them when they get to the jail, but every now and then when it's over-crowded, they mix to a certain degree and they separate themselves. They mix in the dayrooms. In the divisions. You find more gang members in-volved in drug crimes than you do in traffic violations, even murder. In the maximum security units, Divisions 9, 10, 11, you find more gang members and more drug dealers.

Gangs are different today. Gangs control the streets with youngsters from grammar school to high school to college and from one business to another. Gangs are not just running the streets; they're buying businesses. They sell narcotics in the street to buy a barbershop now, to buy a recording studio and produce music. And when they're busted with something else, you find that their gang is related to the music shop. High percentages of the con-tracts of the recording artists—the gangs take money from you from the be-ginning to the end. It's a corporate enterprise now. It's not the "I'll beat you up on the street" thing; it's "I'll take you to court if necessary." It's like ghetto business school.

We have people in here for drug offenses, mostly those who are using drugs rather than those who are making the profits; they're not the higher-ups. Most of the prisoners are here for drug-related crimes. I would say it's pretty close to 65 percent of drug-related charges here in the jail. Crack cocaine, heroin, selling drugs around schools or in different areas. The drug dealers have the cripple selling drugs in a wheelchair. If a guy is here in a wheelchair, it's because he was caught with drugs in the wheelchair. Little kids—they have anybody selling drugs. If you're old enough to talk and walk, then they try to recruit you to sell drugs. Some use and sell; some just sell. We have treatment for them here.

You could end up in Cook County Jail with any kind of narcotics. But you can be cleaned up faster or treated and get back to a normal life faster with some drugs than you can with others. As to the penalties for one kind of drug being harsher than for another, like crack cocaine versus powder co-caine, that's another thing. When you're in jail you go by the law, and the law says this and you do that, even though you might think that this is gonna be different. But, now, we've never been in a fair world, so what do we do? We find that everywhere we go—inside and outside. The state has a problem too. When a person commits a crime, we the public are the first ones to say, put them in jail.

If I were in charge, I would say half of the men would stay here. The other half I'd send to some kind of medical treatment outside the jail. Doctors can give you a physical status of a guy who's using drugs and one who has made it a lifetime of using drugs. You can't get that guy cleaned up who's made it a lifetime of using drugs as fast as you can a guy who's just got in. If you catch them early, you might turn a whole life around as far as drugs are concerned. I'm not saying that our medical clinics aren't full up on the outside, but we know we're overflowing in the jail. And we're sending somebody downstate to a prison with the same problem he had when he came in here, and it's gonna take some changes in prison to get straightened out.

I believe drugs is a crime, and I believe treatment for the crime does not have to be serving time in jail. If you're a user and all of your violent history, all of your negative history, is coming from using drugs, then we ought to try to solve that drug problem and we might not have an inmate. I believe it's a disease like anything else. There's medicine for it; there's treatment for it. A lot of them that are cured go into other things. There is another way to handle drug problems. I would say over 60 percent of the people in Cook County Jail are drug users who are suffering from an illness that should be cured somewhere else. If they didn't have a drug problem, they would probably have a job or probably still be in school, or probably be doing something positive. So I would take them out of the prison, the 60 percent of the inmates, put them in hospitals, in medical programs, clean them up, and get them back into society. It's easier to get an ex–drug addict, an ex-user, a job than it is before he kills somebody for drugs or before he robs for drugs.

The state is getting these people off the street and putting them in prisons, but then they're coming back. Fifty percent of the men who are here are doomed to be in this jail or in a prison for the rest of their lives. They're here till they check out. One circumstance or another they'll be here or they'll come back. And that's sad. This is why we work so hard with the programs in the jail. We have ministers who offer programs in all religions, who take prisoners to Bible class. They graduate from Bible class and they're happier that way. They study their Bible, they study their books for school, and this takes up their mind to a certain extent where they don't have as many fights or misunderstandings between each other. The more programs we have, the better the tension is in the jail. In a Bible class of thirty people, if we can get three or two to continue their religious life when they leave here, we consider that a breakthrough.

We have different programs in the jail now, like art classes, computer literacy, celebrations for ethnic holidays. That's why it's better and quieted down. There are law libraries here. The teenagers have to go to school, and we have a Consuella B. York Alternative High School where they can get their GED. Certain times of the day they're taken out and put in school classes, and they have to come back and do the homework. That helps. And they learn.

Maybe 2 percent or less of the people are here because they're mean and evil and were just born bad. Most of them just didn't have a chance from the word go because of the environment they grew up in. All of them have circumstances to make them what they are. We have guys here ministering today that were gang leaders and criminals yesterday. We have guys here that ran gangs who are now talking against the gang and the narcotics and preaching here every day. Perfect examples how some change and some don't. There's two sides to the story, but the sad story is, there's more that stay and come back than lead successful lives when they leave.

After two years here, I began to see how much trouble the prisoners really were in. And then you say, well, maybe we can find a program to help you; you look like you can be helped. We had two young girls just recently, they went to the store for their mother, and a couple of school friends drove by and said, I'll give you a lift to the store. They jumped in the car. When the police pulled them over, they all got arrested for narcotics. And they can't get out until Mom's come and till they've paid a bond because they were in the car and narcotics was found, and now their record shows narcotics. They were in the wrong place at the wrong time. And after you're in here for a while, things start changing.

We have a musical program for the inmates. We have a guy come in here named Mr. John Wright. He plays classical and jazz piano, and he interested the guys in music, so different people donated pianos and organs for the inmates to play. We have a band come in and play for the programs here. They play jazz and blues and everything else. So it's real nice. These are the types of programs I'm proud of. We have cultural enrichment programs. These are the types of things we didn't have in the jail before, and you can imagine the chaos when you don't have anything to do. Now those guys can say, well, I can go to the library; I can draw awhile, take that tension off. Go play the saxophone, 'cause they used to play it outside; play the piano a little bit.

It's been a change in the whole jail since the programs. Something to occupy the mind and the body. The prisoners make crafts and paintings. Some of them are so creative they don't need a teacher; they're really good. We have a guy so good with charcoal he can draw anybody anytime, anywhere. You think about how much is lost. The talent. We had some singers and piano players in here; man, they was really something. And if people want to donate some books—hardcover, paperback—they can do it.

KALAIS CHIRON HUNT

One Prisoner's Story

Thirty-six-year-old Kalais Chiron Hunt was in the Cook County Jail for the typical reasons: drugs, crime, and gangs. But, he told me, this will be the last time. "I'm gonna get out of here. I'll probably have to do some time in a maximum security prison someplace else, but in any event, I'm not gonna be gone for no long time . . . Before, I was a kid . . . You get back on the street, it was like, man, you was in the county jail—did you have a fight? . . . But now I'm in the mindset where I say to myself, I really don't want and can't come back to this place . . . I have responsibilities now. Now what I thought was making me a man is making me feel less than a man."

I'm under the alias Eric Edwards in jail. My real name is Kalais Chiron Hunt. Eric Edwards is the name I gave to the police so I wouldn't come to jail, but I'm here, so it didn't do me any good.

I was born and raised in Chicago. My mom, she used to work at a rubber company when I was a kid, probably on the North Side of the city. Like my father, I'm in jail. My father didn't do anything. He was just like me, a street person. We got on the streets, sold drugs, did things of that nature. My father now is fifty-eight years old. I'm thirty-six.

I've been in this jail on several occasions. It's a mixture of things that gets me back here. First of all, it's the way I thought. Right now I'm doing something about the way I think, but previously, the things that brought me here was because it was nothing that one person did, or nothing that a million people did, it's just the way that I thought and the environment that I was brought up in. It's easier for me to, say, sell drugs than to go and get a job. I make money faster that way. That's basically why I kept coming back to jail. Using drugs and doing things to get drugs. That's why I keep coming back over and over, because I didn't change the way I thought. And sometimes you get officers in the neighborhood that just say, okay, let's get this guy, let's stop him, and I wind up here.

Where I'm from, a kid who wanted to study or become a professor would be considered a nerd. The average kid growing up on the West Side or the South Side of Chicago, they tend to look at drug dealers, hustlers, players— so-called players—and pimps in their neighborhood. They don't look at the schoolteachers, the firemen, the police officers, or the professors. They don't look at that because they're not around in the neighborhood. And then when you're in a setting as far as your home goes, you've got just a mother or just a father. You don't have two parents; you have one parent. Your mother's at work, so you have to do what you have to do to survive. And nine times out of ten, that means you are either selling drugs or you're doing something that's against the law. It ain't something that you want to do, but if you be around it so much growing up, that's something that you start to take on. You start to say, okay, well, I think this is the norm. It's as easy for me to sell drugs as to ex- pect to go to school. It's as easy for me to sell drugs as it is to expect to play bas- ketball. That's the pain of it all.

School for me was like shooting dice, smoking weed in the bathroom. That's what school was like to me; that's what I went to school to do. I didn't go to school to sit up in the class. Oh yes, I can read, I can write, and I thought that's all I need, but when I pass the bathroom, I hear the music; I go in the bathroom. It was like I should go to class, but no, no, I'm gonna go in the bathroom because I know that's where it's happening. That's what school started being like in high school. 'Cause when you're in grade school, man, it's like you say, school, man, I wanna go to school, 'cause I like the girl that sits behind me. Or in my case, I was crazy about my teacher. Every word she said I just hung on to it like that. So after eighth grade, you know, you kind of like think that you're a man then. You don't want to listen to your mom, and every- thing you do and everything you see, like I said, is in your neighborhood. That's when the gangs kick in. That's when your guys and everybody that you know belong to one certain section or one certain block or neighborhood, and you've got another guy he's belonging to another certain section, a neighbor- hood. That's when gangs kick in, and that's when you'd be like, okay, well, I'm gonna have this gang 'cause this is the most popular gang. Or this is the gang that's in my neighborhood.

I'll say 90 percent of the people here are guilty, even if some are just basically a victim of circumstances. You do have people here because they hang with me and they haven't done anything and they get arrested. Okay, you haven't done nothing. But 90 percent of the people that's here, in the Cook County Jail right now, are here for something they've done or they have knowledge of. Me personally, I've come to grips with what I've done. Ninety percent of the people are guilty. They might say they're not guilty, but they are. They've done something. They took some part in the crime they're being charged with, and that's the honest to God truth.

To get prisoners out of here or keep them from coming back, the men who are here need more information as far as jobs, and they need to be given basically like what we're doing now in this program. This is a life-learning deck now. We study. We study this *Mind of Christ* book. What the chaplain has done was implemented the mind of Jesus Christ into our daily activities. We spend I'd say the better part of the day studying this book. It gives us various Bible verses. It gives us how to change our attitudes towards society and most of all towards our self, and gives us the love of God.

Now I'm not saying that this is the only thing that will stop us, but you have to have other avenues for guys like me that don't have job training and don't know how to fill out an application coming out of these places or coming out of the penal institutions. Don't even know how to be a father, let alone be a friend or a brother. We don't bond with each other. We spend time tearing each other down. We don't spend any time building each other up. So what we're doing here is, we're trying to reconstruct the way we think about society, about ourselves, about our mothers, about our children, about our brother, just anybody walking down the street. You see, in our neighborhoods now, people don't care about that. I don't care about someone being a professor if I have a drug problem; I'm gonna rob you. I don't care about someone being the superintendent of Cook County Jail; if he has something I want, I'm gonna take it. They don't teach us about humanity out there, about being humble and about being peaceful and responsible and, most importantly, responsive, because every action has a reaction. If you've got a bad action, you're gonna get a bad reaction. And most of the times, that's what we're learning out there.

But see right now, what I'm learning here, me personally—I can't speak for everybody else, I can only speak for me—what I'm learning now is what a man's supposed to be. Most of us black males growing up in the neighborhood, we don't have fathers. Our fathers have either ran off or they're on drugs or they're here. And now I'm learning how to be responsible, how to cater to females, my mother, my wife, my children, and all this. How to respect another human being for who they are and what they are and what they think, and not allow that to make me feel inferior or superior, just be comfortable with who I am and working towards our goal, which is the path favored by God—to protect and serve my family. That's what I'm learning.

There's not one single reason that so many black men end up in prison today. It's not just the lack of job opportunities, or just their own responsibility, or just the fact that their fathers are not around and there's a single head of household. It's a multitude of things. What I've learned, it's not the fact that there's not enough jobs, because there's jobs out there. If you look hard enough, you're gonna find a job, I don't care if it's in McDonald's. But the average guy that's over twenty-five is not gonna work at McDonald's. But you could find a job doing something, or you can come up with your own job, as long as it's legal. So it's a number of things that causes African-American males to come to jail. It could be stealing food, it could be drug addiction; man, it could be anything. You can't just pinpoint no one thing, so you have to come up with a scope of things, and a multitude of ideas and remedies to combat that, because if you just focus on the guys that have drug addiction, but what about the guys that don't have jobs? If you just focus on the guys that don't have jobs, what about the guys that's let's just say just victim of circumstances?

You have to set up programs for people here to have ways in getting jobs and really taking up all the spare time that they have. A lot of times you find that people just don't have anything to do. And then they wasn't taught how to be men. We have to start teaching these people how to be men. I mean real men, not a man because of what you've got between your legs, and not a man because you've got a child. It's various things that make up a man—responsibility, protection, being a servant just to the family, let alone the community. These are the things that we should look at that would stop most guys from coming to jail. It took me thirty-six years to figure this out. I wish it would have happened when I was nineteen years old, but I guess that's how I came out.

Basically, all of us come from the same environment, so we know one another from before we got arrested. People know you by your name. Guys in different parts of the jail, H2 or B2 or D2, they know you by your name. It's not a matter of how you hook up with other gang members after you're arrested. They're gonna actually know who you are when you're walking down the walkway, when you're coming down the boulevard, when they see you going to church or on the yard. They know who you are. There's somebody in this place that you know from your neighborhood and then they in turn are going to relay the message that this person is here, this person is there. In jail, the gang members stay in touch with each other through chapel, anything, work, whatever; it makes no difference.

The gangs work the same both inside prison and outside. Let's take the officers of the jail. In all the divisions you have a superintendent, you have a chief, the captain, the lieutenant, the sarge, and then you have the officers. It works the same way with the gangs. You have a guy that's the head, then you have the guys that follow, that will do anything and everything that he asked them to do, no question. You can use the gang structure to get anything you want, besides a female. You get whatever you want. That ain't no problem—cigarettes, grass, food, whatever. It don't make a difference.

On their first day here, the people who aren't a member of a gang get treated. "Treated" means get played. How can I explain this? They don't get nothing. They got to really know somebody to get somewhere. They just get the necessities. They don't get any cigarettes; they don't get any of that. And if they did get it, they'd probably get it took from them by somebody who is a member of a gang. It takes you a lot less than a minute to figure out you should belong to a gang in here. As soon as you walk in that door, you say to yourself, I have to get somebody so I can be somebody.

What the gangs organize to do is nothing that's worth noting. A hypothetical situation is a guy might be in trouble with a guy over here on another deck, and there might not be enough cats on the deck to help him fight this cat. So they'd wait till they get in the yard and they'd say, okay, we've got a problem with this guy; what shall we do? Okay, just hold off, we go, we'll talk about it. If we can't talk about it, then we fight, and then those guys get involved and everybody gets beat up but the problem gets solved. You send the message out, okay, don't mess with them, they're one of my guys. So that's how they do it. There's various ways of getting in contact with a guy you want to talk to that's on another deck.

People can get drugs in here. Of course they can. This is jail. I mean, just 'cause you're in jail don't mean that everything is gonna stop. The only thing you can't do that's actually normal is drive a car and have sex with a woman. That's it. The rest of that stuff you can get. It's here, not for sale on every deck, but in this place. You can get all those things in any penal institution, whether it's the county jail in the Cook County Department of Corrections or IDOC, Illinois Department of Corrections. It makes no difference. The same things that's going on on the streets is going on in here—the same power plays, the same deaths. Everything that's going on out there is going on in here.

There's not so much physical violence today in here, people getting beat up. In the earlier times, like in the late 1980s and early 1990s, I'd say there was a lot of violence. It was real easy to get into a fight. But not so much now. Guys tend to talk now 'cause there ain't nobody too ready to catch cases. Guys don't want to catch another case by being here. And as far as sexual violence goes, well, you can't rape the willing. You've got guys that come in here that's perverse like that. As respects somebody that's willing, somebody that's unwilling, most guys say, well, I'm gonna go with the willing, and you've got guys that would be willing to do stuff like that.

I don't know what percent of the inmates have sex with other men from here, 'cause that can vary, man. I could be talking to someone and they could have homosexual tendencies and I'll not even know it. Your sexual preference is something you don't wear on your forehead, unless you've said it out of your mouth. But I know the percent people say is a lie. It's higher than most people think, probably. It's pretty high. But it ain't true that people who wouldn't sleep with a man out in society will do it here. They do. If you gay in here, you gay in the world. What's the difference? Out there you can do it and not get caught.

If I'm in a cell with three guys and they're having sex with each other, I'm not gonna be one of them. And it's not too likely somebody would try to overpower me. But if they did, it would probably be cases involved, 'cause somebody going to die; somebody going to lose their life. There's certain things that you just can't do to a man, and when stuff like that do happen, somebody gonna wind up being hurt, or somebody wind up changing their name from Steve to Shirley or whatever. Either somebody's gonna lose their life, or somebody's gonna become a woman real soon. Seriously.

The ones who adopt the persona of a woman, I see most of them coming in off the new like that. They come in and the staff knows and I think they separate them guys from the general population. That way they won't be knocking, 'cause there are guys who tend to fight over those kind of people too, as far as the homosexuals versus the heterosexuals. The heterosexual guys, well, they consider themselves heterosexuals, but me personally, I think if you mess with one of them homosexuals, you might as well be gay too. That's homosexual; that's abomination. But they do; some of the heterosexual guys fight over them same as the homosexual people.

In this jail there's three people to one toilet, so you've got to do all your business right there in front of everybody. Right there. What you have to do is become immune to life, like privacy as far as using a bathroom. It's just like the showers: there's only two heads of them. There's thirty-eight people up there who use the same shower. Let's just say that during a lockup the officers say, okay, well, we want you all to take a shower one cell at the same time, for time's sake. I have to get over what I feel as a man and get in the shower if I want to take a shower. Now me personally, I wouldn't take a shower; I'd take a bird bath. I wouldn't get in the shower; that is just something I won't do. But it's hard, man, it's really hard. You don't actually use the washroom while there's a guy there. I mean at school there were females there, but a guy, come on, man, that ain't cool.

I've spent all this time in jail. How am I gonna get this time back; how can I? It's time just lost. Gone. The worst part about being locked up is being away from my daughters, being away from the people that I know, that I can make an impact on, the people that I really, really care about. That's the worst part, and the fact that I'm losing a lot of time doing nothing when I could be using that time for something positive. That's the worst about it. Even other than that, I wouldn't advise this on no man, believe me, I wouldn't.

I thought I could beat the system. I thought I'd never get caught, 'cause I'd never thought about the repercussions behind anything that I've done. We never do; none of us ever do. We never think about what could possibly happen if we do this. We just do it. And then after it happens, then you come back down to like, oh, man, if I'd have known this, I wouldn't have done that. We never think about that. We never think about what might happen, or what could happen. All we want is what we want when we want it and how we want it.

It's hell in here, but you have to understand something. I was always intelligent; I just didn't use the intelligence that God gave me. What I did was trying to be something or mold myself into something that God didn't create me to be or didn't ordain me to be. As a child, most African-American men stand in front of the mirror and try to emulate something that they see growing up. Most people do. I have to keep going back to the role model thing, because if I was seeing like, let's say, a fireman every day, then that could be a role model. I'm not saying there wasn't firemen, but they wasn't around in my neighborhood; they didn't actually live in my neighborhood. If a fire broke out, the firemen would come from a station that's not in my neighborhood to put the fire out. If the ambulance driver come to my neighborhood, he would come from another place; he wouldn't actually live in my neighborhood. I wouldn't wake up in the morning and come outside to play and see a fireman on his way to work or see a policeman on his way to work. I'd see a drug dealer. I'd see someone stealing something. I'd see someone fight and I'd see someone arguing and when I looked to see where my father was, he wasn't there; it was just my mom. So it wasn't that I wasn't intelligent, it's just I wasn't aware of the potential that I had. I grew up seeing those things, so that's the thing that I emulated and that's what I put into my life.

There are people who are more comfortable in prison than out in the world, because they are somebody here and they're nobodies out there. I know a lot of people like that, but they're downstate. There's a lot of people down there that's doing time that would much rather be here because they don't have any responsibility as far as what the normal people have—what we consider normal people, people that don't get in trouble. You know, you get up in the morning, you go to work. You go to work for what? You go to work to take care of your family, to pay your bills right, and having a little few days' necessities for yourself, things on the side. Most of the guys don't have that. They don't have the drive or the will to do that. They'd rather sit in jail and watch TV, play cards, and have the state provide room and food. They don't have no light bills, no gas bills; they don't have to take care of their children. In fact they're having someone else take care of them. For them, the worst punishment might be to throw them out and make them do something. Make them start taking on the responsibilities that they're supposed to have. I mean, I'm ready.

You can't spot people and say, this guy is gonna be here forever, he's gonna stay in the prison system, 'cause you can't tell. And if you've got a person that's acting up, there's a reason for him acting the way he acts. You can't just say, okay, this guy's gonna be here; this is one of the cats I know is not gonna ever do much in life. Look at other people that came in here and turned their lives around. People would say things about them, that they would never change. But you can't say that, because you don't know.

I'm gonna get out of here. I'll probably have to do some time in a maximum security prison someplace else, but in any event, I'm not gonna be gone for no long time. And more so than the previous times I was here, I think about whether I'm gonna be back here six months after I get out. Before, I was a kid. I wasn't really thinking about it; I was having fun. It was cool. You get back on the street, it was like, man, you was in the county jail—did you have a fight? And stuff like that. So you was like a celebrity. I'm serious. But now I'm in the mindset where I say to myself, I really don't want and can't come back to this place. Now I went downhill. I'm getting old. I've got children. I have responsibilities now. Now what I thought was making me a man is making me feel less than a man. So now what I do is, I try to think about things that I need to put in my life, and the things I need to take out of my life, to keep me from coming to this place. And like I said, this *Mind of Christ* has been a big help. It's teaching me and showing me certain things in certain avenues that I can use inside myself—not really getting any help from anybody else, just having the will and the desire inside myself to do something. Not great for the world, but just great for myself. And that's the first and foremost, is to stay out of here and provide for the kids that I have.

I was pretty well literate when I came into prison. But we have some guys that can't read past Go; we have some guys that can't read at all. And it's a shame, because some of them don't ask for help, but we have some that do. I just feel for the ones that don't and then they're my age and I say to myself, why don't they ask anybody for help? I think it has a lot to do with being embarrassed with someone looking at you and looking down on you. And that's another problem that African-American men have. We don't know how to ask for help. We feel that it makes us weaker and inferior, and that's not the case. Everybody needs help; that's something else that I've learned. These are some of the things that I will use at my advantage when I leave this place. I know now that I can reach out and ask somebody, hey, I need some help. I don't understand this; I don't know how to do this.

If you take all the drugs out of the neighborhood, that would be a bit out of hand there. They'll just go to somebody else's neighborhood. Wherever the drugs are, that's where they're gonna go. If you give them better job opportunities, that only helps if you clean them up too. It's the drugs. That's the key to everything. Actually, that's the key to mass murder, to be honest. A guy that commits a murder, do you think he commits a murder because he actually hates the human being? No. Because God don't make people that way. People are not naturally coldhearted people. Drugs turn people that way. Drugs make people think that they're this and they're that. Drugs take people to a different way of thinking. It's drugs. That's the sad thing. If you can get rid of drugs, man, I guarantee 95 percent of our problems would be done with. But then you'd have to deal with greed and stuff like that and we have our ways of dealing with that. Just take their money from them. If you just get rid of drugs, man, you wouldn't have half the people here, not even half.

But if you let everybody out who was busted for doing crack, and you haven't engaged on any kind of help or put them in any kind of program that would deter them from using crack cocaine or whatever drug it is, they'll be back. It's safe to say they'll be back. They think they're not gonna come back if you let them out, but they're gonna go right back out there with no knowledge of what kind of problem they had. They'll go out with a problem, knowing they have a problem but with no answers to fix that problem. So they'll go back living in that same problem; they'll go back doing the same things that they was doing, especially if you just let them go like that and they ain't had no kind of help. That's like coming to jail and they ain't working on nothing. Like I used to do, working on nothing, caring about nothing, playing cards all day, dominoes, chess, and not really giving thought to what's been happening in your life, or with what's going on in your life and what it's about, what's to become of your life. Because when you leave society, that's time that you can never get back. I once heard a man say, if I loan you $100, you can come back and give me $100 back and you've paid me everything that I've given you. But if I give you my time, you can't give me my time back.

First and foremost thing is, I'm gonna get out there and stay out there and find a job, simple as that. It makes no difference what it is, 'cause first I had higher standards and now I'm in here heading way down. I'm gonna get a job and take care of my kids, go to church, build my family around the church structure. I've had three or four jobs. I worked at the Embassy Suites, I've worked at Delaware Cars and Limousines, I've worked at Allied Food. It don't make a difference that I've been in prison several times. Who cares as long as you can do the job? A lot of people use that as a crutch: I've been to jail and I'm not gonna be able to get no jobs, so I'm just gonna do what I've got to do. That's a crutch. That's just telling me that you don't want to do more about it. See, because if you was a real man, against all odds you keep trying. A man is not the man that goes, oh, I got a lot of courage, 'cause courage is not the apple in the field; we already know that. Even if you are afraid and you don't think you're gonna get the job, as long as you try and you keep on trying to keep on, trying to keep on trying until something happens, that's courage. And believe me, if you're persistent and consistent it's gonna happen. You just have to be patient, and we don't have a lot of patience. You have to be patient.

To my knowledge, the only thing that we have in here to give us better preparation is this *Mind of Christ* and studying the Bible, which has an effect on the interior. But now we need things like teaching people how to fill out applications and even just to hold a conversation without acting like a slave or without offending the person that you're talking to, especially when you desire something from them and he's in a position to help you. You've got guys that don't even know how to communicate with those simple skills. We need programs like that set up, designed to help people do those kind of things.

One thing we could do to keep the crime level down, to keep people from going astray, would be to make everything free. I'm just kidding. The people that live in the community are actually their own problems. Say I go back to my community. I could become a professor. I move out of the neighborhood. I know I could become a professor, but I would leave the neighborhood. I wouldn't stay, so who's left in my neighborhood if the professor's not living there, if the police officers are not living there?

If I was Jesse Jackson and I was trying to keep these black men from even going to prison, or trying to get them out of prison, I would encourage everybody that's in the neighborhood who's working on something to grab a person that they feel needs help. Not necessarily a person that they like; it could be anybody. And you take that person and show them and teach them and give them certain avenues. Not actually open the door for them; just point them in the right direction. Don't leave the neighborhood, or if you did leave, then go back to the neighborhood. I'm not saying take all your money and squander it on the neighborhood; no. Show them how you got where you're at. Give them kinds of programs, teach them how to fill out applications, teach them how to hold interviews, teach mothers prenatal care. You've got mothers out there leaving their kids on doorsteps or in hospitals, in garbage cans, for heaven's sake, in alleys. It's not because they don't want the children. They feel that their lives are over. They don't know what to do, so they say, well, I'm gonna give this child up because I know I can't take care of it; I don't even know how. It's not more so the money; it's emotionally. They don't know how to deal with it emotionally.

If I could change daily life in prison to make things better, everybody under the age of twenty-five would have to go to school if they don't have a GED. Everybody that's over thirty-five would be in a separate part of the penitentiary, and the guys that's in between, I'd let them do whatever they want to do, 'cause they don't need anything. They're not thinking to a level to whereas they're gonna be productive for themselves or for anybody else. They can't hear anything. They don't want to hear anything, and they block everything in their self. See, the young people you can reach. The older people you don't have to worry about because they're like me. They've come to a situation in their life where they say, I no longer want to be a part of the problem; I want to be a part of the solution. But the people in the middle, they're the problem, the people that don't care. I'm not saying just do away with them. Let them run their course. Just set them inside of the penitentiary or the jail and let nature take its course. They'll come around. I'm here, and I understand. They don't care about nothing; they mess it up. They get the officers involved with certain things; they don't care about anything.

What I'm saying is that they must let nature take its course. Let old age catch up with you, 'cause once old age sets in, you're too old to do anything. You can't fight, and there ain't nobody here that's gonna listen to you. At least with the younger guys you can scare them straight. You can set up things for them and you tell them like to make certain things, make learning fun to them. Too many times they'll be involved with things that they feel is boring. It's designed to help them, but they can't see themselves take a part in it. But when it becomes fun and they're learning more too, then they want to do it. I would keep the food the same, the TV the same, the phone the same, 'cause that's designed to keep you from not coming back. Every time you go to that phone you have to make a collect call.

So if you take some guys out of here that use drugs, man, and not give them some kind of program, you know, man, you've got a problem. Now, this is what you need to do to fix that problem. You ask, do you want help with this problem? And if they say no, then okay, well, okay, you want to come back? All right; go. That's the thing about it: they want help, give them help, but if you just let them go, know that they'll be back. If you was to let at least 95 percent of the people out of this jail at a quarter to three, at about five o'clock they all be back. You've got to know that to be true. They'll be back 'cause they have nothing else to do. They have no means of being satisfied or fixing their problems, so they just wallow in stuff that they're already in, the mess that they're already in. That's basically what happens, how they've got themselves into everything.

You have to watch what you say in here. Certain things you can say out there in the street, you can't say here. I don't like saying them, but they use words like that. Like if you call a guy a bitch, man, them are grounds for getting beat up. You call a guy a whore, them grounds of getting beat up. If you call him a punk, them's grounds of getting beat up. So you have to really watch what you say. So a guy like me, you see, I know that respect is not something you demand, it's something you share, so I share with them. That way, I deter any of that. And then I'm kind of like a fairly big guy too, so that helps, 'cause people don't want to mess with me. But it's really hard; it is. You have to watch what you say, even when you get angry. You have to be careful of what you say to another inmate. You can't just say anything that comes to your mind. You have to pick your words, because what you might say from minute to minute might cause a fight, a very, very, very, very, very dangerous fight. And then it depends on who you're saying this to. If you're saying it to the wrong guy, it's gonna cost you your life. Yeah. It will cost you your life. You will die in jail, yes, you will. It will happen; it will. You will lose your life by what you say out your mouth to one of these guys that's in these places. So you really have to be careful about that, you know what I mean? It's not normal.

DR. EMIEL HAMBERLIN

Ticket to Success

A 2001 inductee into the National Teachers Hall of Fame, Dr. Emiel Hamberlin has been a renowned teacher at Chicago's Du Sable High School for thirty-six years. Famous for his ability to encourage any child to learn, he asserts that "it's not human to fail." But he remains concerned about the future. "The reason our kids do not value education in the same way we did is that we almost teach them how to be helpless," he said. "We think we're helping them when we do not allow them to attach themselves to some degree of responsibility, and that's what I try to bring out in my classroom."

For people of my generation, education was part of the Civil Rights Movement. We were taught that even in a racist system, we would succeed and be okay if we worked hard. I was born in Fayette, Mississippi, and it was terrible, in terms of what blacks went through. I grew up during the time of Emmett Till, and I know what people in the United States must feel when they think about terrorists. I lived among terrorists, and we could identify them, but nothing was ever done to them. The Klansmen were terrorists.

When I was attending Alcorn State University in Mississippi, my brothers and my sister were living in Chicago. I used to visit them and work in Chicago during the summer months, and then go back to school to study. I didn't like Chicago, and after finishing at the university, I planned to join the Peace Corps. I was waiting for an assignment and my brother said, why don't you come and substitute-teach until you get the assignment from the Peace Corps? And I did. I went to the Chicago Board of Education and they sent me to Du Sable High School as a substitute teacher. And I never stopped teaching.

It wasn't love at first sight. I didn't like the Chicago weather; it was kind of cloudy, and I expected it to be more sunny. There was smog, and the streets were not as clean as where I was coming from. But after about two or three weeks, I said, gee, this is what I like doing. As I continued to teach and to find satisfaction in teaching, that somehow gave me the desire to stay. And now I wouldn't want to live in any other place but Chicago. Kids come out to my house all the time on 85th and Winchester. They landscaped my house. Some of the students are members of the church I belong to.

Being average frightens me. Students realize they don't have an average teacher when they walk into my classroom. If you don't have an average teacher, you're not going to have average students. You're going to have above-average students. Each one of my students also realizes that he or she was born an original; there's no need to dye a copy. You're what you ought to be when you want to be it. And when people misunderstand you, it's because you're great. You're not supposed to be understood; you're not that simple. You're good, you're bad, you're great. You're anything you want to be.

For most of my thirty-six years of teaching at Du Sable High School, my day has started at seven and ended at seven. In the evenings we work in the lab. I get to know more about the children at that time, and I teach more then than I do the rest of the day. The children are relaxed, and I sneak the information in on them. They are in a learning environment, but the structure is such that they don't know I'm evaluating them while they are going through the subject matter—photosynthesis, respiration, adsorption, development, animal behavior, and so on. We have a lot of fun.

Part of my philosophy is, I never fail a child in class. If he comes 80 percent of the time, he's going to pass. It's never his fault that he has not learned. It just so happens that I may not be the right teacher for him, so there's another doctor in the house for him. I would not let a child sit there for ten weeks and then fail. We don't live long enough to fail. It's not human to fail. There's another problem going on, and it's not the child's problem. It's beyond the child, so let's find out what it is. It's not you, I tell them; there's nothing wrong with you. It's I who was not able to teach you, so let's go to another teacher.

The kids are in school about six hours a day, and they have eighteen hours out there in a difficult world, sometimes a nightmare world. But that's the hand we're dealt. And since I'm an educational physician, it's my job to make the students become educationally aware. I'm not worried about where they're coming from; I'm worried about how well I can make them. And if they keep taking my assignments, which are a prescription, they're going to become educationally well. If a student does not get completely well, I'm going to at least make him feel better. This is my charge. This is my duty. This is my passion.

Of course, I am concerned with bolstering the children's self-esteem in the classroom setting. I tell them, do you know how great you are, how wonderful you are? You're an original—don't you feel it, can't you see it, don't you see what I see? Can't you feel what I see? There's the inner part of you, I tell them, that must say yes to what I'm trying to get into you. Once I get your mind and change your attitude, I'll change your behavior, because you can be anything you want to be. It's your mind—it's your attitude—that limits you. And when there's no limit to it, what do you want to be?

So when a child walks into the classroom, it is up to me to hype him up, to pick him up, to energize him, to bring happiness into his life, to enter his morning. And you get the very best you can out of the moments you have.

Many of the children are not being nurtured and praised and prepared for school at home. Where a home is not as happy as it possibly could be, and parents are scrambling and scraping and trying to make ends meet, it stresses the children, even though the parents are doing all they possibly can. The children's attention span is limited, and they're easily annoyed even by someone touching them; they're ready to almost go off. They're constantly under stress and in one or another of these emotional states.

Another thing that happens with the central city children is that when their friends are murdered or killed—and that happens often—they do not know how to grieve. There's no way to grieve. They come right back to school. This is where they find the best possible sanctuary. So not knowing how to grieve, these children many times will hurt another child to get over the grief. They think, I must hurt somebody else. And that is not a positive way of grieving.

The parents are doing all they can do, and many times their spirit is broken because their income is fixed and they wonder, how do I get out of this hole? I'm in a trench; I'm pulling up, trying to get out. At the end of the month you can barely make it out, and by the time you get out and the money comes in, you've become a part of the negativity; you've slipped back into it again.

I involve the family, even where family support is difficult to obtain. I never dwell on negatives and on what can't be done, but seek to discover new ways to do the most difficult tasks. I start where the student is, and in urban areas such as where I teach, it's not always on page one of the biology or horticulture textbook.

One thing I want in my classroom is to surround the students with their subject matter. I have many animals and many plants in the classroom, so once you walk in, it takes your mind completely away from where you're coming from, into another world. And I want to give you something to talk about when you go home other than negativity. I want you to be able to go home and say, this is what happened in the classroom—the alligator was eating, and we fed the piranhas today. The macaws were talking; they have speech teachers. There are many activities that we have in the classroom, and the aim is to over-power the negativity that the students are walking through in terms of getting to school; to counteract the crises that they're going through.

One of the most popular programs I implemented with my students is the Urban Ecology Sanctuary, an indoor-outdoor laboratory where students grew and cared for a large variety of plants and maintained a habitat or ecosystem for peacocks, pheasants, and other exotic birds. The sanctuary won national acclaim as an innovative idea generated by students with school support, and was highlighted in the *New York Times* and other publications around the country. The project was open to the entire community and required many hours of professional consultation, workshops, and seminars for the students as well as collaborations with teachers and community leaders.

Students involved in the sanctuary, along with other teachers and myself, were invited to Cornell University's School of Architecture to share with its students the origin and significance of the project. The Du Sable students also explored the possibility of the sanctuary being duplicated by other urban high schools, and discussed the impact this would have on urban environmental education. All of the students who participated in the project have since gone on to colleges and universities around the United States.

The city of Chicago's Parks Department routinely works with my students when developing wetlands, growing wild grasses, and establishing ecological parks around the city. For many years, my students have worked with the city aldermen in developing abandoned lots into resourceful green areas and com-munity gardens. My classroom's Turn a Vacant Lot Around project was so successful that seniors in our community helped us to continue the program for four years.

Students also went into public housing complexes and decorated the porches with live plants and flowers. They earned many hours of Service Learning credits toward graduation requirements while helping to make life a little better for their families and others. Our Botanical Club earned the high-est award of any such group of environmental education students exhibiting in the Chicago Flower Show over a five-year period. All these programs re-quired tremendous student discipline, dedication, and scholarship.

When students discover the amazing interdependence of people, animals, and nature, they develop a connection to the environment. Conservation, health issues, extinction of species, world pollution, rain forests, food sources, trees, and recycling become as much a part of their daily lives as McDonald's and video games. I want students to know that I can give them some knowledge and skills to protect our global environment, but what they do with their own lives is the real answer. I want students to know that I care what they do with their lives.

The reason our kids do not value education in the same way we did is that we almost teach them how to be helpless. We give them whatever they need, or what we think they need. And that is not their fault. We even supply them with more paper and pencils than they need. We think we're helping them when we do not allow them to attach themselves to some degree of responsibility, and that's what I try to bring out in my classroom.

Teachers lost their authority with kids when parents lost their authority. When children don't come home on time, they don't necessarily come to your class on time. Single mothers try to do most of it by themselves, and they need a helpmate. They're struggling, they're doing it; they're doing the best they can with what they have. I'm not bashing them. If the fathers were not there, it was overwhelming for the mothers to do it all by themselves. So when the family structure fell apart, so did order in the schools.

If the middle class moved back to this area, it would of course help. When you have a heterogeneous grouping of people, economically and educationally, it does help. There are examples to see. There are examples of mothers going to work, of fathers going to work.

I suppose I could get very upset about finding out that a student has dropped out because she's pregnant or another is in the Cook County Jail because he's busted for selling drugs. But then I look at the students as they're walking through the hall, as they're sitting in the cafeteria and in my classroom, and I wonder, if I was in this community, which one of them would I be? Just which one would I be? If I was dealt a hand of an environment that is so negative, that draws so much energy away, that actually reinforces their negativity so well, and they are successful being negative, then how can I offset it with being positive? That's difficult to do, yet it can be done by repeating it over and over again—not bashing a student because of where he's coming from, but helping him to get where he ought to be.

A child who goes to prison, or has to drop out because she's pregnant, or succumbs to drugs, is a lost child. I feel very uneasy about it. I feel for that child with a great deal of compassion, but what I rely upon is what I gave that child while he or she was here with me. I gave him all or gave her all I possibly could give of myself and all the training I could, and tried to guide their life through what they were enduring. So the satisfaction goes with the belief that I did as much as I possibly could do, that I knew how to do—and that if I can't do it, there's another teacher in the house.

Many of the students are in transit when they leave Du Sable High; they're moving to another school in another area of the city. They just don't drop out and that's the end of their career. Where we are is not accepted, and I wouldn't want them to remain here when they can get out. So we don't really lose a lot of students; they transfer to other schools.

Of course, if I see bad behavior in a child, I don't blame that on the child. Children are the reflection of the society in which they live. What they see on television, what they're allowed to hear on radios and CDs, is what they reflect back into the schools. They keep it real.

If I had been born in the Robert Taylor Homes, perhaps I might not be where I am today. That's a real possibility. I said that to a judge when I was being a character witness for a student. I asked him, if you were born where he was born, would you be sitting there or would you be sitting where the young man is sitting? It gave him something to think about. And the young man got probation instead of jail time.

As a black man and as a teacher, I attempt to change lives and mend broken spirits through the power of education. It was not long ago, during my childhood, that my family made its living on the farm. From that humble American beginning, my blackness, my appreciation for nature, and my respect for family and others have given me the power to teach with conviction.

As a teacher and as a man, I am motivated by those around me, and I have been fortunate enough to surround myself with some of America's greatest men and women. Over the course of my career, Du Sable High School has had hundreds of the most talented teachers in America. Many have gone on to higher positions in the education field. I have learned from many of them, I have worked with all of them, and I have become who I am because of them. My students have taught me the most and have given me immeasurable hope and spirit, generation after generation.

Teachers have an incredible influence upon a student, whether it's negative or positive, and most of it is positive. When you've done it well enough and the kids know that you're sincere, that you're dedicated and your passion is for the total development of this child, the entire child himself, they will come back and let you know. They will call you; they will come back. Every day—I can truthfully say this—somebody comes by the school to see me because I made an impact on their lives in some capacity. I helped them develop their academic skills and their survival skills, and I gave them tidbits of inspiration and words of wisdom in the classroom: Do today what others want so you can enjoy life later like others can't.

A critical issue facing education, as I see it, is that we continue to need workers who are trained to use their hands and minds to build the future of America. Many urban youth are not meeting the standards for college entrance, but this does not preclude their making useful contributions to society in other ways. Schools must reflect the needs of the community, and while technology and advanced education are very important, hands-on workers are greatly needed in the fields of medicine, industry and manufacturing, food service and agriculture, building and technical operations, and especially in my field of horticulture and environmental protection.

School districts have few trained vocational instructors and are making no provisions for the future. School boards are stressing "back to basics" in such a way as to eliminate vocational courses in lieu of additional reading and math. Instead of opting for innovative alternative and authentic assessment strategies such as portfolios, demonstrations, or thematic units, they rely on standardized testing as the only method to determine what students know and can do.

I believe that if standardized tests should do anything, they should indicate the vocational capabilities of our students. Students who are either not able to meet the standards set by tests scores, or who are unwilling to do so, would be given the opportunity to investigate vocational fields. Educators would make sure that these are fields that will be needed in the future. Starting in the eleventh grade, students would begin to specialize in a vocation, with sufficient hands-on training to prepare them as capable workers in particular fields.

The Essential Schools research out of Brown University indicates that students involved in small schools where they receive more personalized education do better in their academics. In urban areas, this has meant restructuring large schools into small schools within the present building. Each small school had its own leadership, usually teachers, who were responsible for the progress, selection, and care of their own students. The overall building was run by a building principal who coordinated all the teachers' efforts.

My involvement started with a staff development trip to New York City to visit several small-school programs there that were highly successful. Our faculty became so excited about this education movement that groups of teachers designed several small schools at Du Sable based on academic and vocational themes. The small-schools model worked very well for most of the school's programs. The question is, what can we as educators do to move away from the large urban educational facilities where students are treated as numbers, and where during a school day some students may just slip through the cracks? Many students are so anonymous that they eventually become tremendous discipline problems.

Teachers run the small schools, taking on most of the administrative functions that it took several teams of administrators to do poorly. Children's scores improve, and they want to stay in school. Districts find many excuses and create red tape to hinder the programs, however, and eventually, like the one at Du Sable, they are terminated without even an explanation as to why.

I believe that the future of education in America's cities is in the hands of teachers and that teachers must be empowered to get the job done. Teachers are effective administrators, and they can collaborate to improve schools when given the opportunity.

JASON SMITH

A Different Version

"A lot of the guys didn't want to see my brothers and me make that type of money," Jason Smith told me about his teenage years selling drugs on Chicago's South Side. "I had my mom, but she wasn't always there. I probably would have been proud to have her spend more quality time with me. I wanted to have nice clothes and the jewelry and cars, but I think I missed that quality time more." Remarkably, Jason is now giving quality time to youngsters facing the same dilemmas and choices he once did.

I'm twenty-three years old and I attend Governors State University, where I'm completing my bachelor's degree in business. I'm the former program director of the Evening Reporting Center here in Chicago, for young people who have been in trouble with the law. I recently started working as a probation officer with the Illinois Circuit Court of Cook County Juvenile Justice and Child Protection Division. For the past eight years, I've lived in the Lawndale community.

I was arrested for the first time when I was twelve. The charge was UUW—unlawful use of a weapon. I wasn't guilty. My friend and I were playing in the neighborhood. He had a gun with him. It wasn't a real gun; it was a starter pistol, like a BB gun. We arrived at the house of another friend. The friend's mother was home, and suddenly the kid with the starter pistol pulled it out on her. She called the police and they came to the house and arrested us. I wasn't referred to the juvenile court, and I don't know what they did with the case.

Around that time I started having fights with other kids. I was like most young boys who look up to their older brothers and want to be like them. My two older brothers were part of the Gangster Disciples. I did a good job emulating them and became a member of the same gang. It was an organization with supposedly a family-type atmosphere. I joined for that reason, but I came to find out the gang was involved with violence, drugs, and fast money. By the age of thirteen, I was selling drugs, staying out late, and going to parties—basically what they called back then having fun.

My parents had separated when I was nine years old, and my mom became a single parent. I think my mom had no knowledge of my gang involvement. I was hanging out mostly with one of my two older brothers. She thought he was more responsible and would bring me home at a decent time. We used to sneak in the house through a window, and she was probably asleep in her bedroom.

Once when I was thirteen, I stole a car. It was a bad experience. I was seeing lots of older guys who had nice cars, and I was younger and wasn't making that much money. One night I got together some of my friends to look for a car to steal. We kind of stumbled on one. We knew it belonged to a neighbor, and we figured that since the neighbor didn't work in the morning, it would be a good time to steal their car. I got a screwdriver and broke the neck off the steering column. Inside some cars, under the steering column, there's a little device you can pull up to start the engine.

I stole the car to joyride in it. I got on the expressway with the car. I knew how to drive, but I wasn't an experienced driver. I almost got into an accident. The police chased us and I jumped out, and one of my friends got caught. I got away. My friend went to jail. He spent time in a juvenile detention center.

Around the time I was thirteen and in the eighth grade, the Gangster Disciples killed my cousin, who was a member of the gang. He was sitting in his car and they shot him eight times. We didn't know what it was about, but my brother got angry and became a member of the Black Disciples, a rival gang, to get revenge. I stayed a member of the Gangster Disciples. I was somewhat in the background. My brothers were more out front.

In 1992, I was charged with possession of a .22-caliber gun. I was selling drugs with a friend in the street at the time. Another guy we were selling with had given my friend the gun, because the two of us had to do security at the same time we were selling. We had hidden the drugs behind a house, and when we had a customer, one of us would go back to get the drugs while the other kept watch out front. I was at the back of the house when the cops showed up, and my friend ran to the back and dropped the gun to the ground. He did some time in the detention center and I got off.

It was an older guy that supplied me with my first twenty-five bags of rock cocaine to sell. He had a set that he determined was his, or that was given to him by a member of the gang. A set is a street, sometimes by a school, sometimes by a neighbor's house, where a person's spot to sell drugs is designated by gang members. I was out there on the set with three or four guys I had grown up with. We sold each of the twenty-five bags the older guy had brought us for

$10, and he told us that out of the $250, we had to give him $200 back and we could keep $50.

I was a naïve fourteen-year-old then and I thought $50 was a lot of money, especially because twenty-five bags would sometimes go in twenty-five or thirty minutes. It sounds like a good gig to some young men, but they don't know the dangers that are out there in the streets waiting for them. We got stuck up, police chased us, and we had rival gang members come over and shoot at us to take over the guy's set because it was making a lot of money. They would have killed the guy if they could.

We had guns to protect ourselves. We had security. Four other guys and myself were selling drugs at the set during that time, and there were three guys who carried weapons and watched out for us.

I made enough money to buy my own car, buy my own clothes, and provide for my family. I didn't have to ask my mom for anything. I was making roughly $600 a day. Sometimes my brothers and I would each make even more.

In January of 1993, I was charged with throwing dice in a game of chance in the company of eight other individuals. The case was thrown out. The next month I was charged with unauthorized possession of one clear plastic bag containing twenty-six smaller, pink Ziploc plastic bags thought to be holding cocaine. An older gentleman was arrested with me. "Older" guys were anywhere from seventeen to their mid- or late twenties. That seemed older to me at the time. These were guys I had watched grow up. They were two or three years older than my brothers. We'd all gone to the same schools. Back then the older guys recruited the younger guys to sell drugs. When an older guy and a younger guy got arrested together, the older guy figured the younger one would do less time than he would, and he'd ask the younger one to take the case for him. Sometimes the older guys offered us cash—up to $600—or clothing or jewelry. Most of the younger guys would say no, because if you said yes, you knew the police would remember your face or plant drugs on you.

The cops must have had surveillance on the older guy. They knew the abandoned house where he'd been going to get drugs. I didn't have any drugs on me when the police arrested us on the street, but after handcuffing us both behind our backs and putting us in the police car, they drove to the abandoned house and got some drugs out of it and split them between the two of us. The older guy asked me to take the case for him. He already had other cases and was afraid of doing two or three years, whereas I would have done thirty days. When we got to court the case was thrown out, because the police wrote one location for the arrest in their report and testified to a different location.

We were hiding our drugs pretty well then. It was hard for the police to find us with the drugs on us, unless they sold or bought the drugs as undercover agents. It was harder for them to sell us the drugs because we'd ask if they were an undercover agent. But when the undercover agents bought drugs, they'd pay you with a marked bill, say a fifty. If you kept the bill in your pocket, the police would come back in ten minutes—not the undercover person, because the cops didn't want to give him away—and they'd ask to see the money in your pocket and arrest you. That's why we always looked at the bills that people paid with, and if they were marked, took them to a store right away and bought something to break the bill with before returning to our spot.

About a week after the Ziploc bag case, I was charged with unlawful possession of six pink plastic packets containing cocaine. I was on the street selling drugs, and the police pulled up and started searching me. They handcuffed me and put me in the police car. They got mad because they couldn't find drugs on me. I guess they planned either to find something on me or plant something on me to get me convicted because the case from the previous week had been thrown out. But their story was inconsistent about the evidence, so the judge threw out that case too.

We used to have regular meetings of the Gangster Disciples and talk about what was going on in the streets. Guys used to say they heard that the cops could get extra vacation time or bonuses if they picked up a gun from a gang member. I guess it was true, because sometimes when the cops arrested us, they would try pretty hard to get a gun from us. They'd say, if you turn in a gun, we won't press charges for drugs.

One time I was charged with battery when the mother of a young man I was fighting with slipped and fell while she was trying to pull me off him. There were other charges for battery, and I was charged with damaging property and defacing a firearm—scratching off the serial number.

Lots of the guys smoked weed and drank when they got through for the day. I only smoked weed two or three times. I didn't want to have my mind affected that way. I needed to have my mind right and know my surroundings and know what was going on all the time. I didn't drink vodka or beer or gin. I saw people who were smoking and drinking, and I didn't want to be like them. I figured if I was addicted to alcohol and intoxicated and doing silly things, I'd be no different from the person I was selling to.

I became somewhat of a man roughly around my fifteenth birthday. I was given a set of my own down the street from the set where I'd been working. My brothers and I had guys working for us now. Instead of my brothers and me collecting $50, the guys were taking the $50 and bringing us $200. It was good money.

About a month down the line, we got into a confrontation with our own gang members. We started getting shot at a lot within the Gangster Disciples. I guess it was all the jealousy. A lot of the guys didn't want to see my brothers and me make that type of money. A lot of them wanted to take over the whole area, so they started calling us renegades because we would not participate in some of the meetings or pay our dues. If you were on a set, you had to pay $200 a week dues, sometimes more. Sometimes it was $1,000 a week, for commission and for owning the set in the Gangster Disciples—sort of like rent.

One of my brothers and I were still living with my mom at home, but my oldest brother moved out and got his own place. During this time, a member of the Gangster Disciples gave me some bad stuff. He fronted me some cocaine, and we were supposed to sell it and give him the money back off the sale. It was real cocaine, but they'd mixed embalming fluid or roach spray or something with it to destroy the business we had so the customers wouldn't come back to us.

As a result, we had a set but no customers. We went to Evanston because my cousin had a drug house up there. There were about ten of us, my brother and me and about eight of my cousins. When you keep the drugs within the house, it's called a drug house. The customers came to the crack house and paid for the drugs. You could say I was commuting to work. I was taking the train with the drugs from Chicago to my cousin's house in Evanston. I figured I wasn't going to get caught on the train because there were not going to be any police officers on the train; but if I took the car, they might stop me because of the profile I already had.

There's a big difference between the guys who sell drugs to people on the street and the people who provide the drugs to sell. The guy who sells the drugs to the customer on the street is the one who is constantly out there working. The guy who is supplying the drugs to the guys on the street is the middleman between them and the big-time drug dealers. He's the guy who has the set. The drug dealers are the ones who are moving weight—a kilo of cocaine, a half ounce of cocaine, quarter ounces of cocaine.

If the guy who had the set bought a half ounce of cocaine for $500 or $600, he would divvy up the cocaine into smaller pieces to give to his workers. So he'd probably double his money. I knew the guys who were moving weight. There was always a third party who would help you get to that person, because that person wanted to make sure that the people contacting him weren't police. You didn't want to buy bad stuff either, so that drug dealer had to have a good reputation. If he was in the neighborhood, he was very low key. He didn't want competition from you. If you had good stuff too, you'd be competition for his customers. Nobody ever trusted anyone else. In the beginning I was one of the guys selling drugs on the street, and then I moved up to owning a spot. I wasn't thinking about the dangers much—I was very young, and the money outweighed the fear. I never reached the position of big-time drug dealer.

My cousin in Evanston did. By the time I was sixteen years old, we were making about $10,000 a week from the crack house in Evanston, between the ten of us. Sometimes I'd go home with $1,000 a day. I started buying clothes and spending money on girls and more expensive cars. I helped my family with the rent and continued buying drugs to sell. I had a savings account I had started when I was in the eighth grade. I figured if I put some money in the savings account, it would be safe. But I couldn't put lots of money in the account because if it grew too much, the bank would begin to notice, since I had no job. So I kept some of my money under the carpet in my room at home, but that turned out to be a bad decision. Someone broke into the house and took all the money.

The house in Evanston got raided, and three of my cousins went to jail. My brother and I happened not to be there that day. The police shut down the house, which belonged to my aunt.

I was still living in Chicago. I guess I wasn't looking for a way to sell more drugs during this time, because I started thinking I was going to wind up getting shot or going to jail. I had bought a couple of guns, and I put them in my house. We had to move over to the hill, to the West Side. I was going to Dunbar High School. At some point, my brother who was still in the Gangster Disciples went to work for another guy, who had a different set where my brother thought he could make more money.

One day as I was on my way home from school, I saw some people and didn't know they were detectives. I was standing under the El, and the undercover grabbed me. He said they'd been watching me. I asked how they had been watching me, since I had just left school. He said they knew four guys were under the El selling drugs and that someone had called and said I fit the profile.

The guy they grabbed with me had a gun on him. He was twenty-seven or twenty-eight years old. The police wanted to pin the gun on me, so they said it was my gun. I was charged with possession of a loaded .40-caliber Glock blue steel semiautomatic handgun with nine live rounds.

I don't know what happened to the guy with the gun, because I was in juvenile court and they didn't mention anything about him in my court papers. Maybe it was a setup of some type, but I ended up being charged with another UUW. So I went to court and met Judge Kelly, who placed me on a year's probation and home confinement.

Judge Kelly is a wonderful woman who happens to be Caucasian. She could have sent me up to the detention center and held me until my court date, but she gave me a chance. She said I was going to Pretrial Service, a program designed to prevent youth from picking up new cases. It's a round-the-clock service run by WACA—the Westside Association for Community Action. If I had any problem, I could contact my counselor, James. This guy was also wonderful. He came to my home. He didn't demand anything from me. He valued my ideas. He took me places—Colorado, Boston, Pennsylvania, Niagara Falls—just showing me a different way of life. He happened to be African American.

At first, I was rebellious. I did not like someone coming into my house and telling me what to do. I'd been doing everything on my own. I was the man. But I respected James. In school and on the streets, people talk at you and don't listen to what you have to say. James was willing to listen to me and help me out in any way possible. He helped me get back in school and get my GED. He helped me enroll in college. I went to Malcolm X College, and then I transferred to Richard J. Daley College and completed my two-year degree before moving on to Governors State.

It was hard to change my way of life and turn away from selling drugs. It was hard cutting off friends I had grown up with and known for years. But I didn't travel back to the South Side and visit them. They're the ones who came from the South Side to the West Side to visit me. They tried to apply peer pressure and persuade me to sell drugs and hang out. But somehow my mind was made up. I didn't want to die. I wanted to be able to take care of my family. These are the types of issues we started talking about at the Pretrial Service Program—counselors like James, Vern, Jimmy Alexander, and Ernie, who founded WACA and is now its CEO, and the program's clients, like me. I had never had a positive environment to grow in before, or positive role models like these guys. I was mostly around guys who drank, smoked, and stood on the corner doing nothing all day. I saw something different in the guys at Pretrial Service that made me say, well, maybe I can change. Maybe I can become a normal human being and get a job. All because Judge Kelly sentenced me to the program and gave me a second chance.

It didn't take right away. The counselors had to work on me because, like most young men, I wouldn't accept what they had to say. I thought I knew it all. I thought I had the world at my feet. But they were willing to assist me— to educate me on what was going on in the neighborhood and in society in general. They talked to me about the things that went along with a life selling drugs. People who sell drugs on the street think they're going to retire on the drug money. But most of them don't. They get killed or go to jail or the police take the money away. The government can come in and confiscate your car and your home. You're always looking over your shoulder. You're always exposed to the dangers that go with a life of drugs, drinking, sex, and violence.

It took almost a year and a half for the program to work—for me to turn my life around. I didn't backslide even once. Something buried within me had helped me survive and kept me going. Once I arrived at the Pretrial Service Program, over time I found a meaning to my life. I had proven I had leadership skills and the drive to be successful when I was selling drugs. In the program, I could apply my strengths to something that would make a difference.

Ernie gave me a job. He had me working as a peer counselor for the Evening Reporting Center from four o'clock to eight. I went there directly from school, which kept me out of trouble. I knew I had to be there if I wanted to keep the job. And I had decided I wanted to keep the job. It was a legal way of making money, and I thought the police would stop harassing me. But they still harassed me because of my background as a juvenile. Some of the police knew me. I still hung out in the streets and on the corner. I wasn't doing anything wrong, but they seemed to think I was doing the things I used to do. They would put me up against the wall and have me get out of my shoes, and then they would take out the soles of my shoes, empty my pockets, pull down my pants, and check whether I was carrying drugs in my pants. It was degrading.

I wasn't making much money as a peer counselor, but I figured, how was I going to spend the money anyway if I was dead or in jail from selling drugs? If I'm not here, I thought, how am I going to take care of my mother and my sister? Working as a peer counselor was a different way that I could provide for my family. It took some time for me to grasp that.

In 1996, Ernie told me I could take his daughter to the Thirty-sixth Annual Debutante Cotillion in May, sponsored by the Chicago chapter of Links. There were months of preparation, learning the dance steps, learning where to put the forks and knives on the table at a black-tie ball. The guys I met in the practice sessions were nothing like me. I had just gotten my GED. They were more prestigious. Some were graduating from high school and entering college; others were already attending big-name schools. They had it all. I didn't feel nervous when I met them. I figured that I had been on the street and didn't need their approval. I figured I probably wouldn't be socializing with them anyway.

I had gotten a haircut the night before the cotillion, and the guy who designed my hair didn't make a gang design; it was just a nice design. Still, the coordinator of the cotillion said I couldn't wear that haircut. I guess she thought it was too street—too ghetto. Well, I was going to refuse to dance. I wasn't going to participate. The coordinator was saying I could participate only if I hid my hair or got the design cut out of it. So I was like, all right, I'm not going to participate. What happened was the guys I had practiced with for months before the cotillion came together and said, if Jason's not going to dance, we're not going to dance either. I went and shaved the design into my hair so it wouldn't be as visible, and I participated in the dance.

At the Evening Reporting Center, I moved from peer counselor to a position as counselor and then became the program director. Counselors at the center work hard to keep the kids busy with educational and recreational activities and with life and skills development workshops. They take the kids out to museums and to bowling and basketball games—activities they probably wouldn't do if they were still in the community selling drugs, because they'd be too busy trying to make that money. They probably wouldn't do these things at home either, because most of their parents are busy working or hanging out, not spending quality time with their kids. We enjoyed sitting down like family with the kids and discussing what was going on in their lives and in the world.

We had about twenty-five youths at the center daily when I was program director there. Sometimes it went to thirty. I can remember one winter we had thirty-five kids in the program in one day. Kids enter the program between the ages of ten and eighteen. The counselors try to get the kids to see that the behavior they're displaying is not working; it's not going to get them far. They try to put it out there so the kids can see for themselves where it might lead if they continue down that path.

The kids want to come back. They come back on their own. They go in front of the judge and say they like the program, and after they leave it, some of them stop in and say hi. They feel that the staff members and the kids at the program are their family, their gang. Out there on the streets, they feel they have to take care of their family. In the program, they can be themselves—young people—and not take on that burden. The program has a 91 percent success rate. About 9 percent of the kids don't finish the program. Some of them just drop out; some of them pick up a case.

When I was at the center, we were spending roughly four hours a day with these young people. We got to know them on a personal level. The kids are there every day, four o'clock to eight, Monday through Friday. During the weekend they're on home confinement, with no band around their leg. On some weekends, we picked them up on our own time and took them to the mall, just to see how they were doing. The home confinement officers go out and check up on them. If we could have operated a seven-day-a-week, round-the-clock program, we probably would have.

I try to use myself as an example in any job I have working with kids in trouble. I compare myself with some of those that kept on that path. I explain that when I was a little younger, I looked up to the guys who had all the fancy cars and all the jewelry and all the women, and now I look at them and they're on the corner drinking at age forty and broke and on drugs. Or they're in jail or the grave. I try to explain what really goes on out there. I explain that if Judge Kelly hadn't sentenced me to the Pretrial Service Program, I probably wouldn't have lasted another ten years.

Maybe the biggest reason why kids need the Pretrial Service Program is they don't have that family structure. When I was a kid, I was willing to risk my life because I was told by many people in the neighborhood that I would not survive. I was told by teachers that I would not become anything in life. I had my mom, but she wasn't always there. I probably would have been proud to have her spend more quality time with me. I wanted to have nice clothes and the jewelry and cars, but I think I missed that quality time more. It's that family structure, it's love, that's missing out there now, in our neighborhoods and in society in general.

The hardest thing for the kids in the Pretrial Service Program to believe is that they could get a great education. They feel that a lot of the teachers in the school are not educating them right. They feel like some of the teachers don't care. I tell them that sometimes you have to pick up a book yourself and educate yourself. Many of these kids are functionally illiterate. The counselors hold educational sessions on Tuesday. They try to help tutor the kids. They set aside an hour each day for the kids to do their homework. Sometimes the counselors travel to the schools and make sure the kids bring their homework with them to the program.

When the kids leave Pretrial Service at twenty-one or thirty days, they move on to a different program. Those who are committed to the process can have a rewarding life. We've had some young people come back and say, I've graduated from high school and now I'm going to college. Without this program, we couldn't have made it, they say. We couldn't wait any longer; we had no more time.

I left my job as program director of the Evening Reporting Center to take care of my mother when she got sick. When she recovered, I applied for the position of probation officer with the Cook County Juvenile Justice and Child Protection Division and got the job. Being a probation officer means the world to me. It allows me, as a professional, to demonstrate to others the importance of believing in our children. It allows me to help others better understand the potential of the minors who become involved in the juvenile justice system. I'm in a position to demonstrate what these youth can do when they receive support to develop their talents and succeed.

Index